Riel to Reform

Riel to Reform
A History of Protest
in Western Canada

GEORGE MELNYK
Editor

Fifth House Publishers
Saskatoon, Saskatchewan

Cover design by Robert Grey

Printed and bound in Canada
94 93 92   3 2 1

The publisher gratefully acknowledges the support received for this publication from The Canada Council and the Saskatchewan Arts Board.

Canadian Cataloguing in Publication Data
Main entry under title:

Riel to reform: protest in western Canada
ISBN 1-895618-00-2

1. Canada, Western—History—Autonomy and independence movements. I. Melnyk, George.

FC3209.A4R54 1992. 971.2'03 C92-098103-8
F1060.92.R54 1992
73827

FIFTH HOUSE PUBLISHERS
620 Duchess Street
Saskatoon, Saskatchewan
S7K 0R1

Contents

To the Memory of Howard Palmer 1946–1991
Historian of the Peoples of the West

Acknowledgements

This book has been a collaborative effort from the very beginning. The idea for *Riel to Reform* was generated by Fifth House. The editorial adviser on the project—Dr. William Waiser of the Department of History, University of Saskatchewan—provided insight and assistance, attended numerous editorial meetings, and facilitated the process with his far-sightedness and in-depth understanding of the West. Charlene Dobmeier, managing editor at Fifth House, worked tirelessly in rights acquisition and provided an editorial overview for the project that included copy editing of material written in different styles. June Bradley took on the onerous task of typing the essays and did so with enthusiasm and cheerfulness. Together we formed a team that made this book a reality in only one year. Of course, I accept responsibility for the final text.

I would also like to thank the contributors and their publishers for allowing their work to appear in this collection. During the research for the book, I was fortunate to have been appointed a Research Fellow of the Canadian Plains Research Center, University of Regina. The fellowship provided me with a scholarly context in which to prepare the book and write material for it. I wish to thank Dr. James McCrorie, executive director, and the Board of the Center for their support. The Alberta Foundation for the Arts provided financial assistance.

Finally, I would like to thank my family, who were most understanding and encouraging during the preparation of this, my fifth book.

GENERAL INTRODUCTION

The West as Protest:
The Cycles of Regional Discontent

GEORGE MELNYK

In a recent essay entitled "The Prairies as Region: The Contemporary Meaning of an Old Idea," a leading authority on western Canada stated that "regionalism implies protest." Gerald Friesen equates the West's regional identity with a tradition of political protest. He writes:

> The case for prairie regionalism is usually made by reference to moments of significant public protest: the Metis resistances of 1869–70 and 1885, the farm and labour and religious outbursts after 1918, the rise of third parties in the 1930s and 1940s, the emergence of provincial rights and secessionist sentiments in the 1970s and early 1980s.[1]

This concept of "the West as Protest" is firmly embedded in the public consciousness, and has been for some time. A 1969 booklet, *The Prairies: Alienation and Anger*, written by two journalists from the defunct *Toronto Telegram*, claimed that "for more than eighty-five ... years the people of the Prairies have been shouting their discontent ... Prairie protest has been remarkable in its persistence."[2]

The equation between "the West" or "the Prairies" and "Protest" arises from a certain delineation of regionalism that usually excludes the West Coast province of British Columbia. It is a definition based on the geographical, political, economical, and cultural differences between a region of mountains, forests, and the ocean and a region of prairie grasses, bush, and the Pre-Cambrian shield. Ultimately, it is a division between one kind of history and another; between the British colony on the coast and the territories of the interior. The material in this collection has been selected from that perspective, and its focus is the prairie West.

The authors in this book are historians, political scientists, and journalists. Together they paint a powerful portrait of western regionalism as a movement of political protest that has continued in one form or another for over a century.

The concept of protest is tied to popular upheaval and has generally been associated with historical events such as peasant uprisings in feudal Europe and student demonstrations in this century. It refers to some sense of mass grievance and disenchantment that erupts in peaceful or violent action. Protest often gives birth to new ideologies and new political parties. In the western protest tradition one can find all of these: armed struggle, mass demonstrations, and new political parties. What forges protest politics into a tradition is a connected history and "the memory of past struggles" that continues to rejuvenate new generations.[3]

1

The status of western regionalism as essentially protest-oriented needs to be explored in the context of western Canadian history. The protest tradition is a cyclic one: raging at certain moments, then lying dormant until the next eruption. The affirmation of regionalism and its western priorities leads to confrontation and an attack on the status quo. Historically this has brought about eventual defeat by stronger forces or a temporary channelling of protest sentiment into safe processes, only to rise again from the deep current of dissatisfaction that flows through western Canadian history.

This wellspring of discontent makes western protest a creative force in Confederation, bringing proposals for equality and fairness that are often compromised and skilfully shifted aside by those for whom they are a threat.

Fur Trade Protest

The history of regional discontent in the West began in the fur trade era of the late seventeenth century, when the West's fur resources were being exploited for the European market. By this time, European colonization of North and South America had been in full swing for over a century. White settlement in what became western Canada was transitory and tied to the commerce of trading posts. It was not until the late eighteenth century and the early nineteenth century that the region began to evolve its own identity when an indigenous mixed-white and Native population became established. By 1800 the continent had divided politically in the East into the colonies of British North America, the recently independent United States of America, and the soon-to-be independent Republic of Mexico. But the northwest of the continent was politically undefined. A majority of the area was under the colonial domination of Great Britain and the administrative authority of the Hudson's Bay Company, which had a seventeenth century charter to exploit the region commercially. Political boundaries were soon drawn along the 49th parallel between British North America and the United States of America, but economic and social life was fluid on the frontier until European settlement of the region became more pronounced. It is difficult to speak of a pre-1800 regionalism unless one were to describe the various tribal nations of the plains and their cultures as expressing a "regional" variant of aboriginality. The concept of "protest," then, would have to be reinterpreted, and the idea of "the West" or "North-West" would not fit tribal nationality.

The North-West, as the region came to be called initially, was an economic fiefdom of the Hudson's Bay Company, and it was out of the economic battles waged between the company and its rivals that the first inklings of regional identity and conflict developed. From the earliest stage in its Europeanized history the region was viewed as a battleground to be fought over for both economic and political influence. Colonizing forces outside the region were moulding it, eyeing it, fantasizing about its potential or lack thereof. It was seen as an adjunct of the political forces already established in the eastern part of the continent and for which it was to provide territorial enhancement.

The first representatives of a western perspective, that is, one that stood for regional self-determination, came out of the fur trade economy. These were the Métis or mixed-bloods, descendants of European traders—English, Scots, and French—who had taken Native wives. Scottish settlers, arriving in the Red River Valley in the early nineteenth century, also contributed to the development of a mixed-blood ethnicity through intermarriage.

The Métis stood between the colonial European leadership and the indigenous Indian peoples. All three—Indians, Métis, and Europeans—were tied to the fur trade economy. It was the majority of the Métis community that led the resistance against the Canadian colonial expansion in 1870 and 1885. There are several aspects of this Métis-led regionalism in the nineteenth century that are relevant to the regionalism of today.

First, their regionalism was a product of those who identified with the West and saw themselves as sons and daughters of the area. They did not view themselves as colonists or representatives of foreign interests. Nor did they identify with the outside, but rather, viewed themselves self-consciously as the representatives of the region. They were indigenous and had aspirations for indigenous political control.

Regionalism is not a product of the Indian nations, whose ideology was tribal. To this day western regionalism has little resonance in the aboriginal community, which is much more concerned with its own cultural, economic, social, and political problems than with western autonomy. There may be a meeting ground were western regionalism able to convince aboriginal peoples of its being a vehicle of their self-interest, but that identification is no further ahead today than it was in 1885, when Indian support for the Riel resistance and the Métis was limited. From the start, however, the regionalism of the Métis and their prowestern stance were considered dangerous to the interests of the ruling Hudson's Bay Company and then seen as a problem for the new country of Canada, which bought the region from the company.

Second, Métis regionalism was unsuccessful in creating an independent political entity or in ensuring equality for itself in the Canadian federation, in spite of Manitoba's provincehood in 1870. The negotiations that founded Manitoba also made Riel, its leader, a fugitive from Canadian authority. The failure of western regionalism to ensure that western Canada was an equal partner in the new political order called Canada haunts the region to this day, and the divisions created at that time within the resident community can be detected in the various camps of today. The fact that armed resistance in both 1870 and 1885 was used to express regional aspirations with the end result that the Canadian nation-state was successful in imposing its plans on the West with only minor accommodation has given western regionalism a certain inferiority complex and undermined its claims to legitimacy and autonomous power. Since the time of Riel, western regionalism has been burdened by this failed attempt at self-determination. The same is probably true of Quebec, whose conquest by the British in 1763 has played a negative psychological role in Quebec nationalism. That both Quebec and the West were brought into Canada by force of arms is a reality that cannot be ignored or belittled. It creates an undercurrent that fuels their political demands.

Third, economic discontent as a major characteristic of the resource-based western economy has given western regionalism its major driving force and generated a heritage of protest. The Métis were created by the fur trade, but their political aspirations did not survive the fur trade period. Agrarian regionalism spawned radical farm movements, but their goals faltered after the period of agricultural ascendancy, while postagrarian regionalism resulted in strong provincial leadership that did not survive the downfall of energy prices in the 1980s when the West went into economic decline. In the case of all three regionalisms, the national agenda from the centre prevailed and retained its control.

Socially, Métis regionalism was an amalgam of various ethnic, linguistic, and racial elements. It was the region's first multiculturalism (tricultural and biracial). Multi-culturalism began with the Métis and continued into the period of European multicultu-

3

ral settlement of the prairies. In the mid-twentieth century the region was considered the centre of Canadian multiculturalism in contrast to the supposed uniculturalism of Quebec or Ontario. The multicultural direction that the Métis gave to western regionalism has been transformed in subsequent periods with new peoples and races, but the essential multiplicity of western society has not disappeared and remains an important feature of regional identity.

Politically, Métis regionalism defined western regionalism as standing for the right of regional self-determination, autonomous social and economic development, and opposition to external exploitation and federal government insensitivity to local needs. This theme continued into the agrarian period, reemerging during the energy wars of the 1970s, and has again resurfaced in contemporary political discussion. When David Kilgour, an MP from Edmonton, wrote in 1990 that the West was characterized by "small populations, resource-dependent economies, low political clout and various degrees of regional discontent," he echoed the sense of grievance expressed by the political leaders of the West a century ago.[4]

Culturally, Métis regionalism gave western regionalism a sense of a distinct self. The Métis developed their own indigenous cultural expression in the arts, dress, and dialect. Métis cultural originality was limited because it combined strong influences from outside the region with strong Native influences, and of course it was not allowed to flourish or come to full realization. The Métis elite were also dependent on external educational, linguistic, and religious influences from places such as Quebec. Even today the West has been unable to give the world an original cultural form and has found most of its cultural production derivative, thereby limiting an independent political expression.[5]

Finally, fur trade regionalism established the fundamental feature of western regionalism: its evolving character. It is a regionalism that has advanced through a number of different phases. When the socioeconomic underpinnings of a certain phase of western regionalism dissolved, a new form of regionalism was born, and this has become the historical pattern for the West. But whatever new form this regionalism undertook it retained its basic, Métis-inherited characteristics.

Agrarian Protest

After fur trade regionalism was finally put to rest by the Anglo-Canadian army in 1885, the vacuum was filled with a potent new regionalism based on the agricultural exploitation of the West. The Métis and Indians in the area were, in a matter of only two decades, supplanted by hundreds of thousands of European and North American settlers who homesteaded the unbroken prairie in plots of 160 acres. These small freeholders became the backbone of a new discontent that arose on the prairies.

This new discontent had a number of components similar to the earlier concerns of the Métis. The farmers were unhappy with Canada's National Policy, feeling that it hampered their access to lower-priced goods. They were also critical of the influence the railroad and the grain merchants had on the price farmers received for their products. The Métis had been free-traders, working against the Hudson's Bay Company monopoly, and had also been concerned about the security of their landholdings at the time of the rebellions. The national government's control over trade and land policy continued to be a contentious issue into the agrarian period.

Instead of taking up arms the way the Métis of the frontier society did, the farmers took up mutual aid and cooperatives for economic power, and they built indigenous, regionally based political movements as expressions of their democratic prerogative. They created their own economic and political vehicles and made the West famous for new political parties such as the United Farmers of Alberta, the Progressives, Social Credit, and the Co-operative Commonwealth Federation. W.L. Morton, a leading historian of the West, linked this second wave of regionalism with the earlier fur trade regionalism when he wrote that "agrarian sectionalism . . . had confirmed the tradition of protest begun in the days of political subordination [Riel]."[6]

The mobilization of the West's dominant agrarian sector meant that western regionalism was genuinely a popular manifestation rooted in the new nature of the region as an agrarian hinterland, just as the mobilization of the Métis was rooted in the hinterland status of the fur trade economy. But the sources of this radicalism were not purely agrarian. In the period of agrarian settlement, the West developed five cities, three of which—Winnipeg, Edmonton, and Calgary—became the home of a substantial working class. The labour movement lent its voice to the general discontent and became a prominent player in the formation of parties outside the mainstream.

While a number of changes, such as provincial control of natural resources and the election of farmer-controlled provincial governments, did occur, they did not fundamentally challenge the existence or primacy of the Canadian nation-state or central Canadian domination of the federation. Though the desire for a new society was an undercurrent in all the protest movements, there was no outcry that the West should separate from Canada. The discontent found productive outlets within the national political system, either in the form of new provincial parties, such as Social Credit in Alberta, or in the federal Co-operative Commonwealth Federation (CCF). In most cases there was a strong federal dimension to these political parties, born in the West, but linked to central Canada.

Agrarian regionalism was based on the desire of farmers and workers for economic justice and social reform, just as the earlier Métis regionalism sought a fair deal and a self-determining voice for the West. The inability of the Métis people, the Indian tribes, and then the farmers and workers of the agrarian West to achieve control over the economy is the legacy of subordination that western protest and the history of the region express. Recent moves for aboriginal rights and claims by both Métis and non-Métis aboriginal peoples are indicative of the unresolved issues of the nineteenth century. The current plight of the agricultural community is simply a continuation of its historic struggle for control. What is interesting is that each phase of western protest has been separate from the previous one, so that today's farmers are not interested in supporting aboriginal claims and today's petroleum industry is not interested in supporting western farmers' demands. This is a serious flaw in the protest tradition.

Postagrarian Protest

After World War II agrarian regionalism went into a steady decline as agriculture became less and less important to the regional economy. This was not an overnight phenomenon but a long-term gradual shift, characterized by a new urbanization in the region and the growing importance of natural resource extraction industries. The rural population, which had been in the majority up to World War II, began a steady decline to the point that now not much more than 10 percent of the population in the prairie West is involved directly in agricultural production, and 60 percent of the prairie region's population lives in five cities. This is not to say that agriculture became a nonentity. The fur trade did not disappear in 1885 either. Agriculture continued to play a powerful role as the primary economic generator in Saskatchewan and number two in Alberta. But the agricultural industry became an increasingly subsidized part of the economy and developed a lame image, while the energy industry—oil, gas, and uranium—came to be viewed as the leading edge of the West's economy.

The whole matter came to a head in the 1970s when Alberta led a decade of "energy wars" against the central government and Saskatchewan nationalized its potash mining industry. During this decade a "New West" was born, which had economic muscle and a political elite willing to assert provincial rights vis-à-vis Ottawa.[7] This new regionalism was short-lived, lasting but a decade. In the early 1980s it began to dissolve under the pressure of recession and a dismantling of its regional economic infrastructure through bankruptcy, unemployment, and low commodity and resource prices. Not only did this affect the energy industry that had been such a leader in the 1970s, it also affected agriculture, which suffered through high interest rates, low land values, drought, and an erosion of its subsidy structure.

At the time of this critical turnabout from boom to bust, Roger Gibbins, a University of Calgary political scientist, published an assessment of the state of western regionalism in two books, *Prairie Politics and Society: Regionalism in Decline* (1980) and *Regionalism: Territorial Politics in Canada* (1982). The books covered the agrarian and postagrarian periods specifically from the viewpoint of agrarian regionalism.

Gibbins proceeded on the assumption that the regionalism of the Canadian West lost its reason for being when the agrarian economy that had bound the three prairie provinces together economically and sociologically fell apart. He felt that "a distinctive regional society" had vanished, and he claimed that regional interest in the postagrarian period was not regionwide but rather one of individual provincial rights.[8] It is certainly true that provincial governments led the energy wars against Ottawa under the banner of provincial rights, but it is also true that these rights were made synonymous with regionwide western interests and western grievances. In fact, the provincial orientation of the period paralleled the Métis rights movement of the fur trade economy and the provincially oriented political expressions of the later farm protest movements of agrarian regionalism. What Gibbins did was to equate agrarian regionalism with western regionalism as a whole. *Prairie Politics and Society* appeared at the high point of the western separatist movement (1979-1982). The western separatists never went beyond being a peripheral group, even at their peak, because their ideology was not popular and they were unable to establish themselves on a regionwide basis. This failure of the separatists to become a major regional force would seem to confirm Gibbin's thesis that regionalism had gone into decline.

On closer examination, though, this proves not to be the case. Western regionalism in its postagrarian phase, as Gibbins correctly identified, was very much a western provincial-rights movement. Its leaders were provincial politicians in the region. Their regionalism did not stand for regional unity, the end of western provincial boundaries, separate nationhood, etc., which is what the separatists wanted, but yet it remained prowestern all the same because it expressed and appealed to the western identity as one that was disadvantaged and exploited. The concerns of the western provinces for greater determination and national influence were similar and linked.

The western separatism of this period took regional rhetoric to extreme conclusions and forgot that the essence of the western protest tradition was a striving for control rather than its total achievement: reform rather than rejection. Therefore it was in conflict with this new postagrarian regionalism and its provincial rights focus. The separatists did not realize that the regionalist sentiment out of which their own ideology had sprung was one that stood for a region within Canada rather than a nation-state outside Canada. Their position implied the end of regionalism through its conversion into nationalism and an independent western nation-state.

The end of a pervasive rural agricultural society in the West reoriented the various provincial economies resulting in internal regional differences, but these divisions were no more profound than the division of Alberta's Social Credit government and Saskatchewan's CCF government during the period of agrarian regionalism. What the western separatists failed to comprehend was that the new regionalism of the West was being adequately articulated and well-led by its provincial representatives and that the western separatist attempt to supplant that leadership was doomed to failure. The economic and political basis for this new postagrarian regionalism was real enough, but there were no objective conditions then that would support a successful western separatist movement.

In spite of the loss of the common agrarian economy, the prairie provinces of the West came out as a common front on the question of provincial control of resources and revenues. Provincial self-interest and regional interests came together in the battle with Ottawa over royalty revenues.

In his 1983 book, *The West: The History of a Region in Confederation,* sociologist J.F. Conway of the University of Regina contradicted Gibbins, when he wrote:

> The resource confrontation [with Ottawa] of the 1970s confirmed that regional politics remain in command in the West. In the absence of structural change to alter the West's place in the national economy and its political weaknesses in Confederation, the West has been forced to continue the battle to defend its interests in a subordinate region. This is understandable . . . the Western economy remains vulnerable and fragile, rooted in the exports of natural resources of uncertain world markets.[9]

Conway confirms that whether the export is beaver pelts, wheat, or oil, the fundamental character of the region as an exporter of natural resources to world markets remains its basic characteristic. It is this structural identity that underlies the grievances of western regionalism from the fur trade export period of 1700 to the period of possible water exports in the year 2000. Only when that natural resource export characteristic is finally buried will the disenchantment of western regionalism end and western regionalism as protest disappear.

The American writer, Joel Garreau, in his 1981 book, *The Nine Nations of North America,* recognized that regionalism has been created in North America through the geography of common economic aspirations, a common history and cultural identification, and a shared attitude about a region's relationship to other regions and to the national centre.[10] These elements continued to play a crucial part in postagrarian regionalism of the 1970s and early 1980s. The West as a region has maintained a certain territorial identity that people recognize and comprehend, and the region has been seen to have a distinctive identity in terms of its political, social, and economic heritage.

In a federated nation-state such as Canada, the ongoing elements of regional protest are a sense of regional exploitation and economic injustice, a view that the national government serves regional interests poorly and neglects regional aspirations, and that the region is underrepresented in national decision making.[11] The Triple-E Senate concept that originated in the West in the 1980s was a perfect example of a regional attempt to reform the national political system through an equal and elected upper house, and it was rooted in the attitudes developed during a century and a half of grievance. Its rejection by central Canada, both Ontario and Quebec, in the post-Meech Lake debate on constitutional reform is indicative of the historic resistance to building regional equality in the federation. But if the history of western protest is any indicator some form of Senate reform will occur, but it will not provide the full equality the West has asked for.

But western regionalism does not exist solely in the context of a vast, thinly populated bilingual nation-state known as Canada. It also exists in the context of continentalism and the border it shares with the most powerful nation-state on earth—the United States of America. As an exporter of natural resources, western Canada is a major factor in American geopolitics. When western regionalism insists on autonomous regional development vis-à-vis Ottawa or Washington, both national and continental interests come into play.

Political economist Garth Stevenson of the University of Alberta has stated that "regionalism and continentalism have always threatened the survival of the Canadian state."[12] From the point of view of nationalism, regional discontent is viewed as an ally of American domination. This was particularly true in the Trudeau period when postagrarian regionalism clashed with the central government's nationalization efforts. But in the Mulroney era of national subservience to American interests, regionalists could just as well claim that the Canadian nation-state had become the handmaiden of American continental aggrandizement.

Historian David Bercuson of the University of Calgary once wrote the following about regionalism: "regionalism exists because there are regions."[13] One can expand this further by saying that western protest exists because there are injustices to be protested. The contradictions in the national economy and the different levels of political power on the national scene create regions. Regionalism comes out of the discrepancies created in the nation-state; it is a response. Bercuson went on to state that regional identity coexists with other political identities that people in the region have. One can be a westerner, a Canadian, a Conservative, and a Manitoban simultaneously. One does not preclude the others.[14] In fact, there are elements of all those identities within each of the others—Diefenbaker's messianic sense of Conservatism was certainly different from a Maritime Stanfield sense of Conservatism or a Quebec Mulroney sense of Conservatism, but they all led the same national party.

Constitutional instability, special status for Quebec, economic recession, and continental realignments will create pressures for and against western regionalism. Nevertheless, history shows that western regionalism in its various manifestations is a mainstream ideology that is not easily overcome by either nationalism or continentalism. Perhaps it is its evolving nature and its ability to hibernate that make it resilient.

The equation of regionalism with discontent and protest can end up being a limited, one-sided negative interpretation. Within itself regionalism is content, seeing itself as a force for political equality and reform, for positive social change, for regional security and development, and ultimately for continuation of the nation-state of which it is a part. The enemies of regionalism view its legitimate demands as a permanent challenge and a constant "protest," while the proponents of western regionalism see it as an asset furthering national, social, and political evolution.

The cyclic nature of regional discontent in the West indicates that until the hinterland status and resource-based economy of the region is fundamentally altered protest will continue, but in different forms depending on the political economy of the day. The rise of the Reform Party, coinciding with Free Trade as the latest vehicle of American continentalism, and a renewed crisis over Quebec has heralded a new phase for western protest that can tentatively be termed "Continentalist Regionalism." This regionalism is rooted in the heritage of western protest, but it also relates to the new continental environment, which, itself, is a product of global geopolitical realignment.

The creation of the North American Free Trade bloc is a major feature of the new world economic order of the 1990s, along with the European Community and Japan-led Asia. At the same time, the end of communism in Eastern Europe and the dismemberment of the Soviet Union and Yugoslavia in the 1990-92 period has created a large number of new nations. This spurt of nation-building, coinciding with large new markets for international capitalism and the trend for creating continental trading blocs, has put a host of new ideas and forces into play around the world and in the region—forces both centrifugal and centripetal. The evolution of western regionalism during this period of continentalist integration cannot be predicted, but the heritage of protest and the continued subordinate economic and political status of the region suggest strongly that protest will renew itself once more.

Notes

1. Gerald Friesen, "The Prairies as Region: The Contemporary Meaning of an Old Idea," in James N. McCrorie and Martha L. MacDonald, eds., *The Constitutional Future of the Prairie and Atlantic Regions of Canada* (Regina: Canadian Plains Research Center, University of Regina, 1992), 6. Also see Friesen's *The Canadian prairies: A history* (Toronto: University of Toronto Press, 1984).

2. *The Prairies: Alienation and Anger* (Toronto: McClelland and Stewart, 1969), 3-4.

3. George Rude, *Ideology and Popular Protest* (New York: Pantheon, 1980), 164.

4. David Kilgour, *Inside Outer Canada* (Edmonton: Lone Pine, 1990), 17.

5. G. Melnyk, *Radical Regionalism* (Edmonton: NeWest Press, 1981), 39-46. In 1992 Winnipeg MP Lloyd Axworthy (Liberal) launched a public campaign to explore the concept of "Prairie Integration" by organizing a conference on the subject.

6. W.L. Morton, "The Bias of Prairie Politics," in A.B. McKillop, ed. *Contexts of Canada's Past: Selected Essays of W.L. Morton* (Toronto: Macmillan, 1980), 156. [Also see p. 17 in this volume.]

7. For a detailed discussion of this issue see John Richards and Larry Pratt, *Prairie Capitalism: Power and Influence in the New West* (Toronto: McClelland and Stewart, 1979).

8. Roger Gibbins, *Prairie Politics and Society: Regionalism in Decline* (Toronto: Butterworth, 1980), 200.

9. J.F. Conway, *The West: The History of a Region in Confederation* (Toronto: Lorimer, 1983), 232.

10. Joel Garreau, *The Nine Nations of North America* (New York: Avon, 1981), 1-13.

11. Raymond Breton, "Regionalism in Canada," in *Regionalism and Supranationalism*, 64.

12. Garth Stevenson, "Canadian Regionalism in Continental Perspective," *Journal of Canadian Studies*, Vol. 15, No. 2 (1980), 26.

13. David Bercuson, "Regionalism and Unlimited Identity in Western Canada," *Journal of Canadian Studies*, Vol. 15, No. 2 (1980), 121-22.

14. Ibid.

1

WESTERN PROTEST: AN OVERVIEW

Introduction

The concept of western Canada as a region characterized by protest politics received its classic expression in "The Bias of Prairie Politics," the well-known 1955 essay by Manitoba historian W.L. Morton. Written at a time when the West was moving away from its agrarian-dominated economy and society, this essay established the protest tradition as a fundamental feature of western Canada. Morton sought to connect the politics of the nineteenth-century Francophone Catholic, Louis Riel of Manitoba, with those of the twentieth-century, Ontario-born fundamentalist Christian preacher, William Aberhart, who created the world's first Social Credit government in Alberta.

"The subordinate status of the West in Confederation was the initial bias that set in train the development of prairie politics towards an increasing differentiation from the Canadian standard," Morton wrote. The struggle of the region against economic and political subordination was expressed by the desire for "a new political utopia." When adherents of the Social Gospel tradition preached the need for a "New Jerusalem" on the prairies and the founders of the Co-operative Commonwealth Federation (CCF) dreamed of a day when capitalism would be replaced with democratic socialism, they were expressing this utopian hope.

Although written in a language that is no longer at the leading edge of social science, Morton's thoughts on western protest have created a standard against which all other thinkers on the West continue to be measured.

The contemporary historian of ideas R. Douglas Francis writes about the West as a series of "myths." He identifies one of these myths as "regional protest" and he discusses Morton's role in developing that myth. Francis does not use the term "myth" in the pejorative sense of a lie, but rather in the manner of the great Canadian literary critic and scholar, Northrope Frye, who viewed myth as a powerful story that tells a society what it was and is and how it has operated through time.

Douglas Francis points out that protest is one of several ideas about the West that remain current. He provides an excellent survey of the postwar historiography of the West and illustrates how the protest tradition fits with other themes, such as the affirmation of a distinct regional identity and the emphasis on social reform. A number of historians he discusses appear in this book.

Political scientist David Smith analyses the political dimension of dissent in terms of western-generated parties, movements, and pressure groups from the beginning of the century, when "the culprits were the CPR and the banks," to the Trudeau era, when the enemies were "the National Energy Board and the CBC." His suggestion of administrative "decentralization and devolution" to regional bodies was a moderate western approach at a time of growing alienation between the region and Ottawa, but he makes it clear that "there is no panacea for the region's dissent."

These writers define the major features of the protest tradition. They indicate clearly that the elements outlined by Morton persist to this day. The problems of regional subordination and hinterland status that underlie western protest have yet to be resolved.

The Bias of Prairie Politics

W.L. MORTON

Reprinted from *Transactions of the Royal Society of Canada*, Series III,
Vol. XLIX (June 1955), 57–66, by permission of G. Margaret Morton.

That there has been, and is, some significant difference between the politics of the three prairie provinces and those of other regions of Canada is a matter both of common observation and of academic study. If the existence of the difference is notorious, the explanation of why such a difference should exist is still perhaps sufficiently in question to warrant an attempt at comprehensive explanation. This paper advances the proposition that the explanation is historical and not merely economic or sociological. The proposition implies, as the title is meant to indicate, that the difference between prairie and other Canadian politics is the result of an initial bias, which, by cumulative historical process—the process which takes account of sequence, conjuncture, and will, as well as of logic, category, and necessity—has resulted in traditions and attitudes even more distinctive than the original bias. In short, to pass from the abstract to the concrete, the submission is that in his aims Louis Riel was a more conventional politician than William Aberhart, but that both were prairie politicians.

The proof of that assertion must be postponed for the moment, in order to remark that it has seemed necessary to invoke the notion of bias lest the common error of special studies be incurred, that of exaggerating the significance of one's subject. The difference between prairie and other Canadian politics can be exaggerated, particularly if historical perspective is lost and the study of fundamental institutions neglected. It is more important, if less arresting, to observe that the institutions of the prairie West were Canadian institutions and that the people who worked those institutions and determined the political development of the West were in the overwhelming majority of Canadian birth and ancestry, than it is to discuss the differences of sectional politics. The first laws of the West were largely copied from the statutes of Ontario. There was only one distinctly western group of people, the Métis, and they were broken and dispersed by 1885. The great immigrant groups of the first years of this century, the British, the Americans, and the East Europeans, never endeavoured to change the basic institutions of the country and in the main left politics to the Canadian-born. There seems, in fact, to have been little in the institutional development or the peopling of the prairie West for which some parallel might not be found in the history of western Ontario. It may be said, in short, that old Canada was extraordinarily successful in making the prairie West Canadian.

The effect of Canadian institutions was, of course, modified by the factors of time and distance. The West was colonized some two generations later in time than western

Ontario, and was a distant thousand miles from central Canada. In consequence the West in its years of major settlement was subjected to influences such as Fabian Socialism, the Non-Partisan League, and Social Credit, which the older communities of Canada had escaped, or were better equipped to resist. And the element of mere distance was a powerful agent among those which operated to produce the strong sectional sentiment of the West. But these material factors were modifiers, not determinants, of western history. Despite the lateness of settlement and the barrier of distance, the institutions and people of the prairie West were, or became, Canadian.

If, then, Canadian institutions and ideals prevailed in the West, what was the bias which made prairie politics different? The answer suggested is that the subordinate status given the West in Confederation was the initial bias that set in train the development of prairie politics towards an increasing differentiation from the Canadian standard. The subordination was, of course, in the nature of things, the outcome of the fact that the West was an almost wholly unpeopled wilderness in 1869. The bias was neither necessary nor inevitable; it was historical, the outcome of human will and personality, that of Riel and the clergy, operating in a particular environment. The resistance of the Métis was in many ways pathetic and even comic, but it was sufficient to set a tradition at work, the tradition of western grievance. The struggle of the prairie West against political subordination to central Canada had begun, and it was to go on to merge with the struggle against economic subordination to the capital and corporations of the east. The result of this struggle, both of its failures and its partial successes, was a release of that utopianism which has been endemic in western society since the French Revolution, and indeed in religious form since the Reformation, and which has always found a refuge and a stimulus on the frontiers of settlement. In particular, the revolt against the national political parties between 1911 and 1921, and the shattering of economic conventions by the Great Depression and drought of 1929–39, created a vacuum into which the United Farmers of Alberta and Social Credit rushed.

The assumption that the initial bias of prairie politics was the fact of political subordination in Confederation suggests further a division of the history of the prairie West in Confederation into three periods. The first may be called the colonial period from 1870 to 1905. The second is the agrarian period from 1905 to 1925, and the third the utopian from 1925 to the present. The first is the period of the struggle for political equity in Confederation, not realized until 1930, and the second the period in which the concept of the agrarian bloc dominated western politics. The third period is that in which certain utopian elements, diffused through western society but stimulated on the frontiers of settlement, emerged in prairie politics, and won control of the province of Alberta in 1935. The periodization suggested is, of course, much neater than the facts warrant. The achievement of equality in 1930 was at once made a mockery by depression and drought. The agrarian element is continuous from 1878, when the Grange first appeared in Manitoba, and the utopianism can also be detected from the beginning of extensive settlement. But the periods do indicate the relative importance of the three elements of inequality, agrarianism, and utopianism. Even more important than the periodization is the sequence, for the struggle for equality fed the agrarian revolt, and the agrarian revolt opened the way to the victory of the utopians. The initial bias of inequality, that is, gave a twist to the development of prairie politics which in the historical process has become a major divagation from the run of national development, and which is now a matter for serious concern.

The beginning of the process was the resistance of the Métis of Red River to the annexation of the North-West by Canada in 1869. The resistance was not to union with Canada; it was to union at once and without safeguards that would enable the Métis to survive as a group. On the face of the evidence the resistance was not justifiable. The preparations made by Canada for the acquisition and preliminary government of the North-West were proper and adequate; the one serious omission was the failure to send a commissioner to explain what was to happen, and that was an imperial rather than a Canadian responsibility. The real ground of the resistance was to the beginning of an English-speaking and Protestant immigration, which would become a majority and determine the laws and institutions of the North-West. In that the Métis saw, and correctly, their own destruction. They were resolved not to submit: "Tell them," Riel said to a Canadian, "our great thought is to resist being made Irishmen of."[1] The real blunder of the Dominion government was to regard the acquisition and development of the North-West as a compensation to Ontario for bringing the Maritimes into Confederation and constructing the Intercolonial Railway. Cartier, it is possible, had acquiesced in this surrender of the West to Ontario, on condition that the North-West be a separate government,[2] but some of the missionary clergy of the Roman Catholic church did not.[3] They and Riel determined to oppose the opening of the North-West to the English and Protestant, individualistic and aggressive society of Ontario, a society which would grant equality to the Métis as persons and destroy them as a people.

Their aims the Métis sought to achieve within constitutional limits. The resistance began with a declaration of loyalty to the Crown, and it was continued in the name of British liberty and British justice, though the phrases were mingled dangerously and misleadingly with the rights of man and law of nations. Riel showed himself to be remarkably adept in the English tradition of using the language of constitutional right to justify opposition to authority. But his real problem was to find terms within the limits of the Canadian constitution which would assure the Métis of their object, the preservation of their language, faith, and existence as a group. These Riel was finally convinced were to be found in provincial status, and with that in view the Bill of Rights drawn up by the delegates of the people of Red River was rewritten by the provisional government to demand admission for the North-West, not as a territory, but as a province. What was granted was provincial status, not for the North-West as a whole, but for the old colony of Assiniboia. Thus Riel won a startling, but partial, victory. He had obtained provincial status for no more than a fragment, if a strategic fragment, of the North-West, and even there his victory was incomplete. Small as it was, Manitoba was large enough to hold sufficient Ontario immigrants to outnumber the Métis, and, province though it was, it was not the equal of the other provinces, for it was not granted control of its lands.

This was the beginning of the bias of prairie politics. The fears of the Métis had led them to demand equality for the people of the North-West in Confederation. Unwarranted though the demand was, it had been granted in principle to prevent American intervention and to pacify Quebec. But it could not be wholly granted without driving Ontario to exasperation and imperilling the federal policy of western development by railway construction and homestead settlement. In consequence, the West was left with a sharpened sense of inequality and a tradition of grievance and of special claims, to be embodied in bills of rights from Riel's series of four to that of Mr. Hazen Argue, MP, of May 1955.

14

The subordination of the prairie West, then, to federal control and federal policies, from 1870 to 1905, and even 1930, had confirmed prairie politics in their initial bias. The bias was, however, to be transmitted to, and increased during, the agrarian period. This second phase of the bias sprang from the rapid development of the agricultural economy of the prairie West after 1900. The most easily exploitable resource of the West was the agricultural soil of the prairies, which lent itself to grain growing on an extensive scale. The needs of this economy were few, simple, and imperative: cheap land, cheap transport, and cheap machinery. They were met on a gigantic scale both by private investment and by government subsidy. It was the national policy of the day to develop the West, for the development of the West was the key to national development. The western grain grower was a beneficiary both of the great colonization boom which opened the twentieth century and also of the policies of the national government.

Yet the grain grower developed grievances, which were to be formulated both as a sectional and as a class protest. In part, no doubt, there was an element of human perverseness in this. But there was a strong objective basis to the grain grower's complaints. In the early stages of development both the line elevators and the railways were able to exploit their temporary monopolies; banks and other services were sometimes in the same position. It is not surprising that an attempt should have been made to charge "what the traffic would bear," or that it should have been resisted, as it was by the Farmers' Union, the Patrons of Industry, and the Grain Growers' Associations. These organizations were the grain growers' counter to alleged monopolies.

One other grievance, however, could not be attacked by economic organization alone. That was the National Policy of tariff protection of domestic industry, begun by the Conservative Party in 1879, and continued and refined by the Liberal Party after 1896. The National Policy was not, of course, merely a policy of protection. It was, broadly viewed, also a policy of railway construction and land settlement; in short, its aim was the creation of a national, as opposed to a colonial, economy. All sections were expected to benefit from its realization and, in this broad interpretation, the Crow's Nest Pass Agreement was as much a part of the National Policy as the tariff. But by tradition and interest the western farmer, like many eastern farmers, was disposed to ignore any special or long-term benefits which accrued to him from the National Policy, and fasten on the fact that the tariff operated to increase his costs of living and of production. This disposition was influenced in the prairie West by the defeat of the Reciprocity Agreement in the general election of 1911. The results of that election convinced many western grain growers, suffering from the first slackening of the boom, that the "eastern interests" would go to great lengths to maintain the favoured position in which, in their view, the National Policy had placed those interests.

The 1911 election also convinced a number of grain growers that the national political parties were not reliable instruments for effecting the agrarian voters' wishes. Stimulated by the Progressive movement in the United States and by immigrant British Liberals and Socialists, some western agrarians began to denounce political parties as perverters and corrupters of the will of the people, and to advocate "direct legislation" and "business government" as remedies. The national parties were especially attacked as the facile agents of the "big interests." In this developing agitation there were elements both of sectional agrarianism and of utopianism.

The story has been told elsewhere. Suffice it here to note that the rapid disintegration of the farmers' movement in politics demonstrated the inadequacy of agrarian sectionalism. The weakness of western agrarian sectionalism was threefold.

15

First, there was the weakness of the single economic interest, whether the collective interest of agriculture or the narrower interest of the prairie grain grower. In the complex of the national economic groups, agriculture had to dominate or bargain. Despite its command of numbers, it failed to dominate. The reason was that it could act only through the organized, public effort of many weak and dispersed individuals, whereas industry was able to act privately through a few powerful individuals.

Public agitation competed with lobby influence. Agriculture, which had to bargain, bargained badly because it was of two minds. A powerful and a majority element in its leadership still held to the conventions of liberal economics. A powerful minority was prepared to bargain for government support of agricultural prices, whatever the effect on the struggle to lower the tariff. It was, in short, impossible to obtain agreement among agriculturalists as to what the immediate interests of agriculture were. This fact, of course, betrays the fundamental weakness of the concept of interest or of class, whether used as an instrument of political action or a term of academic analysis: It makes absolute what is in fact relative.

The second weakness was that the prairie West was a minority section. It could not prevail by numbers alone, and the realization of this gave rise to much talk about holding a balance of power at Ottawa. But the balance of power operates only among powers, that is, relatively stable entities. Another condition of its operation is that the powers of a power system be morally and sentimentally indifferent one to another. The farmer representatives at Ottawa from 1922 to 1925 were divided among themselves. Moreover they were not nationalists, like the Irish home rulers, and had no wish to be; and not all had freed themselves from old preferences for the Liberal or the Conservative party. They could not exercise a balance of power at Ottawa, nor can any section which is not on the verge of rebellion and prepared to strike for nationhood.

The third weakness was more subtle. The aims of the farmers in 1921 might have been realized by an agrarian majority in Parliament, but that majority had not been achieved, or even hoped for. They might have been realized, in part, by an agrarian bloc based on the prairie West. But this, possible in the United States, was a delusion under the Canadian constitution. The government in Canada is sustained, of course, not by provisions of the constitution, but by a majority in Parliament. If it is sustained, it can defy a bloc. If it is not, it can seek a majority in a general election. It must, in short, war on blocs and other dissident groups until it has rendered them harmless, or yield the government to them, in which case they have to assume the general responsibilities of government and maintain a majority. The sectional or occupational bloc in Canadian federal politics did not give an economic group opportunity to push its own interests in legislation, or to bring about government by a coalition of groups. It was to begin the destruction of the national parties in the prairie West. It also raised the question whether the parliamentary system is suited for the federal government of a sectional country. The western provinces developed their own political parties, and came to be represented more and more at Ottawa by more or less dissident groups: Liberal Progressive and UFA and, later, CCF and Social Credit. But as the contrary example of the Maritimes suggests, the national parties afforded minority sections perhaps their best opportunity, year in and year out, of influencing national policies. One result, then, of the outbreak of agrarian sectionalism in the prairie West was the weakening of the national parties there and the consequent diminution of western influence in the national government. This diminution would have been much greater had it not been offset by the convention that all the provinces must be represented in the federal cabinet.

16

Thus the bias of prairie politics had carried their development one phase further. Agrarian sectionalism had prevailed, had had its day, and had left its mark. But its concrete political achievements were few, if important, and it had come near to carrying the West out of the national councils. It had confirmed the tradition of protest begun in the days of political subordination, and it had demonstrated the inadequacy in Canadian politics of the sectional or occupational bloc. The bias of prairie politics had either to return to conformity with national political standards, and this return prosperity after 1929 would have greatly helped, or to take one spin of the ball further, beyond agrarian sectionalism to sectional utopianism. The elements of utopianism were already latent; the drought and depression of the early thirties brought them to the surface of prairie politics.

Utopianism, which may be defined for this paper as a readiness to adopt untried methods to achieve ideal ends, was not, of course, of western origin. To cite only the chief example, Social Credit, it is notorious that it was of immediate English origin, and that its roots are to be found in underconsumption economic theories of a century's standing. What the West did was provide a favourable environment for the development of utopian politics: heavy indebtedness, distrust of prevailing political methods and economic conventions, a sense still surviving from the frontier of the possibility of a second chance and a new life—or at least the old life on new terms—a tradition of protest, and the weakness of the old political parties.

While it is true that the West in the early thirties was particularly favourable to the development of utopian elements diffused through the English-speaking world, there had long been elements in its own life which contributed to an outburst of utopianism in the thirties. Most basic of these was the growing strength of evangelical Protestant sects and of the Mormon Church in the "Bible belt" from Winnipeg westwards. No new sect originated on the prairie frontier, but those which had begun elsewhere throve in the rural districts and the small towns of the West. No authoritative study has been made of this phenomenon. It is probable, however, that its origins were twofold. One was the partial failure of the more conventional churches, in particular the Anglican, Methodist, and Presbyterian, to meet the challenge of natural science in any convincing way. By tacitly admitting defeat on the first chapter of Genesis, they seemed to unsubtle minds to have abandoned the Scriptures entirely. The second was that these churches, with the Church of Rome, failed in part, as municipal and educational institutions did also, to solve the problems created by the diffusion of population over enormous areas. As a result, distrust of the "line churches" grew, partly because they were not fundamentalist enough, partly because their efforts to maintain resident clergy and church edifices seemed to be exacting and costly. In these conditions, the growth of fundamentalist religious sects was not surprising, but it created a readiness to listen uncritically to a secular evangelism, to trust bold assurance and to distrust critical doubt, and to accept credulously the promise of a new social order.

The West favoured, too, a ready response to certain idealistic trends, partly rationalist, partly religious, which were also generally diffused, but checked as they were not in the West by the conservatism of an established and sophisticated society. One was prohibition; another, closely related, was the feminine suffrage movement. In the political field, there was direct legislation, and in the economic, socialism. None of these is, of course, to be regarded as merely idealistic, still less as utopian. But the advocates of all tended to present them as offering the possibility of a decisive turn towards a new society. The reform movement of the first quarter of this century in the prairie West was, in short, tinged with millenarianism.

Even in strictly economic matters there was something of this spirit. The great majority of farmers wanted only to increase the farmer's returns. But all the farmers' organizations, from the Grange to the United Farmers, had some touch of uplift, and used the methods and often the songs of evangelism. The doctrine of the Wheat Pool was preached with apostolic fervour and received by the majority of farmers with the abandon of converts. Even socialism, that bleak and scientific analysis of society, was presented idealistically as a creed of social justice. And this superimposition of evangelical idealism on a base of hard materialism was an admirable preparation for the reception of Social Credit.

The way for Social Credit was not less well prepared by its rivals. The United Farmers of Alberta under the inspiration of Henry Wise Wood had committed Alberta to an experiment in group government and had broken the hold of the old parties on that province. Wood's group government, however, was to a great extent a tactical device designed to absorb the radical Non-Partisan League; it was basically conservative, an attempt to strengthen the farmer's position in society as it was. It was found wanting, therefore, when to an electorate made frantic by economic distress some sweeping measures of relief seemed imperative. The instrument for attempting a radical reconstruction of western and indeed Canadian society had already been forged in the Co-operative Commonwealth Federation. This new party, a real political party in organization and intent, was an attempt to bring together those farmer and labour organizations which were ready to undertake a reorganization of Canadian economic society on socialist principles. It embodied the most advanced economic and political thought of the agrarian and labour movements and it systematically condemned the capitalist society from the deficiencies of which, it was alleged, the Depression had sprung. Even the UFA federal members, breaking with the conservative leadership of Wood, were a part, an important part, of the new political movement.

Why did the people of Alberta not turn to the CCF? This is a question which Professor C.B. Macpherson has ably analysed in his *Democracy in Alberta.*[4] The farmers of Alberta were at war with the prevailing economic order; they had rejected the old political parties, the instruments of that order. In their midst a native party had arisen, in part the work of their own representatives in Parliament. They were offered a new political vehicle for their discontents, and new solutions to their economic problems. Yet they turned *en masse* to the leadership of a man who had never been in politics, the advocate of an economic doctrine which was totally untried and severely condemned by all professional economists, whether liberal or socialist. Professor Macpherson's explanation is that the western farmer was a *petit bourgeois.* The term is not a happy one, and one may question the utility of employing in the analysis of a fluid, unformed society a term drawn from an older and stratified society. That may be a class which does not behave as a class, the members of which do not think of themselves as a class, and strongly dislike the idea of class, but surely only in a Marxian sense. But if all Professor Macpherson means is that the purpose of the Albertan farmer and small-town merchant was to achieve economic independence, to make the farm or the store pay, one must agree with him. The western farmer and businessman did not want socialism, which they interpreted as an attack on all property, including their own small concerns. Yet they were vexed and angry with existing economic conditions. For them Social Credit promised an easy and a sweeping reform, without socialism. The

Albertan turned to it and, aided by the war boom and the soil boom, achieved utopia.[5] If it be objected that he did not thereby achieve a new society, it must be admitted that he has attained a new complacency. If one must travel to Nowhere, there is no more comfortable way than on a tide of oil.

Is this, then, the outcome of the bias of prairie politics, the achievement of a new political utopia, which now includes two great provinces and which hopes to extend its political frontiers until the whole nation is remade in its image? To attempt an answer would be to have history hover on the verge of prophecy. The historian must turn back and merely recapitulate the argument. The bias of prairie politics, it has been submitted, began in colonial subordination, continued in agrarian revolt, and went on to the political and economic utopianism of Social Credit. The principal presupposition of the argument has been that there are sections as well as nations, nations as well as civilizations. The sub-society which is a section, it is supposed, possesses some degree of integrity and character. That character, it is assumed, may be defined, and the relations of the sub-society with other societies explored. The prairie West has been defined as a colonial society seeking equality in Confederation. That equality was sought in order that the West should be like, not different from, the rest of Canada. The bias of prairie politics, however, has operated to produce equality with a difference. The emphasis of this paper has been placed on the sectional character of the prairie West. The justification advanced for this emphasis is that the West was a region of political and material differences sufficiently significant to give it the character of a sub-society. That being so, it is the relations of that sub-society with the nation of which it is a part which make significant the history of the prairie West. These relations passed through the phases of colonial subordination to, agrarian revolt against, and utopian rejection of, the political and economic controls, but not the institutional foundations, of the nation. Canadian institutions and the ideals of Canada were accepted and upheld, and in the present stage the purpose of western utopianism is to redeem them by capturing the nation. In a normal development the section would be merged in the nation; the utopian element of prairie politics seeks to merge the nation in the section. The attempt, obviously, is utopian. What is realistic and serious is that the decay of the national political parties and the great alterations in the conventions of parliamentary government in the western provinces are not without parallels in the rest of Canada. Western utopianism, it may be, is an exaggerated symptom of a national malady.

Notes

1. P.A.C., *Volunteer Review*, Vol. IV, No. 1, 3 January 1870, 9, quoting John Malcolm Reid in *London Free Press* of 16 December 1869.

2. A.K. Isbister reported a conversation to that effect with Sir Edward Bulwer Lytton, Colonial Secretary, when Cartier with Galt and John Ross visited England to discuss the confederation of British North America in 1858, in a letter to Donald Gunn of Red River: P.A.M., *Nor'Wester*, 28 December 1859; the letter is quoted (in part) in A.S. Morton, *History of the Canadian West to 1870–71*, 837. Isbister's letter by itself is no more than suggestive, but it is difficult to see how Cartier could have taken any other stand.

3. See the writer's introduction to *The Red River Journal of Alexander Begg* (Champlain Society, 1956).

4. (Toronto: University of Toronto Press, 1953).

5. Professor J.R. Mallory in his *Social Credit and the Federal Power in Canada* (Toronto, 1954) advances the view that Social Credit was taken up as a sectional weapon with which to attack federal control of credit and currency.

In Search of a Prairie Myth: A Survey of the Intellectual and Cultural Historiography of Prairie Canada

R. DOUGLAS FRANCIS

Reprinted from the *Journal of Canadian Studies/Revue d'études canadiennes*, Vol. 24, No. 3 (Fall 1989), 44-69, by permission of the author and the *Journal of Canadian Studies*.

Prairie Canada has produced a rich harvest of books and articles. Yet despite such abundance, the West still remains in some respects a *terra incognita*. While we know a great deal about who came to settle the West, where they settled, which institutions they established, which economic activities they carried on, and which political parties and traditions they established, we know very little about the mental ethos—the intellectual mindset and cultural milieu—of the region. Like in Canada as a whole, intellectual and cultural history in prairie Canada has been a new and limited field of study. This is particularly true if one makes the further distinction, as Brian McKillop does concerning Canadian intellectual history, between "works whose manifest intention is to address themselves to ideas and those that may be brimming with ideas but which have other purposes."[1] In my review of the historiography I have included reference to books and articles which were not written explicitly as intellectual or cultural history but do nevertheless offer insight into the intellectual and cultural life of prairie Canada. As S.F. Wise has noted in his pioneering article "Sermon Literature and Canadian Intellectual History," Canadian intellectual historians "must be concerned primarily with the interrelationship between ideas and actions, and therefore the intellectual commonplaces of an age, its root notions, assumptions, and images."[2] It follows, then, that such ideas can be garnished by historians researching political, economic, or social history from the perspective of the ideas, beliefs, or values motivating men and women to act. If nothing else, intellectual and cultural historians can at least benefit from such research and insights in pursuing their own more clearly defined studies in intellectual and cultural history. This essay will, then, explore what work has been done in the field and suggest new areas of exploration.

Four themes have predominated in the writing of the intellectual and cultural history of prairie Canada. One persistent theme is regional identity. Westerners have been as obsessed with searching for their regional identity as Canadians in general have been with their national identity. Do the prairie provinces constitute a unique region intellectually and culturally, and if so what are the common attitudes, values, and ideas that tie it together? What are the intellectual and cultural roots of the region, and when were they first set down? How are the prairies similar to, and different from, other regions in their attitudes, beliefs, and values, and how does the region relate on an intellectual level to the nation as a whole? These are the general questions addressed by prairie intellectual and cultural historians.

A second theme, and one closely related to that of a regional identity, is regional protest. In many ways, the prairie West has become synonymous with protest and discontent. But while there has been an extensive literature on prairie protest from the political and economic perspective, a great deal less has been written from the perspective of intellectual and cultural history. Virtually no one has studied prairie protest as an intellectual and cultural phenomenon to discover, for example, whether common threads of ideas and assumptions exist beneath the various manifestations of prairie protest. Discontent is as much a product of perception—or imagery—as reality, and this aspect of the subject needs to be explored.

A third and related theme is social reform. This is a relatively recent topic of historical interest, which is surprising given the variety and prominence of social reform movements that have arisen on the prairies. A study of the intellectual roots and underlying assumptions of social reform is a useful way of illuminating attitudes, beliefs, and cultural values of a region, since people involved in reform movements tended to be leaders in their communities and able to articulate the concerns of their fellow citizens. Furthermore, since social reform on the prairies has so often been closely associated with protest and religion, a study of social reform from the perspective of intellectual and cultural history might also shed light on the nature of prairie protest and regional identity.

The final theme is imagery. Imagery relates back to regional identity, for one way to get at that question is to examine how prairie Canadians, and others external to the region, have in the past sought to represent their region through art, literature, and traditional historical sources. Such an approach enables historians to look beyond the conventional means of defining the prairies—by political traditions, economic associations, and social activities—to see it as "a region of the mind" shaped by its literature, art, and myths.

These four themes do not of course constitute the totality of the field of intellectual and cultural history of prairie Canada; indeed, to place works in the field into just one of these four groups is, to some degree, artificial. Nevertheless, they do provide a way of organizing the writing in the field and of focusing the discussion in order to examine the continuities and differences in the approaches of prairie intellectual and cultural historians.

Regional Identity

Regional identity on the prairies dates back at least to the late nineteenth century, when the region was incorporated into Confederation, if not even earlier when the Métis saw themselves as constituting a "new nation." But regional identity as a subject of historical analysis, particularly from the perspective of intellectual and cultural history, is fairly recent. The first attempt was part of the eight-volume Frontiers of Settlement Series, published between 1934 and 1940. C.A. Dawson and E.R. Younge's *Pioneering in the Prairie Provinces: The Social Side of the Settlement Process* (1940) looked at schools and churches as both social and cultural phenomena.[3] The authors defined culture quite narrowly as "institutions" and intellectual assumptions as those ideas that illuminated the settlement process. They set their study into a larger historiographical context of the metropolitan-hinterland paradigm that evolved out of the Laurentian school of thought. Harold Innis, who first enunciated the Laurentian thesis, argued that Canadian history could be understood in terms of the influence of a succession of staple commodities, produced in a hinterland or marginal region, for the benefit of metropolitan centres outside the region that dominated the symbiotic relationship.[4]

The prairies became a hinterland dominated by the cities of central Canada, which shaped not only its economic activities and political institutions but also its cultural values and intellectual perspectives. Intellectually and culturally the prairie West became an extension of central Canada—utilizing the same institutions, and guided by the same beliefs, values, and norms and only modifying them sufficiently to adjust to the new prairie frontier environment. As Dawson and Younge noted: "The present discussion is concerned with the way in which educational institutions are transferred from old to new areas of settlement, with the problems concerning their early development, and with the adjustments which must be made to new physical and social environments."[5] Thus, for them, the prairies constituted a separate region in terms of topography and frontier status, but not in terms of its cultural and intellectual traditions. The region was a mirror-image of Canada as a whole, only less developed because of the "rough edges" as a frontier community.

A second series—"Social Credit in Alberta: Its Background and Development"—began where the Frontiers of Settlement Series left off and challenged its assumption that the prairies were a replica of central Canada. This series of ten studies examined agrarian protest in the West, exemplified through the rise of Social Credit in Alberta, as a unique prairie phenomenon. While none dealt with the intellectual origins of Social Credit or with Social Credit as a cultural phenomenon, two did deal with aspects of Social Credit that might be defined loosely as intellectual and cultural history: John Irving's *The Social Credit Movement in Alberta* (1959) and Jean Burnet's *Next-Year Country* (1951).

John Irving studied Social Credit as mass psychology. He explained why Albertans supported it, utilizing extensive interviews of those who had supported "Bible Bill" Aberhart's movement. Irving, a philosopher at the University of Alberta, saw his study as intellectual history. "Owing to its more limited objectives [in comparison to other large-scale movements based on philosophies such as socialism, communism, fascism, or Nazism]," he wrote, "the Social Credit movement provides an unusual opportunity for a study of the formative role of ideas in the process of social development."[6] By "ideas" he meant opinions, "gut" reactions, and expressions of frustration and desperation rather than "rational" explanations based on party ideology, platform, and intellectual goals. Indeed, S.D. Clark, the general editor of the series, noted in his "Foreword" to Irving's book that the study reinforced the minor role "ideas" and "rational discussion" played in the election of Social Credit in Alberta:

> For someone who believed that political action was the outcome of a rational process of discussion and deliberation, the observation of political developments in Alberta in the years 1932-5 would have been a disillusioning experience. The people truly appeared to have taken leave of their senses, and nothing but disaster, it seemed, could result from the election to office of persons who had so little understanding of the economic and political world as Mr. Aberhart and his Social Credit colleagues. (vii)

Yet Aberhart had his perception of "the economic and political world," and Social

Credit as an ideology was constructed on a comprehensive, albeit biased, view of how the world was unfolding and should unfold, of what was right and wrong with the capitalist system, of how democracy should function, and of how human beings responded in times of crises.

More recently, John Finlay has examined the English roots of Social Credit theory, and David Elliott has explored William Aberhart's Social Credit theories, which were often at variance with those of its founder, Major C.H. Douglas. But there is still a need for a study of the intellectual roots and philosophical assumptions of Social Credit theory and ideas to round out the earlier Social Credit series. Jean Burnet's *Next-Year Country* is a study in social rather than cultural history, but, like social history in general, it overlaps with cultural history in that it looks at the cultural values of the immigrants, particularly eastern Europeans, who settled in Hanna, Alberta (the area chosen for her case study) and the cultural institutions and values they established.[7] Yet Burnet's study only highlights by its absence the need for a study of how Social Crediters disseminated their ideas into local communities through radio, churches, the education system, and local clubs. This aspect of Social Credit—its function as a cultural phenomenon—is still in need of study.

W.L. Morton has been a major figure in the writing of the intellectual and cultural history of prairie Canada, although he never wrote a book that could be classified as such.[8] In articles and papers he presented the ideas necessary to the understanding of his native region. One of those ideas was that the prairie West was not an intellectual and cultural backwater, isolated from the cultural roots of western civilization. Morton rejected Frederick Jackson Turner's popular American frontier thesis for western Canada. The Canadian West, he argued, owed more to the older, established cultural traditions of Britain and Europe than to the frontier. Indeed, Morton saw the prairie West as a cross section of intellectual currents and cultural values that reached back in time to ancient Britain and medieval Europe, including such geographical regions as eastern and western Europe, Britain, the United States, and eastern Canada. This idea he presented in his local history of his own district of Gladstone, Manitoba: "A great heritage has been brought and transplanted with singularly little loss. The Church sprang from a far distant Palestine, local government going back to Robert Baldwin's Ontario, and the New England townships and beyond the seas to Norman and Saxon times; and self-government as the English-speaking people had developed it over the centuries and in new lands."[9]

Morton also emphasized the uniqueness of the prairie West among the other regions of Canada. That particularity lay in its primary relationship to the nation from the very beginning. Its "initial bias" was one of inequality, since from the time of incorporation into Confederation, the West was a colony of central Canada.[10] In this sense Morton's view was consistent with the metropolitan-hinterland theory, which he accepted as a valid interpretation of Canadian history from the western perspective, although ironically it only highlighted and justified the West's long tradition of revolt and protest against the "initial bias" of inequity.[11]

Morton wanted to study that tradition of protest, seeing it as a means to get at the related question of a regional identity. His *Progressive Party in Canada*, published in 1950, was the result.[12] He argued that the Progressive movement was more than a political or economic phenomenon; it had an ideological base and a reform impulse. He outlined the ideological rift between the "Manitoba wing" of the party, as personified in the liberal ideas of Thomas Crerar, and the "Alberta wing," as set out in Henry Wise

Wood's writings on group government.[13] But these opposing viewpoints were part of a larger ideology of progressivism which Morton did not develop and which still needs to be examined before prairie historians can fully understand the agrarian reform movement of the early twentieth century, culminating in the Progressive revolt of 1919 and the Progressive Party of the 1920s.

Morton identified another unique feature of the intellectual life of prairie society—its utopian spirit. Behind both the Riel Rebellion of the 1870s and 1880s and the rise of Social Credit and the CCF in the 1930s stood the spirit of utopianism, which he defined as "a readiness to adopt untried methods to achieve ideal ends." This idea he set out in his address to the Royal Society of Canada in 1955:

> The struggle of the prairie west against political subordination to central Canada had begun, and it was to go on to merge with the struggle against economic subordination to the capital and corporations of the east. The result of this struggle, both of its failures and its partial successes, was a release of that utopianism which has been endemic in western society since the French Revolution, and indeed in religious form since the Reformation, and which has always found a refuge and a stimulus on the frontiers of settlement.[14]

Here was another important theme in prairie history which Morton urged students of intellectual history to pursue.

That challenge has been taken up by one of his students, Anthony Rasporich, an intellectual historian who is at work on a study of utopianism in its various manifestations, including utopian thought, in western Canada. In "Utopian Ideals and Community Settlements in Western Canada 1880-1914," Rasporich examined "the broader role which utopian and quasi-utopian idealism played in the social and intellectual development of the West prior to the First World War,"[15] concluding that utopianism was a pervasive force in western Canada in both its literature and its settlement patterns, evident in the numerous utopian settlement schemes that emerged on the prairies. His study of utopian communities has shed light on this aspect of the social and cultural composition of prairie Canada as well as on the intellectual roots of the region since so many of these utopian communities were based on the ideas of utopian writers. Here then is one means of tracing the intellectual origins of prairie Canada.

While Morton highlighted some of the distinctive ideas and values of the prairies, he also emphasized that the West was like—and wanted to be like—the rest of Canada. "It is more important, if less arresting," he pointed out, "to observe that the institutions of the prairie West were Canadian institutions and that the people who worked those institutions and determined the political development of the West were in the overwhelming majority of Canadian birth and ancestry, than it is to discuss the differences of sectional politics."[16]

One way that the West remained closely linked to Canada was, Morton noted, in the large influx of Ontarians during the formative period of the region's intellectual and cultural development. In "A Century of Plain and Parkland," Morton argued that "modern civilization came to the plains and parkland in the 1870s, but in a specific form, that of Ontario settlement. The next generation was to be dominated by the introduction of the institutions and mores of Ontario into the prairies."[17] Manitoba thus became a cultural replica of Anglo-Saxon Ontario. Once again, Morton only sketched the picture in general terms, leaving the details of the intellectual and cultural links between the two regions to be filled in by later students stimulated by his insights.

At the time that Morton suggested that Manitoba's cultural values could best be understood through a study of their Anglo-Saxon roots, J.E. Rea, another western Canadian historian from Manitoba, offered a similar suggestion but from a different perspective. Whereas Morton tended to think of "culture" in terms of political culture, and "Ontario Anglo-Saxon values" in the context of the metropolitan-hinterland paradigm, Rea was identifying "culture" in terms of social beliefs, ethnic values, and ideological perspective, and seeing Anglo-Saxon Ontario values within the context of the Hartzian thesis.[18] Rea's perspective resulted in a new way of interpreting the intellectual and cultural roots of prairie Canada.

Rea agreed with Morton that the turning point in the emergence of "modern Manitoba" came with the large influx of Protestant Anglo-Saxon Ontarians in the 1870s and 1880s. Using Louis Hartz's *The Founding of New Societies*, Rea argued that these prairie settlers arrived in sufficiently large numbers from an established parent society before the cultural ethos of the new or "fragment" society had "congealed" (or become established); thus, they were able to shape the region's *mentalité*. He maintained that the cultural distinctions the region had enjoyed before the 1870s and 1880s with its native people, Métis, and early French and English settlers were "permanently altered" by the new wave of migrants. Manitoba was reborn in the image of Ontario. Rea also speculated that what happened initially in Manitoba occurred later in the other two prairie provinces. Neither Rea nor any other intellectual or cultural historian since has tested the validity of this latter hypothesis.

The cultural values that Manitoba inherited from its parent Ontario society and that became the "universal" culture of the new society took many forms of bitter dispute: between Protestants and Catholics over separate schools, English Canadians and French Canadians over language rights, and Anglo-Saxons and other ethnic groups over the extent to which Canada was a "British" country. These attitudes were part of the "cultural baggage" of Ontario migrants to the West. In the new society, these values, freed from the ideological evolution and balance that the parent society enjoyed, became even more entrenched and more pronounced. Manitoba, in other words, became Ontario writ large—a more pronounced form of bigoted Ontario than existed in Ontario itself. The Riel Rebellion, in which the indigenous Métis population of Manitoba was supplanted by the newly arrived Ontario migrants, and the Manitoba Schools Question, in which French-speaking Catholics were denied their separate schools and their language rights as had been guaranteed in the Manitoba Act of 1870, were the most obvious examples of ways in which the dominant Ontario culture stamped itself on Manitoba.

This imported Ontario culture became the basis of a late nineteenth-century western consciousness into which other non-Anglo-Saxon individuals and groups had to fit. It also redefined the relationship of the region to the nation. Rea used John Marlyn's novel, *Under the Ribs of Death*, which recounts the frustration, pain, and anger experienced by Sandor Hunyodi, a young Hungarian boy, in growing up in the dominant Anglo-Saxon society of Winnipeg, as a means to identify the prevalence and power of Ontario Anglo-Saxon Protestant culture in the West. He also pointed out that in the typical fashion of a rebellious youth the region soon turned on its parent society to express a strong anticentral Canadian, and especially anti-Ontario, attitude, while at the same time displaying many of the attitudes and characteristics of its parent society.

Recent work by ethnic historian Howard Palmer on nativist attitudes in Alberta suggests that the cultural values of prairie society were shaped as much by British and American beliefs and traditions as by those of Ontario; it was a three-fold melding of dominant Anglo-Saxon cultural groups. Nevertheless, Palmer does reinforce Rea's argument that a decidedly Anglo-Saxon cultural ethos was already in place when other non-Anglo-Saxon immigrants began to arrive at the turn of the century. Palmer's *Patterns of Prejudice* analyses the ideas and assumptions of that prairie nativist tradition.[19]

An idea only suggested by Morton and Rea—that the prairie West reflected the values and attitudes of Ontario—became the focus of Doug Owram's recent, full-scale study, *The Promise of Eden: The Canadian Expansionist Movement and the Idea of the West, 1856–1900*.[20] Here was a major study in prairie intellectual history—an analysis of the idea or image of the West in the minds of an influential group of expansionists in Upper Canada (Ontario) in the 1850s and 1860s, a group that was instrumental in persuading the government of the United Canadas, and after 1867 the Canadian government, to incorporate the North-West into Confederation.

Owram's study is of interest and significance from a number of perspectives, including that of a regional identity. He has shown how the identity of the West was first shaped by the values, attitudes, and ideas of a small but powerful group of Ontario expansionists who transformed the image of the West from that of a semi-Arctic wilderness to a fertile garden and an agricultural hinterland, because it served their own expansionist ambitions as Canadians to imagine the West in those terms. That manipulation of image occurred before Canada acquired the North-West in 1870. What happened after 1870, according to Owram, was a self-fulfilling prophecy: Ontarians moved into the West, which they rightly believed belonged to them, and stamped their white Anglo-Saxon Protestant ("Waspish") values on the region. The expansionist spirit lived on to shape the West into a miniature replica of Canada (read Ontario) and into the "new Britannia."

While Owram's study helps to explain the intellectual and cultural roots of prairie Canada, it fails to explain how this initially Ontario image was transformed into a prairie regional identity which, at one and the same time, served ironically as a replica of Ontario and a defiance—indeed, a denial—of that heritage. Many of the Ontario expansionists who went West later became the strongest exponents of western regionalism and led the struggle of the West to liberate itself from alleged Ontario oppression. Owram suggests that this regional identity was forged out of disillusionment with the expansionist rhetoric, but the nature of that disillusionment and the way it translated itself into a regional consciousness need further analysis.

Gerald Friesen notes in his essay, "The Western Canadian Identity," that a western myth evolved in the late nineteenth century to become the basis of its regional consciousness or identity. The myth was premised on the idea of "the new society which would be created in an 'empty' land. Environmentalism, pastoral and agrarian myths, physiocratic beliefs, and elements now associated with the 'frontier' thesis—democracy, egalitarianism, individualism, cooperation, virility, opportunity, innovation—were aspects of the new society in popular estimation."[21] Friesen does not, however, explain how these ideas became part of a western consciousness and mythology or how they influenced the way westerners saw themselves.

In his essay "Homeland to Hinterland: Political Transition in Manitoba, 1870 to 1879,"[22] Friesen comes closer to explaining when precisely this regional identity took shape. He takes what was a minor political power struggle between English- and

French-speaking Manitobans in 1879 as evidence of a larger cultural struggle between an old and new way of life. In that same year there were, he points out, a number of nonpolitical incidents, which although unnoticed by the politicians were of special significance to the cultural historian of prairie Canada—the change in the perception of time from something to be measured in terms of natural phenomena and bells to measurement by clocks; the shift from cash sales to a credit system; the replacement of a common and open-access land holding system by private property; and the beginning of an agricultural export economy dominated by a small business elite. These changes were indicative of an important cultural phenomenon: the transition from a preindustrial, fur trade economy to an industrial capital culture based on the wheat economy. Friesen argues that the year 1870 may make sense from a political perspective as the point of transition from one era to another. From a cultural perspective, however, it is not so pertinent. Culturally, a new periodization is needed, he argues. The point of transition is the half-century between the 1840s and the 1890s when the society of the western interior went from "a homeland to hinterland culture."

Another article which sheds light on this era of transition is Paul Rutherford's "The Western Press and Regionalism, 1870-96." As the title suggests, he is interested in the role that the western press played in shaping a regional identity during the first generation of prairie settlement. He notes at the outset that Ontarians were "the most influential group among the new settlers" and therefore they "provided the foundation for the new community . . . [But] this did not prevent the growth of a unique western regionalism. Western conditions, primarily economic but also cultural and political, changed the outlook of the newcomers. Very soon westerners became conscious of their own regional identity and of their underprivileged position in the dominion."[23]

The roots of that regional identity, Rutherford suggests (very much along the lines of Friesen), lay in a "myth of the West" perpetuated by the western press. It was a "myth of potential"; the West was "destined to become the granary of the world, the last and richest frontier of European expansion." This myth was not anti-Canadian; on the contrary, it emphasized the role that the new and prosperous West could play in creating a greater Canadian nation. As well, Rutherford notes, the myth was premised on certain conservative cultural values, foremost among them the need for social conformity: "Prairie journals argued the need to preserve the English heritage, to construct a civilized and ordered Christian community. They fostered such authorities as the family, the church, the school, and the police, and such values as religion and morality, law and order, sobriety and cultivation."[24]

Nevertheless, Rutherford notes that the myth turned on itself when its ideals were not achieved. Economic depression and limited growth prevented the West from "becoming the new heartland of Canada; rather it had remained an economic and political colony of central Canada." Thus Rutherford agrees with Owram that the crucible out of which a western regional consciousness was forged was one of failure, depression, and disappointed dreams. It became a defensive identity, seeking to locate blame in institutions and individuals outside the region, namely federal politicians, the Canadian Pacific Railway Company, and the people of Ontario.

Educational historian David Jones also explores the myth of the West. In "The *Zeitgeist* of Western Settlement: Education and the Myth of the Land,"[25] he argues that educators in western Canada during the settlement period perpetuated a myth of the land which eulogized the farmer and elevated farming as a mission. They taught students the importance of gardening and farming, not only, nor mainly, as vocation but also as character building. Jones's study deals with one cultural institution—the school—that helped to develop the myth of the land. What is needed, and Jones points it out himself, is a study of the myth of the land as perpetuated by other moulders of culture, which might include newspapers, popular literature, immigration propaganda, art, music, and social clubs. What Jones might also have called for is a study of a larger "myth of the West," of which the land was only one, albeit an important, component. This larger "myth of the West," I would suggest, constituted "the *Zeitgeist*," the spirit of the time.

Morton, Rea, Owram, Friesen, Rutherford, and Jones have thus all contributed to an understanding of the intellectual and cultural values that formed the roots of late nineteenth-century western Canadian consciousness, but there is still a need for a full-scale study of the subject. Such a project would shed further, perhaps more revealing, light on the unique features of the region that set it apart and have given it a strong regional consciousness ever since.

The aforementioned studies concentrate on the impact of English-speaking Canadians, especially Ontarians, on the intellectual and cultural history of prairie Canada. What impact did French Canadians—or for that matter other non-Anglo-Saxon immigrants—have on the moulding of a regional identity? At the time that the West was incorporated into Confederation, there existed a sizeable French-speaking population in the region. Did francophones influence the region's intellectual and cultural evolution?

Considerably less work has been done on this subject, but two historians have examined the attitudes of French Canadians towards the West and offered insights into western Canadian intellectual and cultural history. Arthur Silver argues in "French Canada and the Prairie Frontier, 1870-1890" that French Canadians in Quebec saw the West "as an infertile land where agricultural failure was almost certain."[26] This negative attitude towards the land was a serious enough indictment, but greater still was the belief that French Canadians would lose their national identity in the West. The West was an alien land culturally, far removed from *la patrie*. Thus Silver argues that in the French-Canadian *mentalité* the idea of the West as expressed in the Quebec newspapers and by Church leaders was a far cry from the view of English Canadians at the time. While Ontarians saw the West as an agricultural paradise and land of opportunity, Quebecers saw it as a cold, barren, desolate area where French Canadians were not welcome. As a result, French Canadians had a limited impact on the West during the critical formative period of its evolution.

Robert Painchaud agreed with Silver's argument, but emphasized the difference in attitude towards the West found in the Catholic hierarchy in the West as opposed to the Quebec hierarchy. The former tried to encourage Quebecers to come West, but their efforts were thwarted by the Quebec clergy who feared losing touch with their parishioners. They maintained instead that "French Canadians should remain in their province lest they lose their majority there and their influence in Confederation."[27] Thus the Church in the West had to rely on its own cultural institutions—colonizing societies, newspapers, social clubs such as the Société St. Jean-Baptiste, and government—to promote colonization to the West. Painchaud had analysed the idea of the West presented by these cultural media. Still, we need to know more about the attitudes and beliefs of those French-speaking Canadians residing in the West in the formative period of its evolution in the late nineteenth century.

What remains of interest is the extent to which the initial regional consciousness moulded in the crucible of late nineteenth-century western settlement lived on or evolved in the twentieth century. Is there an enduring regional identity that transcends time and gives a unity to the region over its historical development? This question has not received much attention, but some ideas have been formulated to date which, while they are not purely intellectual or cultural history, verge on the field.

Political scientist Roger Gibbins argues in *Prairie Politics and Society: Regionalism in Decline*[28] that if a regional identity did exist at one time it no longer does. As his subtitle indicates, western regionalism is slowly being replaced by provincial identities. Gibbins uses prairie politics as the basis for his study, but his book is more than a political analysis. It also tells us a great deal about prairie political culture. He argues that initially the prairies did form a distinct and homogeneous region with a common culture, including a unified political culture, based on a distinctive ethnic makeup, rural lifestyle, and common socioeconomic conditions which manifested themselves in a unique form of political protest. It was the sense of alienation and protest that differentiated the prairies from the rest of Canada, setting it apart and giving it a regional identity. But such differences—expressed in the development of third parties on the prairies—have faded in time as is evident in the integration of the region into the mainstream of Canadian party politics.

From the viewpoint of intellectual and cultural history, unfortunately, Gibbins's study does not explore the uniqueness of political culture in the three prairie provinces. He is more successful in capturing the essence of the unified prairie regional culture in the pre-World War II era than he is in discussing the provincial cultures of the West today. Nevertheless, his thesis is provocative. It challenges intellectual and cultural historians to ask to what extent regional or provincial identities exist today, and, if they do exist, to analyse them.

Nelson Wiseman, another political scientist, has used concepts of ideology and ethnicity to explain the different political traditions in the three prairie provinces.[29] Using a form of Hartzian analysis, Wiseman argues that the liberal ideology of Ontario (with its tory touch) prevailed in Manitoba because of the influx of Ontarians during its formative period of development. In Saskatchewan, by contrast, the dominant ideology was socialism, because of the large number of British socialist immigrants in that province's early history, while in Alberta liberal populist ideas prevailed as a result of the dominant American influence there. Thus Wiseman would agree with Gibbins that on the prairies, political culture is of a provincial nature.

David Smith, a fellow political scientist, challenges Gibbins's and Wiseman's theses in his article "Political Culture in the West."[30] As his title indicates, Smith believes that a unified western Canadian political culture does exist. It is evident in the consistently negative response of westerners to three fundamental questions: what is the West's attitude to cultural dualism? what is its attitude to the central government? and how can it influence decisions of that government? The region has opposed cultural dualism as an affront to its theory of multiculturalism and its practice of Anglo-conformity. It has been suspicious of the central government as the agent of domination of the regions from the beginning of the West's incorporation into Confederation. Finally, the West has never felt that it has had any impact on the federal government whether acting through the dominant party, third parties, or the official opposition party. The consistency of response over time to these questions constitutes, for Smith, "a set of values which derives from the common heritage of western political culture."

Paul Voisey's *Vulcan: The Making of a Prairie Community*[31] is an important study in regional identity which looks at the question of identity from the perspective of local prairie communities. In his study he examines how the region of Vulcan developed and took on its own identity. Historical geographers have long been talking about "functional" regions—areas which function as regions but do not fit the traditional boundaries usually identified as a region; Vulcan is seen as a functional region within the larger region of prairie Canada. Interestingly, Voisey reverses the usual approach to sociocultural studies. Rather than applying a macrocosmic theory to a study, he begins with an exhaustive microanalysis of the region in order to test in practice the validity of various historical theories, including such popular ones as "frontierism" and the "metropolitan-hinterland" paradigm. Such local studies, from the cultural perspective, will prove increasingly useful in understanding the West and its regional identity.

Other "functional" prairie communities are in need of study in the quest for a regional identity. The ranching community has received some attention as a sociocultural phenomenon. David Breen has looked at the British cultural influences, while Sheilagh Jameson and Lewis G. Thomas have looked at the cultural milieu of the ranching elite and the link between the ranching community and the city of Calgary.[32] A quite different area of focus is the culture of prairie women. Veronica Strong-Boag, Susan Jackel, and Elie Silverman have touched on some aspects of the subject, particularly through the lives of prominent women on the prairies, but more work needs to be done before we can talk about a distinctive prairie women's culture and adequately define its characteristics.[33]

Regional Protest

Because protest appears to be a constant in prairie history, a study of the ideology of protest should be a useful means to understanding the intellectual currents and cultural composition of the region. There is, of course, a rich and extensive literature on protest from Riel to the Progressives to Social Credit and the CCF in the 1930s. Indeed, no topic in prairie history has generated more interest than protest. But when one searches for studies of prairie protest from the perspective of intellectual and cultural history, the harvest is less bountiful. In fact, regional protest seems to be an almost neglected subject. There is not, for example, any study which attempts to discover a common thread of ideas or beliefs that underlies various prairie protests, thereby linking them as part of a prairie tradition. Yet a quick glance would suggest that continuity does exist and that an examination of protest movements from this perspective would be a fruitful exercise.

One common underlying thread is religion. From Riel to Social Credit, religious aspirations and beliefs have formed a backdrop to revolt. Until fairly recently, this aspect of revolt had not been dealt with, historians preferring instead to look at the political and economic roots of discontent or to emphasize the constitutional aspects.

Thomas Flanagan's *Louis 'David' Riel: 'Prophet of the New World'* is a study in intellectual history through an examination of the religious ideas of the prairie protest leader. Flanagan maintains that Riel's religious beliefs were central to his actions as the leader of the Métis people, and that, without an understanding of those ideas, we cannot fully appreciate what the rebellions were all about. "Louis Riel," Flanagan writes, "came to believe... during the course of his life that he was endowed by God with a special mission as 'Prophet of the New World'... After the mid-1870s, Riel's mission became the controlling force of his mind. All his actions, whether political or religious, revolved around it."[34]

Flanagan categorizes Riel's religion as a form of millenarianism, a faith "which expects salvation in the form of a millennium." He associates Riel with two categories of millenarian studies: Catholic heresy and nativistic resistance. In his final chapter he shows how Riel's religion fitted into other millenarian cults in four general categories: the social conditions under which it arose, the leader's personality, its doctrines, and Riel's attitude towards violence.

Flanagan's study places Riel's ideas into a larger intellectual context of religious movements, granting them both "respectability"—historians had dismissed earlier his views as the irrational rantings of an "insane" man—and significance. As well, he elevates the rebellions beyond a mere political power struggle or an expression of economic or even social discontent. They had a higher purpose and were motivated by principles and ideas.

The religious ideas behind the agrarian protest movement of the early twentieth century have not received the attention that Riel's ideas have. Richard Allen has measured the contribution that the ideas of the Social Gospel movement made to agrarian reform, to be discussed later under the theme of social reform. Yet the Social Gospel was only one form of religious expression that contributed to agrarian protest in the West. Many of the leaders of the Progressive movement were either religious leaders in their own right or came out of strong religious traditions. Among them were Henry Wise Wood, William Irvine, and Thomas Crerar. Biographies of these men do in some cases touch on their religious beliefs,[35] but no study to date has looked at their religious ideas as a means to understand the religious roots of agrarianism. Since some of them came out of fundamentalist sects and cults, and since, according to W.E. Mann,[36] such sects and cults were numerous on the prairies and were active institutions of prairie protest, a study of the ideas of prairie fundamentalism would greatly assist in our understanding of the intellectual roots of prairie culture and society.

The agrarian protest movement was, however, more than a form of religious revivalism. While religious ideas and values were an integral part of its ethos, there were other significant components to its ideology. David Jones identifies one such element in "The Western Agrarian Press and Country Life Ideology." He argues that this "country life ideology" was based on a positive image of the farmer as a moral, upright, and wholesome individual—God's vicar on earth—and of the land as a permanent, ever-renewing source of sustenance. "The purpose of the country," Jones notes, "was seen as the revitalization of man's spiritual power."[37] Jones's study reinforces the religious nature of agrarian protest, since the farmers' view of themselves and the land was clearly expressed in religious terminology. At the same time it helps to explain the deep distrust of businessmen, labourers, and easterners, for these groups were identified with urban centres, the antithesis of rural values.

A pervasive spirit and philosophy of cooperation also underlay the agrarian protest movement. Ian Macpherson's *Each for All* is a solid comprehensive history of the way in which the idea of cooperation was established in Canada, and particularly on the prairies.[38] It studies the forms it took in various areas of the country and how it evolved and changed in the period from 1900 to 1945. Most of the study cannot be classified as intellectual history, but in various chapters, in sections entitled "The State of the Movement," Macpherson does analyse some of the ideas and beliefs of the cooperative movement at different stages in its evolution. The "ideas" of interest to Macpherson are the practical political and economic ideas that the cooperatives put forward, and his aim is to link those ideas to the social context in which they were expressed. This approach is of particular pertinence to Canadian intellectual history, where, according to Syd Wise, a "pure" form of intellectual history—which might more accurately be called a "history of ideas"—does not exist. In Canada, ideas have always been more sociological than philosophical, expressions of opinions on practical issues of social relevance rather than philosophical discourses on universal themes of enduring interest over time.

What Macpherson's study fails to do is to look at the intellectual roots of cooperative thinking in the writings of socialists or liberal democrats in Britain, the United States, or Scandinavia, the countries from which immigrants with cooperative ideas came. Nor does he probe below the political and economic aspects of cooperative ideas to discover any philosophical outlook on such topics as human nature, society, the role of government, ideas of brotherhood, or the meaning of democracy.

George Melnyk, a prairie writer and critic, probes deeper than Macpherson by studying cooperation in terms of its philosophy or ideology. In *The Search for Community: From Utopia to a Co-operative Society* he examines a wide variety of cooperatives in the world, of which those in Canada in general and western Canada in particular provide but a few examples. He labels western Canadian cooperatives as "liberal democratic" in ideology, and proceeds to explain the label in terms of the ideology of prairie cooperatives. However, Melnyk's study is, of necessity, selective in its analysis. In its penetrating commentary and sweeping overview it reinforces the need for an intensive study of prairie cooperatives from the vantage point of both knowledge about the intellectual sources that the "philosophers" of agrarian reform cited and awareness of the assumptions about man and society implied in their view of the world. Just as man does not live by bread alone, movements do not survive on the basis of practical needs alone. They require justification, a rationale, ideas, and ultimately an ideology, if by ideology we mean what Melnyk defines as "a set of ideas which is generated by a group to defend its self-interest."[39] What was the "set of ideas" generated by prairie farmers to defend their self-interests? And where did these ideas originate? Such questions need to be answered before we can have a basic understanding of the agrarian protest movement. In other words, we still need an intellectual history of progressivism or populism in prairie Canada. Such a study would have a significant section on cooperative thought, but would go beyond that to an analysis of progressivism in general.

E.A. Partridge, the intellectual father of western Canadian cooperatives, has been the subject of two articles which discuss his ideas. In "A Canadian Utopia: The Co-operative Commonwealth of Edward Partridge," Carl Berger examines Partridge's utopian scheme as set out in *A War on Poverty*.[40] He traces the intellectual roots of Partridge's ideas to a variety of utopian writers in Britain, Europe, and the United States, and diagnoses the strengths and weaknesses of his visionary dream. A more recent article by Murray Knuttila utilizes Paul Baran's definition of an intellectual—an individual with the capacity to look at human society as a totality and with the aspiration to serve humanitarian ends—as the litmus test of whether Partridge can be labelled "the farmers' intellectual."[41] He concludes that on both accounts he can. But neither Berger nor Knuttila probe beneath Partridge's political and economic theories to grasp the philosophical principles upon which those theories were constructed.

Seen from the perspective of intellectual and cultural history, the CCF and Social Credit have received some attention, although much more needs to be done. With regard to the nationally oriented CCF, its chief intellectual roots lay in the east—in Toronto and Montreal—where the League for Social Reconstruction, an elite group of socialist academics from McGill and the University of Toronto, drafted the Regina

Manifesto for the party. The LSR had little association with the prairies, as Michiel Horn attests in "The League for Social Reconstruction in Western Canada."[42] But two of its founding members, J.S. Woodsworth and William Irvine, resided in the West. Allen Mills and David Walden have studied Woodsworth's ideas, regrettably, however, from the perspective of his national views rather than his prairie perspective.[43]

While a good deal of research has been done on the League for Social Reconstruction and its leaders,[44] there has been no attempt to show how their ideas were "sold" to prairie farmers who were not socialists and who thought in practical and immediate terms only. How did the CCF manage to bridge the gap between the more "intellectual" approach to reform of the LSR and the more "practical" concerns of prairie farmers who became the political backbone of the party. It would be of interest, for example, to study the ideas and issues debated at the annual CCF conventions to see what concerns farmers at the "grass roots" level had and also to examine how the CCF functioned as a "cultural phenomenon."

Seymour Lipset devotes a chapter to "Ideology and Program" in *Agrarian Socialism*, his study of the rise of the CCF to power in Saskatchewan. Here he explores the meaning of the idea of "socialism" to Saskatchewan farmers, discovering that for some it had a positive connotation and meant simply "cooperative action" while for others it carried a negative meaning and was associated with ideas of "atheism, confiscation of land, and dictatorship."[45] The result, Lipset notes, is that the Saskatchewan CCF dropped the word "socialism" from its program in order to win votes. In this sense, his *Agrarian Socialism* provides strong evidence of an anti-intellectual strain in prairie political protest.

Agrarian Socialism is most successful as a study in cultural history. Lipset emphasizes that the CCF succeeded because it reflected "the general values of the culture in which it has arisen." That culture manifested conservative values. Lipset points out, for example, the opposition that the CCF faced in its attempt to eliminate the "pro-capitalist" values in the province's education curriculum. He also emphasizes the strong religious tradition in CCF thinking. "It is not surprising, therefore," Lipset writes, "that, like British socialism, the Saskatchewan CCF, from the time of its formation and right down to the present, has had a moralistic and religious emphasis."[46] It has long been argued that the CCF, like Alberta's Social Credit, had a strong religious undercurrent, although the religious roots of the party have not yet been explored to any significant degree.

This is not the case of the religious roots of Social Credit in Alberta. In the wake of Irving's and Mann's earlier studies in the Social Credit series, historian David Elliott has more recently explored the religious nature of this protest movement. Elliott has concentrated on the ideas of "Bible Bill" Aberhart, the founder and leader of the movement and party. In "Antithetical Elements in William Aberhart's Theology and Political Ideology," Elliott argues that Aberhart's religious ideas changed once he converted to Social Credit. Once "highly sectarian, separatist, apolitical, other-worldly, and eschatologically oriented," Aberhart's ideas became the pragmatic opposite, and beyond, where his ends seemed to justify the means. To achieve Social Credit, according to Elliott, Aberhart was willing to alter his religious beliefs. Elliott draws a similar conclusion and deals more extensively with Aberhart's religious ideas in his biography of the charismatic "Bible Bill."[47]

Elliott also examines Aberhart's "political ideology" in an article entitled "William Aberhart: Right or Left?" He argues that initially Aberhart's ideology was more left-than right-wing. He drew heavily on the ideas of Edward Bellamy's *Looking Backward* and *Equality*, utopian novels which, as Elliott notes, depicted "a future society in which all land and industry would be nationalized, banks and money abolished, and a credit system substituted." In the end Elliott concludes that "Aberhart's economic and social thought had much more in common with the political left than with the right."[48]

Anthony Rasporich has suggested one common thread in prairie protest, that of utopianism and millennialism. In "Utopia, Sect and Millennium in Western Canada, 1870–1940," he points out that "intellectual continuities [existed] between early sects, utopians and millenarians and the later political movements of the 1930s both at the level of ideas and of certain individuals who bridged the two periods." His article analyses the millenarian response of prairie groups and individuals in the formative period from 1870 to 1885, the communitarianism in the settlement era from 1885 to 1910, millennialism in the Progressive era, and political utopianism in the early years of the CCF and Social Credit. In particular, he suggests links between prairie protest movements and ideas from prominent thinkers in Europe, Britain, and the United States, thus pointing out the strong intellectual undercurrents of prairie thought. He also argues that beneath the apparently diverse political views of the CCF and Social Credit lay a common religious vision: "[b]oth Aberhart's pre-millennial theology and T.C. Douglas's post-millennial vision of the Kingdom of God on earth in the depths of the Depression differed largely in their particulars, but their prophetic vision had a similar liberating promise."[49] Finally, Rasporich suggests that another common strain in prairie radicalism and utopianism is "its nationalist impulse." Throughout its history, the West has played the role of providing national utopian goals:

> First as simply empty space, it held utopian promise for national expansion and growth, and later as a proving ground for political and economic experiments. And throughout its history, the west proved full of moral imperatives for the nation, from the regenerative ideals of wartime in the Winnipeg General Strike, and of the Depression in the Regina Manifesto. The western voice was ever prophetic and millennial in its counsel, if somewhat utopian in its persistent attempts to assimilate the nation into the region.[50]

Such studies show that a continuity of thought does indeed exist in prairie Canada, providing a coherent identity to the region that distinguishes it from other regions in Canada.

Rasporich's approach is indicative of the useful role that the intellectual historian can and should play in the writing of regional and/or national history. Since ideas hold within them the development of thought through the years and beyond political or geographical boundaries, the intellectual historian is able to search for the continuity of thought that exists over time and within a region. While it is true that within Canadian intellectual thought in general and prairie intellectual thought in particular ideas must be tied to a specific social context to give them meaning, ideas do have a way of living on in different manifestations while still retaining a certain "core of thought" which gives them continuity over extended periods of time. The intellectual historian thus seeks to locate consensus rather than discontinuity.

Social Reform

Social reform is the third major theme in the intellectual and cultural historiography of prairie Canada. W.L. Morton first drew attention to social reform on the prairies in the conclusion of his *The Progressive Party in Canada*. Here he labelled the

Progressive movement as a form of social reform and linked it to other social reform movements such as prohibition, women's suffrage, and civil service reform.[51] But Morton did not attempt to explain how they were related, nor did he explore the ideology of reform which, he implied, lay at the root of the Progressive movement.

Richard Allen's *The Social Passion* was one of the first attempts to study the ideas of social reform in Canada by examining one important and underlying aspect of that reform—the Social Gospel Movement. "This book is a study in the history of ideas," he noted in the first sentence of his "Preface," "specifically with reference to the conjunction of the movements of religion and social reform in Canada in the years 1914 to 1928."[52] The book is national rather than regional in scope, although it has a great deal to say about the social gospel movement in the West, particularly about how the movement related to agrarian reform and labour radicalism.

Allen developed the link between the ideas of the social gospel movement and the agrarian revolt on the prairies more explicitly and directly in "The Social Gospel as the Religion of the Agrarian Revolt." He argued that religious ideas and beliefs, more than political, economic, or social factors, explained the cause, aspirations, and meaning of the agrarian revolt. Agrarian reform was more than the ubiquitous, discontented prairie farmer complaining about the weather and "eastern interests"; it operated on a set of ideas which were strongly religious in nature and which provided a rationale and justification for social reform. Religion played a positive and meaningful role in the secular life of prairie Canada. The farmers saw their struggle in terms of such traditional Christian beliefs as alienation and reconciliation, guilt, justification, redemption and ultimately hope. These ideas were tied to practical group, class, sectional, and regional concerns, he pointed out, but they came out of an intellectual tradition that included currents of thought from Britain and the United States. "Agrarian leaders had minds of their own," Allen reminds us; "many of them read widely; and the agencies of press, journal and book brought the world to their doorsteps."[53] The ideas of the social gospel that Allen found unique to agrarian reform included beliefs in cooperative or collective behaviour of farmers that grew out of their perception of themselves as virtuous, moral, and superior beings, their belief in Anglo-Protestant cultural domination and conformity, and their interest in an other-worldly and apolitical philosophy.

In *The Regenerators,* Ramsay Cook challenges Allen's view of the social gospel movement, particularly his assumption that social gospel had "Christianized" Canadian society and in so doing stemmed the tide of secularism. Like Allen's *The Social Passion*, Cook's *The Regenerators* is national rather than regional in scope, bringing together a wide variety of Canadian religious thinkers from all walks of life and various regions of the country as exponents of social gospel thinking. Cook did however connect his views on the social gospel to those of the West in his article "Francis Beynon and the Crisis of Christian Reformism," an analysis of the ideas of Francis Beynon, a prominent Winnipeg journalist and prairie political activist. He points out that at the heart of Beynon's thinking and activities was the belief in a "meaningful Christianity [which] professed a social ethic that would make the complacent uncomfortable and embarrass the corrupt."[54] Such a belief was in keeping with social gospel thinking. Beynon's "meaningful Christianity" involved her in a fight for women's rights as well as for the pacifist cause. Yet in her struggle for everyday social causes, Cook points out, Beynon came close to losing her Christian faith. Like the heroine in her novel *Aleta Dey,* she almost came to believe that the good society could only be built on secular, ethical concepts.

Cook concludes, therefore, that the social gospel movement led to the decline rather than the invigoration of Christianity; it paved the way for secularism. "Indeed," Cook notes, "secularism was implicit in the social gospel."[55] But he also argues that the weakness of the social gospel was its lack of ideas—its failure to have an eschatology which could distinguish its theology from mere sociology or secular reform. The social gospel movement died out for want of ideas; it became too practical and worldly in its aspirations. Nevertheless, by placing social gospel thinking in its social context, and exploring, in the case of Francis Beynon, the beliefs and ideas of one social gospeller in the West, Cook revealed an aspect of social reform which goes a long way to explaining why the movement died out in the post-World War I era. It was part of the general secularization of thought that accompanied a disillusionment with liberal ideas, including liberal Christianity, during the postwar era.

John Thompson has looked beyond the social gospel to other reform movements on the prairies. In "'The Beginning of Our Regeneration': The Great War and Western Canadian Reform Movements,"[56] he examines the impact of the First World War on two reform movements in western Canada: prohibition and women's suffrage. While his study is not intellectual history *per se*, it does analyse the views of the war held by western reformers, views which enabled them to use the war as an effective propaganda for their reform efforts. His study sheds important light on the assumptions and values of these reformers at one stage in the evolution of their movements, namely the war years; in particular, the study shows ideas in the social context in which they were expressed—what Syd Wise calls the "commonplace" of ideas which has been characteristic of Canadian intellectual history.

In his book *The Harvests of War: The Prairie West, 1914-1918*,[57] Thompson broadens his study of the prairie West in the war years. His investigation of "social reform" constitutes one chapter in this larger study. The book is essentially a social history—"a picture of a society during a period of crisis"—but in many places it is social history *cum* cultural history. Thompson is interested in analysing popular attitudes in western Canada towards war, ethnic minorities, and social issues as expressed through such cultural institutions and media as the press, schools, churches, literature, poetry, and songs.

Imagery

The final theme in the writing of intellectual and cultural history of prairie Canada is imagery. Images are "a reflection, a mirror," to use a dictionary definition; thus a study of images particular to the Canadian West is a study of how the region has perceived and defined itself, hence a study in regional identity. Those who have written on this theme have sought the essence of the region—its identity—by looking into the "landscape of the mind" for characteristic symbols, myths, and stories that have shaped its mythology and thus its sense of place. First taken up by a few literary and art critics who saw literature and/or art as cultural expressions which could only be appreciated in their historical evolution, the theme has more recently been taken up by intellectual and cultural historians of western Canada.

In "Nationalism, Identity, and Canadian Intellectual History," Brian McKillop urged intellectual and cultural historians to "bridge the narrowing gap between 'history' and 'literature'" by utilizing literature as a means to study cultural history.[58] His challenge is particularly appropriate for prairie history, which has had a rich "regional literature" (although I use that term reservedly, knowing it is fraught with problems for literary critics) and a number of stimulating literary critics who have themselves been conscious of linking literature and cultural history.

Dick Harrison's *Unnamed Country: The Struggle for a Canadian Prairie Fiction* is a good example of literary criticism *cum* cultural history. Indeed, Harrison notes that what distinguishes his literary study of prairie fiction from that of earlier works such as Edward McCourt's *The Canadian West in Fiction* and Laurence Ricou's *Vertical Man/Horizontal World* is his focus upon the cultural context out of which prairie literature emerges. As he notes, "All literature grows out of a time and a place, and cannot be understood or valued without an understanding of its cultural context."[59] For Harrison, an old culture confronted a new land, and the resulting adjustment in its various stages defines prairie fiction. The "old culture" he defines as essentially Anglo-Canadian–the same cultural context that Owram analyses in *The Promise of Eden* and that Morton, Friesen, and Rutherford allude to in their writings. What Harrison does is to show how the image of the West in prairie fiction changed from earliest writings in which the images reflected a heavily European perspective and form to more recent writings, in which both the form and the images are more western Canadian in orientation. Still, he concludes that the search for an indigenous prairie fiction–a regional identity in literary images–is not yet complete, hence his title–"Unnamed Country."

What Harrison's study lacks from the perspective of intellectual and cultural history is a sufficient understanding of the historical cultural context–which is simply to remind us that Harrison is a literary critic, not an intellectual or cultural historian. That limitation acknowledged, his study is a worthwhile place for the intellectual or cultural historian of prairie Canada to begin since he has highlighted the themes and images of the West over time–the region's *mentalité*–as expressed in its fiction.

Eli Mandel also has a strong appreciation of the historical and cultural context in which prairie literature has been written.[60] Where Mandel differs from Harrison is in his emphasis on prairie literature as an expression of cultural forms which go beyond the region itself to embody universal themes. Mandel reminds us that the West is more than a physical landscape–a unique topography–and in so doing he corrects an earlier imbalance in prairie writing that too readily links literature to its environment; it is a way of seeing that is shaped as much in the mind–in the images, stories, and myths–as in the land. To know the West, to seek its identity, we must therefore look to its intellectual and cultural roots which have been expressed in a creative and powerful prairie literature. Mandel's own literary criticism of prairie literature has already provided the context in which to appreciate that literature not only *qua* literature but as a cultural and historical document, a literary map of the prairie mind.

In art, Ronald Rees's *Land of Earth and Sky*, like Harrison's *Unnamed Country* in literature, is as much an introduction to cultural history as an appreciation of western Canadian art as art. Rees in fact points out that "the landscape art of the prairies chronicles [the] changes in perception [of the prairies]. Landscape paintings and drawings are charts of feeling and attitude as well as records of place. A painting tells as much about the painter and his times as it does about the places painted." Thus a study of prairie landscape paintings over time can be a study in prairie intellectual and cultural history. Rees's study is just that. As he himself claims "The emphasis [of the book] is on culture, in the broad sense of the word, not on art."[61] Accordingly, Rees takes a broad sweep of prairie art from the pre-settlement era to the present, showing as he goes how art expressed the prevailing cultural attitudes of the era. The weakness of the book (the same levelled at Harrison's book) is its failure to provide an adequate understanding of the historical cultural context. Still it is a fine example of the way in which art (like literature) can be seen as cultural expression and can be used fruitfully in a study of intellectual and cultural history.

Gerald Friesen has challenged Mandel's argument that prairie literature does not reflect the prairie region. In "Three generations of prairie fiction: an introduction to prairie cultural history," he shows prairie literature to be a cultural expression of the region at particular times in its historical evolution.[62] The three "generations" he examines are the settlement period, roughly 1850 to 1914; the era of transition from farming as an occupation to agribusiness in the interwar years; and the modern West of the post-1945 period. Each era saw a distinct literary tradition which reflected the cultural values and intellectual concerns of the time. Collectively Friesen's study shows the continuity and consistency within the prairie literary tradition. By sketching out the main themes in that tradition, Friesen offers a challenge to undertake a comprehensive cultural history of prairie Canada through a study of its rich literary tradition.

Clarence Karr's "Robert Stead's Search for an Agrarian Ideal" is a recent example of how intellectual historians can use literature to get at the ideas of an era.[63] By analysing the novels of Robert Stead, Karr is able to show the ways in which one prominent western Canadian intellectual came to terms with the critical issue of the transition of Canada from a rural agricultural to an urban industrial society.

Doug Owram's "The Myth of Louis Riel" examines how perceptions—or what I prefer to call "images"—of Riel in western Canadian historical literature over time reflected the prevailing cultural milieu.[64] He chronicles the evolution of Riel's image from villain to hero, and shows convincingly how that altered perception reflects current cultural and historical opinions and values. The result is as much a study of changing cultural values of western Canada as it is a study of evolving perceptions. Keith Walden has done the same in *Visions of Order*.[65] The book is a fine introduction to prairie cultural history and Canadian cultural history in general as well as an informative account of how the Mounties have been imagined in literature and other historical sources over the years.

My own work on the theme of imagery seeks to examine the changing images of the West over time as expressed in a variety of media including art, literature, poetry, and songs, as well as in traditional historical sources such as fur traders' journals, reports of scientific expeditions, travelogues, and government immigration propaganda. In "Changing Images of the West," I examined the secondary literature on the subject to see what has been done, what approaches have been taken, and what still needs to be done; "From Wasteland to Utopia: Changing Images of the Canadian West in the Nineteenth Century" explores the theme in nineteenth-century sources, while my recent book, *Images of the Canadian West: Responses to the Canadian Prairies 1690–1960*, takes the subject both back in time to the early fur trade era and ahead to the current period.[66] Obviously such a sweep in time and the use of a wide variety of sources attest to the very general nature of my treatment of the subject. Thus it too, like Friesen's work, stands as a challenge to pursue the subject in greater depth from a host of sources which have not yet been examined to any great extent.

In conclusion, there is a prairie intellectual and cultural history. A number of important studies have already carved out a distinct field. To date they have dealt generally with one of four themes—regional identity, protest, social reform, and imagery—but the themes are themselves interrelated and integral, thus giving a unity to the field. That underlying unity is an ongoing search for a prairie myth, some *Weltanschauung* which can be said to be uniquely western Canadian, of which these four themes are a component. We have only begun to shape that myth. Much unexplored territory still remains. Prairie intellectual and cultural history thus remains a relatively new and exciting field of historical research.

Notes

*I wish to acknowledge my appreciation to Gerald Friesen of the University of Manitoba; David Marshall, Howard Palmer, and Anthony Rasporich of the University of Calgary; and George Melnyk of Calgary for their helpful comments on this essay.

1. Brian McKillop, "So Little on the Mind," in his *Contours of Canadian Thought* (Toronto: University of Toronto Press, 1987), 24.

2. Syd Wise, "Sermon Literature and Canadian Intellectual History," in J.M. Bumsted, ed., *Canadian History Before Confederation: Essays and Interpretations*, 2nd edition (Georgetown, Ont.: Irwin-Dorsey, 1972), 254.

3. C.A. Dawson and E.R. Younge, *Pioneering in the Prairie Provinces: The Social Side of the Settlement Process* (Toronto: Macmillan, 1940). For a discussion of Dawson's ideas, see Marlene Shore, *The Science of Social Redemption: McGill, the Chicago School and the Origins of Social Research in Canada* (Toronto: University of Toronto Press, 1987), 68-120.

4. On the metropolitan-hinterland theory, see J.M.S. Careless, "Frontierism, Metropolitanism, and Canadian History," in Carl Berger, ed., *Approaches to Canadian History* (Toronto: University of Toronto Press, 1967), 63-83; and Careless, *Frontier and Metropolis in Canada: Regions, Cities, and Identities to 1914* (Toronto: University of Toronto Press, 1989).

5. Dawson and Younge, *Pioneering in the Prairie Provinces*, 159.

6. John A. Irving, *The Social Credit Movement in Alberta* (Toronto: University of Toronto Press, 1959), x.

7. John Finlay, *Social Credit: The English Origins* (Montreal: McGill-Queen's University Press, 1972); David R. Elliott and Iris Miller, *Bible Bill: A Biography of William Aberhart* (Edmonton: Reidmore, 1987).

8. On W.L. Morton, see Carl Berger, *The Writing of Canadian History: Aspects of English-Canadian Historical Writing since 1900* (Toronto: University of Toronto Press, 1976), 238-58; and Brian McKillop's "Introduction" to *Contexts of Canada's Past: Selected Essays of W.L. Morton* (Toronto: Macmillan, 1980), 1-11.

9. Quoted in Berger, *The Writing of Canadian History*, 243.

10. W.L. Morton, "The Bias of Prairie Politics," *Transactions of the Royal Society of Canada*, Series III, XLIX (June 1955), 57-66. [Also see pp. 12-19 in this volume.]

11. See W.L. Morton, "Clio in Canada: The Interpretation of Canadian History," *University of Toronto Quarterly*, XV (April 1946), 227-34.

12. W.L. Morton, *The Progressive Party in Canada* (Toronto: University of Toronto Press, 1950).

13. See W.L. Morton, "The Social Philosophy of Henry Wise Wood," *Agricultural History*, XXII (April 1948), 114-23.

14. Morton, "The Bias of Prairie Politics," 63, 58. [Also see pp. 17, 13 in this volume.]

15. Anthony Rasporich, "Utopian Ideals and Community Settlements in Western Canada 1880-1914," in H. Klassen, ed., *The Canadian West: Social Change and Economic Development* (Calgary: Comprint, 1977), 37.

16. Morton, "The Bias of Prairie Politics," 57. [Also see p. 12 in this volume.]

17. W.L. Morton, "A Century of Plain and Parkland," in R. Allen, ed., *A Region of the Mind* (Regina: Canadian Plains Study Center, 1973), 168.

18. J.E. Rea, "The Roots of Prairie Society," in D. Gagan, ed., *Prairie Perspectives* (Toronto: Holt, Rinehart & Winston, 1970), 46-55.

19. Howard Palmer, *Patterns of Prejudice: A History of Nativism in Alberta* (Toronto: McClelland and Stewart, 1982).

20. Doug Owram, *Promise of Eden: The Canadian Expansionist Movement and the Idea of the West 1856–1900* (Toronto: University of Toronto Press, 1980).

21. Gerald Friesen, "The Western Canadian Identity," Canadian Historical Association Annual *Report* (1973), 15.

22. Gerald Friesen, "Homeland to Hinterland: Political Transition in Manitoba, 1870 to 1879," Canadian Annual Report: *Historical Papers* (1979), 33–47.

23. Paul Rutherford, "The Western Press and Regionalism, 1870–96," *Canadian Historical Review*, LII, 3 (September 1971), 288.

24. Ibid., 294–95.

25. David Jones, "The *Zeitgeist* of Western Settlement: Education and the Myth of the Land," in J.D. Wilson and D.C. Jones, eds., *Schooling and Society in 20th Century British Columbia* (Calgary: Detselig, 1980), 71–89. For a general and popular discussion of the subject of a "myth of the land," see as well Jones, *Empire of Dust: Settling and Abandoning the Prairie Dry Belt* (Edmonton: University of Alberta Press, 1987).

26. Arthur Silver, "French Canada and the Prairie Frontier, 1870–1890," *Canadian Historical Review*, L, 1 (March 1969), 11–36. See as well his *The French-Canadian Ideas of Confederation 1864–1900* (Toronto: University of Toronto Press, 1982), 67–87.

27. Robert Painchaud, "French-speaking Settlers on the Prairies, 1870–1920," *Canada's Visual History*, Series I, Vol. 19; and his "French-Canadian Historiography and Franco-Catholic Settlement in Western Canada, 1870–1915," *Canadian Historical Review*, LIX, 4 (December 1978), 447–66.

28. Roger Gibbins, *Prairie Politics and Society: Regionalism in Decline* (Toronto: Butterworths, 1980).

29. Nelson Wiseman, "The Patterns of Prairie Politics," *Queen's Quarterly*, 88, 2 (Summer 1981), 298–315.

30. David Smith, "Political Culture in the West," in D.J. Bercuson and P.A. Buckner, eds., *Eastern and Western Perspectives* (Toronto: University of Toronto Press, 1981), 169–82.

31. Paul Voisey, *Vulcan: The Making of a Prairie Community* (Toronto: University of Toronto Press, 1988). On the subject of "functional regionalism" see William Westfall, "On the Concept of Region in Canadian History and Literature," *Journal of Canadian Studies*, 15, 2 (Summer 1980), 3–15; G.W.S. Robinson, "The Geographical Region: Form and Function," *Scottish Geographical Magazine*, LIX (1953), 49–58; and J. Wreford Watson, *North America: Its Countries and Regions* (New York: Praeger, 1967).

32. David Breen, *The Canadian Prairie West and the Ranching Frontier, 1874–1924* (Toronto: University of Toronto Press, 1983); Sheilagh Jameson, "The Social Elite of the Ranch Community and Calgary," in A.W. Rasporich and Henry Klassen, eds., *Frontier Calgary: Town, City, and Region 1875–1914* (Calgary: McClelland and Stewart West, 1975), 57–70; and Lewis G. Thomas, "The Rancher and the City: Calgary and the Cattlemen, 1883–1914," *Transactions of the Royal Society of Canada*, Series IV, VI (June 1968), 203–15.

33. See the relevant sections in Veronica Strong-Boag, *The New Day Recalled: Lives of Girls and Women in English Canada, 1919–1939* (Toronto: Copp Clark Pitman, 1988) and her "Ever a Crusader: Nellie McClung, First-Wave Feminist," in V. Strong-Boag and Anita Clair Fellman, eds., *Rethinking Canada: The Promise of Women's History* (Toronto: Copp Clark Pitman, 1986), 178–90; Susan Jackel, ed., *A Flannel Shirt and Liberty: British Emigrant Gentlewomen in the Canadian West, 1880–1914* (Vancouver: University of British Columbia Press, 1982); and her "Introduction" to Georgina Binnie-Clark, *Wheat and Women* (Toronto: University of Toronto Press, 1979); and Eliane L. Silverman, *The Last Best West: Women on the Alberta Frontier, 1880–1930* (Montreal: Eden Press, 1984).

34. Thomas Flanagan, *Louis 'David' Riel: 'Prophet of the New World'* (Toronto: University of Toronto Press, 1979), vii.

35. On Henry Wise Wood see W.K. Rolph's *Henry Wise Wood of Alberta* (Toronto: University of Toronto Press, 1950) which touches on Wise Wood's religious background in the Campbellite

Church, but does not develop it to any extent. Anthony Mardiros's *William Irvine: The Life of a Prairie Radical* (Toronto: Lorimer, 1979) deals only in a cursory fashion with Irvine's early religious life and hardly at all with his religious ideas. Howard Palmer deals with Irvine's religious and political life, and to an extent his ideas, during Irvine's Calgary years in "William Irvine and the Emergence of Political Radicalism in Calgary, 1916-1921," *Fort Calgary Quarterly*, 7, 2 (Spring 1987), 2-19. Reginald Whitaker's "Introduction" to *The Farmers in Politics* (Toronto: McClelland and Stewart, 1976) provides a very good analysis of Irvine's ideas as expressed in this major publication. Thomas Crerar still awaits a biography. On the ideas of Wise Wood and Irvine see William Stabler, "The Progressive Ideology of Henry Wise Wood and William Irvine," B.A. Honours Thesis, University of Calgary, 1980.

36. W.E. Mann, *Sect, Cult and Church in Alberta* (Toronto: University of Toronto Press, 1955).

37. David Jones, "'There Is Some Power About the Land'—The Western Agrarian Press and Country Life Ideology," *Journal of Canadian Studies*, 17, 3 (Fall 1982), 99.

38. Ian Macpherson, *Each For All: A History of the Co-operative Movement in English Canada, 1900-1945* (Toronto: Macmillan, 1979).

39. George Melnyk, *The Search for Community: From Utopia to a Co-operative Society* (Montreal-Buffalo: Black Rose Books, 1985), 28.

40. Carl Berger, "A Canadian Utopia: The Co-operative Commonwealth of Edward Partridge," in S. Clarkson, ed., *Visions 2020: Fifty Canadians in Search of a Future* (Edmonton: Hurtig, 1970), 257-62.

41. K. Murray Knuttila, "E.A. Partridge: The Farmers' Intellectual," *Prairie Forum*, 14, 1 (Spring 1989), 59-74.

42. Michiel Horn, "The League for Social Reconstruction in Western Canada," in R.D. Francis and H. Ganzevoort, eds., *The Dirty Thirties in Prairie Canada* (Vancouver: Tantalus Research, 1980), 65-76.

43. Allen Mills, "The Later Thought of J.S. Woodsworth, 1918-1942: An Essay in Revision," *Journal of Canadian Studies*, 17, 3 (Fall 1982), 75-95; David Walden, "'Following the Gleam': The Political Philosophy of J.S. Woodsworth," in J. William Brennan, *'Building the Co-operative Commonwealth': Essays on the Democratic Socialist Tradition in Canada* (Regina: Canadian Plains Research Center, 1984), 43-56.

44. See M. Horn, *The League for Social Reconstruction: Intellectual Origins of the Democratic Left in Canada 1930-1942* (Toronto: University of Toronto Press, 1980); R. Douglas Francis, *Frank H. Underhill: Intellectual Provocateur* (Toronto: University of Toronto Press, 1986); and Sandra Dwja, *The Politics of the Imagination: A Life of F.R. Scott* (Toronto: McClelland and Stewart, 1987).

45. Seymour Lipset, *Agrarian Socialism: The Co-operative Commonwealth Federation in Saskatchewan. A Study in Political Sociology* (Berkeley: University of California Press, 1971), 161.

46. Lipset, *Agrarian Socialism*, 160, 170.

47. David Elliott, "Antithetical Elements in William Aberhart's Theology and Political Ideology," *Canadian Historical Review*, LIX, 1 (March 1978), 39; Elliott and Miller, *Bible Bill: A Biography of William Aberhart.*

48. David Elliott, "William Aberhart: Right or Left?," in Francis and Ganzevoort, eds., *The Dirty Thirties*, 11-32.

49. Anthony Rasporich, "Utopia, Sect and Millennium in Western Canada, 1870-1940," *Prairie Forum*, 12, 2 (Fall 1987), 217, 237-38.

50. Ibid., 238.

51. Morton, *The Progressive Party in Canada*, 267ff.

52. Richard Allen, *The Social Passion: Religion and Social Reform in Canada 1914-28* (Toronto: University of Toronto Press, 1971), xxiii.

53. Richard Allen, "The Social Gospel as the Religion of the Agrarian Revolt," in C. Berger and R. Cook, eds., *The West and the Nation: Essays in Honour of W.L. Morton* (Toronto: McClelland

and Stewart, 1976), 174–86. [Also see pp. 138–47 in this volume.]

54. Ramsay Cook, "Francis Marion Beynon and the Crisis of Christian Reformism," in Berger and Cook, eds., *The West and the Nation*, 187–208.

55. Ibid., 202.

56. John Thompson, "'The Beginning of Our Regeneration': The Great War and Western Canadian Reform Movements," Canadian Historical Association, *Historical Papers* (1972), 227–45.

57. John Herd Thompson, *The Harvests of War: The Prairie West, 1914–1918* (Toronto: McClelland and Stewart, 1978).

58. Brian McKillop, "Nationalism, Identity, and Canadian Intellectual History," in *Contours of Canadian Thought*, 17.

59. Dick Harrison, *Unnamed Country: The Struggle for a Canadian Prairie Fiction* (Edmonton: University of Alberta Press, 1977).

60. See, for example, Eli Mandel, "Images of Prairie Man," in Allen, ed., *A Region of the Mind*, 201–209; Mandel, "Romance and Realism in Western Canadian Fiction," in A.W. Rasporich and H. Klassen, eds., *Prairie Perspectives* 2 (Toronto: Holt, Rinehart and Winston, 1973), 197–211; and Mandel, "Writing West: on the road to Wood Mountain," *Canadian Forum*, LVII (June-July 1977), 25–29.

61. Ronald Rees, *Land of Earth and Sky: Landscape Painting of Western Canada* (Saskatoon: Western Producer Prairie Books, 1984), 1, 2; see also his *New and Naked Land: Making the Prairies Home* (Saskatoon: Western Producer Prairie Books, 1988).

62. Gerald Friesen, "Three generations of prairie fiction: an introduction to prairie cultural history," in Bercuson and Buckner, eds., *Eastern and Western Perspectives*, 183–96.

63. Clarence Karr, "Robert Stead's Search for an Agrarian Ideal," *Prairie Forum*, 14, 1 (Spring 1989), 37–57.

64. Douglas Owram, "The Myth of Louis Riel," *Canadian Historical Review*, LXIII, 3 (September 1982), 315–36.

65. Keith Walden, *Visions of Order: The Canadian Mounties in Symbol and Myth* (Toronto: Butterworths, 1982).

66. R. Douglas Francis, "Changing Images of the West," *Journal of Canadian Studies*, 17, 3 (Fall 1982), 5–19; and Francis, "From Wasteland to Utopia: Changing Images of the Canadian West in the Nineteenth Century," *Great Plains Quarterly*, 7, 3 (Summer 1987), 178–94; R. Douglas Francis, *Images of the West: Responses to the Canadian Prairies, 1690–1960* (Saskatoon: Western Producer Prairie Books, 1989).

Western Politics and National Unity

DAVID E. SMITH

Reprinted from David J. Bercuson, ed., *Canada and the Burden of Unity* (Toronto: Macmillan of Canada, 1977), 143–168, by permission of the author.

There is nothing unusual in the benefits of a federation being unequally distributed among its constituent units—it happens in all existing federations and contributed to the disintegration of several that failed (i.e., the West Indies and Malaysia). But as a rule, in a federal polity the least-favoured areas are the seat of the greatest resentment. What is unusual in Canada is that the four western provinces, who are materially better off than the five eastern provinces, and two of whom rival Ontario in per-capita wealth, should be marked by a long history of antifederal sentiment. Moreover, on the prairies, political action accompanied dissent. This has manifested itself most visibly in support given, first, to new parties, and, later, to the major federal opposition party. Unlike the residents of Quebec, with whom westerners have shared some grievances, prairie voters have in recent years effectively excluded themselves and their region from the ranks of the governing Liberal Party.[1] This collective rejection of the dominant party of this century in federal politics has in turn exacerbated the region's sense of isolation.

To the outsider, the legacy of western Canadian resentment of the federal government is mystifying. In the eyes of the resident of Ontario, the West, in the energy-conscious seventies, is both economically and politically potent. For Quebecers, the region constitutes a significant part of English Canada's dominant majority. Indeed, they view it as the hostile heartland of anti-French feeling. And to the envious easterner, the western provinces, even "have-not" Manitoba, share a material prosperity never found in the Atlantic region.

The continuing disaffection of the West is the result of no single factor but stems from grievances that are economic, political, and even cultural in origin. If there is one element common to each, however, it might be termed "unfulfilled expectations." The prairie West (which is the subject of this paper) at the opening of the twentieth century was a land of superlatives. When its great potential went unrealized, frustration, not doubt, replaced optimism. On the prairies there was never any question but that the region's promise was thwarted by federal policies that alternated between neglect and exploitation. Most recently, after a decade of singular devotion to Quebec's problems, the federal government is viewed from the prairies, in the conflict over oil and natural gas, as once again turning its guns and not its ear to the West.

Roots of Dissent: Economic

The economic grievances of the prairies have arisen from the role assigned them by

43

several generations of federal policy-makers. For most of this century, westerners generally accepted their designated place as primary, especially wheat, producers but rejected the restrictive conditions under which they were expected to function. In recent years, however, prairie residents and their governments have begun to press for new federal policies that would allow them to diversify their single-crop economy. Three Farmers' Platforms, adopted in 1910, 1916, and 1920 by the Canadian Council of Agriculture, and virtually every statement made by a western politician before the Depression, demanded lower tariffs (preferably free trade in natural products with the United States), more equitable freight rates, government operation of terminal elevators, and a government-owned and operated Hudson Bay Railway.[2] The platform of 1921 and the Progressive Party's stand during its years in the House of Commons demonstrated an additional concern for good government, more particularly the reform of institutions like the Senate and the electoral system, which were viewed as iniquitous. But it was trade and transportation, as it affected the region's and the nation's major crop—wheat—that aroused the West.

Policies that would lower the cost of growing wheat were necessary, it was argued, if prairie farmers were to be encouraged to stay on the land. And that, the Farmers' Platform of 1910 said, was what they should do, because "the greatest misfortune which can befall any country is to have its people huddled together in great centres of population."[3] Two decades later, this antimetropolitan sentiment was echoed by Conservatives in Saskatchewan who feared Anglo-Saxon farmers would lead the exodus to the cities if conditions did not improve, and leave the countryside to the foreigner.[4] Concern for maintaining the family farm, about which so much is heard today, only assumed prominence when the mechanization of agriculture made it an endangered institution after the Second World War.[5]

The demands of the western farmer before the First World War generally received a sympathetic hearing by the federal governments of the day. As difficult as that may be for westerners to believe now, the explanation then made good economic sense. According to Vernon Fowke, there was a tremendous national investment in the wheat economy that had to be protected:

> The prospect for the profitable employment of capital and labour in the production of wheat on the Canadian plains attracted millions of immigrants to the continent and to the region, and prompted the investment of billions of dollars not only in the prairie provinces but throughout the entire nation. The prairie provinces constituted the geographic locus of the Canadian investment frontier in the first three decades of the twentieth century . . .
>
> An investment frontier may be geographically diffused but it nevertheless has tangible, concrete expression in the process of real-capital formation. The establishment of the wheat economy required the assembly in the prairie provinces of a massive structure of capital equipment without which the large-scale production and marketing of wheat would have been impossible. This included not only the equipment of the farms but also the equally indispensable equipment of the market centres throughout the region and of the transportation routes between.[6]

Gradually, at agrarian urging, the federal government assumed responsibility for the inspection, quality, transportation, and (in some instances) storage of prairie wheat. But federal intervention on behalf of the farmers was as much the result of Ottawa's calculation of the national interest as it was a victory for agrarian pressure politics. It

44

should be remembered that "all parts of the Dominion with the exception of the maritime provinces expanded their industrial and other economic activity in direct response to the opening of the prairie market."[7]

Both of the federal parties appreciated the need to secure the wheat economy, but the Liberals in 1911, with their stronger agrarian but weaker business ties, were willing to go further than the Conservatives. They pledged themselves to reciprocity with the United States. Although manufactured goods were not included, the proposal was feared and fought by commercial groups as the first step to economic union of the two countries. For the Tories, the wheat economy had made the dream of a successful national economic policy a reality. Reciprocity, they believed, would enrich western wheat farmers but at the expense of central Canadian industrialists. When the naval issue weakened Laurier's support in Quebec, the Liberals could not carry reciprocity—identified as it was with the interests of the West—on western support alone. In the 1911 campaign the interests of three of Canada's regions were directly in conflict, but when the votes were counted, only those of one—Ontario—had been satisfied. The effects of the failure to secure reciprocity with the United States can be overemphasized. Had the agreement been achieved, it would have moderated but not removed western dissent. The other grievances—freight rates and elevators—would have remained, and its defeat did not bring an immediate agrarian revolt. The years before the war were a time of expansion and the war itself buoyed the wheat economy. Indeed, the federal government, using its emergency power under the War Measures Act in 1919, created an extremely popular but short-lived wheat board whose restoration became the elusive goal of the next generation of farmers.[8]

It was the adjustment to peacetime that definitely marked an end to the period of uninterrupted growth that had existed on the prairies since the opening of the century. From the appearance of the Progressives as a political force in 1920 until the creation of the Canadian Wheat Board in 1935, the western farmers fought for better treatment on several fronts. Initially, they pressed the federal government to create a peacetime wheat board with the same broad powers to set prices as enjoyed by its "wartime" predecessor. But court decisions after the war denied to the federal government the sole constitutional authority to act. The best Ottawa could do was create a board that required supplementary legislation on the part of two or more prairie provinces to endow it with powers comparable to the old one. Nevertheless, Manitoba never acted and the other two provinces failed to find sufficient personnel. By the mid-twenties, in any case, interest in a wheat board waned as farmers were caught up in the crusade for a voluntary wheat pool. The pool was based on the principle of cooperation which was much respected and practised on the prairies. Farmers who signed five-year contracts with the pool were committed to sell all the grain they produced through its facilities. The story of the pool's success and then collapse in 1931 has been told before and is not relevant here, except to note that while it operated, wheat ceased to be a subject of political friction.[9] With wheat removed from politics and the economy prosperous, regional dissent was minimal.

One sign of a return to something approaching prewar harmony was the decline of the Progressive Party. The number of prairie seats in the House of Commons increased from forty-three in 1921 to fifty-four in 1926 but the number of Progressive members declined from thirty-eight to eighteen. The government of W.L. Mackenzie King, after an uncertain beginning, had managed to placate prairie critics and undermine the Progressive revolt. The tariff, against which westerners of all partisan stripes had r~:led, was reduced in 1924. The same year the old Crow's Nest Pass rates, which guaranteed reduced freight charges on grain and certain other commodities and which had been suspended in 1918 under authority of the War Measures Act, were restored.[10]

The transfer of natural resources to the prairie provinces by Ottawa in 1930 was interpreted in the West as the final step in achieving provincial autonomy. Retention of the resources by the federal government in 1870 and 1905 had acted as a continual irritant in federal-provincial relations even though, in the case of Saskatchewan and Alberta, the financial settlement in lieu of resources had been generous. Ironically the year 1930 did not inaugurate a period of prosperity on the prairies, with the provinces using the resources to further their individual development, but was, instead, the beginning of depression and drought that were to destroy the prairie economy. Rather than a decade in which the region began to loosen its ties to the centre, the thirties witnessed first collapse and then total dependency of the three prairie provinces upon Ottawa. According to the Rowell-Sirois Report, Saskatchewan, Alberta, and Manitoba (in that order) led the provinces of Canada in the decline of provincial per-capita incomes between 1928–29 and 1933.[11]

The single most important policy development of the thirties, as it affected the prairie provinces then and later, was the creation in 1935 of the Canadian Wheat Board. By this action, the federal government began a course that would eventually lead it to assume sole responsibility for the orderly marketing of wheat. The political ramifications of this decision and its contribution to regional dissent became apparent only over time. Wheat was no longer depoliticized, as it had been in the period of the pools, but neither was it open to legislative manipulation as in the prewar years. The provinces were now free to criticize the federal government's policies towards the board, while the board was generally free of federal government intervention in its activities. In this triangular relationship of board, farmer, and federal government, the government appeared vulnerable. For the board there was a reservoir of good will among farmers that grew from memories of the high wheat prices of 1917 through 1920 when grain had previously been controlled by a wheat board. But the farmers were congenitally suspicious of the government.

For nearly twenty years the new system worked well. The farmers were happy with the good, stabilized prices the board secured for them and the federal government took the credit. But if their wheat policy brought acclaim to the Liberals it also, eventually, brought criticism. The massive harvests of the fifties which saw the volume of farm-stored wheat triple created a problem that price stabilization could not solve. The Liberals' answer to the wheat glut was to have the farmers bear the storage charges, aided by low-interest loans. The board was the responsibility of C.D. Howe, minister of trade and commerce. His reputation for business acumen rang hollow to farmers when wheat sales declined and he refused to consider any but hard currency, non-Communist customers. His reputation for arrogance struck home when he threatened to withdraw the low-interest-loan legislation if opposition members of Parliament delayed its passage by criticizing its terms.[12]

More than any other single issue, the government's wheat policies were responsible for its loss of support on the prairies in 1957. The Liberals won only six of forty-eight seats, down eleven from 1953. Wheat delivered the region to the Progressive Conservatives and has held it for them. In its first session of Parliament, the Diefenbaker government introduced the Prairie Grain Advance Payments Act, which provided advance payment to producers for grain in storage, a policy the Liberals had refused to initiate.[13] Large grain sales to Communist countries followed and the Progressive Conservatives "ingratiated [themselves] with thousands of electors."[14] Between 1958 and 1974, there were 327 constituency contests in general elections on the prairies and the Tories won 267 of them. Of the remaining 60, the Liberals won only 25.

The policies that proved so electorally successful for the Progressive Conservatives preserved the institution of the Canadian Wheat Board as it had operated during the Liberal hegemony of 1935 to 1957. The wheat glut, and its resulting storage problems of the 1950s, was a technical question that was eliminated by moving wheat. The first substantive policies to alter the western grains industry appeared only in the late 1960s during the Trudeau government. These policies, which have been identified with the minister responsible for the Wheat Board, Otto Lang, have included a program to reduce wheat stocks and diversify western agriculture (Lower Inventories for Tomorrow), a grain income stabilization plan, and removal of feed grains from the Wheat Board's control. Each of these ideas, along with a suggestion that the Crow's Nest Pass rates be reexamined, has been received with alarm on the prairies and has had to be amended, withdrawn, or curtailed.

The evolution of Canada's wheat economy, especially the federal government's assumption of responsibility through the creation and operation of a wheat board, has increased regional dissent. The board and the institutions and policies that surround it have come to possess an aura of sanctity that deters change or even suggestions of change. Distrust and suspicion of those who propose reforms, especially when they are in the central government, are heightened when the Liberal Party is in power. That party has deteriorated as a political force in western Canada at the same time as its hold on the central region of the country has increased. Changing party fortunes have made the Liberal Party's few prairie members appear unrepresentative of the West. By contrast, the Progressive Conservative Party seems unable (and, in truth, at times unwilling) to divest itself of its western "image." The detrimental effect of this alignment upon national policy is obvious, but equally damaging is its implication for regional policies which have to be negotiated or extorted, not developed in "a spirit of cooperation."

The experience of the prairie provinces in the last decade, as they have sought to diversify their economies, testifies to the absence of harmony in the relationship between the West and Ottawa (especially Liberal Ottawa). Some of the most bitter obloquy was voiced by Saskatchewan Liberals, in power between 1964 and 1971, led by W. Ross Thatcher. Unlike their NDP opponents, who favoured state direction and control, Thatcher's Liberals were committed, at least publicly, to an unplanned private enterprise economy. And, like the classic entrepreneur, they sought to spread benefits and risks among as many investors and businessmen as possible. Saskatchewan's natural resources were the province's major attraction and Thatcher soon found himself locked in combat with the federal Liberals over policies to develop them. The premier never accepted the priority given in the sixties to constitutional reform by Pearson and later Trudeau. Financial problems, he said, were "the major challenge to the continued existence of our country."[15] He was particularly incensed by the federal government's white paper on taxation, issued in 1969, which he described as "the most damnable piece of legislation" he had seen since becoming a Liberal.[16] The Saskatchewan government attacked the cancellation of exemptions previously enjoyed by mining companies on the grounds that it would discourage new mining ventures in the West

47

at a time when Saskatchewan desired just such investment.

But Thatcher was not alone in his criticism and rejection of national policies. The recent debate, between Saskatchewan and Alberta on the one hand, and Ottawa and the rest of the provinces on the other, over the use and cost of energy resources and the Saskatchewan government's decision, late in 1975, to nationalize the potash industry (while the constitutionality of its resource taxation policy was still before the courts) is evidence of the continuing conflict that has marked the economic history of the prairie provinces. These events confirm in the minds of westerners the image they have of an "imperial" federal government which, when the need arises, will sacrifice their interests and patrimony in the name of national unity but, in reality, for the good of central Canada. This is the distribution of power that westerners believe exists. Any other interpretation they believe to be window-dressing, including the prime minister's plea to the Western Economic Opportunities Conference in 1973, "for a new approach to national development wherein our goal must be to seek balanced and diversified regional economies across the country."[17] At the conference, the four western provinces sought changes in federal policies (as they affected the region's agriculture, economic and industrial development, transportation, and financial institutions). The lack of progress since belies Trudeau's claim that "it is no longer essential for our survival to think of a single industrial heartland and a resource-based perimeter."[18]

Roots of Dissent: Politics

The dissent found in western Canada today stems almost as much from grievances that arise out of its political culture as it does from economic unrest. Here, because of a singular combination of events among which must be numbered the influx of an ethnically heterogeneous population settling on homesteads spread over thousands of square miles where services were expensive and attainable only through local initiative, a unique set of attitudes, beliefs, values, and skills developed. Consider the place of cooperatives, which, from the great provincial elevator companies to the village store, were a pillar of the prairie community; or the interrelationship of politics and religion as witnessed in the Social Gospel of T.C. Douglas and J.S. Woodsworth or the Social Credit of William Aberhart. The prairie experience with both has no Canadian equivalent. Nor is labour's turbulent history in the West duplicated elsewhere in Canada, although of course this is no measure of its respective import for the nation's history. At the same time, although the prairie provinces share a regional political culture, each of them can claim its own distinctive set of characteristics. It is this very pluralism which explains the region's rich heritage of protest.

Politics, in the form of party, movement, and pressure groups, has been both an expression and a cause of western dissent. Until the end of the First World War, when the Progressives burst upon the federal scene and the farmers captured power in Winnipeg and Edmonton, the politics and parties of the prairie provinces were an integral part of the national political structure. Regional dissent, as seen in the Farmers' Platform of 1910 and 1916, was expressed either through pressure-group activity or through one of the two original national parties. Western farmers had established their provincial organizations (the United Farmers of Manitoba, the United Farmers of Alberta, and the Saskatchewan Grain Growers' Association) early in the history of their respective provinces and these bodies quickly assumed a powerful position in provincial politics as well as an articulate and united voice in the federated Canadian Council of Agriculture. Pressure-group activity in this period succeeded because governments at both the federal and provincial levels responded to the demands of the developing West. In the conflict of interests which is the hallmark of politics and the raison d'être of federalism, the West and its farmers lost only one major battle—reciprocity in 1911. The old party structure helped simplify the job of the pressure groups. As long as there were Liberals or Conservatives in power in Ottawa and in the provinces, grievances could be transmitted directly through the partisan pipeline. From local constituency officials through to the federal cabinet minister, who was the acknowledged spokesman for the province in the national capital, provincial and federal parties (this distinction is itself misleading since it was not made at the time) sought to serve one another.

Before 1921, integration of the federal political system developed through reciprocal support of each level's policies as well as politicians primarily because the major federal programs of interest to the West concerned the development of the wheat economy. But other federal policies, whatever their subject, were bound to evoke response from provincial politicians; then too the federal party dichotomy was not, as C.B. Macpherson has argued, "extraneous" to Alberta and the other prairie provinces.[19] Even if prairie society was overwhelmingly petit bourgeois, as Macpherson contends, parties were not solely mediators of class conflict. There were other issues where national parties took positions which had nothing to do with class conflict but on which prairie parties and voters were forced to align themselves. One example concerned religion and education. Manitoba's politics had been thrown into turmoil in the 1890s by legislation, considered by some to be a violation of the spirit of its terms of union, to create a public school system that did not provide denominational schools for Roman Catholics. Despite a partial compromise that quelled some passions, Manitoba's government got what it wanted. Yet the issue was not laid to rest and continued to reassert itself provincially into the 1960s. In Alberta and Saskatchewan, a similar dispute arose in 1905 when it appeared that the autonomy legislation would extend denominational rights in education beyond former territorial practice. There had been little acrimony over separate schools in the Territories but the events of 1905 injected a degree of emotion to the subject that abated only slightly after the Laurier government removed the offending clause. A cleavage had been formed in provincial politics where none existed before. It assumed increased prominence, especially in Saskatchewan, during the First World War as a result of jingoistic campaigns against foreigners (many of whom were Roman Catholic) and at the end of the twenties due to the abuse of the immigrant by the Ku Klux Klan.[20]

Integration of the parties on both levels of government was irremediably damaged in 1917 with the creation of the Union government led by Sir Robert Borden. Except at its birth, that government, which included the minister responsible for the successful Liberal Party organization in Saskatchewan (J.A. Calder) and the Liberal premier of Alberta (Arthur Sifton), was viewed in the West as essentially Tory in complexion and therefore hostile in design. The political significance of this judgment may be better appreciated in company with the returns of the four federal elections between 1900 and 1911: in the area between Ontario and British Columbia the Liberals won fifty-four of the eighty-six seats at stake. But coalition also indicated partisanship generally because its calculated disregard of past politics strengthened those critics of the system whose fortunes had waxed and waned since the turn of the century. Liberals and Conservatives were never so entrenched on the prairies that they could afford to forget the original non-partisan base of territorial politics or ignore the periodic threat of groups like the Non-Partisan League who challenged the utility, as well as ethics, of partisan politics.[21]

The temporary eclipse of prairie Grits in Parliament opened the way for disillusioned westerners in the House of Commons to coalesce in a new Progressive Party. Although the Progressives attracted much attention in 1921 when they demanded a new national policy and won thirty-eight of the prairie provinces' forty-three seats, they were essentially reformist Liberals whose momentum was halted when the Liberals, under Mackenzie King, adopted some planks in their platform and co-opted their first two leaders, T.A. Crerar and Robert Forke.

Because both their accomplishments and failures are so ambiguous, the place of the Progressives in Canadian political history remains enigmatic.[22] Their legislative record, in terms of policies successfully carried through Parliament, was meagre. Depending on the observer's partisan leanings, the Progressives were either the taskmaster or handmaiden of Liberal politicians, some of whom saw the new party as a retribution for their indiscretion with Borden's Tories. The Progressives were not a protest party of the West only—over 41 percent of the victories in 1921 were outside of the prairies (mainly in Ontario). In addition to its prairie strength as "a sectional protest against a metropolitan economy, it was also [on the prairies as elsewhere] an agrarian protest against the growing urban domination of the Canadian economy and of national politics."[23] For the westerner, the Progressive movement offered an opportunity to repudiate those economic terms of Confederation that made the region a captive of the centre and which were aggravated by postwar inflation for all commodities except wheat, whose average annual price fell from $2.51 a bushel (as set by the temporary wheat board) in 1920 to $1.65 (on the open market) in 1921.[24] Eastern as well as western Progressives opposed the transformation of Canada from a rural-agricultural to an urban-industrial society. Antimetropolitan sentiment, heightened by further growth of the large cities during the war, had been evident for some time, even on the prairies, which were the least urban of Canada's regions.

The Progressives failed to reverse the forces against which they protested just as they failed to secure most of the legislation they promoted. Yet their short-lived revolt was significant for subsequent protest groups in western Canada. First, it stimulated the provincial farmers' associations to consider entering politics directly as electoral organizations. The United Farmers of Alberta in 1919 and the United Farmers of Manitoba by 1922 decided to follow the federal Progressives' example, to the extent that the organized farmers in both provinces deserted the old parties. Once into electoral politics, the theory of group government set the Alberta farmers apart from their brothers elsewhere, but the effect of that initial decision was as disruptive for traditional parties there as in other provinces.[25]

The farmers of Saskatchewan, organized in the Saskatchewan Grain Growers' Association, made a hesitant entry into provincial politics in 1922 but reversed their decision two years later. This agrarian indecision was the result of the Liberal Party's success since 1905 at co-opting prominent leaders and advocating popular policies with a critical eye for simple solutions. When Saskatchewan farmers wanted public ownership of elevators, as in Manitoba, the government responded with legislation to promote cooperatives, and when the Non-Partisan League's cry for cheap money was echoed by "responsible" farmers, the province's Liberals provided long-term, low-interest loans. The Saskatchewan Co-operative Elevator Company and the Farm Loan Board were among the most popular and financially successful enterprises that Saskatchewan Liberal governments ever introduced. Thus, during the twenties, Saskatchewan's politics and parties survived the farmers' revolt, while in Alberta and Manitoba, the old party systems were destroyed. The Liberals, who had held power in Edmonton ever since the province was created, were displaced and never returned while in Winnipeg the success of the UFM initiated an era of non-partisan and then coalition government that was to last for thirty-five years. Rebellion against the traditional party alignment thus loosened the bonds of Confederation by increasing the opportunities for regional dissent.

The Progressives influenced the course of western protest in a second, but this time negative, way. Both Social Credit and CCF enthusiasts considered the old Progressive revolt ineffectual, although each learned a different lesson from the episode. Social Credit, like the UFA before it, distrusted brokerage politics and interpreted the Progressives' fate as confirmation of the danger inherent in cooperation. The CCF, however, sought cooperation with other groups (but not the Communists) and blamed the Progressives' weaknesses on poor organization, a failing the CCF never displayed. This, however, was the extent of the connection between the Progressives and these later protest movements. Some Progressives, it is true, did join Social Credit or the CCF but many more returned to the Liberal Party from whence they had come.[26]

Social Credit and the CCF represented a new form of dissent. W.L. Morton describes them (particularly Social Credit) as "Utopian" in the sense that they sought "to merge the nation in the section."[27] Unlike the Progressives, who wanted to reform the existing economic and political system, the new parties each sought to replace the old order with one constructed according to new principles. At its English inception, Social Credit was an economic theory that saw politics as a means to attain a goal, but later, in Alberta, because of the Canadian constitution, this idea was abandoned. Social Credit quickly emerged as a regional protest party whose political ambitions led it to clash most resoundingly with Mackenzie King and his Liberals and with the federal government and its offspring, the Rowell-Sirois Commission.

Because of its socialist doctrine and diverse origins, the CCF was never a regional party like Social Credit. In Saskatchewan, the strong base provided by the United Farmers of Canada (Saskatchewan Section) and the eventual victory of the CCF over the ruling provincial Liberals gave the new party an agrarian aura. Yet its urban-industrial supporters always exerted great influence in the party's organization. The achievement of the CCF and its successor, the New Democratic Party, was the revolution it wrought in political and social thought after the Regina Manifesto—governments and individuals today accept as reasonable many of the movement's principles. But this national success deprived the party of any special claim to representing regional interests, particularly those of the West. Even in its Saskatchewan bastion, the assertion could never be supported by electoral results. In the period between 1935 and 1957 (including the elections of those years), 117 federal seats were contested in the province and the Liberals won fifty-three to the CCF's fifty-one. The Progressive Conservatives won nine and other candidates four.

By the early fifties, the protest parties of the West had become "provincialized." Prairie voters who wanted to vent their wrath at Liberals and who also hoped to change government policies had to look elsewhere. Eventually they focused on the one party that had never been popular in the West, the Progressive Conservatives. In the fifty years before 1958, the party had won only 22 percent of prairie seats at stake in general elections. This, however, increased to 81 percent of the region's seats in the period 1958 through 1974. It was a dramatic swing in partisan sympathy and is all the more remarkable because of its apparent permanence. Equally impressive, however, has been the rejection of the Liberals in all three provinces. Only in Quebec is there a similar alignment of the old parties, although there it is the Progressive Conservatives who are unpopular.

The Tories' success in the West is not the subject of this paper except as it is interpreted to be a continuation of the tradition of prairie political protest. With the passing of each recent general election, the hold of the Progressive Conservatives upon the region becomes more notable. Neither the competence nor record of the Diefenbaker government can explain it. It is, rather, a dissentient vote directed against the centre and the Liberal Party, which today is identified with the centre. Western Progressive Conservatives are generally more Progressive than Conservative. They articulate the same values and interests that supporters of the Progressive, Social Credit, and CCF parties once did. This "floating" protest vote has been attracted, at different times, to different parties which have almost always been in opposition in Ottawa. Nothing reveals more accurately the political impotence of the region or the lack of hope for improvement. The burden of unity, which the West believes it has borne for so long, will lighten only if the region can secure policies more favourable to itself. For this to happen, the West must secure a greater voice at the centre in federal decisions or it must have more autonomy to formulate its own policies.

The First Alternative

A great voice at the centre requires, in effect, more participation by westerners in the deliberations of the Liberal Party. Because there is only a handful of Liberals to represent the West's interests, Liberal governments have generally been unreceptive to the region's demands and, even when sympathetic, unable to carry legislation through because of lack of popular or parliamentary support. There are ways in which the current situation could change. Western voters could elect more Liberals which, in light of the party's national electoral success, would be reasonable. But given the region's recent voting preferences this is unlikely. An alternative would be to reform the electoral system so that the Liberals' popular vote (which, as a proportion of the party's national vote, has ranged in the last fifteen years from a low of 10 percent in 1974 to a high of 13 percent in 1968) would be translated more accurately into elected members (which, as the proportion of the party's seats in Parliament, have ranged in the same period from 2 percent in 1962 to 7 percent in 1968). Reform of the electoral system is scarcely discussed in Canada except in isolated instances, such as in Quebec by Parti Québécois supporters after the last provincial election. Nevertheless, the fact remains that the absence of strong western representation in recent Liberal governments explains the party's plight in the West. It is also clear that without a vocal expression of concern for the West's interests in caucus and in support of the few prairie ministers who do speak for the region, the area's concerns receive relatively low priority. One may argue about the comparative impact of caucus, cabinet, and the senior civil service upon the formulation of policy but low visibility in at least two of these key areas effectively mutes the prairies' voice.[28]

A political party is more than an electoral organization, even though that is its principal function for the Liberals and Progressive Conservatives. One of the jobs of a party is to act as a transmission belt, alternatively conveying constituency matters to the legislator and governmental policy to local supporters. The role of the riding association therefore becomes extremely important for it is continually required to evaluate interests and, in the first instance, legitimize government policy which, when found acceptable, is propagated and defended by the party faithful to the electorate. One of the Liberal Party's greatest weaknesses in the West today is that the local organization is so often absent, atrophied, or suspicious of federal attachments.[29] Instead of audiences that are critical but ultimately concerned about the party, ministers frequently find themselves having to explain government policy to hostile interest groups. Repeated Progressive Conservative electoral sweeps have discouraged all but the truest prairie Grits who usually persevere because of personal motives that include, among others, ideology and hope for a share of federal patronage. The work of the local associations in promoting the party has increasingly been taken over by "communications specialists" who have substituted public relations for partisanship.

A striking contrast between federal Liberal governments since 1963 and their predecessors of a quarter of a century ago is the absence of dominant provincial spokesmen. The change is particularly noticeable to a westerner because, as recently as the King and St. Laurent periods, J.G. Gardiner and Stuart Garson acted like barons whose authority in matters affecting their provinces was absolute. Today there is no minister of similar political stature. The tradition of co-opting prominent provincial politicians was not begun by King, nor was it unique to the Liberal Party: Laurier invited three provincial premiers into his 1896 cabinet and Borden searched for regional talent especially for his Union government. As it affected Saskatchewan, however, the practice was particularly marked. Indeed, until 1971, all but one (W.J. Patterson) of eight provincial Liberal leaders sat in Parliament at some point during their public careers.[30] Co-optation did not signify provincial party subservience nor ministerial parochialism. The party mobilized provincial grievances which the minister could vent in cabinet. At the same time, and perhaps more important in terms of promoting unity, the ministers acknowledged the importance of national policies through their continuing allegiance and participation.

Co-optation, which was one manifestation of what is now referred to as "elite accommodation," declined in significance for several reasons.[31] Although the Progressive Conservatives practised it, they were never as good at it as the Liberals, partly because there were fewer Progressive Conservative governments to draw from, as Diefenbaker discovered when he became prime minister. The evolution in federal-provincial relations of the last two decades has enhanced the status of provincial governments and made their politicians, of all stripes, less malleable to federal direction. But the principal reason for the decline of co-optation was the Liberal Party's abandonment of the practice.

Even before the Diefenbaker era opened, Liberal Party strength on the prairies had begun to decline. When the demands of the burgeoning urban middle-class electorate of southern Ontario captured the party's attention after the Second World War, the western voter felt ignored. In the aftermath of 1958, the regionalization of the party was intensified with the Liberals of central Canada coming to dominate its councils. In an attempt to restore the party, they set out to refurbish its image, rebuild its organization, and reform its practices. Professing as their goal the greatest participation by the greatest number, they created federally appointed organizations to promote the interests of the federal party in each province. The first casualties of this innovation (as indeed was its intent) were the old provincial war-horses who had dominated the region's politics.

These changes, which were far more sweeping than this brief reference suggests, caused the Liberals special problems in the West where their hold was precarious in any case. On principle, the local faithful resented what they interpreted as dictation from the centre, while in practice they fought to maintain their traditional voice in patronage distribution. Internecine squabbles between federal and provincial Liberals, most of whom had never won an election, broke out in Alberta and Manitoba. In Saskatchewan, rancour spread between Thatcher and his supporters, who believed they should have a share of federal patronage, and the Ottawa loyalists, who viewed the methods and style of the new premier as quintessential "old politics." Seized by a desire to control the party, each camp of Liberals in Saskatchewan did little else than fight the other, while "those who believe[d] that policy had some importance . . . stay[ed] away from any meeting that sound[ed] organizational."[32]

The strategy of the sixties dictated that the Liberals should direct their appeal to where most of the voters lived. In fact, this tactic garnered votes in Ontario and, in turn, sharpened the party's metropolitan image. The isolated urban support it received on the prairies, where the few seats won were in the major cities, strengthened this impression. The absence of rural members made the Liberals appear the least representative party in the region. Representation is a notoriously slippery concept open to varied interpretation and, the theory of group government aside, there is no logical reason why farmers must represent farmers for agriculture to secure the legislation it wants or deserves. The fact remains, however, that although only the Liberal Party can offer the prairies access to federal policy-making, it has failed to make its case. The old conflict between region and nation thus remains unresolved, even heightened. For the party, no obvious escape exists from the impasse, but for the region there is another option.

The Second Alternative

In the Canadian political system, where policy is the preserve of ministers and their advisers, the individual MP, especially an opposition member, has few opportunities to influence its formulation. Thus a region of the country that withholds support from the government cannot realistically expect Parliament to accommodate its interests. As an alternative, it must lay claim, on its own behalf, to a broader range of powers and control than has been customary in Canadian federalism.

All provinces in one way or another have done this in recent years as they have raised their sights and finances. Indeed, this collegial assertiveness has transformed traditional federal-provincial relations into quasi-diplomatic negotiations.[33] While no division of jurisdiction or of institutions in a federal system is immutable, any province or group of provinces seeking a redistribution of power must recognize that federalism is based on the existence of rival sovereign powers. Thus a proposal to alter the status quo necessarily requires adjustments and counteradjustments on the part of both levels of government. And, in the context of this discussion of alternatives, suggestions which have, as their ultimate goal, the extension of a province's or region's control of its development will inevitably be viewed as threatening by the federal government. The proposals must therefore be realistic in terms of their objectives and method of implementation. Otherwise they will be rejected both by Ottawa, which will view them as damaging to the political system, and by prairie residents, who are not "Rupert's Land nationalists" seeking hinterland independence.

Westerners view themselves as Canadians, maybe even "ideal" Canadians who, if left to their own devices, would ignore the myths and prejudices that obsess their eastern compatriots. In many respects, the West was never an extension of Central Canada except perhaps in its very earliest settlements. Later, it was a new land for hundreds of thousands of foreign immigrants ignorant of the passions of Canada's history. Yet, as creatures of the federal government, the prairies' political and economic development was tied closely to events at the centre. The West was made the testing ground for Confederation and the patronizing attitude that underlay this assumption stimulated resentment as much as any specific program—be it for tariffs or freight rates, bilingualism or energy policies.

The prairie provinces distrust the federal government, especially now that they have so little influence on its policies. The West has, to a large degree, achieved political autonomy in that the fortunes of its parties and politicians are nearly free of federal entanglements. In federal-provincial negotiations the prairie premiers, regardless of party, share to a remarkable degree interests that are essentially regional in scope. The Western Economic Opportunities Conference in July 1973, when the premiers of the four provinces west of Ontario prepared joint statements on a range of subjects, constituted the clearest evidence of this mutual concern.

Of course it is obvious that the problems confronting each province are not the same. Alberta's prosperity and growth, for instance, require a different set of policies from those needed to check the population decline and economic stagnation of Saskatchewan and Manitoba. When one speaks of the West, therefore, it does make a difference which province is being discussed. There is, nonetheless, sufficient common ground among the provinces in their disagreements with Ottawa to encourage three suggestions for change in the operation of the federal system. They are policies that would promote, first, decentralization, second, devolution, and third, control.

Decentralization implies a transfer of federal instrumentalities to the region. Several possibilities exist. At the most visible level would be the establishment of local offices of major federal departments like Agriculture and Regional Economic Expansion, large proportions of whose clientele live in the region. The purpose of this proposal quite simply is to give broader access to and thus encourage more local participation in the making and carrying out of those federal governmental policies of special importance to the prairies. Decentralization of another sort (which has actually begun in limited areas) is to move federal enterprises like the Royal Canadian Mint and Air Canada's overhaul base to the West. As an indication of federal commitment to redress a policy of neglect, such actions are commendable. They are not welcome as token gestures. The ultimate purpose of such developments must be to generate skills and talents, not just jobs.

One of the significant contrasts between Canada and the United States is the continuing unrivalled dominance of a few large old cities here and the growth of regional "technological" centres (Detroit after the First World War, and Houston, Kansas City, and Seattle after the Second World War) there. Indeed, given the language division in this country, Toronto's hold on the life of Canada's West has no equal in the United States. This concentration of wealth and knowledge starves the rest of the country and contributes to the antimetropolitan sentiments already mentioned.[34] One example of how this works is federal research policies and their effect on industry and universities. Increasingly these policies favour a "centres-of-excellence approach" which, given the disparity of local resources in Canada, cannot help but favour the centre over the periphery.

But there is no reason why westerners should be only consumers of research, especially when much of it is the work of "expatriates." Because the federal government's contribution to research and development, while regrettably meagre by international standards, is nonetheless the major source of funds, this would appear a promising subject for federal-provincial negotiation. A change in policy, which saw research and development decentralized, would have long-term benefits for the areas of relocation. In view of the West's sudden but certainly transitory prosperity arising from energy sales, this is a field where hard bargaining could pay rich dividends.

Devolution differs from decentralization because it delegates authority to subordinate agents who thereby acquire the right to take initiatives. For a region isolated from political power at the centre, this is surely a most attractive feature. Decentralization limits choice by expanding government; devolution increases freedom by conferring power. Students of federalism might question the need to introduce devolution in a system where powers are already divided and institutions exist to make it work. The answer is that federalism does not work as far as the West is concerned. The integration once provided by political parties is gone. Cabinet government, as understood by all Canadian politicians save the Progressives, will not deviate from single-party rule (witness the NDP's abhorrence at even the suggestion of coalition in 1972). And Parliament is not nor, given our political culture, can it be a congress. Yet the West must find some means of accommodating its interests in the federal system.

The traditional alternatives—Senate reform or a constitutional amendment to revise the division of powers—while reasonable in the abstract are politically impracticable. First, there must be an amending formula adopted, and then there must be agreement to change. Senate reform, which is perennially popular, never succeeds because any change that would actually convert it (even moderately) into a chamber of the provinces is critically studied by both federal and provincial governments who fear rivals. The advantages of devolution are that it is permissible constitutionally and benign legislatively (that is, power devolved or delegated is retrievable).

How then might it be used to the region's advantage? Two illustrations are the creation of a Western Canada Planning Council and a Western Canada Resources Development Council. These bodies would function as intermediaries between the provinces and the federal government where discussion, debate, and decisions could occur on subjects of immediate importance to the region.[35] Composed of individuals selected for a term by the provincial legislatures and Parliament or perhaps with a proportion appointed by the provincial and federal governments, the councils would exercise powers conferred by the legislature and cabinet and, ideally, would provide the atmosphere for accommodation now lost to the anti-Liberal West. The conference of first ministers is staged on too grand a scale for true discussion. Instead, negotiations are conducted between semisovereign leaders who seek to influence each level's policies, which are already formulated and maybe even announced.

Decentralization aims to give the region influence on federal policy as it is being formulated, while devolution seeks to provide control of policy when it is being implemented. This proposal recognizes the administrative revolution that has taken place in Canadian politics in the last fifty years. Where once "the culprits were the C.P.R. and the banks. Now, it is more likely to be the National Energy Board, the C.B.C., the Department of Transport (or any other choice of agencies) which appear as the decision-makers who ignore the aspiration of Western Canadians."[36] But the transformation has still broader implications for the political system. Regulatory bodies have been created in the main to deal with matters that require special knowledge or that are politically contentious. In each instance, it is believed that "parliament ought to ensure that politics is taken out of those decisions." The problem is that "any time there is a choice open to an administrator, [it] is by its essence a political choice."[37] Where the choice has definite regional implications, say the regulation of energy exports or the abandonment of rail lines, the potential for sectional conflict is increased.

To be sure, federal regulatory bodies, like all national committees, are constituted on a regional basis. But by virtue of its operation, this practice is no guarantee of equity. Moreover, the agencies' isolation from political supervision heightens the sense of impotence and injustice the region experiences when its interests are once again assumed to coincide with those of the nation. Whatever changes occur at the federal level, it would be desirable for the West to be able to assert some regional control, if only through the requirement that regulatory bodies report annually (documenting the reasons for their decision) to a body like the Planning Council referred to above.

The aim of these proposals is to reduce the suspicion of the federal government that currently thrives in Western Canada. This distrust has serious implications for the region and the nation, especially now that the economic terms of Confederation have shifted so strongly in favour of Alberta and, to a lesser extent, Saskatchewan. Governments, like individuals, fear uncertainty, and it was for this reason, as much as it was to protect mineral tax revenues, that the Saskatchewan government announced its plan in 1975 to nationalize the potash industry. Provincial governments cannot plan without some assurance that their predictions of the future are reasonably sound. The Blakeney government feared a repetition of Alberta's conflict with Ottawa. They judged that in the battle to control and develop the oil industry Alberta's government and people lost.

There is no panacea for the region's dissent. The hoary grievance about freight rates is evidence of that.[38] These are only symptoms of the West's malaise. The problem goes much deeper because as the prime minister has perceptively noted: "There is a different culture in the West than there is in Central Canada... It's not a different civilization but certainly it's a different form of culture than exists elsewhere."[39]

Notes

1. To the list of political histories yet to be written should be added a comparative study of the West and Quebec in Confederation. For a reason, see Ramsay Cook, *Canada and the French-Canadian Question* (Toronto, 1966), 95-96.

2. The Platforms are in Appendixes A, B, and C of W.L. Morton, *The Progressive Party in Canada* (Toronto, 1950), 297-305.

3. Ibid., 298.

4. David E. Smith, *Prairie Liberalism: The Liberal Party in Saskatchewan* (Toronto, 1975), 137-43.

5. John Stahl, "Prairie Agriculture: A Prognosis," in *Prairie Perspectives*, ed. David P. Gagan (Toronto, 1970), 58-76; Smith, *Prairie Liberalism*, 318.

6. Vernon C. Fowke, *The National Policy and the Wheat Economy* (Toronto, 1957), 71.

7. Ibid., 72.

8. P.C. 1589, 31 July 1919.

9. The campaign for the pool is described in *The Diary of Alexander James McPhail*, ed. Harold A. Innis (Toronto, 1940), Chap. 2. See, too, H.S. Patton, *Grain Growers' Co-operation in Western Canada* (Cambridge, Mass., 1928).

10. Morton, *Progressive Party in Canada,* 156.
11. Canada, *Report of the Royal Commission on Dominion-Provincial Relations* (3 vols. in one, Ottawa, 1954), Vol. I, 150.
12. *Montreal Star,* 9 February 1956.
13. *Statutes of Canada.*
14. Norman Ward, "The Contemporary Scene," in *Politics in Saskatchewan,* eds. Norman Ward and Duff Spafford (Toronto, 1968), 287.
15. Province of Saskatchewan, "Opening Statement," Federal-Provincial Constitutional Conference, Ottawa, 10 February 1969, 1.
16. Saskatoon *Star Phoenix,* 18 February 1970, 1.
17. Pierre E. Trudeau, "Social and Economic Objectives of the West," statement tabled at Western Economic Opportunities Conference by the prime minister of Canada, 24 July 1973. See, also, the "Verbatim Record" of the three-day, Calgary meeting for an amplification of the prime minister's views as well as pertinent comments by the four western premiers.
18. Ibid.
19. C.B. Macpherson, *Democracy in Alberta: Social Credit and the Party System* (2nd ed., Toronto, 1962), 24.
20. Smith, *Prairie Liberalism,* 146.
21. See D.S. Spafford, "'Independent' Politics in Saskatchewan before the Non-Partisan League," *Saskatchewan History* (Winter 1965), 1-9; and Paul F. Sharp, *The Agrarian Revolt in Western Canada: A Study Showing American Parallels* (Minneapolis, 1948), Chaps. 5 and 6.
22. The dilemmas of the Progressives are extensively chronicled in Morton's *Progressive Party in Canada.*
23. Ibid., 292.
24. Fowke, *National Policy,* 200.
25. The best single explanation of the theory of group government is in Macpherson, *Democracy in Alberta,* Chap. 2.
26. Walter Young, *The Anatomy of a Party: The National CCF, 1932–61* (Toronto, 1969), 15; Smith, *Prairie Liberalism,* 213.
27. W.L. Morton, "The Bias of Prairie Politics," in *Historical Essays on the Prairie Provinces,* ed. Donald Swainson (Toronto, 1970), 300. [Also see p. 19 in this volume.]
28. For comments on the relative importance to policy of party caucus and cabinet, see Alan C. Cairns, "The Electoral System and the Party System in Canada, 1921-1965," *Canadian Journal of Political Science* (March 1968), 55-80; and J.A.A. Lovink, "On Analysing the Impact of the Electoral System on the Party System in Canada," *Canadian Journal of Political Science* (Dec. 1970), 497-516. See, too, J.A.A. Lovink, "Parliamentary Reform and Governmental Effectiveness in Canada," *Canadian Public Administration* (Spring 1973), 35-54.
29. Although made more than fifteen years ago by an Alberta Liberal, the following description of the party's decline is still accurate and is not limited to this province. "I tried to call a nominating convention and only five people came. At that meeting our president resigned as he is leaving town and there were not enough present to elect another president . . . No candidate came forward. The feeling among the five present was that no person with any self-respect wants to run unless he is sure of winning. I have run and disagree." F. Olson to "Federation," 15 June 1959, National Liberal Federation Papers, P.A.C.
30. It is true that A.H. McDonald, leader from 1954 until 1959, only made it as a senator and W. Ross Thatcher was elected as a CCF candidate in 1945 and sat as a socialist until 1956.
31. On the theory of elite accommodation, see *Consociational Democracy: Political Accommodation in Segmented Societies,* ed. Kenneth McRae (Toronto, 1974); and Robert Presthus, *Elite Accommodation in Canadian Politics* (Toronto, 1973). An unpublished paper that deals in passing with elite accommodation and the West is Joseph Wearing, "Mutations in a Political Party: The Liberal Party of Canada in the Fifties and Sixties," prepared for the Annual Meeting of the Canadian Political Science Association, Edmonton, June 1975.

32. Otto Lang to Keith Davey (National Director), 29 September 1970, National Liberal Federation Papers, P.A.C.

33. Richard Simeon, *Federal-Provincial Diplomacy: The Making of Recent Policy in Canada* (Toronto, 1972).

34. Toronto is also the communications centre for English-speaking Canada.

35. Lloyd Axworthy, "Administrative Federalism and the West," paper presented to Liberal Conference on Western Objectives, Vancouver, July 1973.

36. Ibid., 5.

37. Canada, House of Commons, *Third Report of the Special Committee on Statutory Instruments, Session 1968–69* (Ottawa, 1969), 35. The speaker was the then minister of justice, John Turner.

38. Howard Darling, "What Belongs in Transportation Policy?" *Canadian Public Administration* (Winter 1975), 665–66.

39. "Transcript of the Prime Minister's Speech at the Liberal Party Convention, Vancouver, July 15, 1973," 8 (in author's possession). Two pieces which explore the theme of regional culture are: Gerald Friesen, "The Western Canadian Identity," *CHR Historical Papers* (1973), 13–19, and *A Region of the Mind: Interpreting the Western Canadian Plains,* ed. Richard Allen (Regina, 1973).

2

RIEL AND RESISTANCE (1850–1885)

Introduction

Louis Riel and the "rebellions" of 1870 and 1885 have become synonymous with the birth of the protest tradition. Donald Swainson describes the process that brought the West under Canadian control as "annexation" and maintains that it resulted in colonial status for the region in Canadian federalism.

He outlines the context of this annexation by describing the rise of the Métis people and their economic role in the pre-Canadian period and then details Canadian attitudes towards the West during the transfer of power from the Hudson's Bay Company to Ottawa. The unequal status of this vast area controlled directly by Ottawa, except for the tiny new province of Manitoba won by force of Métis arms, ensured that grievances would continue. The West was not a partner in the original formation of Confederation, nor did its population freely vote to join Confederation the way Newfoundland did in 1949. It had no official father of Confederation; its most famous political leader was an exiled rebel who was hung for treason.

The indigenous perspective on the Riel period is expressed by the Métis historian and political thinker, Howard Adams. His analysis of the events of 1885 is taken from his ground-breaking 1975 book, *Prison of Grass* (revised edition). He describes the war of 1885 as "the culmination of a complex struggle" involving many groups in the North-West from the starving tribes on reserves to politically frustrated white farmers and settlers. He interprets the protest as a broadly-based, popular movement and downplays the role of Riel, which, under an older interpretation, had been viewed as paramount.

Douglas Owram's discussion of regional discontent in the 1880s deals specifically with the new agrarian settlement forces unleased by the building of the railway. These new westerners, who had come westward after annexation and were destined to replace the Métis as regional leaders after 1885, were already developing constitutional and economic concerns that would maintain agitation for responsible government in the North-West until the formation of Saskatchewan and Alberta as provinces in 1905.

As the fur-trade based Métis and the buffalo-dependent Plains Indian tribes lost their power, a new agrarian society was quickly taking hold in the West. In two decades it would come to dominate the region and so relegate the legacy of Riel to historical memory. But agrarianism was to develop its own disillusionment with Ottawa.

Although not always remembered or honoured, the events of 1870 and 1885 continue to generate controversy and new interpretations. The blood of martyrdom has given them a legendary quality that cannot be easily erased. They are the protest tradition's solid foundation.

Canada Annexes the West:
Colonial Status Confirmed

DONALD SWAINSON

Reprinted from Bruce Hodgins, Don Wright, and W.H. Heick, eds.,
Federalism in Canada and Australia: The Early Years (Waterloo: Wilfred
Laurier University Press, 1978), 137-157, by permission of the publisher.

The early history of the Canadian West[1] is characterized by dependence and exploitation. The area and its resources were controlled from outside, for the benefit of several distant centres, whose relative importance changed from time to time. London, Montreal, and Toronto, the major and competing metropolises, were flanked by such lesser competitors as Minneapolis-St. Paul, Benton, and Vancouver. A prime result of this pattern of development has been a continuing resistance to outside controls. At the same time, the character of western people and institutions has been heavily influenced by forces outside western controls. Even indigenous peoples were largely defined by the forces that controlled the region. The interplay of these factors has played a large part in moulding the character of the West and in determining fundamentally its role in Canadian federalism.

The pattern of dependence preceded federal union and for the West is the context within which federalism must be viewed. It began in the seventeenth century when English traders established themselves in posts around Hudson Bay. Chartered in 1670 as the Hudson's Bay Company, this "Company of Adventurers of England tradeing [*sic*] into Hudson's Bay"[2] tapped an enormously profitable trade in furs. To this prestigious and powerful firm the Crown delegated vast responsibilities and valuable privileges:

> [T]he Company was granted the "sole Trade and Commerce of all those Seas Streightes Bayes Rivers Lakes Creekes and Soundes in whatsoever Latitude they shall bee that lye within the entrance of the Streightes commonly called Hudsons Streightes together with all the Landes and Territoryes upon the Countryes Coastes and confynes of the seas Bayes Lakes Rivers Creekes and Soundes aforesaid that are not actually possessed by or granted to any of our Subjects or possessed by the Subjects of any other Christian Prince or State." They were to be the "true and absolute Lordes and Proprietors" of this vast territory, and they were to hold it, as had been envisaged in the grant of October 1669, in free and common socage ... These lands were to be reckoned as a plantation or colony, and were to be known as Rupert's Land; and the Company was to own the mineral and fishing rights there as well as the exclusive trade and the land itself.[3]

For two hundred years, the Hudson's Bay Company was the (more or less) effective government of Rupert's Land, an enormous territory stretching from Labrador through the shield and the prairies and into the Arctic tundra in the West. It included most of what are now the provinces of Manitoba, Saskatchewan, and Alberta. Control over the West was thus vested in a firm centred in London and exercised in the interests of commerce.

Montreal businessmen (whether French before the Conquest, or British after) refused to recognize the HBC's trade monopoly, and wanted to share in the profits. In spite of enormous overhead costs French traders penetrated the West in the middle of the eighteenth century, and entered into competition for the favour of the Indian fur gatherers. After the Conquest Montreal's challenge to the Hudson's Bay Company's monopoly was even more serious. Numerous Montreal-based traders entered the field, but the most famous and effective were organized late in the eighteenth century as the North-West Company. This marvel of capitalist organization exploited the wealth of the shield and the prairies. It opened the rich Athabasca country and its agents penetrated north to the Artic and west to the Pacific. The Nor' Westers introduced the influence of Montreal into the mainstream of western life. The vicious competition between Montreal and London for the control of the western trade, however, proved too costly; in 1821 the Hudson's Bay Company and the North-West Company amalgamated. But both Montreal and London continued to exercise great influence in the West. And, of course, the officers and men of the reorganized Hudson's Bay Company remained a powerful force in the West until Canada annexed the area in 1870.

Children of mixed white and Indian blood were an inevitable result of the presence of fur traders in the West. By the late eighteenth century these people were a numerous group on the prairies. They can be very roughly divided into two subgroups: English-speaking half-breeds and French-speaking Métis. The former tended to be relatively settled and to have close ties with the white communities in the Red River Valley. The Métis were more autonomous and distinctive. During this period, they developed into a powerful force.

As a people, the Métis were very much a product of the fur trade. Like many other unsophisticated and indigenous peoples, they were manipulated by the great business firms that exploited the natural resources of their area. The North-West Company employed them first as labourers and hunters. The trade war between the fur trading giants increased their utility, especially after Lord Selkirk established his famous settlement in the Red River Valley in 1811–12. Selkirk's colony and the HBC functioned as interdependent units, and challenged the viability of the NWC operations west of the Red River. The NWC could not declare war on one without fighting the other. Consequently it declared war on both, and the Métis became its prime weapon. The leaders of the NWC encouraged the growth of a primitive nationalism; the Métis were encouraged to believe that the Red River settlers threatened their claim to western lands, a claim inherited from their Cree and Saulteaux mothers. Cuthbert Grant, a Scottish educated half-breed, was appointed Captain of the Métis by the North-West Company, and his followers became a small private army. They harassed the Selkirk settlers, a process that culminated in 1816 in the battle of Seven Oaks where Grant's men massacred Governor Robert Semple and twenty of his settlers. But in spite of its superior military strength, the NWC, primarily for geographical reasons, could not sustain a protracted campaign against the Red River colonists and HBC. Consequently, the firms united in 1821; the West was pacified.

The four-year struggle (1812–1816) against the Selkirk settlers was a decisive event in western history. It marked the beginning of the Métis as an organized and self-conscious group. After 1821, they continued to accept Grant's leadership. They founded Grantown on the Assiniboine River west of the restored Selkirk settlement and made that village their capital; for the next seventy years they were at the centre of prairie history.

After the union of the firms, Cuthbert Grant and his people were co-opted by the controlling interests. The Métis defended the growing and prosperous community of Selkirk settlers, their former enemies, from the Sioux. In 1828, Grant was made Warden of the Plains of Red River, with responsibility for enforcing the Hudson's Bay Company trade monopoly. During these quiet years of the 1820s and 1830s the Métis of Grantown organized and refined their most important institution, the famous buffalo hunt, which provided important food reserves for settlers and traders alike, and an economic base for the Métis.[4] The implications of the hunt were endless. It was organized along military lines and was easily adaptable to military and political purposes. The Métis, self-confident about their identity and proud of their place in western society, referred to themselves as the "New Nation" but nonetheless they remained dependent on buffalo and fur traders.

The Métis were created as a people only after the arrival of white traders in the West; the Indians had peopled the prairies for several millennia. It might be argued, however, that European influences recreated Indian society; these forces certainly revolutionized Indian history. When white men first came to North America the Indians who inhabited the western plains lacked horses and guns. The acquisition of these items, combined with trade, radically altered Indian society. In some instances, and for a brief period, the result was startling. A recent historian of Alberta illustrates:

> For a few vivid decades Blackfoot culture, based upon horses, guns and unlimited buffalo, rose rapidly into the zenith of the rich, colourful and glamorous life which many regard as the apogee of plains culture. Prior to 1730, during the long era which the Blackfoot called the dog-days they travelled on foot and used dogs for transport. About that year, the acquisition of horses and guns swept them rapidly onward and upward until slightly over a century later they were at the peak of their spectacular horse-based culture... Though horses and guns had made the Blackfoot aggressive, they also provided the leisure which led to the flowering of their social life.[5]

Revolutionized Indian societies were highly vulnerable to external forces. They could not manufacture either guns or ammunition; traders could (and did) cause social calamities through the introduction of liquor and a variety of diseases; trading patterns could not be controlled by Indians. More important, the buffalo could be liquidated and settlement could destroy the basis of Indian independence. In the mid-nineteenth century these successful western Indian societies were in a delicately balanced position. European contacts had changed the very character of their society; at the same time they were dependent upon and vulnerable to white society. Further white encroachment in the West could destroy them. Then encroachment of course quickly occurred, and in the 1870s the western Indians were swamped. A recent student of Canadian Indians comments: "For the sake of convenience, and recognizing the arbitrariness of the choice, we may use the date 1876, that of the first Indian Act, as the beginning of what we call the 'colonial' period. From the point of view of the European, the Indian had become irrelevant."[6]

The full complexity of mid-nineteenth-century prairie society cannot be revealed in a few paragraphs. The main characteristics, however, can be delineated. The West was inhabited by French-speaking Métis, English-speaking half-breeds, officers and men of the Hudson's Bay Company, Selkirk settlers, and a handful of missionaries, retired soldiers, and free-traders. Except for the Indians, these groups were all centred around the forks of the Red and Assiniboine Rivers, where a pluralistic society emerged. Reasonable amity usually prevailed, although the Métis could not be controlled against their will by the aging and increasingly ineffective HBC regime. This was a civilized society with its own churches, schools, and law courts. Its various components produced their own indigenous middle-classes, leaders, institutions, and traditions. Several religions were sustained within the settlement and promoted amongst the Indians.

At the same time, these diverse western societies were fragile and derivative. W.L. Morton describes the Selkirk settlers as "Scottish crofters on the banks of the Red."[7] Indian society had been recreated through European contact and persons of mixed blood were a product of liaisons between fur traders and Saulteaux and Cree women. Employees of the HBC were often of British birth. None of these groups had sufficient cultural integrity or autonomy to retain their distinctiveness and independence without a considerable degree of isolation from the larger North American society. As Bishop Taché observed about immigration into the West: "The movement (of immigration) is an actual fact, and we must cease to be what we have hitherto been, an exceptional people."[8]

They were dependent on more than isolation. Economically they needed the fur trade and the buffalo hunt. Buffalo products were sold to traders, settlers, and Americans at Minneapolis-St. Paul. The fur trade supplied cash, employment, and markets. Agriculture, "subsistent, riparian, and restricted,"[9] was nonetheless an important enterprise. Markets were obviously extremely limited. The large-scale export of commodities was hardly reasonable and, even within the West, Red River Valley farmers had no monopoly on food production as long as the buffalo survived. The agricultural sector of the western economy thus remained modest.[10]

Within the West some of these groups, particularly HBC officials, Indians, and Métis, could exert tremendous authority; their futures, however, were in the hands of forces that could not be contained. They had sufficient group-consciousness to defend collective interests, and to varying degrees they were all willing to resist encroachments from the outside. The Métis revolted against the locally enforced trade monopoly; HBC officials became dissatisfied with the treatment meted out to them by their London superiors. The Scots settlers resented the suggestions that the area could be disposed of without prior consultation. A willingness to resist in spite of dependence and relative weakness was a striking western characteristic long before the West was annexed by Canada. It is an important component of the western context of federalism.[11]

The central Canadian context is equally important. French-Canadian explorers penetrated the West in the eighteenth century, and thereafter the West was always a concern of at least some central Canadians. The connection became somewhat tenuous after the union of the fur companies in 1821, but it was never lost; there was always full cognizance of the fact that Rupert's Land was British territory.

A more pointed interest became evident in the late 1840s and the nature of that interest illuminated central Canadian attitudes about what the West was, what it should become, and how it should relate to what was then the province of Canada. This interest, while by no means partisan in nature, centred in the Upper Canadian Reformers. It can be illustrated by an examination of two of its representative manifestations: the campaign of the Toronto *Globe* to annex the West and organization of the North-West Transportation Company.[12]

The *Globe* was the organ of George Brown, who emerged in the 1850s as the Upper Canadian Reform leader. It was a Toronto newspaper that spoke to the farmers of what became western Ontario, but at the same time represented many of the metropolitan interests of Toronto's business elite. Its interest in the North-West tended to be economic and exploitative. Underlying this early tentative interest in the West was the assumption that the West would become an economic and social adjunct of Upper Canada. On 24 March 1847, for example, Brown reprinted Robert Baldwin Sullivan's lecture, "Emigration and Colonization." While primarily concerned with Upper Canada, Sullivan also discussed settlement possibilities in the North-West. He viewed the West as a potential settlement area of Upper Canadians. In 1848 the *Globe* claimed the West for Canada, and dismissed the rights of the Hudson's Bay Company. The West, it argued, was "capable of supporting a numerous population. This wide region nominally belongs to the Hudson's Bay Company, but in point of fact it does not seem to be theirs."[13] The *Globe's* interest petered out in 1850, but revived after a few years. In 1856 it published a series of revealing articles by an anonymous correspondent, "Huron": "I desire to see Canada for the Canadians and not exclusively for a selfish community of traders, utter strangers to our country; whose only anxiety is to draw all the wealth they can from it, without contributing to its advantages even one farthing."[14] He pronounced that charter of the Hudson's Bay Company "null and void" and declared that "the interests of Canada require that this giant monopoly be swept out of existence..." "Huron" was emphatic on this point:

> The formation of a Company in opposition to the Hudson's Bay Company would advance the interests of Canada; it would consolidate and strengthen the British power on the continent... In the organization of [opposition to the HBC], every patriot, every true Canadian, beholds results the most important to his country.

According to the *Globe*, westward expansion was an urgent need because of a shortage of settlement land "south of Lake Huron." "(Canada) is fully entitled to possess whatever parts of the Great British American territory she can safely occupy..."[15]

Interest in westward expansion was by no means confined to the *Globe*. In 1856, the Toronto Board of Trade indicated interest in western trade.[16] Various politicians took up the cause and the matter was aired in both houses of Parliament.[17]

In 1858 a Toronto-based group made a "quixotic" and "abortive"[18] attempt to penetrate the West through the incorporation of the North-West Transportation, Navigation and Railway Company (known as the North-West Transit Co.).[19] The project, designed to link central Canada and the Red River Valley by a combination of rail and water transport, was premature and unsuccessful, but its promoters' attitudes towards the West were both representative and persistent.[20] The objects were the exploitation of such likely and unlikely western possibilities as buffalo hides, furs, tallow, fish, salt, sarsaparilla, and cranberries, "the opening (of) a direct communication between Lake Superior and the Pacific..." and the opening of trade with the Orient. "We place before us a mart of 600,000,000 people (in China) and (our project will) enable us geographically to command them; opening the route, and leaving it to the guidance of commercial interests, Canada will, sooner or later, become the great tollgate for the commerce of the world." By "Canada," of course, was meant Toronto, and these promoters dreamed of controlling a great empire: "Like the Genii in the fable (the East Indian trade) still offers the sceptre to those who, unintimidated by the terms that surround it, are bold enough to adventure its embrace. In turn Phoenicia, Carthage, Greece, Rome, Venice, Pisa, Genoa, Portugal, Holland and lastly England, has won and worn this ocean diadem; Destiny now offers (the East Indian trade) to us."

During the 1850s a dynamic and expansive Upper Canada saw the North-West as its proper hinterland. It was regarded as a huge extractive resource, designed to provide profit for the businessman, land for the farmer, and power for Toronto.

While cultural attitudes are sometimes difficult to identify, it was probably assumed that the North-West would be culturally as well as economically dependent on the St. Lawrence Valley. J.M.S. Careless, for example, suggests that "Brown used the North-West agitation to complete the reunification of Upper Canada's liberal party merging Toronto urban and business leadership with Clear Grit agrarian strength in a dynamic party front."[21] Brown's "party front," which wanted "French Canadianism entirely extinguished,"[22] was dedicated to majoritarianism and the sectional interests of Upper Canada. While the nature of Reform attitudes towards French Canada is debatable, it is hardly likely that the same men who strove to terminate duality in central Canada sought to extend it to the North-West. Some Lower Canadian leaders (both French- and English-speaking), especially those identified with Montreal business, were interested in westward expansion for economic reasons. There was, however, little French-Canadian enthusiasm for expansion westward.[23] French-Canadian attitudes emanated from the nature of Lower Canadian society, which was profoundly conservative and lacked the buoyant and dynamic qualities of Upper Canada: "Not movement but stasis, enforced by the very nature of the task of 'survival', was the keynote of French-Canadian Society."[24] French Canadians lacked confidence in the economic viability of the North-West, in major part because of pre-Confederation missionary propaganda that emphasized difficulties relating to the West. It was generally assumed that "western settlement was the sole concern of Ontario,"[25] and the large-scale French-Canadian emigration would threaten French Canada's ability to survive. Thus there existed a Lower Canadian force to counterbalance Upper Canada's drive westward or Upper Canadian assumptions about how the West should be used. The only additional British North American region that could have possessed western ambitions consisted of the Atlantic colonies: New Brunswick, Nova Scotia, Prince Edward Island, and Newfoundland. Their traditional orientation was towards the Atlantic, not the interior. The Atlantic colonies were not about to launch an imperialistic venture in the 1860s.

Apart from Montreal business ambitions the field was clear for Upper Canada, but little could be done until a new political order was established in central Canada. The constitutional settlement embodied in the Act of Union of 1840 broke down during the 1850s. The complexities of central Canadian politics during the 1850s are not germane to this discussion, although it should be noted that a prime reason for the breakdown of Canadian government was the incompatibility between the uncontrollable dynamism and expansionism of Upper Canadian society on the one hand, and the conservative and inward-looking society of Lower Canada on the other.

The new order was worked out by the Great Coalition of 1864 that was committed to the introduction of "the federal principle into Canada, coupled with such provision as will permit the Maritime Provinces and the North-West Territory to be incorporated into the same system of government."[26] The solution was Confederation, which was established by the British North America Act of 1867. It created a highly centralized federation that included the province of Canada (divided into Ontario and Quebec), Nova Scotia, and New Brunswick, and that made explicit provision for the inclusion of the remaining British North American territories:

> It should be lawful for the Queen, by and with the Advice of Her Majesty's Most Honourable Privy Council, on Addresses from the Houses of the Parliament of Canada, and from the Houses of the respective Legislatures of the Colonies or Provinces of Newfoundland, Prince Edward Island, and British Columbia, to admit those Colonies or Provinces, or any of them, into the Union, and on Address from the Houses of Parliament of Canada to admit Rupert's Land and the North-western Territory, or either of them, into the Union ...[27]

Confederation was thus the constitutional framework within which the West was destined to relate to central Canada.

The nature of the new confederation had profound implications for the West. The system was highly centralized, so much so that in conception it hardly qualified as a federation in the classic sense. The Fathers of Confederation wanted a strong state that could withstand American pressure. Heavily influenced by trade considerations, they saw federation in mercantilistic terms. As children of the empire as it existed prior to the repeal of the corn laws, it is not surprising that their federal model was the old colonial system, modified to involve "the citizens of the provinces ... in the government of the whole entity":[28]

> The purpose of the Fathers of Confederation—to found a united and integrated transcontinental Dominion—was comparable with that of the mercantilists: and in both designs there was the same need that the interests of the parts should be made subordinate to the interest of the whole. The Dominion was the heir in direct succession of the old colonial system. It was put in possession of both the economic and political controls of the old regime. On the one hand, it was given the power to regulate trade and commerce, which had been the chief economic prerogative of Great Britain; on the other hand, it was granted the right to nominate provincial governors, to review provincial legislation and to disallow provincial acts, the three powers which had been the chief attributes of Great Britain's political supremacy.[29]

In his more optimistic moments, John A. Macdonald went so far as to predict the demise of the provinces: "If the Confederation goes on, you, if spared the ordinary age of man, will see both local parliaments and governments absorbed in the general power. This is as plain to me as if I saw it accomplished."[30]

It is true that Lower Canada and the Atlantic colonies were part of the new Dominion, but the effective pressure for the new settlement came from Upper Canada. French Canada realized the inevitability of change, but generated little enthusiasm for Confederation. She could offer no better alternative and hence acquiesced (not without considerable protest) in the new arrangement.[31] The creative role was played by Upper Canada, and for that section Confederation was a great triumph. The new system was posited on the abandonment of dualism and, through representation by population in the House of Commons, the acceptance of majoritarianism, albeit with limited guarantees for French-Canadian culture within the province of Quebec. Majoritarianism was very much to the advantage of Ontario, which, according to the 1871 census, had 1,600,000 persons—or 46 percent of Canada's 3,500,000 people. This translated into 82 of the 181 seats in the House of Commons. The first prime minister was an Ontarian, as were the leading lights of the opposition—George Brown, Edward Blake, and Alexander Mackenzie. In the first cabinet Ontario, the wealthiest province, had five of thirteen places. Even the capital was an Ontario city.

The Ontario Liberals became the leaders of the nineteenth-century provincial rights agitation and Ontario emerged as the bastion of provincial rights sentiment, but while the federal scheme was being defined most of Ontario's leaders, regardless of party, concurred on the utility of this "quasi federal" scheme.[32] This is hardly surprising. The Reformers or Liberals were the larger of the two Ontario parties, and doubtless looked forward to a great future as the rulers of *both* Ontario and the Dominion. Although they realized this aim by 1873 and ruled simultaneously in Toronto and Ottawa for five years, they suffered humiliating defeats in 1867 at both levels. The deep autonomist drives within Ontario society quickly reasserted themselves, and Ontario's Liberals began their protracted assault on Macdonald's constitutional edifice. This should not obscure the fact that quasi-federalism met with little Ontario opposition during the mid-1860s.

The acquisition of the North-West would take place within the context of Canadian federalism. The Fathers of Confederation tended to assume that the "'colonial' relationship with the provinces was a natural one ... It therefore seems more appropriate to think of the dominion-provincial relationship at that time as similar to the relationship of the imperial government with a colony enjoying limited self-government."[33] Ontario Liberals quickly adopted a different approach to federalism; federal Conservatives did not. The West was to be "annexed as a subordinate territory."[34] Ontario's leaders were anxious that expansion take place quickly, and assumed that Ontarians would benefit through the creation of a miniature Ontario in the West. At the same time the settled portion of the West, shaken by the breakdown of its isolation and possessing a tradition of resistance to outside control, was accustomed to colonial status, exploitation, and dependency.

Canada's first Confederation government was anxious to honour its commitment to annex the West. William McDougall and George Cartier went to London in 1868 to negotiate the transfer to Canada of Rupert's Land and the North-West Territory. Their mission was successful. The Hudson's Bay Company agreed to transfer its territory to Canada; the Dominion agreed to compensate the company with one-twentieth of the fertile area in the West, land surrounding HBC posts, and a cash payment of 300,000 pounds. The initial transfer was to be to the Crown, which would immediately retransfer the area to Canada.

In preparation for the reception of this great domain, Canada passed "An Act for the temporary Government of Rupert's Land and the North-Western Territory when united with Canada."[35] This short act provided that the West, styled "The North-West Territories," would be governed by federal appointees—a lieutenant-governor assisted by a council. It also continued existing laws in force and public servants in office until changes were made by either the federal government or the lieutenant-governor. The act was to "continue in force until the end of the next Session of Parliament."

It had been suggested that this statute does not reveal much about the intent of the federal authorities because it was preceded by such phrases as: "to make some temporary provision" and "until more permanent arrangements can be made."[36] At the same time P.B. Waite notes that it was not a temporary provision at all. After the creation of Manitoba, "the rest of the vast Northwest Territories remained under the Act of 1869, that 'temporary' arrangement. It was re-enacted in 1871 as permanent without any alteration whatever."[37] There is no reason to assume that in 1869 Macdonald and his colleagues intended any very radical future alteration in the statute, which, with the appointments made thereunder, revealed much about Ottawa's attitude towards the West. The area, not a Crown colony in 1869, was to join Confederation as a federally controlled territory—not as a province. It was not assumed that the West was joining a federation; rather, Canada was acquiring a subservient territory. Local leaders were neither consulted nor considered. These assumptions emerge even more clearly when the initial appointments under the act are studied. Ontario's ambitions to control the West were symbolized by the appointment of William McDougall as lieutenant-governor. He was a former Clear Grit who represented Ontario Reformers in the first Confederation government. An imperious and sanctimonious expansionist, he had neither the ability nor the desire to take local leaders, especially those who were not white, into his confidence. Certainly the federal government's request that he search out westerners for his council[38] would hardly inspire local confidence. McDougall was regarded as anything but impartial.[39] Initial executive appointments were not likely, with the possible exception of J.A.N. Provencher,[40] to inspire local confidence in a regime that was organized in central Canada. Two appointments were flagrantly political. A.N. Richards was the brother of a minister in Sandfield Macdonald's Ontario government and Captain D.R. Cameron was Charles Tupper's son-in-law. Even if one accepts the argument that the "temporary" act was indeed temporary, it is difficult to argue that Lieutenant-Governor McDougall, Attorney General Richards, or Chief of Police Cameron were temporary.

These various decisions made in distant capitals caused an upheaval in the Red River settlement, the only really settled part of Rupert's Land. Red River was, in fact, on the verge of expansion—a point forcibly made to federal and imperial authorities by Anglican Bishop Machray, HBC Governor of Assiniboia Mactavish, and Roman Catholic Bishop Taché.[41] The unsettled state of Red River was a product of many factors. By the end of the 1840s the commercial authority of the HBC had been irretrievably eroded. During the 1850s the isolation of the area was just as irretrievably lost. American traders pushed up from St. Paul and by the late 1850s a Canadian party, allied with the anti-HBC agitation in Canada, had emerged in the settlement. These Canadians, whose attitudes had been previewed in the 1840s by Recorder Adam Thom and were later to merge with those of Canada First, were arrogant, threatening, and racist. They led a concerted assault on the authority of the company, and were instrumental in producing political chaos at Red River during the 1850s. To the Métis, especially, they represented a threat to their rights and way of life. These justified fears[42] were confirmed by Canadian government officials who entered the area prior to the transfer and offended local sensibilities. Instability was abetted by a "breakdown of the traditional economy of the Settlement" during the late 1860s. In 1868 Red River "was threatened by famine."[43]

The people of Red River could assess Canadian intentions only on the basis of Canadian activities, appointments, and laws. The response was resistance, spearheaded by the Métis but reluctantly supported to varying degrees (or at least tolerated) by most people at Red River, except the members of the Canadian Party: "Riel's authority, although it originated in armed force, came within a few months to be based on the majority will of the community."[44]

The details of the resistance of 1869–1870 are well known and are not germane to this paper. What is important is that Louis Riel's provisional government was in such a strong strategic position that it was able to force the federal authorities to negotiate on terms of entry. The results were embodied in the Manitoba Act that created the province of Manitoba.

Provincehood was a victory (more, it might be noted, for the Métis than for the other sections of the Red River community), but Manitoba nonetheless entered Confederation as a dependency, not as a full partner with a federal system. Two broad circumstances explain the continuation of "subordinate"[45] status. First, Manitoba was not constitutionally equal to the other provinces. The Métis leaders and their clerical advisers placed great emphasis on cultural problems. Anticipating an influx of Ontarians, they demanded and obtained educational and linguistic guarantees. The federal authorities were concerned primarily with such larger issues as the settlement of the West and the construction of a transcontinental railroad. To facilitate these policies, in the formulation of which Manitoba had no say, Ottawa retained control of Manitoba's public lands and natural resources "for the purposes of the Dominion."[46] Professor Eric Kierans comments:

> The ownership of the land and resources belong [sic] to the people collectively as the sign of their independence and the guarantee of their responsibility. By British law and tradition, the ownership and control of the public domain was always handed over to the political authority designated by a community when the citizens assumed responsibility for the government of their own affairs . . . During the . . . hearings [related to the *Report of the Royal Commission on the Transfer of the Natural Resources of Manitoba* (Ottawa, 1929)] Professor Chester Martin . . . testified: "The truth is that for 35 years, (i.e., until the creation of the Provinces of Saskatchewan and Alberta), I believe that it will be correct to say, Manitoba was the solitary exception within the British Empire to accepted British practice with regard to control of the crown lands and it still remains, in respect of public lands, literally not a province but a colony of the Dominion." . . . In substance, any attempt to grant responsible government to a province or state, while retaining for the Imperial or Federal authority the control of crown lands and revenues, was held to be a "contradiction in terms and impossible."[47]

Just as serious as Manitoba's inferior constitutional position, was her effective status. She was in no way equipped to function as a province with the full paraphernalia of responsible government. She was ridiculously small, limited in 1870 to some 12,000 persons and 13,500 square miles. The province had an extremely limited tradition of representative government and, to complicate matters further, several of her key leaders were fugitives from justice because of their roles in the resistance. As Lieutenant-Governor A.G. Archibald explained in 1872: "You can hardly hope to carry on responsible Government by inflicting death penalties on the leaders of a majority of the electors."[48] Perhaps even more important, provincial finances were hopelessly inadequate; the federal government granted "provincial status to an area which was essentially primitive; and it gave financial terms modelled improperly upon those given to the older provinces."[49] Under the Manitoba Act the province received $67,104 per annum in grants. Her own revenue came to only about $10,000. Even by 1875, 88 percent of provincial revenues were federal subsidies. "During the whole period from 1870 to 1885 Manitoba was little more than a financial ward of the federal government ... "[50] The province could not even afford public building to house the lieutenant-governor and assembly until Ottawa advanced the necessary funds. In 1871 about one-third of provincial expenditures were used to cover legislative expenses.

Thus provincehood was granted prematurely to a jurisdiction that could sustain neither its responsibilities nor the kind of status it ought to have occupied with a federal state. The primary fault lay with the federal leaders: "The Manitoba Act bears on its face evidence both of the inexperience of the delegates from the Red River settlement and of the lack of mature consideration given to the measure by the federal government. The former circumstance was unavoidable; the latter can hardly be condoned."[51] During the early years of Manitoba's history even the outward trappings of real provincehood were absent. For several years the province's immaturity prevented the development of responsible government and the first two lieutenant-governors, A.G. Archibald and Alexander Morris, functioned as effective governors rather than as constitutional monarchs. Until 1876 the lieutenant-governors even attended cabinet meetings.

Early Manitoba was a colony of central Canada because of constitutional discrimination and because she had neither the maturity nor the resources to support provincehood. But that was not all. With the advent of formal provincial status came an influx of settlers from Ontario, a process that started with the arrival of the Anglo-Saxon Ontarian hordes that dominated Colonel Garnett Wolseley's expeditionary force of 1870. That small army had no real military function. It was sent west in 1870 to appease Ontario—to serve as symbolic compensation for the inclusion in the Manitoba Act of cultural guarantees for the Métis. In extreme form, the expeditionary force was a model of what the later central Canadian influx was to mean. Local traditions were shunted aside as agriculture was commercialized and society revolutionized. The Indians were unable to assimilate themselves; many Métis sold the land they had been granted to unscrupulous speculators and moved into the North-West Territories. In a symbolic action a group of Ontarians who arrived in 1871 seized some Métis land on the Rivière aux Ilets de Bois. In spite of Métis protests they kept the land and sharpened the insult by renaming the river "the Boyne"! Some Scots settlers sympathized with the Canadians, but like the HBC traders they had to watch the old society die. Within a few years Manitoba was a colony of Ontario demographically as well as constitutionally, politically, and economically.

The province of Manitoba was only a minuscule portion of the territory annexed by Canada. The remaining enormous area was organized as the North-West Territories. With virtually no permanent white settlement, it received even shorter shrift than Manitoba. Its initial government was provided under the "temporary Government" act. That statute was "re-enacted, extended and continued in force until ... 1871" by the Manitoba Act.[52] Prior to its second automatic expiry in 1871 it was again reenacted without major change, this time with no expiry date. Until 1875, therefore, government for the North-West Territories was provided under the initial legislation of 1869. During these six years the administration of the territories was somewhat casual. There was no resident governor—that responsibility was simply added to the duties of the lieutenant-governor of Manitoba. Most of the members of the council were Manitobans who did not live in the territories. The Indians, the largest group of inhabitants, were managed not consulted.

The Mackenzie government overhauled the administration of the North-West in

1875 by securing the passage of "The North-West Territories Act." Although not "fully thought out"[53] it did provide a fairly simple system of government consisting of a separate governor and a council that was initially appointed but that would become elective as the non-Indian population grew. The capital was established at Battleford until 1882 when it was moved to Regina. Mackenzie appointed David Laird, a federal cabinet minister from Prince Edward Island, as the first full-time lieutenant-governor of the North-West Territories. His first council included neither an Indian nor a Métis who resided in the NWT. There was no elected councillor until 1881.

Prior to 1869 the West was a dependent area, ruled (if at all) in a casual, chaotic but paternalistic manner for the benefit of a huge commercial firm centred in London. Westerners feared that the transfer involved simply a change of masters, not a change of status. The Métis feared that in the process they would lose their lifestyle and culture through an inundation of Ontario settlers. The result was a movement of resistance led by the Métis, but with broad support within the Red River settlement. For the bulk of the West the resistance resulted in no change whatsoever. For a small district on the Red River the result was a tiny anaemic province incapable of functioning as a viable partner within a federal system.

After 1867 Macdonald and his colleagues were not able to maintain "quasi-federalism" over the original components of Confederation, but for the West annexation to Canada involved the confirmation of colonial status. The fifteen years after the transfer was the launching period for the West in Confederation. During those years federal sway on the prairies was virtually unchallengeable.

Ottawa's most powerful instrument was federal possession of the West's public lands "for the purposes of the Dominion." This enabled Ottawa to implement two policies that were crucial to the Canadianization of the West: rapid settlement and the construction of a transcontinental railroad. Extreme difficulties did not prevent the execution of these policies. Public lands were made available to settlers in a variety of ways. Although settlement did not proceed as quickly as the federal authorities desired, Manitoba experienced rapid growth during the 1870s and 1880s. Within a generation of the transfer the territories west of Manitoba had been populated by Ontarians, Americans, and Europeans. Consequently the provinces of Saskatchewan and Alberta were established in 1905. The federal authorities had recognized from the outset that a transcontinental railroad was required if the West was to be properly Canadianized. After several false starts, the Canadian Pacific Railway was chartered in 1880. The CPR was heavily subsidized, receiving from the federal government some $38,000,000 worth of track constructed at public expense, $25,000,000 in cash, a railroad monopoly in western Canada for twenty years, and 25,000,000 acres of prairie land. The land grant was considered indispensable to the line's success and the success of the railroad was one of the fundamental "purposes of the Dominion." The federal government designed its transportation policies to suit the needs of central Canadian business, and was not particularly tender towards western interests. As Charles Tupper, minister of railroads, put it in 1883: "The interests of this country demand that the Canadian Pacific Railway should be made a success . . . Are the interests of Manitoba and the North-West to be sacrificed to the interests of Canada? I say, if it is necessary, yes."[54]

Federal Conservative strategists, who were in power during 1867–73 and 1878–96, tied tariff policy to settlement and transportation. They saw the West as central Canada's economic hinterland. The area was to be settled quickly and become an exporter of agricultural products and an importer of manufactured goods. Central Canada was to be made the manufacturing centre. The CPR was to haul eastern manufactured goods into the West and western agricultural produce to market. High tariffs were designed to protect the manufacturing industries from foreign competition and at the same time guarantee freight traffic to the CPR by forcing trade patterns to flow along east-west, not north-south lines. These basic decisions determined the nature of post-1870 western development. They were made by federal leaders to serve central Canadian interests and they perpetuated the status of the West as a colonial region.

Federal management of the West during these years should be looked at in micro as well as macro terms, although it is clear that federal authorities had little interest in day-to-day western conditions. If settlement was to proceed in orderly and rapid fashion the Indian "problem" had to be solved. That task involved extinguishing Indian rights to the land and rendering the tribes harmless by herding them onto reserves. The instrument used for these purposes was the Indian "treaty." During the 1870s a series of agreements was negotiated between the Crown and the prairie tribes. Through these treaties the Indians gave up their right to their traditional lands in return for reserves and nominal concessions, payments, and guarantees. However, they tended to resist being forced onto reserves as long as the buffalo, their traditional source of food, remained plentiful. By 1885 the buffalo were on the verge of extermination and most Indians had been coerced to settle on reservations.

In 1873 Canada founded the North-West Mounted Police, another instrument of federal control.[55] The Mounties constituted an effective federal presence on the prairies, chased American traders out of southern Alberta, policed the Indians and Métis, and symbolized the stability and order desired by white settlers. In bringing effective federal rule to southern Alberta they abetted the termination of the international aspect of Blackfoot life. This breakdown of regional international societies was part of the process of Canadianization.

The federal political structure also functioned as a control instrument. Until 1887 Manitoba's handful of MPs constituted the West's entire representation in the House of Commons. These members tended to support the government of the day because of its immense patronage and fiscal authority.

> Dependent upon federal largesse yet suspicious of eastern dictation, the western attitude towards national politics was often a curious mixture of ministerialism and defiance. Some papers seemed to believe that the electorate should always give a general support to the government, for such support would ensure a continuous supply of federal monies for western projects. At the same time these papers admitted the need to champion regional interests.[56]

During the 1870s and 1880s the West was Canadianized. By the end of the century massive immigration (which incidentally produced a distinctive population mix that helped differentiate the region from central Canada) combined with basic federal policies had produced a new West, but its status had changed little. The process generated resistance. The government of Manitoba challenged the CPR's monopoly and sought to obtain better financial terms. Farmers in Manitoba and along the Saskatchewan River organized unions and began their long struggle for a host of reforms including lower tariffs and a transportation system sensitive to their needs. Under Louis Riel's leadership a minority of Indians and Métis rose in 1885 in a pathetic and ill-led rebellion. Territorial politicians crusaded for representation in Parliament and responsible government of the North-West Territories.

By the end of the century western resistance to federal control and leadership was a well-established tradition. The West, however, was not strong enough to challenge Canada's great national policies successfully. Consequently the West has remained a subordinate region; the Canadian federation retains its imperialistic characteristics. As W.L. Morton suggested: "For Confederation was brought about to increase the wealth of Central Canada, and until that original purpose is altered, and the concentration of wealth and population by national policy in Central Canada ceases, Confederation must remain an instrument of injustice."[57]

Notes

1. In this essay, the "West" refers to the territories that became the provinces of Manitoba, Saskatchewan, and Alberta. Rupert's Land consisted of the Hudson's Bay Company territories. The North-West Territory included the other British lands in the northwest. British Columbia was separate and is not considered in this essay.

2. E.E. Rich, *Hudson's Bay Company, 1670–1870*, 3 vols. (Toronto, 1960), 1: 53.

3. Cited in ibid., 1: 53–54.

4. For a superb account of the buffalo hunt, see Alexander Ross, *The Red River Settlement* (London, 1856), Chap. XVIII.

5. James G. MacGregor, *A History of Alberta* (Edmonton, 1972), 17, 24. For further illustrations see Stanley Norman Murray, *The Valley Comes of Age: A History of Agriculture in the Valley of the Red River of the North, 1812–1920* (Fargo, 1967), 13: "By 1800 the Sioux and Chippewa tribes also had acquired horses. Because these animals made it possible for the Indians to hunt the buffalo over great distances, these people soon spent most of the summer and fall roaming the vast prairie west of the Red River. As they became more nomadic, the Indians placed less emphasis upon agriculture, pottery making, weaving, and the idea of a fixed dwelling place. In years when the buffalo were numerous, they could live from the hunt alone. Such was the case between 1800 and 1840 when the Sioux and Chippewa experienced degrees of luxury and leisure they had never known."

6. E. Palmer Patterson, *The Canadian Indian: A History Since 1500* (Don Mills, 1972), 39–40. Different dates apply in different areas: "Thus, by 1865 the plight of the Indians in the Red River Valley was a pathetic one, and for the most part their culture no longer had any effect upon this area" (Murray, *The Valley Comes of Age*, 15).

7. W.L. Morton, "Introduction to the New Edition" of Alexander Ross, *The Red River Settlement* (Edmonton, 1972), xx.

8. Cited in A.I. Silver, "French Canada and the Prairie Frontier, 1870–1890" *Canadian Historical Review* 50 (March 1969): 13.

9. W.L. Morton, "Agriculture in the Red River Colony," *CHR* 50 (March 1969): 13.

10. Murray, *The Valley Comes of Age*, 44, 48: "[T]here can be little question that the economy of the Selkirk colonies stagnated soon after they were able to produce a surplus. The major reason for stagnation in Red River agriculture was the limited market for farm produce, and this situation developed primarily out of the economic prerogatives of the Hudson's Bay Company ... [I]t continued to rely upon supplies brought from England and pemmican furnished by the metis hunters." In short, "agriculture did not become really commercial under the fur company regime ... " Morton points out that Red River agriculture lacked both "an export staple and transportation" ("Agriculture in the Red River Colony," 316).

11. There has recently been considerable discussion of western "identity." Debate on this question will doubtless continue. It can be argued that this persistent willingness to resist is one of the most distinctive western characteristics and is certainly a part of any western "identity," and that it long antedates Confederation. P.F.W. Rutherford, however, dismisses Métis influence:

"Unlike other regions in the dominion, the western community was essentially a product of events set in motion by Confederation" ("The Western Press and Regionalism, 1870–96," *CHR* 52 (September 1971): 287). Morton, however, comments: "Louis Riel was a more conventional politician than William Aberhart . . . " and "[t]his was the beginning of the bias of prairie politics. The fears of the Métis had led them to demand equality for the people of the Northwest in Confederation" ("The Bias of Prairie Politics," in *Historical Essays on the Prairie Provinces*, ed., Donald Swainson (Toronto, 1970), 289, 293). [Also see pp. 12,14 in this volume.] What is more "western" than this recurring "demand" for "equality"?

12. For a more detailed discussion by the present author see *Ontario and Confederation*, Centennial Historical Booklet No. 5 (Ottawa, 1967) and "The North-West Transportation Company: Personnel and Attitudes," Historical and Scientific Society in Manitoba *Transaction*, Series III, No. 26, 1969–70.

13. *Globe* (Toronto), 14 June 1848.

14. Quotations from articles by "Huron" are from *Globe*, 18 and 31 October 1856.

15. Ibid., 10 December 1856.

16. Ibid., 4 December 1856.

17. Province of Canada, *Journals of the Legislative Council of the Province of Canada*, Being the 3rd Session of the 5th Provincial Parliament, 1857, Vol. XV, 60, 80, 184, 195; Province of Canada, *Appendix to the Fifteenth Volume of the Journals of the Legislative Assembly of the Province of Canada*, Being the 3rd Session of the 5th Provincial Parliament, 1857, Vol. XV, Appendix 17.

18. Joseph James Hargrave, *Red River* (Montreal, 1871), 143.

19. Province of Canada, *Statutes*, 1858, 635ff.

20. Material that follows is from *Memoranda and Prospectus of the North-West Transportation and Land Company* (Toronto, 1858); Allan Macdonnell, *The North West Transportation, Navigation and Railway Company: Its Objectives* (Toronto, 1858) and *Prospectus of the North-West Transportation, Navigation and Railway Company* (Toronto, 1858).

21. J.M.S. Careless, *The Union of Canadas: The Growth of Canadian Institutions, 1841–57* (Toronto, 1967), 206.

22. P.A.C., George Brown Papers, George Brown to Anne Brown, 27 October 1864, cited in Donald Creighton, *The Road to Confederation* (Toronto, 1964), 182.

23. For an analysis of French-Canadian attitudes see Silver, "French Canada and the Prairie Farmer."

24. Ibid., 29.

25. Ibid., 15.

26. Cited in Chester Martin, *Foundations of Canadian Nationhood* (Toronto, 1955), 314.

27. British North America Act, Section 146.

28. Bruce W. Hodgins, "Disagreement at the Commencement: Divergent Ontarian Views of Federalism, 1867–1871," in *Oliver Mowat's Ontario*, ed., Donald Swainson (Toronto, 1972), 55.

29. Donald Creighton, *British North America at Confederation* (Ottawa, 1939), Appendix II, *The Royal Commission on Dominion-Provincial Relations* (Ottawa, 1940), 83.

30. P.A.C., John A. Macdonald Papers, 510, Macdonald to M.C. Cameron, 19 December 1864, cited in Creighton, *The Road to Confederation*, 165.

31. See Jean Charles Bonenfant, *The French Canadians and the Birth of Confederation*, Canadian Historical Association booklet No. 10 (Ottawa, 1967).

32. See Hodgins, "Disagreement at the Commencement."

33. J.R. Mallory, "The Five Faces of Federalism," in *The Future of Canadian Federalism*, eds., P.A. Crepeau and C.B. Macpherson (Toronto, 1965), 4.

34. W.L. Morton, "Clio in Canada: The Interpretation of Canadian History," in *Approaches to Canadian History*, ed. Carl Berger, Canadian Historical Readings I (Toronto, 1967), 44.

35. This act is reprinted in W.L. Morton, ed., *Manitoba: The Birth of a Province* (Altona, 1965), 1–3.

36. See Ralph Heintzman, "The Spirit of Confederation: Professor Creighton, Biculturalism, and the Use of History," *CHR* 52 (September 1971): 256-58. Heintzman comments: "Now even a cursory examination of the text of this Act of 1869 would cast serious doubt upon the worth of this argument" (p. 256)—i.e., that the act revealed the "real intentions of the federal government" (p. 247). "The purely temporary character of the Act is made clear in the preamble . . . But all of this informed speculation is quite unnecessary. We have an explicit statement of the intentions of the government from the mouth of John A. Macdonald himself. Macdonald told the House of Commons flatly that the 1869 Act was 'provisional' and 'intends to last only a few months' . . . " (p. 257). Heintzman's chief concerns are educational and linguistic rights.

37. P.B. Waite, *Canada 1874-1896: Arduous Destiny* (Toronto, 1971), 65. See also Lewis Herbert Thomas, *The Struggle for Responsible Government in the North-West Territories 1870-97* (Toronto, 1956), 48. It is clearly possible to debate the implications of the act, but a document that Macdonald's government made the permanent constitution for the North-West Territories cannot simply be dismissed as meaningless. It is interesting to note that when the statute was made permanent in 1871, with only insignificant modifications, and, of course, the exclusion from its provisions of the new province of Manitoba, it was justified in its preamble as follows: "whereas, it is expedient to make provision for the government, after the expiration of the Act first above mentioned [i.e., An Act for the temporary government of Rupert's Land], of the North-West Territories, that being the name given . . . to such portion of Rupert's Land for the North Western Territory as is not included in . . . Manitoba . . . " (An Act to make further provision for the government of the North-West Territories, 34 Vict. Cap. XVI).

38. "Instructions issued to Hon. Wm. McDougall as Lieutenant Governor of the North West Territories, Sept. 28, 1869," in *The Canadian North-West: Its Early Development and Legislative Records,* ed., E.H. Oliver (Ottawa, 1914-15), II: 878-79.

39. For his earlier hopeless insensitivity concerning Red River see W.L. Morton, "Introduction" to *Alexander Begg's Red River Journal* (Toronto, 1956), 23.

40. Provencher, a nephew of Bishop J.N. Provencher of St. Boniface (1847-53), was a central Canadian newspaperman. He had only minimal contact with the West and was described as "a pleasant sort of a man who had come up altogether wrongly informed regarding this country . . . " (*Alexander Begg's Red River Journal,* 176). Provencher's relationship with the bishop was his only tie with the West, unless it is assumed that the Métis were French Canadians and therefore identified closely with other French Canadians. The Métis, of course, assumed no such thing, regarding themselves as a New Nation. To assume that the Métis were French Canadian is to commit a sort of historiographical genocide. Heintzman, "Spirit of Confederation," 253, for example, comments: "This awareness of the 'canadien' community at Red River was one reason to rejoice in the annexations of the North-West: it meant that the French of the west would be welcomed back into the fold and raised the possibility that colonists from Lower Canada would find themselves 'at home' on the prairies." Presumably, for Heintzman, these 'canadiens' included the Métis. Alexander Begg held the members of McDougall's party in very low esteem. McDougall was characterized as "overbearing," "distant," "unpleasant," and "vindictive." Richards "does not appear to be extraordinarily [sic] clever on Law Subjects although appointed Attorney General," Cameron was "a natural ass," and Dr. Jacques "an unmannerly young fellow" (W.L. Morton, "Introduction," *Alexander Begg's Red River Journal,* 176). Is it any wonder that Canada's initial attitude towards the North-West was looked at through a jaundiced eye?

41. George F.G. Stanley, *The Birth of Western Canada: A History of the Riel Rebellions* (Toronto, 1936), 63-64.

42. Morton, "Introduction," *Alexander Begg's Red River Journal,* 29, 40-42, 45.

43. Ibid., 17.

44. M.S. Donnelly, *The Government of Manitoba* (Toronto, 1963), 10.

45. Morton, "Clio in Canada," 44.

46. Manitoba Act, Section 30.

47. Eric Kierans, *Report on Natural Resources Policy in Manitoba* (Winnipeg, 1973), 1. The

severity of this kind of analysis has been questioned. See, for example, J.A. Maxwell, *Federal Subsidies to the Provincial Governments in Canada* (Cambridge, Mass., 1937).

48. Cited in Donnelly, *Government of Manitoba*, 16.
49. Maxwell, *Federal Subsidies to the Provincial Governments*, 37.
50. Donnelly, *Government of Manitoba*, 161.
51. Maxwell, *Federal Subsidies to the Provincial Governments*, 37–38.
52. Section 36.
53. R.G. Robertson, "The Evolution of Territorial Government in Canada," in *The Political Process in Canada* (Toronto, 1963), 139 note.
54. Cited in Chester Martin, *"Dominion Lands" Policy* (Toronto, 1938), 470.
55. See S.W. Horrall, "Sir John A. Macdonald and the Mounted Police Force for the North-West Territories," *CHR* 53 (June 1972). Horrall notes, 182–83: "To Macdonald the problem of policing the Northwest resembled that faced by the British in India."
56. Rutherford, "Western Press and Regionalism," 301.
57. Morton, "Clio in Canada," 47.

Causes of the 1885 Struggle

HOWARD ADAMS

Reprinted from Howard Adams, *Prison of Grass* (Saskatoon: Fifth House
Publishers, 1989), 70–80, by permission of the author.

The term "Riel rebellion" for the hostilities of 1885 is not only misleading but incorrect because it implies that Louis Riel alone was responsible for the hostilities. The truth is that he entered only the later stages of a long struggle involving many groups in the North-West. The war of 1885 was the culmination of a complex struggle that had arisen over the previous two decades between the people of the North-West and the industrial rulers of Ottawa. Western protests were made by local merchants, farmers, settlers, workers, Indians, and Métis, and their demands essentially centred around the need for a responsible government to make economic and land reforms. The hostilities of 1885 proved to be an important turning-point in the social and political development of Canada. The new rulers established capitalism in the North-West, and the way was clear for modern agriculture and industrialism to expand through the private enterprise system.

Although responsible government had been granted to the small province of Manitoba in 1870, including the authority necessary for provincial administration, the federal government had not imposed its constitutional authority on the remainder of the North-West: "The Territories in 1870 were wholly without government of any form. The institutions of law and order, as understood in civilized communities, were non-existent."[1] Nominal control remained solely in the hands of the lieutenant-governor of Manitoba until 1873, when the governor general of Canada appointed a council to help him. The council and the new lieutenant-governor, Alexander Morris, urged the government to create a police force, the NWMP (North-West Mounted Police), which they did in 1873. Control of Indian Affairs and of the NWMP was retained by Ottawa at this time, and has never been relinquished. Finally, the North-West Territories Act of 1875 reorganized the North-West Council and named a lieutenant-governor exclusively for the North-West Territories, whose population of about 20,000 at that time included 13,000 Indians, 5,000 Métis, and 2,000 whites. The appointed council of five members and a lieutenant-governor had the power to pass ordinances relating to taxation for local purposes, public health, highways, and the administration of justice; however, they did not have a judicial system or a police force of their own capable of carrying out these functions. Ottawa reserved the right to disallow any ordinances passed by the North-West Council. This pseudofederal administration was imposed on the North-West people without their participation and had no connection to their local political development, but, since federal troops did not move beyond Manitoba after the civil war, the North-West people were able to establish a certain degree of local autonomy.

As early as 1873 there was already considerable regional interest and involvement in local political affairs. Unlike the Indians, some Métis were still relatively independent within their communities, and their Native councils acted as their local government. At St. Laurent, Saskatchewan, for instance, the Métis population of approximately 800 people became highly organized and very involved in local politics. By 1875 the Métis of St. Laurent had established their own local government, including a five-member council and a president.

Apart from the injustices suffered by the Indians and Métis, discontent among all people in the North-West, both Native and white, began in the early 1880s, mainly centring around economic issues. The cost of machinery was 40 percent higher on the prairies than in the East. Local wholesale merchants charged a high price for all goods, regardless of whether they were imported or not, while farmers received low prices for their products. Freighting companies, like the Hudson's Bay, imposed excessively high transportation rates. Many farmers who were forced to live on credit were charged high interest and fell increasingly into debt. By 1884 the economic crisis was at its worst: the North-West land boom had collapsed, CPR construction had almost come to a standstill because the federal treasury was empty, and immigration to the prairies slowed to a trickle as prices for western goods dropped seriously. Moreover, the increasingly authoritarian leadership of Lieutenant-Governor Dewdney discouraged local participation in the political and economic concerns of the community. The people felt themselves to be voiceless victims in a corrupt system; discontent accelerated, with the centre of agitation at Prince Albert, where many land investors had lost large sums of money in 1882 when the CPR route was diverted from Prince Albert to Regina. Throughout the North-West, the generous grants of land given to the CPR by the federal government angered the people. For example, in one transaction, 17,000,000 acres were given to the CPR even though some of the woodlots in that area had been promised to settlers. These injustices were perpetrated without warning or consultation with residents of the area, leaving many embittered and hostile.

Supporting the North-West struggle were many different groups. Farmers and Métis felt a bond of mutual oppression and wanted a redress of their shared grievances. Following the recession in the West in 1882, white settlers began to petition for better conditions, but, although they presented their demands to the Macdonald administration on frequent occasions, their requests were ignored each time and they became increasingly annoyed. People at a mass meeting in Prince Albert dealing with the sale of local land to the CPR stated:

> Another sale is shortly to be held, when we may expect just such another outburst of popular feeling. In some parts the settlers threaten bloodshed rather than ejectment and should it come to this, the Dominion Government will be powerless to enforce the law as neither Mounted Police nor Canadian Volunteers will be willing to engage in the work of driving Canadians from their rightful homes in order that the land grabbers may have quiet possession thereof.[2]

A typical conflict arose over the construction of a telegraph line between Humboldt and Prince Albert. A small group of local businessmen favoured by Ottawa received the contract. When the official town committee selected a route contrary to the one chosen by these businessmen and had the poles moved to another location, a member of the group became exceedingly angry. He charged the men who removed the poles with unlawfully and maliciously removing property of the Dominion government. But, when the six defendants appeared in court, they were accompanied by 300 local supporters, many of them armed. The case was immediately adjourned by the presiding judge and the town remained in a state of near-riot for ten days. On 15 November 1883, when the six accused reappeared in court, the judge quietly dismissed charges because police reinforcements had not arrived to quell the disturbances. Feelings of resentment towards these prominent businessmen and the Hudson's Bay Company had been festering for some time: a militant mood was revealed as early as April, when "rumours were heard of a bizarre plot to seize the Dominion Lands Office in Prince Albert, and hold Governor Dewdney as a hostage until every settler got his patent."[3]

White settlers became insistent in their demands for responsible government throughout the North-West Territories, not just in the Saskatchewan area. Settlers throughout the North-West made four basic demands of the Ottawa authorities: first, lower the tariff rates; second, cancel the CPR monopoly at once; third, give provincial status to the North-West; and, finally, construct the railway to the Hudson Bay. In Manitoba general labour strikes and expressions of protest warned of serious trouble. However, the major weakness of the North-West people's confrontation was a lack of effective leadership above the local level that could provide systematic organization of the various groups into one integrated force. Emerging from the local white population and shaping the direction of the agitation was William Henry Jackson, a white farmer who was a liberal militant and an effective spokesman. He became one of the major leaders of the white settlers and worked closely with the Native people's movement. Together with Charles Adams, president of the English Halfbreeds Association, Thomas Scott, a white farmer, and others, Jackson helped organize the settlers' and farmers' unions throughout the North-West. Operating at the local level, these groups arranged for the election of delegates to a central committee, which became the governing body of confrontation activities.

In the spring of 1884, a delegation of three, including Gabriel Dumont, was sent to fetch Riel from the United States, where he had lived in exile since 1873. Macdonald now had someone to blame personally for the agitation: if shooting began, the Métis would be the victims and Riel was a made-to-order scapegoat. Propaganda was circulated that described Riel as an advocate of hostilities and a leader of the "poor ignorant" Métis who would do what he commanded. Finally, Macdonald began to show a personal interest in the western political scene, although he still pleaded ignorance of Métis grievances: "A month after Louis's arrival Sir John sent a couple of observers to Saskatchewan and informed the Governor General of Canada that he was watching the situation."[5]

The prime minister had taken steps to make sure that his opinions of the North-West troubles would be circulated to the local people by assuming financial control of the Prince Albert *Times* newspaper. On 18 July 1884, he wrote to Lieutenant-Governor Dewdney: "I forget whether I told you that I had arranged to secure the Prince Albert paper, so if any little patronage can be sent them from below, it will be appreciated."[6]

Thus, in control of the only Prince Albert communications medium, the Macdonald regime began its task of putting out propaganda against the white settlers' movement. Exaggerations of potential Indian and Métis uprisings were headlined and used to justify the recruiting of police in the area. The presence of a greater number of soldiers and police intimidated the people and threatened the militant leaders.

By the summer of 1884, the Métis and Indians were becoming isolated from the white people's organizations and forces. The leaders realized that some sort of scheme seemed to be working against the whole North-West people's movement, but they became more determined to resist whatever action Ottawa might launch. A manifesto was issued through the central committee's secretary, William Jackson, on 28 July 1884, which outlined their intentions and actions, and pointed out the need to keep all groups working together:

> To the Citizens of Prince Albert:
> Gentlemen: We are starting a movement in this settlement with a view to attaining Provincial Legislatures for the North-West Territories and, if possible, the control of our own resources, that we may build our railroads and other works to serve our own interests rather than those of the Eastern provinces. We are preparing a statement of our case to send to Ottawa as a matter of form. We state the various evils which are caused by the present system of legislation showing:
> 1. That they are caused by the facts that the Ottawa legislators are responsible to Eastern constituents, not to us, and are therefore impelled to legislate with a view to Eastern interests rather than our own; that they are not actually resident in the country and therefore not acquainted with the facts that would enable them to form a correct opinion as to what measures are suitable to North-West interests, consequently liable to pass legislation adverse to North-West interests even when not favorable to their own; lastly that they have not the greater part of their immediate private interests involved in the interest of the said Territories, and are therefore liable to have their judgement warped by such private interests.
> 2. That the legislation passed by such legislators has already produced great depression in agricultural, commercial, and mechanical circles, and will continue to increase that depression unless the system is revised; that is to say, unless our legislators are chosen by and responsible to ourselves actually resident in the country and having the bulk of their private interests involved in the interests of the country.
> We give the complete list of our grievances, but instead of asking the redress of each of them separately, we ask the remedy to the root of the evil, i.e., Provincial Legislatures with full control over our own resources and internal administration, and power to send a just number of representatives to the Federal Legislature whatever and wherever that may ultimately lie. Possibly we may settle up with the East and form a separate federation of our own in direct connection with the Crown.
> Louis Riel of Manitoba fame has united the halfbreed element solidly in our favour. Hitherto, it has been used . . . [by] whatever party happened to be in power in the East, but Riel has warned them against the danger of being separated from the whites by party proposals.[7]

Throughout the summer of 1884, settlers' and farmers' unions organized and agitated for their cause. Representatives from Qu'Appelle and Assiniboia visited Ottawa to make their demands heard, and the people of the North-West were clearly prepared politically for organized confrontation with the federal government. They talked as well of secession from Canada and possible annexation to the United States. There was certainly a large number of people in the North-West Territories who were prepared for annexation, and all that summer more people joined them.

It was a political necessity for Macdonald's government to hold onto the North-West, since western settlement and the trans-Canada CPR were part of the Conservative Party's promise. The federal government also knew that they had to crush the secession movement and the North-West agitational forces in order not to lose this valuable land and its resources. The plan constructed by the federal authorities was that they would make certain concessions to the white residents of the North-West, while at the same time allowing the Métis and Indian situation to aggravate itself to the point of desperation and hostility. In this way, Ottawa could justify troop movements to the North-West by saying that savages had created an uprising and were massacring innocent settlers. Military occupation of the troubled North-West in the eyes of the whites of eastern Canada would be not only an urgent necessity but an act of justice on behalf of all Canadians, and Macdonald would be hailed as a hero.

At the North-West Farmers' Union convention held in Winnipeg in early January 1885, a declaration of rights was drawn up. Basically, it condemned the "oppressive duty on agricultural implements, the monopolistic operation of the C.P.R., and the vexatious methods in the administration of public lands." The members denounced the federal government for its deceitful practices in luring immigrants to the West as "the promised land" when in fact they experienced only hardships and failure. The farmers complained that the price of grain was so low it did not allow even a subsistence living. They claimed that agriculture had been in "a fair state" a few years earlier, but that lately the lands were deserted and overgrown with weeds and the buildings were fast decaying. Their declaration demanded the right to autonomous local government, provincial control of railways and public lands, the removal of custom duties on farm machinery and building materials, representation in the Dominion cabinet, and the construction of a Hudson Bay railway. They wanted greater authority for the North-West Territories Council; they insisted that council members should be elected by local residents rather than appointed by friends of John A. Macdonald, and they demanded lower tariffs, systematic marketing of their goods, better homestead laws, and local control over large land companies. In short, they wanted an end to the corruption of the North-West administration. These requests were ignored by the Macdonald government.

Although the white farmers and settlers were experiencing serious problems, the Indians and Métis were suffering even greater economic difficulties in the early 1880s. Chiefs complained that many of the great promises made by Ottawa during treaty negotiations had not been kept. Councillor Fine Day of Battleford Reserve stated that "most Indians had come into reserves by 1882, but it was very much against their wishes. It was either come in, or starve to death."[8] He claimed that his people were trying to make a living by cutting cordwood, but they received so little pay for their wood that it barely kept them from starvation: "The Government's policy could be summed up in six words: feed one day, starve the next."[9]

> From the Touchwood Hills, the Interpreter reported a similar state of starvation: "I beg to inform you that the Indians around here are starving very badly . . . I fear that many of these people will not see spring."[10]

Indian Affairs officials apparently felt that once the Indians were placed on reserves they would become totally conquered people who could be treated as subservient children. Some of the worst Indian Affairs officials were those at Frog Lake. The Hudson's Bay factor there stated: "They ill-treated these poor people in a most brutal manner. They kicked them, beat them, and cursed them in a most revolting fashion. Two stood out as particularly miserable beasts."[11] The local minister held a similar opinion of these officials: "in numerous instances, the way they treated the natives could not but produce harmful effects. Certain men treated the Indians like dogs."[12] The fort officials also exploited their positions:

> At the beginning of winter, the Government agents halved the Indians' rations and sold the excess for their own profit. The Indians could not complain of this shameful practice because all the Government representatives did the same thing, right from the Governor of the Territories down to the sub-agents on the Reserves.[13]

By the spring of 1884, the economic conditions of the Indians were so serious that Chief Poundmaker called an assembly of Indians of the North-West. He claimed that Indians realized they had made a serious mistake in agreeing to treaties with the federal government. Superintendent Crozier of the Mounted Police attempted to arrest the Indian chiefs for assembling, but they were so desperate that they defied Crozier's authority.

The Métis, likewise, were close to starvation, since their means of livelihood had practically disappeared, and in 1878 they began petitioning the federal government for assistance. As Riel had stated, these lands belonged to them once through original title, twice for having defended them at the cost of their blood, and thrice for having cultivated and inhabited them. The Métis had requested assistance in obtaining seed grain and farm implements, but, instead, they were asked by the federal government to pay two dollars per acre for their own farms, which they had improved and developed. Between 1878 and 1884, the Métis submitted eighty-four petitions to Ottawa requesting better conditions and better services. Not one was answered. According to an Ontario newspaper: "The Half-Breeds of the plains have not been dealt with by the present government. On the contrary, steps were expressly taken in the direction of delay."[14] Not even Mounted Police requests for assistance to the half-breeds stirred the government. Sergeant Kennan explained the serious economic conditions and the need for government action in a letter to Superintendent Crozier in September 1884:

> The crops here are almost a total failure and everything indicates that the halfbreeds are going to be in very straitened conditions before the end of the coming winter which of course will make them more discontented and will probably drive them to an outbreak and I believe that trouble is almost certain before the winter passes unless the government extends some aid to the halfbreeds during the coming winter.[15]

Such concern was unusual, coming from the Mounted Police. According to popular explanation, the Mounted Police force was established to prevent whiskey traders from buying Indian furs, which the Hudson's Bay Company claimed as its exclusive right. However, it is not just a coincidence that the Mounted Police were established during the development of Indian reserves to ensure the "success" of the treaty negotiations with the Indians and "help" relocate Indians and half-breeds to their reserves and colonies. The Mounted Police had the responsibility of patrolling the reserves and Métis communities but proved instead to be a source of oppression and agitation, much disliked by the Native people. Councillor Fine Day claimed that the Indians suffered brutality under the Mounties, who frequently paraded through Native settlements in order to intimidate the people and remind the Natives that they had to "stay in their place." When the Hudson's Bay factor at Fort Carlton complained to the Mounties that the half-breeds were becoming lawless and threatening a rebellion, fifty Mounties marched into the Métis community of Batoche and threatened the entire population.

They attempted to arrest Gabriel Dumont, Chief of the Batoche Halfbreed Council, and at the same time terrorized the people. This display of force successfully intimidated most of the Natives, as it was intended to.

The Indians, who had lived in the area for thousands of years without police, saw no reason for the establishment of a force in the North-West since there was no serious disorder or lawlessness in the country. To the Native people, this military force was similar to the federal troops who had invaded Fort Garry in 1870. The Mounties were not ambassadors of goodwill or uniformed men sent to protect Indians; they were the colonizer's occupational forces and hence the oppressors of Indians and Métis. The volumes written about how helpful and understanding the Mounties are towards Native people are sweetheart myths written by "WASP"s who have never experienced insults, beatings, and bullets from a Mountie.

The attempt to arrest Dumont was particularly resented by the Métis, since the Batoche Halfbreed Council was a representative body elected by the local people of Batoche, St. Laurent, and St. Louis, which they felt should be respected. The council had fifteen members, a president, and a constitution:

> The inhabitants of St. Laurent held a public assembly to draw up laws and regulations for the peace and tranquility of their community. In the absence of any form of government among them to administer justice and to judge the differences that may arise among them, they have thought it necessary to choose from among their number a Chief and Councillors invested with power to judge differences and to decide questions and matters affecting the public interest.
>
> The Chief with the members of his Council is elected for one year and during their term of power, the president and the members of Council are empowered to judge all cases that shall be brought before them. The Chief, by the advice of his Council, can convoke the general assemblies of the public, in order to submit for their decision matters of higher consequence, concerning which they would hesitate to pass orders without knowing the opinion of the majority of the public.[16]

Since most Métis people were directly involved in the difficult political issues of their community, they had a fairly good understanding of the struggles they encountered in making a living and in dealing with the federal government. A specific issue that had generated considerable anxiety among the Batoche Métis was the land claim of the Prince Albert Colonization Land Company, which was attempting to seize a vast tract of land in St. Louis on which several half-breed families had settled. The company was composed of cabinet ministers' relatives and top government officials. The confrontation became serious; the Métis decided "to protect [the land] with guns, if necessary." The situation remained largely a stand-off until after the half-breeds' defeat at the battle of Batoche. In the confusion that followed, it is likely that most half-breed families lost their land, as some of the men were sentenced to penitentiary terms.

Another source of agitation in the North-West was Governor Dewdney, a corrupt and arrogant man who encouraged similar attitudes among his subordinates. Besides cheating the Indians of their rations, Dewdney and his government generally held these people in contempt and were likewise corrupt and dictatorial in their dealings with white people. He neglected his duties as governor and spent his time dealing in lands, mines, and timber. Although Dewdney had been approached by the people of the North-West concerning their grievances, he did little to alleviate their suffering: his response was a message to Macdonald suggesting that more troops should be sent west if the agitation continued. The governor also retained a great deal of personal power over the people within his jurisdiction. Individuals were unable to keep liquor in their homes unless Dewdney personally granted them this privilege and he reserved the right to revoke these permits at any time if he was dissatisfied with the permit-holder's behaviour. Because the North-West Territories Council was subservient to him, Dewdney made himself virtually an absolute ruler in the North-West.

Contrary to the traditional interpretation, Louis Riel was not the main source of agitation in the North-West struggle of 1885. The Batoche half-breeds had a local government whose council members and president were democratically elected. Under these circumstances it was not possible for Riel or anyone else to come to Batoche and take over individual control of the people and their government. The decision to invite Riel to Saskatchewan was taken after the matter had been discussed by people in several districts, both Native and white. The invitation specified what Riel would have to do and his main function was to aid the people of the North-West in their constitutional struggle. He was responsible to the people and therefore took direction from them: "That there is anything in Mr. Riel's ability as a leader to cause alarm is not believed by those who have had the opportunity of judging him . . . his own statements are so pacific in nature that no one could be surprised to hear of his volunteering for missionary work."[17] Riel was working for the North-West people's movement, not leading it. He was not in a position to command the forces of confrontation, and he tried to persuade the Métis people to avoid violence and separation from the white people's forces. As William Jackson said in his formal statement to the citizens of Prince Albert:

> . . . in regard to his public attitude it is better to accept his services *as long as he works for us* . . . As long as both elements work on the square, doing justice to each other, there will be no clash, but a marked advance toward our end, i.e., justice in the North-West. [Emphasis added][18]

Notes

1. G.F.G. Stanley, *The Birth of Western Canada*, University of Toronto Press, Toronto, 1936, 190.
2. Prince Albert *Times*, 20 June 1883.
3. Ibid., 15 November 1883.
4. R.E. Lamb, *Thunder in the North* Pageant Press, New York, 1956, 137–38.
5. J.K. Howard, *Strange Empire*, Morrow, New York, 1952, 317.
6. Public Archives of Saskatchewan, Macdonald Papers, Macdonald to Dewdney, 18 July 1884.
7. Stanley, 300–301.
8. "The Cree Rebellion of 1884," *Battleford Historical Publications*, Vol. 1, No. 1, 1926.
9. Stanley, 270.
10. Ibid., 271.
11. A.H. de Trémaudan, *Histoire de la Nation Métisse dans l'Ouest Canadien*, Albert Levesque, Montreal, 1935, 415. (Author's translation.)
12. Ibid.
13. Ibid., 417.
14. London *Advertiser*, 31 March 1885.
15. Macdonald Papers, Kennan to Crozier, 26 September 1884.
16. "Copy of the Laws and Regulations Established for the Colony of St. Laurent on the Saskatchewan," Documents and Articles about Métis People, Indian and Métis Department, University of Saskatchewan, Saskatoon, 1972, 42.
17. Prince Albert *Times*, 19 September 1884.
18. Stanley, 301.

Disillusionment:
Regional Discontent in the 1880s

DOUGLAS OWRAM

Reprinted from Douglas Owram, *Promise of Eden: The Canadian Expansionist Movement and the Idea of the West, 1856–1900* (University of Toronto Press, 1980), 168–191, by permission of University of Toronto Press, © University of Toronto Press, 1980.

Practically every indicator of the economy in the West showed marked improvement in the years surrounding 1880. Land sales, homesteads, and preemptions rose from 132,918 acres in 1876 to over a million acres by 1879 and an astonishing 2,699,145 acres by 1882.[1] Grain exports, first begun in 1876, continued to increase in value with each succeeding crop. Settlers, encouraged by this prosperity, pushed westward from the fertile soil of the Red River Valley onto land that had only recently been declared suitable for agriculture. The long-awaited destiny of the North-West seemed at last to be imminent.

In the centre of this prosperity was the city of Winnipeg and, as befitted the "gateway to the West," it experienced the most heady effects of growth. Its population doubled between 1875 and 1878, and by 1882 it was more than six times the 1875 figure.[2] The general prosperity of the West was magnified in the city until optimism and economic growth touched off a wave of activity that continually astonished visitors. J.S. Dennis, in Winnipeg in the summer of 1881, wrote in a tone of amazement that "the excitement here as to lands is astonishing approaching nearly to a craze—that is in the matter of city, town and village lots."[3] J.B. McLaren, recently arrived from the East, wrote his acquaintance, George Grant, that the city of Winnipeg was as much a unique feature of the West as was the prairie. He was fascinated by "the craze that exists there for the West, for locating towns on the line of railway and selling town lots by auction before there is a settler within one or two score miles."[4] Canadians had often looked with a combination of jealousy and derision upon American land booms. Now, it seemed, they were experiencing one of their own. *Grip*, the satirical Canadian version of *Punch*, was not about to ignore such an easy target simply because of its national origin:

> Sing a song of millions,
> Spent like random shots,
> Up in Manitoba,
> Buying corner lots.
> Fancy paper city—
> Pretty Indian name—
> Is it very naughty,
> Playing such a game?[5]

While the years of good grain crops, growing shipments to the East, and a buoyant world economy all helped to create the speculation on lands in Winnipeg, the boom also fed upon itself. As with most other booms, much of the excitement was internally generated: speculators purchased property not because of the integral worth of the land but because they believed that the boom atmosphere would allow them to make a quick profit and sell out; each time the property changed hands the price was increased and each sale created stories of fast profits and easy money. The basic underpinning of the heady atmosphere that prevailed in Winnipeg in these months, however, was the arrival of that long-awaited symbol of development and progress, the railway.

In December 1878 Winnipeg was connected to the outside world by rail. It was true that the first link was not with the east but the south, and that the facilities were so crude that a locomotive could not turn around at the Winnipeg end of the line. Nevertheless, the Pembina Branch heralded the long-awaited end of an era of isolation for the settlements on the banks of the Red River. As one contemporary put it, "the 'golden gate' to an immense country" seemed to have been opened "and thousands, eager to participate in a share of the undeveloped treasure, poured into the land."[6] The Pembina Branch was but the first of several railway-related developments in the later 1870s and early 1880s: a new railway, the Manitoba and South Western, was chartered in 1879, and in 1880 the greatest railway of all, the Canadian Pacific, decided to take its line through Winnipeg. Such events as these led westerners to feel that the time had come when potential would be translated into development.

There were those who expressed nagging doubts as to the direction that this development was taking. The heady speculation of the land boom was hardly the means to the sturdy agricultural economy and society thought essential. The whole speculative market was based on quick profits and rapid footwork rather than hard work, and men at the time recognized this fact. Dennis warned that "some people will before long I fear come to unmitigated grief" and a visiting reporter from the Toronto *Globe* noted that he often heard the same prediction made in the streets of Winnipeg.[7] Not many people heeded these warnings, however, in the years of 1881 and 1882.

The desire to speculate in land seems to have been practically irresistible. Even Sandford Fleming, a man who had known the West for a long time and who was fairly cautious in financial matters, could not resist the temptation to make some investments while in Winnipeg in 1882. Nor was Fleming looking to the solid, long-range possibilities of such a purchase: he bought two lots in Rat Portage on 2 February and sold them six days later at a profit of $200.[8] Even the respectable and conservative Anglican bishop of Saskatchewan, John McLean, yielded to the worldly race after quick profits. Writing to Charles Mair in Prince Albert on almost the same day that Fleming purchased his lots, McLean asked on what terms he "could secure a few lots for my own *private account*, not for church or school or any other Diocesan purpose."[9] Unfortunately, McLean's choice of investments was not as sound as Fleming's; land prices in Prince Albert did not rise to nearly the same extent as they did in Manitoba.

The Winnipeg land boom was an aberration in the trends of western development. It was, nevertheless, a significant event in many ways. It reflected the optimism of the age and meant that the reality of development in the North-West seemed to coincide with the increasingly utopian visions that had gained acceptance over the years. If the West was portrayed in extremely favourable terms it could also be said that the region was developing as rapidly as such images might suggest it should. Even in its most extreme phase, then, the expansionist image of the North-West seemed only to be a reflection of the actual course of history. Such a pleasant state of affairs did not last for long.

As with most land booms, the one centred in Winnipeg collapsed suddenly. A good many people who held their property too long or who purchased at too high a price suffered as a result. The investment, which had seemed so sound at the time, suddenly proved practically worthless. In retrospect, there were many to be found who had condemned the boom and pointed to it as a well-learned lesson concerning the necessity of stable development. John Schultz, writing in 1884, could even take comfort from the fact that "the bursting of the Boom has weeded out all the speculative and weakly ones and left a better element behind."[10] "W.F.C.," writing in the Toronto periodical, *The Week*, in 1883, took the same position and interpreted the collapse of the boom as a swing of the economic pendulum now thankfully returning to an equilibrium.[11]

In spite of such hopeful statements, the end of the boom had a decidedly negative impact on the West. The collapse of land prices signalled the beginning of trouble in a number of economic areas. More significant than the price of land in Winnipeg was the decline of crop prices, commercial transactions, and, most central of all, the rate of settlement. Beginning in 1883 all of these key indicators fell. In 1883, 1,831,982 acres of land were alienated, down over 800,000 acres from the year before. Thereafter things got worse instead of better. In 1884 this figure dropped to 1,110,512 acres and in the troubled year of 1885, 481,814 acres.[12] The collapse of Winnipeg land prices marked the beginning of a serious and widespread depression that was to hang over the West for the next several years. Periodic recoveries proved to be only temporary and not until 1896 did the North-West again really experience long-term prosperity.

The depression had a profound effect on those who had gone west on the premise that expansionist optimism was justified. For more than a generation Canadians had been led to believe that practically anyone who was willing to work would be able to live comfortably in Canada's illimitable granary. So long as it was thought that the West was moving towards the realization of its potential, this belief went unchallenged. The collapse of 1883, however, meant that reality and image no longer coincided. As Charles Mair wrote to George Denison, "matters instead of improving in the North West are getting worse. To use an old phrase the bottom seems to have fallen out."[13] The archetypal expansionist, the man involved in the West for nearly fifteen years, suddenly found himself wondering if the region was going to live up to the promises that had been made for it. Mair, as with many who had shaped their lives according to expansionist arguments, now faced bitter disillusionment.

Mair's disillusionment was with the economic conditions in the West and did not extend to the land itself. "That matters will recover is certain," he wrote on one occasion, for "the country is there."[14] This combination of faith in the land and disappointment with the actual state of things was widespread in the West in the 1880s. Those who had accepted the basic expansionist argument on the worth of the land never rejected it. George Patterson, writing in 1885 to explain the depression in the West and the discontent that existed, still maintained that the farmer in the region began with a great many advantages over farmers elsewhere.[15] More than a decade after the collapse of the land boom the faith still remained. In 1895 George Grant wrote to lament the continued lack of development in the North-West. "The most disheartening feature to the visitor," he maintained, "is the enormous quantity of land round the city which remains virgin prairie or is cultivated in a slovenly fashion." It was especially discouraging because Grant felt that "there is no such soil in the world for the production of cereals."[16]

This mixture of faith and disappointment characterized the mood of the West in the 1880s and early 1890s. Those who had accepted the idea of expansionism were not willing to accept the qualifications that Henry Youle Hind had insisted were necessary. Even when westerners found that their actual lives had failed to live up to expectations, they retained their image of the North-West as a fertile garden. Blame for the depression of the 1880s would not be directed towards the land itself. It would take another, much more severe, depression before there arose any serious challenge to the optimistic conclusions of John Macoun.

There were two possible explanations for the problems of the 1880s other than a stingy land. One was that those who had settled in the West had not applied themselves sufficiently to the task of building up a livelihood. Settlers, who had undergone great discomfort and put in long hours carving a farm out of the quarter section they had been allotted, rejected this explanation out of hand. There was thus only one possible explanation left. The men who had gone west as part of a great national and even imperial project had been betrayed by those who had remained behind. While expansionism had always been metropolitan in tone, it had also presumed that the relationship between the East and developing West would be beneficial to both regions and to the nation as a whole. As economic reality clashed with the expansionist image, however, many began to wonder whether the East, and particularly Ontario, was not concerned only with the exploitation of the West for its benefit.

In a speech given in honour of the lieutenant-governor of the North-West, Charles Mair summed up this new attitude: "To pass from the old state of things to the present is like going from warmth into chill air." That this disillusionment was not with the land made the situation all the more intolerable: "We find ourselves in the heart of a rich country, yet, through no fault of our own, confronted by a material outlook which bristles with difficulties." Such a situation existed, he continued "not through our own supineness, not through indolence or lack of industry, but through circumstances over which we have had no control and which we have fought in vain." Mair's words revealed a sense of powerlessness and frustration that has since become a classic component of regional grievance.

The problem was not that there was no remedy but that only in the East could that remedy be found. We "came here through public maps, through public declarations, and through public charters," said Mair, "every one of which we have lived to see cut down." Expansionism, he felt, was a two-way contract. One party consisted of those who had responded to the call to settle the West. The other half of the agreement was made up of those in the East and the federal government who had depicted the development of the region as part of a great national campaign that would benefit all. These parties, however, had betrayed the contract by working against the prosperity of the West. "Like many others," Mair "was constrained to attribute the delay to eastern jealousy."[17] The man who had dismissed the sectional and social concerns of Red River in 1869 found it necessary by the 1880s to assert western rights in the face of eastern indifference.

The particular thrust of the argument presented by Mair and others in these years was not against expansionism but against those who had failed to live up to its implications. They felt that the development of the West was being deliberately hindered by easterners who, in their short-sighted selfishness, failed to understand either the value of the West or the aspirations of the people. As the Edmonton *Bulletin* said on 19 January 1884: "It is quite apparent that papers and politicians in the east have utterly false ideas as to the relationship of the North-West to Canada as a whole and the position to be taken in confederation by its people." Even John Schultz wrote confidentially of his own party that "if we had men in Ottawa instead of [?] like Daly and jackasses like some of the rest of them we might have an enormous aid in this development."[18] The easterner was to blame for the failure of the West to live up to its promise. Nevertheless, many were discontented enough that they gave clear warning of their willingness to turn on expansionism itself if their grievances were ignored. In a significant resolution in 1884, the Farmers' Union attacked a basic tenet of expansionism when it recommended that until things improved in the West immigrants should not come to the region.[19]

The expansionist movement had always had regional overtones. Canada West had spawned it and provided it with its main personnel. In the 1880s, however, a new regionalism began to develop. Westerners, including many from Ontario, found a new focus for their interests in the land they had adopted. These interests, while still thought to be part of a plan to develop the nation as a whole, were not necessarily congruent with those of eastern Canada. Government agents and others still turned out enthusiastic pamphlets in praise of the North-West, but it had become apparent that the expansionist movement had fragmented under the pressure of regional discontent. For westerners at least, the enthusiasm of earlier years had been replaced with a reserved scepticism.

Those who had gone west in the name of expansionism were not the only ones to suffer as a result of the depression of the 1880s. The Métis and the Indians, those remnants of the old order, had their own complaints. Over the last few years things had gone from bad to worse for both these groups. They had been seriously affected by the dwindling herds of the buffalo in the 1870s and, in some cases, had come close to actual starvation. Governor David Laird's lament to Mackenzie in 1879 that "the disappearance of buffalo has suddenly brought thousands of Indians to the verge of starvation," was all too typical of reports from the North-West in the late 1870s and early 1880s.[20] In addition, incompetent and corrupt government officials, questions of land titles, surveys, and the advancement of an alien civilization itself, all contributed to the discontent of these two groups. In the early 1880s this discontent began to be expressed in increasingly vocal protests and isolated outbreaks of defiance to Canadian authority. As Ottawa continued to ignore these protests, the attitude of both Indians and Métis became more and more extreme.

Initially the Métis came close to forming an alliance not only with the Indians but with the white settlers as well. Several prominent farmers and political leaders in the North-West attended joint protest meetings with the Métis; petitions to Ottawa often had as many signatures of white settlers as they did of Métis.[21] The return of Louis Riel in the summer of 1884 and the drift of the Métis towards violent resistance in early 1885, however, prevented the continuation of that alliance. Riel was already tainted with the aura of violence and most white settlers, even given their grievances, were not about to follow him in yet another attempt to defy Canadian governmental authority. Thus when, in March 1885, Métis protest flared into open rebellion, few white settlers were involved. Nevertheless, western analysis of the rebellion reflected a continued degree of sympathy for the ends, if not the means, of the Métis.

"It is a mistake to suppose the rising is factious and sudden," an anonymous correspondent to *The Week* wrote from Calgary in April 1885. "It is the growth of years. In fact," he continued, "the whole country sympathizes with the rebels."[22] Such a sweeping generalization required a certain alarmism or partisanship, but there was widespread sympathy for the position of the Métis. Frank Oliver, the thirty-two-year-old native of Peel County and editor of the *Edmonton Bulletin*, felt that while Riel could not be condoned for his actions neither could it be said he was the cause of the violence. "A match will not fire a pile of greenwood," he wrote, "but it will a pile of dry. Had the Saskatchewan country been in a satisfied condition a hundred such men as Riel might have come into it." Given the treatment of the region in the past years, however, "the pile was ready made for the fire-brand, and the fire-brand ready lighted came in the person of Riel."[23] The *Manitoba Free Press*, its regional perspective reinforced by the partisan Liberal outlook of its editor, W.F. Luxton, came to a similar conclusion on 7 April. "Wherever it is known that the half-breeds and Indians are in rebellion," Luxton wrote, "it is known that they were first deceived and wronged, then neglected, finally allowed to prepare openly for an appeal to arms without a step being taken to hinder them."

Major James Walsh, the well-known retired officer of the North-West Mounted Police, warned that such attitudes were not uncommon in the West. In an interview for the Toronto *Globe* he urged the government to appoint a commission to treat with the Métis. "Don't forget," he commented, "that these people have the hearty sympathy of all the white settlers in their district." Even in the midst of violence Walsh maintained, as did many others, that "these people are not rebels, they are but demanding justice."[24] Even Charles Mair, whose personal antipathy to Riel went back to 1870 and who on hearing of violence regretted that Riel had not been hanged, directed his anger not at the half-breeds but at the government. "I would not damage the Govt. openly," he wrote George Denison, "for the railway completion is of vast importance." In his private correspondence, however, he had no such reservations: "Had there been an energetic, patriotic fellow sent out as Lieut. Governor of the Territories instead of this lump of selfishness and greed—Dewdney—all this difficulty would have been avoided." Later that day, after he saw the casualty lists from Duck Lake, Mair was even more explicit in his denunciation of the government: "The Govt. and Dewdney are responsible for all this. Every species of warning was given and thrown aside."[25]

While the western sense of discontent was strong and led to sympathy for the Métis, there were also emotions and forces at work which to some extent countered that sympathy. Faced with violence, many felt that challenge to Canada's authority outweighed all other matters. *Grip*, the satirical magazine that had so often criticized the government for its handling of the North-West, dropped both its criticism and its satire as the first troops headed west. "The departure of our gallant men for the scene of the rebellion in the Saskatchewan country," it editorialized on 4 April, "was perhaps the most stirring event which Toronto has ever witnessed." There were doubts as to the government's handling of the situation but a time of crisis was not appropriate for their discussion: "It will be time enough to debate the cause and affix the blame when the rebels have been subdued."

Western Canadians were not exempt from this spirit of martial enthusiasm. The *Manitoba Free Press* took time out from its criticisms of the government to write enthusiastic editorials about Canada's "citizen soldiers."[26] Charles Mair, in spite of his harsh condemnation of the government, joined George Denison's force of the Governor General's Body Guards in order to fight for his country and, not incidentally, to continue the old quarrel with Riel. Nicholas Flood Davin, who represented the North-West Territories in the federal Parliament and had often complained of the

government's treatment of the West, was inspired to write a poem calling for national
unity in the face of armed rebellion:

> Upon the field all rancour healed
> There's no discordant hue
> The Orange marches beneath the Green
> The Rouge beneath the Bleu
>
> One purpose now fires every eye
> Rebellion foul to slay
> Forward for Canada!'s the cry,
> and all are one to-day.[27]

Loyalty to country overcame regional protest, and most westerners felt compelled to
take their stand with the nation.

While the patriotism that prevailed in the spring of 1885 muted the sympathy that
existed for the Métis position, it did not lead many westerners to assume that Riel was
the real cause of the rebellion. Even as they marched to subdue the Métis they
continued to point an accusing finger at the government in the East. Charles Pitblado,
a Presbyterian minister in Winnipeg, volunteered to act as chaplain to the troops. On
his return, however, he preached not of the evils of rebellion but of the evils that had
caused that rebellion. The life of the Indian and half-breed "has been paralyzed by our
presence," he charged. "They have been robbed by our unprincipled traders. They have
been corrupted by our vices. They have been pauperized by our charities. They have
been demoralized and wasted by our neglect." It was not surprising that violence should
occur when "on the vast prairies, where his fathers dwelt in ease, and lived in plenty,
the aborigine of the western land roams an idle, naked, starving outcast."[28] Daniel
Gordon, who also acted as a chaplain, felt much the same, and later wrote to Grant that
"if I were an Indian I would take all the risks of an uprising and have done with it."[29]
The Anglican bishop of Saskatchewan, John McLean, found himself caught between
national fervour and regional grievance: on the one hand he was noted in Prince Albert
during the rebellion for "the most deliciously jingo sermons";[30] on the other hand he
saw the violence as an indication of the nation's failure to do its duty in the West.[31]

The pulls of national enthusiasm on the one hand and regional sympathy for the
Métis on the other affected many westerners. In 1869 and 1870 Riel's actions were an
attempt by the old order to protest the seeming intolerance of the new in Red River; as
such, the new order, and those who supported its aims, had opposed the Métis. The
1885 rebellion has been interpreted as another, and final, attempt of the old order to
halt the march of a foreign civilization.[32] It has also been seen, in an argument that
focuses not on the rebellion but on the controversy surrounding Riel's execution, as a
significant setback to the French-English cooperation implied by Confederation.[33]
While both of these arguments have their place in any analysis of the rebellion, there
is a third factor in the Métis and Indian resistance of 1885. Their discontent represented
to some extent the discontent of the West in the face of eastern domination and eastern
indifference. To this extent the settlers in the West were sympathetic to the Métis in a
way that was not possible in 1870.

The Riel rebellion was simply a crisis that dramatically illustrated a longer-run
trend towards regionalism. It was a movement that had begun before 1885 and would

continue long after the Métis had been defeated. More and more people who had come west with a strong sense of association with Ontario would reject that background and identify with the West. Years after the rebellion, Charles Mair found his sympathy for the Métis had not disappeared. "It is monopoly has raised up any outcry there is here," he wrote, "and well it might. I would have taken up the musket fast enough myself on that question." Later he went further and implied in a letter to Denison that at some future time he might find himself on the rebel side, "potting at you and Merritt and Dunn, not to say Baldwin from behind some coteau or bluff."[34] It was a humorous remark, but the point was made nonetheless. By the time of the second Riel rebellion, western complaints had gone beyond specifics to a general sense of grievance. This, easterners did not completely understand. Even those such as George Grant who were extremely sympathetic to the western position tended to blame matters on particular evils such as "party" and "patronage."[35] In contrast, those in the West were beginning to see a general eastern indifference and selfishness as being at the root of their problems.

By the summer of 1885 the editor of the Macleod *Gazette* so despaired of eastern understanding that on 13 June he called for a direct appeal to Great Britain and hinted that secession might prove the only real solution to "an overbearing and unscrupulous federal authority." The tone was not all that extreme in the troubled days surrounding the 1885 rebellion. Such discontent, even if exaggerated by the rhetorical flights of newspaper editors, indicated that the problems were perceived to have gone beyond questions of immediate policy and beyond the failures of the specific party in power. Rather a widespread feeling had developed that the West was being exploited by the East, and those in the "new Canada" being treated as less than full partners in Confederation. As the Edmonton *Bulletin* warned on 1 November 1884, even before the rebellion, "the idea that the North-West is to eastern Canada as India is to Great Britain is one that will, if not abandoned, lead to the rupture of confederation at no distant date."

In this context the attitude of any particular party was simply a manifestation of the larger problem, and thus there was no paradox in voting for the Conservatives in overwhelming numbers only two years after the Riel rebellion. The Liberal government, with its record of hesitancy and delay over the Canadian Pacific, had long ago lost any legitimacy as a vehicle for western interests; there was little reason to vote for it even though the Conservatives had proved themselves indifferent. Western grievances did not lead immediately to political shifts because, for many westerners, there seemed no place to go.[36] A disenchantment with the traditional party structure was growing, however, and this would contribute to both intra-party strife and, eventually, to the shattering of traditional party lines in the West.

The growing disillusionment implied a collapsing faith in the ability of current expansionist strategy to reconcile eastern, western, and national interests. It had originally been assumed that the immigration of a large number of English Canadians to the prairies would ensure a common sense of identity and interests between old and new English Canada. In the face of economic adversity and depression this had failed to materialize. By 1885 westerners were beginning to view their own region as distinct from the East. Conscious of their disagreements with Ontario, western Canadians began to look at national issues from a regional perspective. More and more it was argued that such issues could not be resolved without looking at them within the context of regional inequities in Canada. Some issues, such as imperial federation, took on different ᵣuances. How, asked one writer, could Canada talk about joining a larger federation without first readjusting its own: "It must be on a readjusted basis, having full consent of the loyal inhabitants of the Province [Manitoba] to cement the terms."[37] Other issues, important in central Canada, seemed less so from a western perspective. Even the great Canadian pastime of anti-Americanism suffered in this regard. When Denison wrote Mair excitedly in 1888 on the current fisheries crisis, the former Canada Firster replied that the main danger to Canada was internal not external. "There is more danger in the North West to the Dominion from the reign of monopolies and Eastern self-seeking than in Yankee bluster, and unless the freest measures of development are applied in this country there will be antagonism roused of deeper note than Cleveland's message."[38]

The collapsing sense of unity between eastern and western Canada in the achievement of the national destiny was two-sided. Throughout the 1870s Edward Blake had represented a stream of Ontario resistance to such costly schemes of western development as the Canadian Pacific Railway. As long as the West seemed about to offer Canada a glorious future, however, such protest was both qualified and limited. In the 1880s, however, as the West continued to prove to be an expensive and undeveloped burden, more and more easterners tended to criticize the cost of development. Western protests simply aggravated the situation and broadened eastern criticism to include comments on western selfishness and provincialism. In 1884 Goldwin Smith summed up, as he often did, the pessimistic side of Ontario's attitude when he asked: "What will she gain by the Pacific Railway? Merely, as it would seem, the gratification of staring like a cow at the passing train." *Grip* found itself in agreement with Smith's comment and set it in cartoon form.[39] The Riel rebellion accentuated these Ontario doubts over the great expansionist idea. Suddenly, it seemed, the annexation of half a continent presented more difficulties than had been thought: "This affair brings home forcibly to us the remoteness of the North West from Old Canada and the magnitude of the natural barriers which lie in between. The same degree of military strength and compactness is perhaps not necessary to cohesion here which is necessary in Europe, but some degree is necessary even here. We have annexed a continent on the moon."[40]

Moreover, it seemed as if Ontario was the only province with enough sense of loyalty to Canada to make a real effort to save the nation. In an editorial that unfairly reflected on the efforts of the rest of Canada, *The Week* complained that other provinces were showing a deplorable lack of enthusiasm for the suppression of the Métis rebellion. "Alone, or with only the British quarter of Montreal to assist her, Ontario will have to do it; and some day she will grow tired of doing it alone." The West, like French Canada and the Maritimes, seemed to draw on the strength of the nation without contributing to it. Though *The Week* represented only one segment of Ontario opinion, it, at least, was disenchanted enough by 1885 to adopt for some time thereafter an unenthusiastic and even hostile attitude towards the North-West.[41] There was, then, disillusionment in Ontario as well.

While segments of Ontario opinion might grumble about the cost of the Canadian Pacific Railway, however, there was none of the deep-seated feeling of resentment that existed in the West. If nothing else, Ontarians still sensed that their province played a key role in government circles in Ottawa. The West, in contrast, had no such feeling and no assurance that the present state of economic depression might not continue permanently. It was thus in the West that the first concerted campaign began to readjust expansionist economic strategy in order, as the argument went, to put the West into a better position relative to the rest of the nation. The western sense of regionalism contained within this campaign made it contrast sharply with the centralist assumptions of earlier expansionist rhetoric.

Western discontent manifested itself in a number of ways through the 1880s. Questions of control of lands, Dominion-provincial rights, railway charters, and financial arrangements, all became issues as those in the West challenged the current relationship between their region and the rest of Canada. Of them all, however, perhaps none better summed up the mood and aspirations of westerners than the great vision of a railway to Hudson's Bay. Its place in the panoply of western grievances was given recognition when, in one of the last petitions to the government before the rebellion, Riel and his fellow petitioners had given a prominent place to the complaint that "no effective measures have yet been taken to put the people of the North-West in direct communication with the European markets via Hudson's Bay."[42] It was a matter of little importance to the Métis and Indians, but it was of the utmost significance to those settlers whom they hoped to ally to their cause. As much as the rebellion itself, the demand for the railway was a product of western discontent.

The revival of interest in a transportation outlet via Hudson's Bay seemed to run contrary to the trends of the last quarter century. Even before annexation the Hudson's Bay Company ceased to employ the route as a major transportation link to the southern prairie, turning instead to the more economical land route via Minnesota. The growth of a Canadian presence in the West simply confirmed the abandonment of the route. Expansionist strategy made the use of an east-west route via Lake Superior essential. Initially by enlarging the canoe route of the North West Company in the shape of the Dawson Road and then by the projected all-land route of the Canadian Pacific Railway, Canada sought to compete with and eventually supplant the dominant southern route. Thereby, it was hoped, an integrated national trade pattern would emerge. In this contest the old route to the North-West via Hudson's Bay was but a bystander. It seemed nothing more than the relic of an archaic economic and political era. Then, quite suddenly, interest revived in this traditional means of access to the North-West.

Initially the revival of interest in the Hudson's Bay route reflected the optimism of the later 1870s about the prospects of the North-West. Estimates of the region's potential had grown so great that even before the primary link had been completed men began to look for auxiliary means of transport to handle the future traffic of the region. The exports and imports of the North-West, the argument ran, would be so great in the future that no single rail line could possibly handle them all. The answer, it seemed, was another railway running in this case to a port on Hudson's Bay; this rail line would then connect to ships running between the bay and the ports of Europe.

The original enthusiasm for the project was largely fostered by Robert Bell of the Geological Survey. In 1875 and 1877 Bell visited James Bay and in 1878 he explored the Nelson and Hayes rivers. Bell was a colleague of Macoun's and he possessed the same irrepressible sense of optimism when it came to the future of the North-West. The Hudson's Bay route was his own particular contribution to the enthusiasm of the age. In reports, letters, pamphlets, and speeches this scientist argued the feasibility and practicality of a railway to Hudson's Bay.[43] By 1878 he had acquired two important allies. J.S. Dennis, seemingly willing to support any new project for the West, wrote Macdonald urging consideration of the route. Even more significantly, Henry Youle Hind testified, he later said reluctantly, that "the establishment of a cheap and speedy means of communication between the North West and the open Atlantic via Hudson's Straits, would not only secure the rapid settlement of Manitoba, but open to successful immigration a fertile area twenty times as large as that Province."[44]

In 1880 the connection of the bay and the prairie came a step closer to reality with the chartering of two companies with the avowed purpose of building a railway to Hudson's Bay. Each of these companies reflected different origins, different personnel, and, before long, different purposes. The first company was the Nelson Valley Railway and Transportation Company and was based on Montreal men and money; its founders included Montreal senator and businessman Thomas Ryan, George Drummond of the Canada Sugar Refining Company, and Alfred Brown, a director of the Bank of Montreal. The second company was based in Winnipeg which, for obvious reasons, had its own aspirations towards the bay. Hugh M. Sutherland, president of the Rainy Lake Lumber Company and future member of Parliament for Selkirk, was the moving spirit behind the organization but it also included a number of prominent Winnipeg figures such as John Schultz. Initially the two companies did not receive a great deal of encouragement. John A. Macdonald's Conservative government had gambled its future on the completion of the Canadian Pacific Railway, and it did not welcome any scheme that would divert money and attention towards a second outlet. The Hudson's Bay railway would have to wait until the Canadian Pacific became a reality.[45]

The approaching completion of the Canadian Pacific did provide a new impetus for the Hudson's Bay railway but not in the way that had originally been thought. Rather, the same commitment which the government made to the completion of the railway by closing the deal with the syndicate signalled the beginning of doubts as to the boon the railway would confer on the North-West. The long-awaited Pacific railway suddenly possessed an ominous degree of power and before long the great hope of the West would become its greatest source of complaint. These complaints provided new and compelling reasons for the construction of a railway to Hudson's Bay.

The control of the Canadian Pacific by a private company had in itself raised questions among those interested in the West. George Grant, admittedly biased because of his friendship with deposed chief engineer, Sandford Fleming, complained in 1880 of the contract that had been made with the syndicate. "The Govt. is giving too much, and putting too much power in the hands of the Syndicate . . . I have been doubtful all along. I am rather more than doubtful now."[46] The sober-minded principal of Queen's University was joined in his concern by Jesse Beaufort Hurlbert who took time out from his optimistic writings on Canada's climate to protest to Macdonald that many Conservatives in the West opposed the syndicate bargain.[47]

Opposition was based not only on the specific details of the arrangement but also on a more general suspicion that the development of such a crucial national enterprise by a private company would raise up a dangerous power in the North-West, and for that matter all of Canada. As Grant said, "It looks as if now there would be no check on the plunderers."[48] Not only was the syndicate a powerful company but, according to the agreement, it was given a monopoly of railway lines to the south of its own main line. Peter Imrie, in a long letter to the secretary of the Department of Agriculture, perhaps best summed up the range of fears which was shifting western opinion on the railway. "The monopolist has the whole realm of the possible to work upon," he wrote, "and the few detailed arguments which precedent, or reason, or fancy, may enable anyone to adduce against monopolies can hardly represent anything but a mere tithe of the possible evils which may be put in operation." The unknown as much as the known made the whole arrangement loathsome. "It is to my mind, this very indefiniteness of the danger that makes it overwhelming, because otherwise—i.e., if we could imagine the precise manner in which the monopolist would use his opportunities—we could no doubt take some steps towards obstructing him. Probably enough your Railway Company will discover some quite new way of taking the cream off the country—some way that nobody even thought of before."[49] By the time the railway was completed across the prairies many were convinced that Imrie's fears had been proven completely justified.

Many western interests felt themselves injured by the policy of the government towards the Canadian Pacific. The withdrawal of prime areas of land from settlement in order to allow the Canadian Pacific to choose its land grants was one of the first sources of complaint. It was also one of the most persistent. Even the North-West Council, often accused of quietly accepting direction from Ottawa, felt constrained to pass a resolution condemning the "Mile Belt." It was, said the council "detrimental to growth and prosperity—large blocks of land being held by the Government, and settlers being disbarred from locating on them." By leaving large tracts in visible locations along the line of railway the immigrant was given "a false idea of the North-West, and an inadequate and sometimes misleading impression of the character of the soil."[50] The other major complaint against the railway was directed at the so-called monopoly clause. Even before the Canadian Pacific was complete, Manitoba had taken issue with the federal disallowance of provincial railway charters. The nature of the issue mixed economic policy with provincial rights and thus exacerbated the whole problem. Moreover, it seemed to many to prove that the Canadian Pacific had undue influence over the federal government. Immigration and development were still central to western growth and anything that might hinder these processes was bound to become a source of complaint. As soon as the Canadian Pacific appeared as an obstacle to western aspirations, it found itself with many opponents in western Canada.

If, at first, the term "monopoly" related to a specific clause in the agreement between the government and the syndicate, it was not long before it took on a much more general meaning. The very dominance of the Canadian Pacific in the western Canadian economy, whether because of the monopoly clause or simply because it was the only means of transport, made the railway a symbol of eastern exploitation at western expense. The campaign against the monopolistic control of the Canadian Pacific became, in essence, a campaign against the general dominance of the western economy; as such, the railway became a scapegoat, and not completely without reason, for the ills of the West. Charles Mair summed it up tersely when he wrote in 1891 that "the country is killed with C.P.R. extortion."[51]

The growing antipathy towards the Canadian Pacific revolutionized the purpose behind the Hudson's Bay railway. What had begun as an expression of western optimism became, by the mid-1880s, an almost desperate attempt to escape from dependence on the Canadian Pacific Railway. That railway, based on an east-west trade axis, served only itself and eastern Canada. The Hudson's Bay railway, however, would challenge both the Canadian Pacific and the dominance of eastern Canada in the western economy. As Goldwin Smith pointed out, "no point of commercial geography can be more certain than that nature has placed the commercial outlet of the prairie region to the south. But first, for political purposes, it was wrested round to the east; and now to break the monopoly thus established, an attempt is made to fix the outlet to the north."[52] Far from denying this, proponents of the bay railway argued that the opportunity to break the power of the Canadian Pacific was one of the most compelling reasons behind the project. "The Canadian Pacific Railway and its branches west, south and south-west of Winnipeg," wrote bay supporter William Murdoch, "are all tributary to the Hudson's Bay Railway, it being the shortest route to the sea; no corporation, however powerful, can coerce the channels of commerce, and the outlet is via Hudson's Bay."[53]

The challenge to the Canadian Pacific was thus a challenge to the expansionist premise that an east-west flow of trade was essential for the sake of the nation. The whole idea of a major outlet via Hudson's Bay implied a direct connection between the West and Europe, bypassing eastern points and, not incidentally, eastern control. Proponents of the bay scheme, while admitting their repudiation of past economic strategy, gave indications that they felt their idea to be a means of preserving the expansionist ideal—the rapid development of the West and thereby the nation. The bypassing of the East was, in terms of this principle, a minor readjustment. In fact, in the imagery, sense of zeal, and even in the personnel involved in the Hudson's Bay railway scheme, one can sense an attempt to transport the expansionist idea to new, western soil.

Two things stand out about the individuals involved in the Hudson's Bay railway scheme in the 1880s. The first is that, not surprisingly, the majority of them had strong connections with Manitoba and the North-West. The chairman of the federal select committee on the railway, for instance, was Joseph Royal of Manitoba. The secretary to the committee was Charles Tuttle, a transplanted Nova Scotian living in Winnipeg and founder of the Winnipeg *Daily Times*. Moreover, much of the strongest support for the idea came from Manitoba itself. A select committee of the Manitoba Legislature and the Winnipeg Board of Trade both reported favourably on the plan. Their efforts received the support of numerous individuals such as Charles Bell and Thomas Scoble of Winnipeg, Hugh Sutherland, Charles Mair and, in Edmonton, Frank Oliver. The Montreal-based group which had chartered a company in 1880 still existed, but by the middle of the decade played little part in what was essentially a regional discussion.

The second notable feature of the group was the number of members with expansionist affiliations. In some cases, such as Charles Mair and John Schultz, this affiliation was both immediate and strong. A good many others, however, also revealed their expansionist leanings in less spectacular ways. Thomas Scott, for instance, member of Parliament for Winnipeg between 1880 and 1887, was a supporter of the railway. Born in Lanark County in 1841, Scott had edited the expansionist *Perth Expositor* in the 1860s. He had gone to Manitoba in 1870 with the Red River expedition and in 1873 had settled permanently in the province.[54] Charles Napier Bell had also been born in the expansionist Ottawa Valley town of Perth and went to Manitoba with the Red River expedition. Bell accepted the promises that had been made for the country and remained there permanently. By the later 1880s he was both a supporter of the Hudson's Bay railway and president of the Winnipeg Board of Trade.[55] Hugh Sutherland's background was in Prince Edward Island rather than in Ontario, but he too was an easterner who had chosen to cast his lot with the new West. In 1874 he had been sent west by the Department of Public Works as their superintendent for the North-West Territories; he remained in that position until the change of government in 1878 left him out of work. It was then that he applied himself to a career in the West and to the Hudson's Bay railway.

Those who did not live in the West but who did support the Hudson's Bay railway almost invariably had expansionist backgrounds. Typical was S.J. Dawson, who was on Royal's committee, as was Thomas White. Robert Bell's enthusiasm has already been mentioned. Even the elderly English writer, Joseph Nelson, who had turned out expansionist tracts in the 1860s, renewed his contact with the movement by compiling a collection of speeches and statements favourable to the bay route.[56] Western aspirations and expansionist enthusiasm thus came together in the 1880s to promote a new campaign, this one directed to the north.

The basic argument in favour of the Hudson's Bay route rested on a straightforward geographical fact: Hudson's Bay was the closest body of water to the wheat lands of the North-West. Moreover, if one measured the distance from any port on the bay to England, it was found to be the shortest route to the interior of Canada. "The fact of a seaport existing in the very heart of the continent more than 1500 miles nearer than Quebec to the centre of the North-West Territory, has scarcely begun to be noticed by the public," lamented one writer. Unnoticed though it may be, however, "its importance can hardly be over-stated. Churchill Harbour is only four hundred miles from the edge of the greatest wheat field in the world."[57] If this route was developed, said Colonel Thomas Scoble, "the centre of our vast fertile area would be as close to Liverpool as the present grain emporium of the United States—Chicago."[58] Any map, as supporters of the bay constantly repeated, led one unavoidably to the conclusion that the potential of the route was immense.

In the same way that the expansionists had pointed to the prairie as a sign of destiny, the supporters of the bay turned the geographical situation of the bay into proof that nature intended it to be used. "Should we not, as Canadians," asked William Murdoch, "anxious for the full development of the great national resources of our country, take what nature offers so freely, and make use of her bountiful gift?"[59] Canada had been given not only a vast west but also a "great Mediterranean sea," and destiny pointed to the future importance of it. Geography easily became converted into mythology as the myth of the north was given new application by the enthusiastic Charles Tuttle: "The directive magnetic force that controls the mariner's needle is not a more attractive problem than is the not less unerring north-westerly trend of human progress. Westward and northward have the marching orders been, until the people of the present generation must look southward and eastward for the homes of their ancestors. The greatest deeds have always been accomplished in high latitudes, because the highest latitudes produce the greatest men." Tuttle's enthusiastic statement was, however, qualified. "Strange as it may seem," he concluded, "the north is always underrated."[60] This tendency again revealed itself, promoters felt, in the case of the Hudson's Bay route. The main obstacle to their scheme was the lack of knowledge concerning the ports on the bay and the route from these ports to the Atlantic Ocean. The general image of the entire region was that of an arctic wasteland and the effort to overcome this impression occupied a great deal of the time of those who supported the route.

In spite of its northerly position, promoters argued, the Hudson's Bay route provided a feasible passage for ships. The history of the last two centuries had proven the bay to be one of the safest water systems in the world. Charles Napier Bell, in a report presented to the Winnipeg Board of Trade in 1884, pointed out that "with the exception of one occasion (1779), Moose Factory has been visited by a ship in every year since 1735."[61] Charles Tuttle concurred, recounted the history of the use of the bay, and concluded that "Hudson's Bay and Strait has been utilized for more than two centuries, with a regularity that furnishes no insignificant recommendation of the route."[62] If the men of the seventeenth century in their small sailing craft and with rudimentary navigational aids could regularly and successfully use the route, then there seemed no reason to doubt that the men of the nineteenth century could do so. E.P. Leacock, a member of the Manitoba Legislative Assembly, argued this point in 1888: "If Cabot in 1498, Hudson in 1610, Gibbon in 1613, Baffin in 1614 and hundreds of others since . . . felt no fear and were able to venture through the Hudson's Bay, then the nineteenth century, with its steam, its iron ships, its thousand modern appliances, cannot be afraid to venture where men went fearlessly so many years ago."[63]

Promoters of the route did not rest all their arguments on history. Once again scientists and popularizers reinterpreted geography and climate to support their own positions. In the case of Hudson's Bay, it must be admitted, the task of dissociating the region from the Arctic was not so easy as it had been in the case of the North-West. Nevertheless a valiant attempt was made to do so. "In the popular mind," said Robert Bell, "Hudson's Bay is apt to be associated with the polar regions, yet no part of it comes within the Arctic circle, and the southern extremity is south of the latitude of London." James Bay could be seen as practically temperate in its climate for it was "in the latitude of Devonshire and Cornwall."[64] Another former expansionist, William Kennedy, testified that "we have the larger half of a continent teeming with animal, vegetable and mineral wealth, only awaiting the hand of labour to draw it forth and enhance its value a thousand fold; and nature opens the gateway by which this wealth may be sent to the remotest quarters of the globe, and the produce of other countries be brought into our midst."[65] Charles Bell went even further and pictured the climate of the bay as both comfortable and attractive: "Robson, Dobbs, Ellice, Hearne and other writers state that when Europeans have once lived in the country about the Bay, that they are never content to live out of it again." In order to prove this, Bell cited some comparative statistics of dubious value to prove that that climate at York "is but very little colder than at Winnipeg, and during the summer it is warmer there than in this Province." Things seem to have changed a great deal since the 1840s when Robert M. Ballantyne had described York Factory as "a monstrous blot on a swampy spot, with a partial view of the frozen sea!"[66]

The praise of the climate of Hudson's Bay was part of the general attempt to make the idea of a railroad to that point seem attractive. Beyond the general image of the region, however, there was a very specific question that had to be answered. The Hudson's Bay Company, it was known, had sent only one or two ships a year to its ports on the bay; this could be done within the constraints of a relatively short navigation season. If a railway was to be worthwhile, however, the navigation season had to be long enough to allow a considerable carrying trade. Proponents of the route argued that this was no problem and that, as Robert Bell argued, only the freezing of the harbours would limit navigation.[67] Nevertheless, as even the most enthusiastic admitted, hard evidence was wanting, especially concerning the navigability of Hudson's Strait.

In order to provide information on this crucial question the Canadian government commissioned an exploring expedition under Lieutenant Andrew Gordon of the Royal Navy. Robert Bell accompanied the expedition as geologist and Charles Tuttle went along as an "observer."[68] He was also unofficially to act as a popular writer who could record the work of the expedition for public consumption. In the end the expedition did little to resolve the problems that existed. Unlike the Hind and Palliser expeditions, the efforts of science failed to provide the final proof needed by supporters of the route to convince those who took a more neutral position. If the uncommitted remained uncommitted, the supporters of the route found much in the conclusions of the expedition to support their case. In part this has to be attributed to the triumph of wishful thinking. Even Charles Tuttle found the bias of individuals such as Robert Bell somewhat amusing: "He could not be persuaded it rained when it poured; or that there was any wind, when it blew at a gale of thirty miles an hour; or that there was any ice, when the Neptune was rearing and plunging in the midst of it like a mad bull; or that it was cold, when the mercury was down to 32 degrees above, and when he was pacing the deck, compelled to wear a good coat of reindeer; in fact he was prepared to believe that the propellor had hit a whale rather than ice." Beside such enthusiasm John Macoun looked like a sceptic.

Tuttle's perceptive comments on Bell's attitude did not, however, stop him from himself adopting an extremely optimistic stance in his writings on the expedition. In the end the vision of the route dominated any untoward experiences of the voyage. Entry to the west via Hudson's Bay, Tuttle argued, was not only feasible but also preferable and more comfortable than the regular route from the east. In fact, the immigrant coming in by the St. Lawrence River would gain an unfavourable impression of Canada, for he would see "wretched shanties" and "half-fed cattle gazing upon sterile fields." In contrast, the immigrant who came via the bay would have the opportunity to see the "glory and grandeur of Greenland's icy mountains" and perhaps even "a sporting whale."[69]

With such a long history of successful use and a pleasant, even, spectacular voyage before the person who undertook it, the sceptic might be prompted to ask why the route had not been developed before. In explaining the bay's lack of use, supporters of the route turned to the company that had been so long associated with it. Conspiratorial forces were seen to be at work in the propagation of the image of the bay as they had been in the image of the West. Charles Bell theorized that earlier in the century the Hudson's Bay Company had realized that "it was highly desirable to keep any adventurous persons from trying to gain a foothold in the future, and the best means to be adopted were those of magnifying the dangers of navigation."[70] The negative image of the route was thus of relatively recent origin and the product of a deliberate policy on the part of the monopolistic Hudson's Bay Company. "Why," asked one writer, "has this route remained so long unused and ignored? The answer is: for the same reasons which untill [sic] now kept the fertile lands of the North-West unsettled and imperfectly known. The Hudson's Bay Company have until lately held the whole of the North-West as a hunting ground for its Indians, and the interests of the Company lay in discouraging settlement or intrusion on its domain."[71]

Such charges were a direct extension of the expansionist rhetoric of the 1850s and 1860s. New conspirators were arising, however, to compete with the old. "Is it not astonishing," wrote Leacock, "that the great corporations in eastern Canada, and the great corporation running through our midst should all unite with the Provinces and States in the East and oppose a scheme which will turn the channels of western trade away from them." Not surprisingly it was the Canadian Pacific Railway, the "great corporation running through our midst," that became the focal point of the new conspiracy theory. "It is no longer a secret," Tuttle wrote the premier of Manitoba in 1884, "that the eastern Provinces generally and the Canadian Pacific Railway in particular are opposed to the Hudson's Bay Railway."[72] Four years later, on 10 January 1888, the *Winnipeg Free Press* warned that "the C.P.R. will bring its powerful influence to bear for the defeat of a more dangerous rival to its through traffic than even the abolition of monopoly would call into existence." When Charles Mair was visited by some representatives of the giant railway, he noted with suspicion their dislike of the bay route: "They pooh-pooh Sutherland's H.B. scheme and I think they mean to oppose it."[73]

Given the purposes behind the bay route, the Canadian Pacific was much better suited to the role of conspirator than was the Hudson's Bay Company. The latter was, after all, but an obsolete monopoly which had unsuccessfully conspired against eastern expansion. The Canadian Pacific, on the contrary, represented those forces of eastern control and exploitation which westerners felt hampered their efforts to develop the region. At the same time, there was a depressing continuity in the whole process. As Charles Mair complained, government policy allowed a "stall fed monopoly," the "Hudson's Bay Company in its new shape the C.P.R.," to dominate the North-West and frustrate its proper aspirations.[74] The bay route, however, would allow the West finally to break free of the powerful and exploitative corporations. By setting the bay against the transcontinental line the scheme became, on a symbolic level, the means of acting in a positive manner against all those remote forces that oppressed the West.

The Hudson's Bay route thus became a method of assailing the unassailable and overcoming the helplessness that many westerners felt. By rendering the West independent of the East it would remove all those injustices of which the West complained. It was, to put it simply, seen as a panacea for all western problems. "The hope of Manitoba," wrote Tuttle, "is in the Hudson's Bay route."[75] Support for the railway was, in fact, a statement of faith in the West itself. The railway thus took on mythical qualities and, as one commentator noted, belief in it "can be likened only to St. Paul's definition of faith: 'It is the substance of things hoped for, the evidence of things not seen.'"[76]

Given such an attitude it is not surprising that the railway took on a moral dimension; it was not simply an economic venture but a means to remedy the unjust exploitation of the West and as such its triumph would be the triumph of justice. "The people of Manitoba are fully justified in their determination to secure free and untrammeled railway and water communication with all parts of the world," wrote Tuttle. As the inhabitants of Red River had been thought to deserve the blessings of British freedom and as Canada had deserved the opportunity to develop the West, so the West now demanded the opportunity to alter the original expansionist strategy to ensure that they obtained their due. National destiny and human justice demanded the construction of the railroad. "Let the walls of monopoly be broken down, and let us have competition in railway traffic."[77] Destiny and justice displaced economics as Charles Mair warned angrily of the avarice that sought to block the opening of the bay:

> Open the Bay! the myriad prairies call;
>   Let homesteads rise and comforts multiply;
> Let justice triumph though the heavens should fall!
>   This is the voice of reason—manhood's cry.
>
> Open the Bay! Who are they that say "no"?
>   Who locks the portals? Nature? She resigned
> Her icy reign, her stubborn frost and snow,
> Her sovereign sway and sceptre, long ago,
>   To sturdy manhood and the master, Mind!
> Not these the foe! Not Nature, who is fain

When earnest hearts an earnest end pursue;
But man's old selfishness and greed of gain;
These ancient breeders of earth's sin and pain—
These are the thieves who steal the Nation's due![78]

The Hudson's Bay railway was not built within the lifetime of most of those who became its advocate in the 1880s. The concrete problems of navigation and the question of its economic viability could not be shunted aside as many would have wished. Nevertheless, many of the delays and broken promises concerning the route did reflect an eastern indifference and Canadian Pacific hostility that, in the extreme, nearly justified the conspiratorial images that circulated among the proponents of the bay. John A. Macdonald, for instance, was so sceptical of the worth of the bay route that he was willing to deal it a nearly fatal blow for the sake of political control within one Manitoba constituency.[79] Other eastern politicians showed an equal, if less spectacular, aversion to this particularly western scheme. Eventually the increased political power of the West, rather than any new interest in the scheme in the East or any new evidence of its viability, would lead to the construction of the railway. Only then did westerners find that the bay route would not magically free them from eastern control.

The indifference of the East simply deepened the western sense of alienation from the original expansionist idea. The call for the Hudson's Bay route had been a demand for a major readjustment of east-west relations in order to revive and strengthen the national sense of unity while ensuring the achievement of the original expansionist goal of the rapid development of the West. When people in the West perceived that the East was ignoring their demands, whether on the railway or other issues, their earlier suspicions were deepened. The East seemed to have betrayed the original promises of the expansionist movement; in response, many in the West turned their back on the older perception of Canada and began to look for their identity in the land around them.

Notes

1. *Annual Report of the Department of the Interior*, 1887, xii.
2. A.F.J. Artibise, *Winnipeg: A Social History of Urban Growth, 1874–1914* (Montreal, 1975), 130.
3. P.A.C., Macdonald Papers, Vol. 209, Dennis to D.L. Macpherson, 17 Aug. 1881.
4. P.A.C., Grant Papers, Vol. 4, McLaren to Grant, 9 June 1881.
5. *Grip*, 18 March 1882.
6. J.C. McLagan, "Description and History of Winnipeg," in John Macoun, ed., *Manitoba and the Great North-West* (Guelph, 1882), 492.
7. Macdonald Papers, Vol. 209, Dennis to Macpherson, 17 Aug. 1881; W.H. Williams, *Manitoba and the North-West: Journal of a Trip from Toronto to the Rocky Mountains* (Toronto, 1882), 40.
8. P.A.C., Fleming Papers, Vol. 83, "Journals of Trips," entries for 2, 4, 8, 16 Feb. 1882.
9. Queen's University Library, Mair Papers, McLean to Mair, 3 Feb. 1882.
10. Public Archives of Manitoba, James Gemmel Papers, Schultz to Gemmel, 27 Dec. 1884.
11. "W.F.C.," "Manitoba Farming," *The Week*, I (6 Dec. 1883), 4.
12. *Annual Report of the Department of the Interior*, 1887, xii.
13. P.A.C., Denison Papers, Mair to Denison, 21 March 1885.
14. Ibid., 20 June 1884.
15. *The Week*, III (6 May 1886); letter to the editor from George Patterson.
16. *Globe*, Toronto, 5 Sept. 1895; letter from Grant.
17. Mair Papers, Vol. 7, "Speech of Mair at Banquet to Lieutenant Governor," undated.

18. Denison Papers, Schultz to Denison, 7 Oct. 1895.
19. Charles Tuttle, *Our North Land: Being a Full Account of the Canadian North-West and Hudson's Bay Route* (Toronto, 1885), 391.
20. P.A.C., Alexander Mackenzie Papers, Microfilm Reel #M-199, Laird to Mackenzie, 1 July 1879; see also on the extermination of the buffalo, F.G. Roe, *The North American Buffalo* (Toronto, 1951), 467-88.
21. G.F.G. Stanley, *The Birth of Western Canada* (Toronto, 1960), 266-68.
22. *The Week*, II (9 April 1885), 296; letter to the editor from 'C.'
23. Cited in ibid. (4 June 1885), 426.
24. Cited in Charles P. Mulvaney, *The History of the North-West Rebellion of 1885* (Toronto, 1885), 88.
25. Denison Papers, Mair to Denison, 28 March 1885.
26. 28 April 1885.
27. *Herald*, Halifax, 18 May 1885.
28. *Witness*, Montreal, 10 June 1885.
29. Grant Papers, Vol. 6, Gordon to Grant, 1 Feb. 1886.
30. John C. Donkin, *Trooper and Redskin in the Far Northwest* (London, 1888), 142.
31. P.A.C., Church Missionary Society Archives, 2/0, McLean to Fenn, 15 June 1885.
32. Stanley, *Birth of Western Canada*, vii.
33. Mason Wade, *The French Canadians, 1760-1967* (Toronto, 1968), I, 393-446.
34. Denison Papers, Mair to Denison, 8 May 1888, 13 Aug. 1889.
35. See speech by Grant cited in Halifax *Herald*, 20 May 1885.
36. Although it might be argued that one seemingly meaningful course was to encourage a greater concentration of political power in the local government. It is interesting that concern over the powers of the North-West Territories government began to develop simultaneously with the growing problems of the region around 1883-84. See Lewis H. Thomas, *The Struggle for Responsible Government in the North-West Territories, 1870-97*, 2nd ed. (Toronto, 1978), 117-45.
37. P.H. Atwood, *Jubilee Essays on Imperial Confederation as Affecting Manitoba and the North-West* (Winnipeg, 1887), 7.
38. Denison Papers, Mair to Denison, 6 Nov. 1888.
39. Smith in *The Week*, I (28 Feb. 1884); *Grip*, 8 March 1884.
40. *The Week*, II (26 March 1885), 257.
41. Ibid., (9 April 1885), 257; 3 and 17 Dec. 1885, 21 Jan. and 25 March 1886.
42. P.A.C., Colonial Office Records, 880: North America, print 113, "Canada. Rising in the North-West Territory; Correspondence," #25 Landsdowne to the Earl of Derby, 21 April 1885; enclosure #1.
43. Howard A. Fleming, *Canada's Arctic Outlet: A History of the Hudson's Bay Railway* (Los Angeles, 1957), 9.
44. *Navigation of Hudson's Bay* (Ottawa, 1878), Dennis to Macdonald, 11 Nov. 1878, 1-2; 5.
45. Fleming, *Canada's Arctic Outlet*, 11-14. For Sutherland's aims, see Sutherland, *The Hudson Bay Railway; an open letter from the President of the Hudson's Bay Railway to members of the Parliament of Canada* (Ottawa, 1890).
46. Fleming Papers, Vol. 18, Grant to Fleming, 14 Dec. 1880.
47. Macdonald Papers, Vol. 127, Hurlbert to Macdonald, 17 Dec. 1880.
48. Fleming Papers, Vol. 18, Grant to Fleming, 21 June 1880.
49. Macdonald Papers, Vol. 373, Peter Imrie to John Lowe, undated [1880].
50. Ibid., Vol. 105, "Resolution of the North West Council," 1883.
51. Denison Papers, Mair to Denison, 15 Aug. 1891.
52. "A Bystander," *The Week*, I (20 March 1884), 243.
53. Murdoch, *Report on the Winnipeg and Hudson's Bay Railway* (Winnipeg, 1884), 27-28.
54. J.K. Johnson, ed., *The Canadian Directory of Parliament* (Ottawa, 1968), 523.

55. *Winnipeg Free Press,* 6 March 1971.
56. Nelson, *Proposed Hudson's Bay and Pacific Railway and New Steamship Route* (np 1893).
57. *New Route to the Interior of North America* (Montreal, 1881), 13.
58. Scoble, "Our Crop Markets," *Historical and Scientific Society of Manitoba,* Transaction no. 15, 8 Jan. 1885, 9.
59. Murdoch, *Report on the Winnipeg and Hudson's Bay Railway,* 26.
60. Tuttle, *Our North Land,* 17.
61. Bell, *Our Northern Waters,* (Winnipeg, 1884), 5.
62. Tuttle, *Our North Land,* 241.
63. Leacock, *Hudson's Bay Route* (np 1888), 3–4.
64. Robert Bell, "On the Commercial Importance of Hudson's Bay, with Remarks on Recent Surveys and Investigations," *Proceedings of the Royal Geographical Society* (London), III, 10 (Oct. 1881), 577–86, 578, 581.
65. Province of Manitoba, *Report of the Select Committee of the Legislative Assembly of the Province of Manitoba Appointed to Procure Evidence on the Practicability of a System of Communication with this Province via Hudson's Bay* (Winnipeg, 1884), 12.
66. Bell, *Our Northern Waters,* 48; Ballantyne, *Hudson's Bay* (Edinburgh, 1848), 137.
67. Canada, Journals of the House of Commons, 1884, Report of the Select Committee on Hudson's Bay, 5.
68. For the official report on the expedition, see Canada, Department of Marine and Fisheries, *Report of the Hudson's Bay Expedition of 1884 under the Command of Lieutenant A.R. Gordon* (Ottawa, 1884).
69. Tuttle, *Our North Land,* 103–104; 554–58.
70. Bell, *Our Northern Waters,* 28.
71. *New Route to the Interior of North America,* 3–4.
72. Leacock, *Hudson's Bay Route,* 4; Tuttle to John Norquay, 22 Dec. 1884, cited in Tuttle, *Our North Land,* 464.
73. Public Archives of Manitoba, Schultz Papers, Mair to Schultz, 26 April 1891.
74. Denison Papers, Mair to Denison, 6 Nov. 1888.
75. Tuttle, *Our North Land,* 396.
76. "Garry," "The Hudson's Bay Railway," *The Week,* III (25 Nov. 1886), 831.
77. Tuttle, *Our North Land,* 470.
78. Mair, "Open the Bay!" in *Dreamland and Other Poems, Tecumseh: A Drama* (Toronto, 1974), 169–70.
79. Macdonald Papers, Vol. 262, Scarth to Macdonald, 3 Feb. 1884; Stephens to Macdonald, 6 Feb. 1887; Scarth to Macdonald, 18 Feb., 25 June, 13 Sept. 1887; Macdonald to Scarth, 15 Sept. 1887.

3

AGRARIAN AND LABOUR REVOLT (1885-1919)

Introduction

From 1885 to the First World War and beyond, western Canada became one of the breadbaskets of the world. Immigration from the United States and Europe resulted in a large new population of both rural and urban dwellers. This new society was divided into classes, and although ordinary farmers and workers formed the majority of the population they felt that they had the least power and derived the fewest benefits. Their attempts to redress this inequality gave western protest a new face.

Vernon C. Fowke's analysis of relations between central Canada and the West, "Western Protest and Dominion Policy," taken from his classic work *The National Policy and the Wheat Economy*, continues to be a powerful tool in our understanding of this period. Written in the 1950s, it explains how the western farmer felt exploited by the railway, the grain merchants, and the Ontario manufacturers, who were protected by a high tariff wall. While the price a farmer received for his grain was unprotected, set by a fluctuating world market, the price of the goods he bought remained protected.

The farmers of the West attempted to counter this situation by creating farmer-owned elevator companies and cooperatives that marketed their products, allowing them a measure of control. But the demand for justice and equality continued to grow. The West was a new society, full of hope and expectation, and people had immigrated with visions of a new and better life. The exploitation and inequality they were experiencing angered and embittered them.

While the agrarian sector was taking its own initiatives, workers in western cities were fighting for improved income, shorter hours, and social benefits. Through radical organizations such as the One Big Union (OBU), through various fringe political parties, and through the established trade union movement they sought to create a society that offered them dignity and advancement.

The watershed event in this struggle was the Winnipeg General Strike of 1919. In his interpretation of the strike David J. Bercuson explains what caused the strike, why it failed, and what the results were. Because of the strike Winnipeg became a symbol of class polarization in the West.

One movement that influenced both farmers and workers, rural communities and cities, was the Social Gospel. Combining Christian morality with the desire for social reform, this movement called for prohibition, an end to class exploitation, an empowerment of the weak, and a system of social justice that would eliminate poverty and ignorance. Richard Allen discusses the impact of Social Gospel ideas on the farm movement and its leadership, but he also makes it clear that the urban roots of Social

Gospel resulted in a new class of intellectual and political leaders in the West who were schooled in a social change-oriented Christianity. These leaders dominated reform politics until World War II.

This was a formative period, as fresh and new as the agrarian society that dominated the region at the turn of the century. Its economic struggles and demands for social reform laid the groundwork for the golden age of agrarian protest discussed in the next chapter.

Western Protest and Dominion Policy

VERNON C. FOWKE

Reprinted from Vernon C. Fowke, *The National Policy and the Wheat Economy* (University of Toronto Press, 1957), 153–157, by permission of University of Toronto Press, © University of Toronto Press, 1957.

Local and terminal elevators, along with railways, formed the costly but indispensable physical equipment for the marketing of western grain. The Dominion government had no philosophical aversion to monopolistic control either of elevator or railway facilities, but by 1900 it was possessed of a firmly established pragmatic aversion to monopoly of any sort which threatened to interfere with western development or with national policy. Despite the cancellation of the monopoly clause, the Canadian Pacific Railway Company inevitably retained a strong measure of monopoly within the area contiguous to its lines and shipping points. Towards the end of the century the railway had extended the monopoly privilege to the elevator field by agreeing with any party who would build a standard elevator at a loading point that it would prohibit the loading of cars at that point either over the loading platform or through a flat warehouse. Agrarian protest against this practice, voiced in the House of Commons, prompted governmental investigation and regulation. Legislative controls over grain trading agencies were immeasurably broadened after 1900 by new legislation and by repeated amendment to the old.

Legislative control in the grain trade was by no means new. Governmental inspection and grading of grain as one of the groups of "staple articles of Canadian produce" was well established in Canada prior to Confederation. It was translated into federal law in a General Inspection Act of 1873,[1] and, through repeated revision, this act was kept in conformity with changing circumstances. The revisions of 1885, 1889, 1891, and 1899[2] effected the necessary legislative transition to harmonize with the shift from an eastern grain trade in winter wheat to a national trade in spring wheat of western origin. Various grades of Manitoba "hard" wheat headed the list of descriptions in the revision of 1885. The amendments of 1889 and 1891 provided for the establishment of a western as well as an eastern standards board, and for the establishment of "commercial" grades for western grain, these grades to be applicable in cases where crop conditions prevented the inclusion of a considerable proportion of the crop in the statutory grades. The General Inspection Act of 1899 created the inspection district of Manitoba, defined to include Manitoba, the North-West Territories, and Ontario as far east as the head of the Lakes.

Changes in the legislative provision for inspection and grading, instituted in response to the petitions of boards of trade and grain trading interests,[3] went a long way to improve the Canadian system of the sale of grain by official grade. They did not prevent the recurrence of farmers' criticism in the matter of inspection, and they did not even touch the question of governmental control of grain handling agencies.

In 1898 James Douglas, member for East Assiniboia, introduced a bill into the federal House "to regulate the shipping of grain by railway companies in Manitoba and the North West Territories." The main purpose of the bill was to secure for farmers the legal right to load grain over loading platforms or through flat warehouses. Its premise was that the powerful element of monopoly inherent in the position of the Canadian Pacific Railway Company—even after the cancellation of the monopoly clause—was being extended to the elevator field by agreement between the railway and elevator companies, and must be broken. The bill made no progress in the 1898 session but was reintroduced in 1899. Its original introduction prompted the Canadian Pacific Railway Company to provide cars for platform loading for the crop of 1898. Discussion of the bill before a special committee of the House in 1899 led the government to appoint a royal commission "on the Shipment and Transportation of Grain in Manitoba and the North-West Territories."

The commission of 1899 was the first of half a dozen federal royal commissions to investigate the grain trade of western Canada within the next forty years,[4] and the first of two appointed before 1920. In 1906 a farmers' delegation appeared before the Agricultural Committee of the House of Commons to protest the inadequacy and injustice of the inspection and grading of western grain as carried on under existing legislation. On the basis of requests thus presented, the federal government appointed a second royal commission to investigate the farmers' complaints and to recommend changes in the Grain Inspection Act and the Manitoba Grain Act. Since royal commissions were used repeatedly by Dominion and provincial governments after 1900 in the development of policy concerning the wheat economy, and since such investigating bodies may have a variety of uses, it is well to note certain features of these two commissions. This is of particular importance because of contrasts in regard to the type and purpose of the royal commissions appointed by the federal government before and after 1920.

The chief point of interest concerning the two federal commissions of 1899 and 1906 is that their personnel was made up almost exclusively of western grain growers.[5] The central purpose of the commissions was, it may be presumed, to hear and evaluate the complex of grain growers' complaints concerning grain handling facilities. Yet no attempt was made by the government to observe, in the selection of personnel, any of the usual rules concerning a proper representation of the various parties vitally interested in the dispute, or of the various geographic areas of the national economy. The commission of 1899 consisted of three Manitoba farmers under the chairmanship of Judge Senkler of St. Catharines, Ontario. When Judge Senkler retired on account of ill health he was succeeded by A.E. Richards (afterwards Mr. Justice Richards) of Winnipeg. It is clear from the records that C.C. Castle, one of the farmer members, dominated the group. The commission of 1906 was made up of three western farmers including the chairman, John Millar of Indian Head.

The facts noted above suggest that the early federal commissions on the grain trade were not regarded as instruments for the impartial evaluation of agrarian protest against the elevator and milling companies and the railways. They also suggest that the governments which appointed them were not seeking to weight the scales against the protesting western wheat growers, and that there was no attempt to select royal commissioners who could be counted on to reduce the farmers' protests to the level of ridiculous tirade by the refinements of economic sophistry. The Dominion government was, apparently, prepared to take seriously the wheat growers' protests and was not, in fact, willing to run the risk of having these protests effectively countered by the presence of representatives of any of the defendant interests. This characteristic of royal commission membership before 1920 was not typical of the commissions appointed by the Dominion government to investigate the problems of the West. The membership of such royal commissions after 1920 was of a different character and this difference provides one of the sharpest of the contrasts between the policy-making devices employed in the two periods respectively.

The partisan nature of the membership of the pre-1920 royal commissions on the grain trade makes it clear that they were not appointed primarily as impartial fact-finding bodies. The facts and the fancies which were likely to be encountered were well known and the commissions were used as a device for putting them on the record. In doing this, they were to serve two purposes: they were to perform the well-recognized safety-valve function so common to royal commissions; and they were to educate the public and the Dominion Legislature on the necessity for a certain type of legislative enactment. The first purpose is self-explanatory. The explosive pressures which the commissions were designed to release harmlessly are readily apparent in the record of the history of western development. The second purpose requires a brief comment. Its implication is that the royal commissions of 1899 and 1906 were not so much expected to formulate policy or even to advise on the formulation of policy as they were to establish the need and rationale for policy already awaiting application. They recommended a single solution to the problems created by the existence of monopolistic elements in the grain trade over the turn of the century. Their recommendations called only for licensing and supervision by a permanent governmental agency.

The royal commission has too well earned the reputation in Canada of being an excellent alternative to effective governmental action, an instrument to justify procrastination. While the governmental use of later royal commissions on the Canadian grain trade may have contributed to that reputation, this was by no means true of the commissions of 1899 and 1906. The commissioners applied themselves diligently to the recording of information relevant to their terms of reference, they reported their recommendations in some detail, and the government promptly implemented these recommendations by legislation—each time, it may be said, on the eve of a general election.

Reporting on its investigations of the charge that local elevators had secured a monopoly position by the aid of the railways, the commission of 1899 indicated that the refusal of the railways to accept grain from flat warehouses or to furnish cars directly to farmers had forced the growers either to ship their grain through the elevators or to sell to them. The resultant "lack of competition," the commission stated, had given to elevator owners the power to depress prices. "It would naturally be to their interest," the commission added, "to so depress prices; and when buying to dock as much as possible."[6] The only adequate remedy for the specific failure of competition at local shipping points, it appeared to the commission, lay in the fullest possible freedom of shipping. It therefore advised that the railways be required by law: (1) to permit the construction of flat warehouses at loading points; (2) to construct loading platforms themselves on the basis of farmers' petitions; and (3) to provide farmers with cars "as a legal right" and not as a matter of privilege. For the proper regulation of the trade in general it recommended the adoption by the Dominion government of the system already well established in Minnesota, where a state commission, the Railroad and Warehouse Commission, was responsible for the administration of a general supervisory act relating to the shipment of grain.

The Manitoba Grain Act[7] was passed by the Dominion government in 1900 to implement the recommendations of the commission. Apart from the general question of grain trade regulation, the major emphasis was on the provision of alternative opportunities for the disposal of grain at local points in order that some effective degree of competition might be restored. This emphasis, so pronounced in western protest, had been translated directly into the recommendations of the commission and was the basis of the central legislative requirements of the act of 1900. It provided for the licensing, bonding, and supervision of all grain dealers, and established the office of warehouse commissioner for administration.[8] It required the railways to supply cars without discrimination for loading through flat warehouses or elevators, or over loading platforms. Furthermore, the railways were required, on the receipt of a written application of ten local farmers with a certain minimum acreage in crop, to construct a loading platform and to make it available without charge. Standard forms were established for recording the various transactions involved in the transfer, storage, and sale of western grains.

Neither the entire act nor any one of its sections would be of benefit to grain growers if interested parties were to be allowed to circumvent the legislation passively or in open defiance. Construction of loading platforms and permission for the erection of flat warehouses as required by the act were indispensable to the creation of alternative local opportunities for the disposal of grain. These provisions, however, could be frustrated in their purpose unless they were accompanied by the assurance that cars would be provided with complete impartiality for loading through the various agencies, so the car distribution clause (s. 44) proved to be of crucial importance in the implementation of the federal policy of grain trade regulation in the early years of the century. Adequate observance of this legislative requirement was not established until the Sintaluta test case of 1902 wherein the agent of the Canadian Pacific Railway Company at Sintaluta was found guilty of a breach of the relevant section of the act. The decision was upheld by the Supreme Court of Canada on appeal and the validity of the law was thus made certain. Remaining ambiguities in the car distribution clause were further reduced by a legislative amendment in 1902 which embodied new wording almost identical with that recommended by the Territorial Grain Growers' Association.[9] The Manitoba Grain Act and the Sintaluta judgment fell far short of a complete removal of the dissatisfaction of grain growers with local shipping conditions but they went a considerable distance in that direction.

Shortly after the turn of the century the attention of western growers was shifted increasingly to the terminal market and to the activities carried on in terminal elevators at the head of the Lakes, to the processes of inspection and grading in Winnipeg, and to the conduct of business in the Winnipeg Grain and Produce Exchange. In response to a request from the Territorial Grain Growers' Association, the Territorial Department of Agriculture had milling and baking tests conducted at the Ontario Agricultural College, Guelph, in 1903 and 1904, to determine the bread-making qualities of the various grades of western grain. The report of the expert showed variations in baking qualities which had little relation to typical price spreads between the grades.

The publication of the results of these investigations intensified the demands for further changes in the system of governmental inspection and grading. The federal Grain Inspection Act of 1904 consolidated existing legislation in this field but dissatisfaction continued unabated. The Grain Growers' Grain Company, organized in 1906, sought to operate within the established system and to break the monopoly elements which appeared to characterize the private trade.[10] What a farmers' commission agency might accomplish in the terminal market was far from clear in 1906. Certain points, however, were evident. Such an agency could neither alter the inspection system appreciably nor, without terminal elevators of its own, could it modify the method of operating the terminal elevators. The farmers' delegation that appeared before the Agricultural Committee of the Dominion House in 1906 protested particularly against the inspection and grading system. The royal commission appointed following these representations was instructed "to take into consideration all or any matters connected with the Grain Inspection Act and the Manitoba Grain Act..."[11] The commission, reporting in 1908, recommended approximately fifty specific amendments to these laws in order that they might constitute "a more thorough system of supervision and control." The Dominion government promptly implemented the recommendations *in toto*.

The reaction of the commission of 1906 to the question of ownership of elevators by the Dominion government is of particular interest. The question was raised in a preliminary way at the hearings and was summarily dismissed. The proposal put forward by the Grain Growers' associations of Manitoba and Saskatchewan was that the Dominion government should construct and operate a number of conveniently located interior terminal elevators. It was argued that such facilities would relieve car shortages by shortening the turn-around time and would provide growers with official grade and weight with a minimum of delay. The commission advised against the expedient as excessively costly and one which would involve shippers in unnecessary expense. Its opinion was that the option of shipping to an interior terminal was one that few shippers would choose since "spot grain was the objective except for local mills."[12]

The associations also urged that the Dominion government take over the terminals and operate them as a public utility. On this point the commission reported as follows:

> To prevent the evils that are made possible by operation of the terminal elevators under the present system, we do not think it wise to advise the Government to go to the length of taking over the terminal elevators or of prohibiting persons engaged in the grain trade being interested in such terminals. We believe it possible to obtain a good service from these elevators under the present ownership by having a more thorough system of supervision and control.[13]

The three farmer commissioners of the 1906 investigating group were clearly out of sympathy with the representatives of the Grain Growers' associations in regard to the question of socializing the terminals. They were, however, in harmony with the views of the Dominion government of that day and those of many years to come. The views which they expressed may also have been acceptable to a large majority of western grain growers at the time, for the agitation for government ownership of grain handling facilities was as yet only in its initial stages.

Although the Canadian Pacific Railway Company did nothing by way of providing local grain buyers with elevator facilities, it did construct terminals at the head of the Lakes. From 1884, when it built the first terminal at Port Arthur, until 1904, the terminal facilities at Fort William-Port Arthur were exclusively operated by the company. In 1902 the Canadian Northern Railway, just beginning its expansion throughout the West, built large terminals at the Lakehead, which it leased to grain companies in 1906. In 1904 two of the grain companies, the Ogilvie Flour Milling Company and the Empire Elevator Company built public terminals.[14] Thus, after 1904, the terminals gradually came into the hands of the grain companies and became part of their integrated systems.

Integration, both regional and functional, has characterized Canadian grain handling agencies from the early days. Companies which served as warehousemen through the ownership of local and terminal elevators ordinarily bought and sold grain and thus acted as merchants also. Farmers came increasingly after the turn of the century to believe that this combination of functions was detrimental to their interests, particularly when it occurred in the terminal field. It was considered that a terminal operator who bought and sold grain on his own account could not be expected to offer disinterested service to patrons whose grain he was called on to handle on a storage or transfer basis. The chief charges against such operators were those of mixing and undercleaning of grain, both of which practices allegedly had the effect of diluting Canadian export grain to the minimum of each respective grade and thus of lowering its reputation as well as its price in the overseas markets.

With these circumstances in mind it is not difficult to realize that the complaints of the western grain growers were not silenced by the "more thorough system of supervision and control" of the elevator system which was provided in 1908 by amendment to the Grain Inspection Act and the Manitoba Grain Act in conformity with the recommendations of the federal royal commission of 1906. In May 1909, a delegation from the Interprovincial Council of Grain Growers' and Farmers' Associations urged federal operation of terminal elevators before Sir Richard Cartwright, federal minister of trade and commerce. In this representation the farmers' delegation was supported by the Dominion Millers' Association. Investigations conducted officially by Commissioner Castle and independently by the Manitoba Grain Growers' Association late in 1909 confirmed the long-standing allegations of the farmers that terminal elevator operators mixed and undercleaned the grain which they handled. The views of officials of western farm organizations were summed up in an editorial in the *Grain Growers' Guide* of 28 December 1909: "Just so long as these [terminal] elevators remain in private hands, there will be the temptation to private gain. There is only one possible method by which the system of robbing the farmers' grain at the terminals can be abolished. That method is by federal government ownership."[15]

The agitation continued unabated throughout 1910. In January the Manitoba Grain Growers' Association presented a memorandum to Cartwright embodying the same proposal as before. On this occasion the association was supported by representatives of eastern millers and by a number of independent grain dealers of Winnipeg. Among the various demands presented repeatedly to Sir Wilfrid Laurier on his western tour of 1910 was the demand for federal operation of terminals and for the prevention of mixing therein. The prime minister expressed his willingness to discuss the terminal matter further, and in October, on his return to the capital, he wrote to the Grain Growers' associations saying that the government would hear their representations. The associations decided against further separate appearances in this matter in view of the march on Ottawa planned by the Canadian Council of Agriculture.[16] One of the major petitions presented by the massive delegation of 500 western grain growers and 300 eastern Grangers in December 1910, was, therefore, a repetition of the demand for federal operation of terminals.[17] Additional support was given to this memorial by the Dominion Millers' Association, the Toronto Board of Trade, and eastern and western exporters.

The representations of 1910 may be regarded as the climax of the pressure put on the federal government to operate the terminal elevators. The government refused to yield except by way of partial compromise. The well-established policy of attacking abuses by legislative control and improved supervision was continued in the Canada Grain Act which was introduced by the Liberals in 1911 and enacted by the Conservative government in 1912. This act consolidated the Grain Inspection and Manitoba Grain acts, it replaced the office of warehouse commissioner with a board of grain commissioners and provided for the mixing of grain in "hospital elevators." As a concession to the persistent western demands for socialization of the terminals the act provided for the construction or acquisition of terminals at the head of the Lakes by the Dominion government and for the operation of such elevators by the Board of Grain Commissioners.[18] The government built a terminal at Port Arthur in 1913 with a capacity of 3 1/4 million bushels and, on the recommendation of the Board of Grain Commissioners, constructed interior terminal elevators at Moose Jaw, Calgary, and Saskatoon beginning in 1913-14, and, a decade later, one in Edmonton.[19] These elevators were placed under the management of the Board of Grain Commissioners.

The mixing of grain in terminal elevators remained a troublesome matter for years after the passage of the Canada Grain Act but it, along with the more general question of terminal operation and control, assumed less and less relative importance after 1912. A number of factors contributed to this result. The elaboration of control and supervision provided for by the Grain Act inspired greater confidence. The government's lakehead terminal provided an alternative channel for western grain. More important still, however, was the fact that the terminal field was no longer controlled exclusively by nonfarm interests. In October 1912, the Grain Growers' Grain Company, which until that time had operated as a terminal commission agency without elevator facilities, leased a terminal at Fort William from the Canadian Pacific Railway Company and immediately assumed operation.[20] In January of the following year it purchased another terminal at the same place. Presently the Saskatchewan and Alberta Co-operative Elevator companies were organized and the former company entered actively into terminal ownership and operation. The truth of the matter is that the farmers lost much of their aversion to a number of the practices of the terminal elevator companies by becoming terminal elevator operators themselves. This is notably true of the long-protested practice of mixing grain. The royal commission which reported on the Canadian grain trade in 1925 pointed out that the farmers' grain marketing companies of the day, the Saskatchewan Co-operative Elevator Company, the United Grain Growers Limited, and the three provincial wheat pools with their joint Central Selling Agency, were all engaged in the mixing business.[21]

By 1914, the Dominion government was well on the way towards the fulfilment of the national policy in terms of western economic development, an achievement made with but slight modification of the elements of that policy as originally evolved. Western lands had contributed substantially to the financing of the first transcontinental railway and had offered the major attraction for settlers to become established in the western provinces. Tariff policy remained essentially unchanged from that of the firm protection which had been made effective a generation earlier. The British preferential schedules, adopted over the turn of the century, modified this system to a certain extent, but they made no breach in the concept of an east-west transportation universe of which the St. Lawrence community formed an integral part. The view that a shortage of private capital or a reluctance on the part of private investors should not be allowed to prevent major development had cost the Dominion heavy expenditures for the first transcontinental railway, but had not involved the taint of socialism. Similarly, for the second and third transcontinental systems, the Dominion government had assumed tremendous commitments for security guarantees and for the construction of the National Transcontinental from Moncton to Winnipeg. The free-enterprise system of railway construction was nevertheless regarded as still intact. Monopoly in the railway field, originally regarded as essential to the national policy, was found to be incompatible with that policy and had given way to governmentally sponsored competition and governmentally imposed regulation.

The difficulty encountered in marketing western grain did not appear to be primarily due to a shortage of developmental capital. Elevator facilities were inadequate before the turn of the century, but they were rapidly multiplied thereafter by private capital until in 1910 a royal commission could report that country elevators existed greatly in excess of requirements throughout the West. Western farmers' demands after 1905 were not for governmental assistance in the building of elevators in order to overcome a shortage of such facilities, but, rather, for outright socialization of the local and terminal elevator system of the West in order to break the private monopoly elements which appeared to dominate its activities. Farmers appointed as royal commissioners were able to tell the Dominion government what it was reassured to hear, that adequate regulation rather than socialization was the remedy needed for the real and imaginary abuses of the existing elevator system. In spite of direct and persistent agricultural representations to the contrary in the years 1909 and 1910, the government maintained this conviction and policy and renewed its pledge to that effect in the Canada Grain Act of 1912 as well as in later revisions of that act.

The outbreak of war in 1914 created the emergency which for the first time in the history of the Dominion placed the national military obligation foremost regardless of possible incompatibility with national economic development. The pace of western expansion had faltered before the war. Economic conditions were uncertain. The outbreak of war reduced immigration to negligible proportions and impeded the entry of capital. The country's energies turned from the promotion of immigration and economic development to the solution of the manifold problems of recruitment and military training.

It became evident, as the crisis of the war became more clearly defined, that the economic development of the West in the tradition of the national policy was not contradictory to the requirements of the new situation but was, on the contrary, of the utmost positive importance to it. The popular slogan came to be, "Food will win the war." Because of the problems of shipping, food in this context meant wheat from non-European countries but, more specifically, from countries in the Northern Hemisphere. While further immigration for the occupation of new lands was out of the question for the time being at least, there were in the Canadian wheat economy millions of acres of good land which were occupied but not as yet under cultivation. A major part of the Canadian contribution to the Allied effort in the First World War consisted of a maximization of wheat exports and the fostering of the agricultural effort which made such exports possible.

The Dominion government entered the war and, for the most part, fought through it to the end without seriously questioning the assumption that economic policies which sufficed for peace would suffice for war.[22] Essentially the belief was in "business as usual" or in business according to free-enterprise principles for the allocation of the factors of production. Price served as a satisfactory guide for the allocation of labour, capital, and land in peacetime. The use of the factors of production might well be guided by the same directive during war, with one modification—patriotism. Price and patriotism, so it was argued, would adequately serve to guide the economy and determine its goals. "Recruit rather than conscript" expressed the economic as well as the military philosophy of the Dominion government as, indeed, of the Allies generally.

Modification of this viewpoint was forced upon the Canadian as upon other Allied governments. For the Dominion government at least it was a modification founded on expediency rather than on principle, and an alteration to be reversed as quickly as possible. In regard to manpower, conscription became essential, but only for military purposes and for the latter part of the war. In railways, a chaotic situation, with no possibility that the two incomplete transcontinental systems could either be left as they were, or completed and operated on the basis of further governmental guarantees, compelled the eventual nationalization of more than half the Canadian railway mileage. This measure occurred without hope of later reversal but also without the acceptance by the government of the principle that nationalization was anything but an undesirable necessity. As to the market structure for goods and services other than those for the military and for a part of the railway system, few modifications were regarded as necessary at any time during the war—with the eventual exception of wheat.

Even in regard to the marketing of Canadian wheat the traditional laissez-faire policy was maintained for upwards of three of the four war years. The only changes demanded of the wheat economy were quantitative ones. It was a question of more and more. Western Canada was a wheat exporter of marked significance to western Europe well before 1914 and the prompt exclusion of Russia from western markets by the closing of the Dardanelles early in the war focused Allied demands on North America. In contrast to the food policies developed during the Second World War, the Allies' demands for food were concentrated on wheat on a general assumption that an effective war effort required above all that bread be plentiful and cheap.[23] The major shift in the world demand for wheat was, however, left for a considerable time to work itself out through ordinary market channels. While governmental purchasing was established in Italy, the grain trade in Britain and France was left strictly in private hands. Cash and futures markets remained open, and private importers, millers, and other agencies carried on the trade as before. With the market system left to its own devices in the major importing countries and in the United States, it would have been surprising to find any early modification in the Canadian grain marketing system, the "open market" system with its focal point in the Winnipeg Grain Exchange. For two years after the outbreak of the war the Allies secured necessary foodstuffs through the ordinary import channels in reasonably ample quantities and without pronounced advances in price.[24] The Canadian bumper wheat crop of 393.5 million bushels in 1915, grown on an acreage increased by five million acres over that of 1914, contributed materially towards that end.[25]

However, drastic alterations in supply and price during the summer months of 1916 compelled an alteration in food policy, first concerning Allied procurement and, second, by resultant pressures, in the overseas producing countries. Under conditions of unrestricted submarine warfare, the price of wheat in Britain advanced by one-half from June to October 1916. On 10 October the Liverpool futures market was closed and the British Royal Commission on Wheat Supplies was appointed as an agency for investigation and for control of the procurement, first of wheat and flour, and, shortly after, of all cereals. By the end of November 1916, the United Kingdom, France, and Italy had signed the Wheat Executive Agreement to purchase all wheat requirements jointly, under the agency of the British Royal Commission on Wheat Supplies. Private trading in wheat and flour virtually disappeared in the three countries. The predominant position of the single purchasing agency forced the purchasers of other countries into a position of almost total dependence. Greece joined the buying pool in April 1917, Portugal and Belgium at a later date, and eventually Norway, Sweden, Holland, Iceland, and Switzerland came to rely heavily on the Wheat Executive of the Allies for supplies of wheat and flour.

Centralized purchasing on the part of the Allies was projected into overseas export markets by the establishment of agencies to secure wheat for the commission. In the United States the Wheat Export Company, a buying and exporting agency, was incorporated to secure wheat for the Wheat Executive, and the Wheat Export Company of Canada was incorporated under Dominion charter for the same purpose. These companies replaced the regular exporters in the respective countries. For a number of months, however, the regular grain markets remained open in Canada and the United States and the Wheat Export companies purchased in cash and futures markets alike as ordinary buyers. It is clear that while the markets remained formally unchanged, their structure was fundamentally altered by the predominance in each of them of the single overseas buyer with unprecedented resources at its disposal. It was only a matter of time until formal alteration was made to accord with realities.

During the winter of 1916–17 the British government made an attempt to negotiate the purchase of wheat outside the newly established purchasing agency. In February 1917, an offer was made to Hon. George Foster, minister of trade and commerce for Canada, for the purchase of the entire Canadian crop at $1.30 per bushel for No. 1 Northern in store at Fort William and other grades in proportion. The Canadian Council of Agriculture advised the government that the offer was unsatisfactory, since the price had averaged more than that over the preceding six months, and it countered with a proposal to the government that the crop be offered at prices between a minimum of $1.50 and a maximum of $1.90, or a flat $1.70 per bushel. The British offer was repeated and no agreement was reached.

Circumstances sufficiently disruptive to induce the formal alteration of the open market system of trading in the Winnipeg Grain Exchange occurred for the first time in the spring of 1917. The crop of 1916 in the United States was small, and the Canadian crop, although fairly large,[26] was badly rusted and of poor quality. Much of it proved on delivery and inspection to be below contract grades, that is, below those grades deliverable at the seller's option on a futures contract.[27] The respective Wheat Export companies in the United States and Canada, acting as purchasing agencies for the British Royal Commission on Wheat Supplies, bought wheat and wheat futures heavily throughout the winter, the latter purchases being made without speculative intent but rather to assure the necessary supplies of wheat. By the spring of 1917 these agencies were in possession of great quantities of May and July wheat, that is, they had negotiated contracts to secure delivery of substantial quantities of wheat of any one of the contract grades during the months of May and July.

It became increasingly clear that the available supplies of wheat of contract quality were inadequate to meet the commitments held in good faith by the Allied purchasing agencies. An unpremeditated but nonetheless effective corner had been created in May wheat in the Winnipeg and Chicago markets. Although the purchase of futures by the purchasing agencies had, in effect, comprised hedging rather than speculative transactions, these agencies desired to obtain wheat of satisfactory milling quality and were by no means willing to waive their contractual rights by accepting grain of quality lower than the contract grades. Near panic developed in the Winnipeg market by April as "the shorts attempted to cover." During the month of April, May wheat rose in Winnipeg from $1.90 to over $3.00 per bushel.[28]

Faced with unmistakable proof that the futures market as constituted was inadequate to the circumstance of the day, and in order to avoid its complete collapse, the Council of the Winnipeg Grain Exchange made emergency arrangements on its own authority and requested intervention by the Dominion government for the longer run.[29] On 28 April 1917, the council forbade trading in futures for speculative purposes and on 3 May the May and July futures were withdrawn from trading entirely. The Dominion government negotiated with the Wheat Export Company for a settlement of the impossible position of the short sellers of futures and the British purchasing agency accepted noncontract grades at a discount.

The Dominion government quickly made plans for the establishment of adequate control over the movement of Canadian grain, and the open market system of trading in the Winnipeg Grain Exchange came to an end for the duration of governmental control. On 11 June 1917, an Order in Council established the Board of Grain Supervisors, an agency of the federal government, and endowed it with monopoly control over Canadian wheat. The purposes of the board, as expressed in the Order in Council, were to control the distribution of Canadian grain as between domestic requirements and the Allied purchasing agencies, and to regulate domestic distribution "in such manner and under such conditions as will prevent to the utmost possible extent any undue inflation or depreciation of values by speculation, by the hoarding of grain supplies, or by any other means."[30] The board's principal powers were to acquire Canadian grain; to fix prices for it which would be uniform throughout the country with due regard for position, costs of transportation, quality, and grade; and to resell it to domestic millers and to Allied purchasing agencies. The board handled no grains other than wheat because the purchasing agencies would not guarantee to take them at fixed prices.

The board handled the remainder of the 1916 Canadian wheat crop and the crops of 1917 and 1918. The prices which it established were $2.40 per bushel, basis No. 1 Northern, Fort William, for the portion of the 1916 crop which remained unsold at the time it commenced operations, and, on the same basis, $2.21 for the 1917 crop and $2.24 for the 1918 crop. An order of the board terminated trading in wheat futures in the Winnipeg Grain Exchange starting 1 September 1917. This order remained in effect until 21 July 1919.

It may be noted in passing that governmental control replaced the open market system in the United States as well as in Canada in the summer of 1917.[31] The United States Food Administration was established on 10 August 1917, and four days later the Food Administration Grain Corporation was created with power to buy wheat to support or guarantee a "fair price" to be set by a committee appointed by the president of the United States. The corporation operated for the 1917 and 1918 crops, buying heavily in the autumn months to maintain the guaranteed price and selling its stocks throughout the remaining months of each year. At the end of June 1919, the Food Administration Grain Corporation was dissolved, and replaced by the United States

Grain Corporation,[32] which stood by to guarantee a floor price for wheat as had its predecessor. The basic guaranteed price for wheat in the United States throughout the three crop years was $2.20 per bushel. For the 1919–20 crop year the guarantee was largely inoperative due to the fact that market prices ordinarily ranged well above it.

The armistice of 11 November 1918, came at a time when the new crop year was well started. There was no question but that the Board of Grain Supervisors should continue to market Canadian wheat for the balance of the crop year. The policy to be pursued for succeeding years, however, remained to be decided. Joint Allied purchasing disappeared shortly after the armistice although governmental procurement and distribution of grain in most of the countries of western Europe persisted. There were influential groups in Canada actively interested in the restoration of the pre-1917 system of open market trading on the Winnipeg Grain Exchange. In general terms it was the view of the Dominion government that, with the war now over, prewar principles and practices should be restored to effectiveness with a minimum of delay, and that the Canadian economy should return to "normal" as quickly as possible. There appeared considerable likelihood that the government would withdraw from the grain business and permit the "private trade" to operate as before.

The government permitted the reopening of futures trading on the Winnipeg Exchange on 21 July 1919, but the erratic speculative activity which followed indicated that the action was premature to say the least. Within the few days during which the futures market remained opened, the price of October wheat advanced from $2.24 1/2 to $2.45 1/2.[33] By Order in Council of 31 July the Dominion government established the Canadian Wheat Board with the exclusive responsibility of handling and marketing the 1919 crop along with any part of the 1918 crop which had not been delivered to the Board of Grain Supervisors by 15 August 1919. In August, the Supreme Economic Council, organized by the Paris Peace Conference, restored the Royal Commission on Wheat Supplies as the joint purchasing agency for Great Britain, France, and Italy. The purchase and distribution of wheat continued on a national basis in the other countries of northwestern Europe.

The constitution of the new Canadian Wheat Board is described in the records of the United Grain Growers as "almost identical with that submitted by the Canadian Council of Agriculture."[34] The plan was worked out by the United Grain Growers Limited and the Saskatchewan Co-operative Elevator Company and was submitted to the Dominion government on acceptance by the council.[35] The original resolution of the council had called for the establishment of a board "similar to the U.S. Grain Corporation with like power and functions and with the financial accommodation adequate to its operations."[36] The constitution as finally drafted and submitted to the government, however, must have departed from the resolution, for the resultant Canadian Wheat Board differed markedly in function from the United States Grain Corporation. The latter, as noted above, was purely a minimum-price support board and bought wheat only when necessary to that purpose. The Canadian Wheat Board was given a monopoly in the sale of the Canadian crop both in domestic and foreign markets and, in the latter markets, exclusive control of the sale of flour as well as wheat. It differed from its Canadian predecessor, however, in that it did not buy and sell at fixed prices but rather received all Canadian wheat at a fixed advance or initial payment and distributed the additional funds secured from its total sales in the form of interim and final payments. The total proceeds, grade by grade, were thus "pooled" as at Fort William[37] regardless of the actual proceeds of any individual consignment or of the time of delivery. This feature of the plan which, according to the board, "resembled very closely that which was in existence in Australia,"[38] was of the utmost significance in its influence on agricultural agitation and organization during the 1920s.

The initial payment made by the board was $2.15 per bushel, basis No. 1 Northern in store at Fort William. Along with this payment went participation certificates which entitled the seller of the wheat to a proportionate share in the total net proceeds of the crop. The initial payment was slightly below the price guaranteed to farmers in the United States ($2.25 per bushel) and farther still below the maximum to which prices had risen in the brief July interval of open market trading on the Winnipeg Grain Exchange. Since they had no experience in the disposal of their crop on the basis of partial payment, and no certainty about the additional payment to be secured, the western growers were far from unanimously favourable to the new marketing arrangement. Some would have preferred to dispose of their grain at a higher fixed and final price, as they had been able to do under the Board of Grain Supervisors, some urged the adoption of the United States system of a guaranteed floor price at a higher level and without pooling, and many would have been willing to take their chances with the open market. Participation certificates were poorly regarded and were in many cases disposed of throughout the year for trifling sums. In May 1920, the board announced that the certificates would be redeemed for not less than 40 cents per bushel. An interim payment of 30 cents per bushel on 15 July and a final payment of 18 cents on 30 October 1920, brought the total payment for the compulsory government pool—for that, in effect, was what it was—to $2.63 per bushel, basis No. 1 Northern, Fort William.

Late in the session of 1920 the Dominion government passed an enabling act to permit continuance of the Wheat Board for the crop of 1920 should it be found necessary. Resumption of futures trading in the United States grain exchanges on 15 July 1920, and the concurrent relaxation of centralized buying, however, provided the government with the opportunity to announce that the operations of the Wheat Board would not be continued for the 1920 crop. The Wheat Board, in its report for the crop year 1919-20, pointed out that since it had been designedly a one-year board, it had used the facilities of the private grain trade as far as possible in order that "the trade would be better able to resume the handling of the wheat at the expiration of the controlled period."[39] By the early autumn of 1920 the "controlled period" was at an end.

Notes

1. *Statutes of Canada,* 36 Vic., c. 49 (1873).
2. Ibid., 48-49 Vic., c. 66 (1885); 52 Vic., c. 16 (1889); 54-55 Vic., c. 48 (1891); and 62-63 Vic., c. 25 (1899).
3. See V.C. Fowke, *Canadian Agricultural Policy* (Toronto, 1946), 243.
4. Commissions were appointed in 1899, 1906, 1923, 1931, and 1936. An additional commission was appointed by the federal government in 1921 but its investigations were halted by an injunction sought and secured by the United Grain Growers Limited and upheld by the Supreme Court of Canada. For the citation of the reports of these commissions seriatim see V.C. Fowke, "Royal Commissions and Canadian Agricultural Policy," *Canadian Journal of Economics and Political Science,* Vol. XIV, No. 2, May 1948, 165 n.
5. For a comparison with the interwar commissions, see Chap. x, 188 ff.
6. Canada, *Sessional Papers,* 1900, No. 81a, 10.
7. *Statutes of Canada,* 63-64 Vic., c. 39 (1900).
8. C.C. Castle, one of the farmer members of the commission of 1899, was appointed first warehouse commissioner.

9. See H.S. Patton, *Grain Growers' Coöperation in Western Canada* (Cambridge, Mass., 1928), 34–35.

10. See Chapter VIII, 136–38.

11. From Order in Council appointing the royal commission, 26 July 1906 (*Report of the Royal Commission on the Grain Trade of Canada, 1906*, Canada, *Sessional Papers*, 1908, No. 59, 3). That the investigation was meant to be thorough is indicated by the power extended to the commission "to visit the grain growers, the elevators all over the wheat-growing region, the methods of handling the grain at the various stations, farmers' elevators, as well as companies' elevators, the distribution of cars, methods of the grain dealers in Winnipeg, Toronto and Montreal, and the system of government inspection and collection of fees, selection of grades and the methods of handling the grain at Fort William and Port Arthur, at the lake ports, at Montreal, St. John and Halifax, and also the conditions existing as to the manner of handling the grain upon its arrival in England" (ibid.). The commission conducted its investigations in western and eastern Canada, in the United States, and at a dozen centres in the British Isles.

12. Ibid., 14.

13. Ibid., Appendix E, 39.

14. See *Report of the Royal Grain Inquiry Commission, 1925* (Ottawa, 1925), 76.

15. As cited in Patton, *Grain Growers' Coöperation in Western Canada*, 135 n.

16. The Canadian Council of Agriculture was formed in February 1910. D.W. McCuaig, president of the Manitoba Grain Growers' Association, was its first president.

17. Other demands made by the delegation were for tariff reductions, increased British preference, reciprocity with the United States, completion and operation of the Hudson's Bay Railway and its terminals by the government, the establishment of a chilled-meat industry, federal cooperation legislation, etc.

18. In outlining the intentions of the government in relation to the section of the grain bill which provided for government operation of terminal elevators, Hon. Mr. Foster said: " . . . we do not intend to undertake the financial or experimental responsibility of taking the whole terminal elevator system under government operation for the present, but we wish to give to the people of the West a choice between the terminal elevators that are run by corporations or individuals and those that are run by the government either as owners or lessees." Canada, *House of Commons Debates*, 28 Dec. 1912, as cited in Patton, *Grain Growers' Coöperation in Western Canada*, 145.

19. For an analysis of the reasoning on which the construction of the interior terminal elevators was urged and accomplished see R. Magill, *Grain Inspection in Canada* (Ottawa, 1914), 54–58. For an analysis of the extent to which these elevators achieved their purposes on the basis of their first decade of operation see *Report of the Royal Grain Inquiry Commission, 1925* (Ottawa, 1925), 42–43.

20. United Grain Growers Limited, *The Grain Growers Record, 1906 to 1943* (Winnipeg, 1944), 15–16.

21. It cannot be inferred from this that there was general approval, among the membership of these companies, of the practice of mixing. "Hon. J.A. Maharg, then president of the Saskatchewan Grain Growers' Association, and a director of the Saskatchewan Co-operative, of which company he is now president, said that the directorate of his company, with perhaps one or two exceptions, were individually opposed to the practice of mixing, but because the practice had become prevalent, the company found that they had to go into it to make money to compete with their competitors, and they were forced into it. His personal view was that mixing was done by the farmer on the farm, it was done in the country elevator, it was done by all who handled wheat, and he believed Canadian wheat to be mixed in the United States; and, therefore, since it could not be stopped, mixing in the private elevators at the head of the lakes should not be stopped." *Report of the Royal Grain Inquiry Commission, 1925*, 105. For an extended discussion of the mixing problem see ibid., 75–109.

22. This attitude was in sharp contrast to the approach of the Dominion government to the

Second World War; substantial measures of governmental control were drafted before the fall of 1939 in anticipation of the war, and other restrictive measures were matured and made effective month by month as the war progressed.

23. The British Royal Commission on Wheat Supplies stated that bread was "the only diet which sufficed in isolation and was therefore, indispensable" (as cited in Mitchell W. Sharp, "Allied Wheat Buying in Relationship to Canadian Marketing Policy, 1914–18," *Canadian Journal of Economics and Political Science*, Vol. VI, No. 3, Aug. 1940, 372).

24. A single exception to the ordinary open market procurement of wheat supplies by the Allies in the first two years of the war was a secret joint purchase effected by the governments of the United Kingdom, France, and Italy in the winter of 1915–16. Ibid., 374.

25. The average yield of wheat per acre in the prairie provinces in 1915 was 24 bushels, approximately 50 percent above the long-time average, and a figure unequalled in western Canadian crop experience until 1952, when the average yield in the prairie provinces was 26.3 bushels per acre. See W. Sanford Evans Statistical Service, *Canadian Grain Trade Year Book* (Winnipeg, annually).

26. At 262.8 million bushels the Canadian wheat crop of 1916 was above the ten-year average, 1911–20, of 238.4 million bushels. Ibid., 1920–1, 4.

27. Contract grades of wheat in Canada at that time were No. 1 Hard, and Nos. 1, 2, and 3 Northern.

28. From 1 April to 3 May 1917. Sharp, "Allied Wheat Buying," 381.

29. Ibid., 381–82.

30. As cited in *Report of the Royal Grain Inquiry Commission, 1938* (Ottawa, 1938), 31. Dr. Robert Magill, chairman of the Saskatchewan Elevator Commission of 1910 and first chief commissioner of the Board of Grain Commissioners under the Canada Grain Act of 1912, was appointed chairman of the Board of Grain Supervisors.

31. For a discussion of the wartime control of wheat in the United States see Frank M. Surface, *The Grain Trade during the World War* (New York, 1928); and Surface, *The Stabilization of the Price of Wheat during the War and Its Effect upon the Returns to the Producer* (Washington: United States Grain Corporation, 1925).

32. The United States Grain Corporation came to an end 31 May 1920. It purchased over 138 million bushels of the 1919 crop in the course of its stabilization activities. See Surface, *The Stabilization of the Price of Wheat*, 18, 24.

33. United Grain Growers Limited, *The Grain Growers Record, 1906 to 1943*, 25.

34. Ibid., 25.

35. Joseph C. Mills, "A Study of the Canadian Council of Agriculture," unpublished M.A. thesis, University of Manitoba, 1949, 125.

36. Resolution of the Canadian Council of Agriculture, 9 July 1919. The resolution contained the statement that: "The Canadian Council of Agriculture is strongly opposed to the opening of the Canadian markets for unrestricted trading in wheat, and would reiterate its recommendations of August 19, last year [1918], that the Government of Canada create, without delay, a body similar to the U.S. Grain Corporation with like power and functions and with the financial accommodation adequate to its operations." As cited in Mills, "A Study of the Canadian Council of Agriculture."

37. Freight from the local point to Fort William was deducted from the initial payment and was accordingly not pooled.

38. The pooling idea was new to the Canadian West and had only recently been introduced for trial in Australia. The board reported (*Report of the Canadian Wheat Board, Season 1920* [Ottawa: King's Printer, 1921], 6):

In the first place, the board in adopting the plan of operation outlined in the Government's instructions, had to blaze a new trail. There was no precedent to follow. While a wheat 'pool' was being tried in Australia, its success had not been established, and it seemed to be regarded with more or less disfavour by some important sections of that country. In North America nothing of the kind had even been attempted. Some of the ablest men in the North American grain trade considered the plan as too 'communistic,' and doomed to failure. This impression was not confined to grain trade men alone, but was quite prevalent among our bankers and in other business circles. Large sections of the rural communities in the various provinces too, protested, by resolution or delegation, against the creation of the board, and as an alternative seemed bent upon having the Government either purchase the crop outright at a fixed price, or establish an organization similar to the United States Grain Corporation.

In the rural districts along the international boundary, particularly in southern Manitoba and southeastern Saskatchewan, the cry during the autumn months of 1919 was for an open market ...

39. Ibid., 5.

Confrontation in Retrospect

DAVID J. BERCUSON

Reprinted from David J. Bercuson, *Confrontation at Winnipeg: Labour, Industrial Relations, and the General Strike* (Montreal and Toronto: McGill-Queen's University Press, 1974), 176–195, by permission of the publisher.

The Winnipeg general strike was one of the most complete withdrawals of labour power ever to occur in North America and dealt a mighty blow at one of trade unionism's strongest bastions. The strike, from the labour viewpoint, was a complete failure in the short run and no amount of poststrike rhetoric could cover up this fact. As international organizer Fred Varley observed in early June 1919: "There never was in history a strike in which the workers answered the call so spontaneously, and there never was a strike in which the workers were so badly trimmed."[1]

After eight weeks of struggle with the owners and operators of the contract shops, the metal workers won nothing more than a reduction in the work week from fifty-five to fifty hours at the same rate of pay. Deacon, the Barretts, and Warren had signed a declaration, published on 16 June, undertaking to recognize individual craft unions in their plants; but they never lived up to the pronouncement. They knew they had beaten the union and the withering away of both machinists Lodge 457 and the Metal Trades Council[2] in the months following the strike was mute evidence of their total victory. They fought the metal unions for thirteen years and in the end smashed their power. In November 1919, T.R. Deacon capped this success by introducing a works council plan into his shop which closely followed a scheme in use by the International Harvester Company. These councils had power to make recommendations concerning matters of interest to employees but no power to take effective action—they were glorified advisory boards, nothing more.[3]

Building trades workers were more fortunate; their dispute was never as bitter as the struggles in the contract shops and their past relations with employers had been much more amiable. In large measure, wages paid in this industry reflected the state of construction in the city and the summer of 1919 was no exception. After the general strike was over the Builders Exchange entered into negotiations with individual unions and by the end of August signed agreements with a number of them which, in every case but one, set new rates retroactive to 1 July higher than those offered prior to the strike. The same builders who had claimed vehemently in May that they would like to meet the demands of their workers but could not pay a penny more than they were offering, paid more than a few additional pennies. In May the construction industry was in the same depressed condition it had been in throughout the war years, but by the end of August construction was booming in Winnipeg and the demand for skilled tradesmen was high. The building trades unions went on strike on 1 May because they could not wrest substantial wage increases from their employers and the demand for a living wage, based on this dispute, turned into a major rallying point. But in late summer they were given increases that in most cases amounted to 15 cents per hour. The state of the economy was responsible—the general strike itself played no role in their good fortune.

The building trades was the only bright spot in an otherwise gloomy picture. Varley commented that the only thing to do was "kneel in reverence before the employers"[4] and that was precisely what many did. Prospective applicants for positions in the city's civil service were forced to sign an oath promising not to join a union connected with other labour bodies and not to participate in sympathetic strikes.[5] General Ketchen noted on the last day of the strike that approximately three thousand veterans had found jobs while the walkout was in progress and there was no reason to believe any would be dismissed so that strikers could be rehired.[6] The way was eventually cleared for the reemployment of postal workers though the process was not completed for over a year and even then the men were forced to reapply and start at the bottom.[7] Railway workers who had answered the general strike call were almost all taken back but lost their seniority and as late as 1945 were engaged in a fight to regain their pension rights.

The general strike drained much of the vigour from the city's unions. Winnipeg was almost completely free of work stoppages in the eighteen months following the general strike and there were only two walkouts of any significance.[8] This was the least in many years and shows graphically that workers had had their fill of strikes. A labour force that had expended every possible effort to win a six-week general strike but had been totally defeated was certain to be more docile in the months and years ahead; the workers were simply too exhausted mentally and economically to offer much industrial resistance. The unions' vitality was also sapped as a result of the OBU secessionist movement. Efforts to line up organized labour in the city behind the OBU reached a climax when the Trades Council voted to affiliate with the new union on 29 July.[9]

Thus the battle which many had pinned their hopes on, the struggle which would culminate in better wages, union recognition, and management's acknowledgement that workers were a power to be dealt with, had ended in total failure. The union leaders who led the Trades Council to the brink in early May, many believing there would be no need for a strike because the employers would surely back down, were proven wrong. They made several grave miscalculations and in many cases were so convinced of the righteousness of their cause that logical and concise thinking and planning were notably absent. Many workers knew only that the hour for confrontation had finally come and religiously believed in their own ultimate victory.

The strikers were not revolutionaries and did not seek the violent overthrow of the existing social and political order. The leaders of the city's labour movement did not attempt to solve their problems by wiping out the opposing class, but they did want to assert a comparable authority. What they did not see in their enthusiasm, however, was that a general strike must create great social chaos and by itself brings society crashing down unless special measures are taken. It is an admirable weapon for revolutionaries but those who do not want social collapse must work to undermine its effectiveness. This is what the Citizens' Committee tried to do but were not nearly as effective as the General and Central Strike committees. The workers themselves became the chief strikebreakers when they accepted a responsibility to keep society functioning at the very beginning of the walkout. They undermined the effectiveness of the strike, prolonged it, and contributed immeasurably to their own defeat. All this was done because they were not revolutionaries and had made the grave mistake of assuming that the general strike was a viable and effective industrial weapon. It was not an industrial weapon but a political one because workers' families needed milk as much as the sons and daughters of the employers.

Once the workers began to assume a partial administrative responsibility for the maintenance of water, heat, light, power, and food distribution, their position in society was radically altered and their power greatly enhanced. They were now as important to the everyday directing of society as was capital and they began to rival capital's power to exert leverage on the government. They became directly involved in the operation of essential services, though their authority was exercised in cooperation with civic officials and, in certain cases, owners and managers. They never intended to create a revolutionary situation but were trapped into appearing to be doing so by their own inexperience and lack of planning. Permit cards read "by authority of strike committee" but should also have mentioned the municipal administration and the managers. This would have been more accurate and would have undermined charges that the strike committee had taken control of municipal government.

By carrying on in the manner that they did, labour appeared to be assuming governmental authority and was not equipped or prepared to cope with the political or military implications of this new situation. By launching a general strike the workers had embarked on a radical course but were not radical enough to escape the consequences of their action. They were providing governments with an obvious excuse to intervene and were unable or unwilling to meet the challenges of the intervention. Once the unions had decided to shut down the entire city and keep it shut until they had won, they ran directly into the power of all three levels of government and had to choose to either "get guns" or give in. All their life experiences would not allow them to take the former course; thus the latter was forced on them. When the federal government decided to involve itself in countering a revolution which never existed the workers were lost. Their only choice was between unacceptable compromise, complete defeat, or direct, perhaps armed, resistance.

The Winnipeg general strike was not a revolution and was never planned to be one. It did, however, raise basic questions concerning the nature and composition of "constituted authority" as well as what qualifies as a *bona fide* challenge to that authority. There can be no doubt that the strikers intended to enhance their own position at the expense of the normal political and economic power of capital. In using as blunt an instrument as a general strike, however, they also ran the risk of challenging the *de facto* power of at least one level of government. General strikes are intended to bring the normal functions and activities of society to a standstill and they therefore transfer to the workers part of the option of what will continue to operate and what will not—this is inevitable if anarchy is to be avoided. To this degree the existing order is undermined, whether by accident or design and whether on a purely local level or a more national one. The rapid increase of labour's power in Winnipeg was a shock to the cosy arrangements and alliances that had existed for at least four decades. This threat to the status quo was compounded by the belief in some quarters that the workers were embarked on a campaign to supplant the municipal and even the provincial and national governments. The charge was not true but reflected the unions' rapid rise to new positions of power. Thus, the political implications of a general strike were far more widespread and potentially serious than those of more ordinary industrial disputes, a fact the workers failed to realize.

The roots of the general strike are intricately intertwined with the social and industrial development of the city and bitter animosities between labour and management can easily be discerned as early as 1906. The disputes of that year which wracked the contract shops and street railway were marked by the use of professional strikebreakers, military aid to the civil power, and the injunction. In both episodes labour and management were willing, possibly eager, to test out the limits of their own power; industrial development was still at an early stage in the city and both sides were probably attempting to set precedents for the future. The street railway dispute was a standoff and the antagonists fought each other constantly through the succeeding years. This was probably beneficial, since each learned to respect the strength of the other. But the contract shops dispute was a disaster for the union and the experience created hatred and enmity for years to come. Here there was no respect, only scorn and fear.

The contract shop employers were of that special breed of self-made men who tended to be intolerant towards the members of the classes from which they themselves had risen. To a man like Deacon the union was merely another obstacle to overcome in any way possible if success was to be achieved. Such a man was loath to accept what he would have called "dictation by his employees" and the Barrett brothers, who had built upon the early successes of their father, were of the same stripe. They had, after all, declared at one point that they would never allow a union to tell them what to do. These men were not apt to forget that they had been strong enough to defeat the union in 1906 and would not give way easily in the future.

The unions also did not forget, but their memories were bitter ones, of defeat aided by court injunction and long legal battles. These workers were also strong-minded men, many experienced in the socialist politics and industrial struggles of their native Great Britain and they came back again and again to challenge the power of their employers. Each time they did so defeat became less acceptable and the stakes were raised on both sides. When the machinists realized they could not win on their own in 1917, they combined with other metal workers in the Metal Trades Council and when that failed in 1918 they called upon all the unions in the city to back them. They successfully convinced the majority of Winnipeg's trade union members and many nonunion workers as well that general principles were involved and that the strike was a crusade for collective bargaining in all industries.

Winnipeg was Canada's largest and most important rail centre. Key to three transcontinental railroad systems, the city was home to sprawling marshalling yards and repair shops. By the beginning of the First World War the men who worked in these yards and shops were highly organized and their unions were among the most powerful in Canada. These same unions, however, could not make a dent in the city's independent contract shops—a situation they found unacceptable. They were powerful against the largest railroads in Canada but impotent when challenging three relatively small establishments. This pushed them in their unceasing efforts to organize the contract shops and to obtain the same wages and working conditions enjoyed in the railway shops. Power and prestige were just as important as economic gain.

The situation in the building trades was different because relations in this industry were never marked by the rancour and bitterness evident in the metal trades. The dispute in the spring of 1919 was almost solely an economic one, even though in the context of a general unrest both sides attempted to make of it a holy crusade. The Builders Exchange were parroting the contract shop owners when they declared in late

127

April that they would have nothing more to do with the Building Trades Council. This was a tactic that further clouded the main issue but was only to a small degree motivated by ideological considerations. Though complicated by an atmosphere of mistrust, the dispute was initially caused by the rising cost of living, the small pay increases earned by construction workers during the war, and the inability of the employers to grant wages as high as those demanded by the unions. Building trades workers were not given substantial wage increases during the war largely because their employers were starving for business. At first there was a great number of tradesmen unemployed and the unions were unable to press their demands for higher pay. Later, when many construction workers had joined the army and the unions were in a better position to put pressure on their employers, the Norris government stepped in to stabilize conditions in the trade and the industry was upset by only one strike of any real consequence in the entire wartime period. When the unions approached the Builders Exchange in the spring of 1919 they were impatient. There was no war now to blame the situation on and they were determined to improve their position in relation to prices. Their employers, however, who were probably unable to pay the new wage scales set by the unions, refused to meet the demands, thus creating militancy in an industry noted for the lack of it.

When the call for a general strike was issued every union but one willingly answered and, more significantly, many thousands of nonunion workers responded as well. The war placed great strains on the social fabric by aggravating old problems, creating new ones, and setting the stage for the five months of uncertainty and unrest which immediately preceded the general strike. Wartime inflation, scandals, the government's treatment of large numbers of new Canadians, and its tight controls on the use of foreign languages were compounded by the conscription crisis and the government's attempt to ban the use of strikes and lockouts. The war created conditions favourable to the rapid growth of the trade union movement and that expansion itself created militancy as a by-product.

The government of Prime Minister Robert Laird Borden did almost nothing to aid the growth of Canadian unions during the war. The most significant and openly favourable action, its informal sanction of the creation of Division 4 and the extension of the McAdoo Award to Canada, came late in the war. For the most part unions in Canada grew through immense organizing efforts conducted among workers growing more and more dissatisfied with their lot. In order to attract new members the unions had to demonstrate they could offer tangible gains in return for union dues, and they had to show prospective members as well as workers already in the fold that they were respected by bosses and governments. To make tangible gains they had to demand more and be unwilling to settle for less. These conditions create militancy. Those who are more militant are less willing to compromise because in many cases they deeply believe in the virtue and justice of their own cause. Thus power and prestige became interrelated with a crusading, evangelistic spirit.

The events of the summer and fall of 1918 played a significant role in the creation of an atmosphere conducive to a general strike. The success of the sympathetic strike in May, combined with the victory of the western postal workers in August and the failure of the contract shops' strike, gave radical union leaders a powerful and convincing argument. Though moderates such as McBride, Robinson, and Winning were always in the majority on the Trades Council it was radicals such as Russell and Johns who called the shots. They could and did point to the 1918 disputes to prove their contention that militancy paid off and the lack of it was bound to be disastrous. They impressed the moderate majority with the argument that extraordinary times demanded extraordinary actions, including the organization of "industrial" unions and the use of the general strike. Russell and his followers challenged the moderates to accept their responsibility as union leaders and sanction more radical action. The power and persuasiveness of the radicals grew in direct proportion to the growth of war-related problems and the demonstrated inability or unwillingness of governments to cope with them. The radicals tended to present their arguments in black and white terms and combined deep and thoughtful analysis with simplistic solutions. One was either for them or against them. They carried the fight to the moderates and forced them to choose.

These radical leaders were well known, respected, and liked. So they successfully convinced the moderate majority that the One Big Union type of organization and the general strike were logical and necessary answers to the workers' problems. Many moderates were swept up in the growing enthusiasm for radical solutions with little or no thought to the consequences of such action. They began to look upon the general strike as merely another tool to be used in industrial disputes, a larger strike, nothing more. In the year prior to May 1919 the call for a general strike was heard with increasing frequency, but not a single page of the *Western Labor News* or *The Voice* was devoted to a discussion of its social and political ramifications. Some leaders may have believed they would never have to resort to the use of the general strike, that the very threat would suffice, while others thought the power of the workers combined with the righteousness of their cause would assure quick, easy, and relatively painless victory. Why should one trade have to endure a long, costly struggle when the massive, combined power of every union member in the city could quickly win a dispute with little risk to the workers? The victory of the 1918 sympathetic strike was, in reality, disastrous in the long run.

There was much on the line during the 1919 general strike—the high stakes help account for the length of the affair and the tactics used on both sides. In downing their tools on the morning of 15 May, the unions in Winnipeg laid their power and prestige on the line—this was the long-awaited confrontation. There was now no higher level of escalation, all the bets were on the table, nothing held in reserve. The idea that the continuous application of greater power was bound to result in success was to receive its greatest test. Once they had gambled everything they must win or lose all. The thought that compromise on the main issues might still be a viable alternative was no more acceptable to them than to their employers. It no longer really mattered whether the aims were justifiable, the cause righteous; it was a matter of total victory or total defeat.

The employers and their allies were fully cognizant of this—they had never been willing to compromise and were always determined to smash the union. In the past they had used every weapon at their disposal and knew that if they were defeated by the general strike they would lose the last and most important battle. The contract shop owners were the leaders in this but others, members of the Citizens' Committee, closed ranks behind them in a show of solidarity calculated to match that of the unions. If the strike could be defeated the power of the unions would suffer a heavy and perhaps mortal blow. For some the fear of revolution and the spirit of crusade was undoubtedly genuine, but for the most part the belief that a union victory would set society on its head and place workers in a position where they would sit as equals with management at the bargaining table spurred them on. This thought was intolerable to the leaders of the business community.

Governments also had a great deal at stake in the general strike. Some public officials, panicked by the fear of Bolshevism and the Russian revolution, genuinely believed they were meeting a challenge to constitutional authority. The prime minister was content to listen to the explanations and follow the advice of Meighen and Robertson, but appears to have had little to do with their conduct. The minister of the interior and the minister of labour were at least as interested in preserving the status quo in labour-management relations as they were in countering a revolution. They wanted to nip the One Big Union movement in the bud, shore up the position of the international unions, and ensure the survival of craft unionism. They were willing to see the strike ended peacefully as long as there was no recognition of the Metal Trades Council, but if this could not be accomplished then the strike must be decisively crushed.

The advocates of the One Big Union took up the government's challenge and adopted the position that once the strike had been identified with the OBU it must be won. Johns was perfectly aware of what he was writing when he told Midgley that they could not afford to let the strike be lost. There was precious little reason for W.A. Pritchard's presence in the city other than as an observer for the Central Committee appointed by the Western Labor Conference. The strike was certainly not an OBU effort. The OBU was not founded until after the strike had started and the various provincial committees responsible for organization which were struck in March 1919 took no part in any of the decisions to call the strike. There can be no doubt, however, that the OBU loomed in the minds of many men—strikers and their opponents—and was made an issue before the strike was over.

Two groups played key roles in events leading to the strike and were of crucial importance after 15 May. The returned soldiers, pro-strike and loyalist, were determined to collect what they thought was due them from society, and the new Canadians undoubtedly believed they would gain a new human dignity through victory. The impact of the veterans is relatively easy to determine, for they were loud in proclaiming their sympathies and the reasons for them. But the eastern Europeans stuck to their traditional silence and, though blamed as the driving force behind the strike, played a relatively passive role.

There were probably two basic desires burning inside most veterans when they returned to Canada in late 1918 and 1919—the wish for peace in their own lives and the determination to avoid further wars. Veterans voiced their aspirations by demanding that society make good on its promises of a better postwar world and some made ready to do battle with those individuals they believed were threatening the civilization just saved from the Kaiser. A returned soldier, therefore, decided to join the strikers or the Citizens' Committee, depending on which desire was strongest and how he wished to see it fulfilled. Those who tended to sympathize with the Citizens' Committee were probably of more well-to-do families, while those who supported the strikers were former workers or trade union members. They were all men of action—they had just finished proving this—and saw little sense in "sitting tight and doing nothing."

The part played by new Canadians remains a matter of some mystery. At the time of the strike and for a short period afterwards every event that smacked of radicalism was blamed on enemy aliens, who were usually described as anarchists and Bolsheviks capable of the most sinister deeds. Both anti- and pro-strike veterans paraded under banners damning the alien enemy. Nevertheless, a careful study of the key names in the Winnipeg Trades Council from 1913 to 1920 reveals only three men with non-British or Canadian names—Harry Veitch, Abraham Heaps, and Sam Blumenberg. The last man was a figure of minor importance, whereas both Veitch and Heaps were born in Britain. One may also look in vain for articles or letters submitted to Anglo-Saxon trade union newspapers by eastern Europeans; they simply did not get involved in the political or trade union activities of British and Canadian workers, though they often supported groups of their own.

Before August 1914, new Canadians suffered the trials and tribulations undergone by most immigrants in a new land; but after the outbreak of war many also became "illegal" and were forced to register and carry cards proclaiming them to be "enemy aliens." Some were wrenched from their houses and sent to detention camps in northern Ontario. With the passage of the Wartime Elections Act in the summer of 1917 they lost their political rights, and when veterans began to return to Canada in increasing numbers many were physically assaulted and dismissed from their jobs. By the spring of 1919 they, too, were ready to participate in the crusade to build a new society, and many of the approximately 30,000 to 35,000 workers who joined the strike must have come from this group.

The opponents of the strike had compelling reasons to smash it with all the powers at their command. The cooperation of all three levels of government with the Citizens' Committee was the key factor determining the strike's outcome. When Meighen and Robertson laid the prestige of the federal government on the line, the outcome could no longer be doubted; the strikers' cause was lost. They worked closely with Norris, Gray, and the Citizens' Committee to put every obstacle in the path of the strikers and force them into impossible situations. It is hard to judge the degree of collusion but its presence is undeniable; the governments identified their interests with those of the employers and sided with them almost from the start.

There were five key steps which led to the final defeat of the general strike and the federal government was deeply involved in all of them. The dismissal of the regular police and their replacement by the specials put a large anti-strike, pro-Citizens' Committee force into the hands of municipal authorities. At the same time as this was taking place the federal government was quietly but quickly building up the militia and RNWMP forces at its disposal so that by 16 June Winnipeg was virtually an occupied city. This set the stage for Robertson's intervention in the proceedings of the mediation committee and the arrest of the radical strike leaders—two closely connected events. The minister of labour was anxious to have contract shop employers make concessions and probably thought their 16 June declaration was reasonable, but the Strike Committee was not given a chance to discuss these proposals because the arrests were carried out less than twenty-four hours after their publication. Robertson probably hoped a strike committee devoid of Russell, Johns, and their colleagues would be more pliable.

It is impossible to determine whether or not Russell or any other of the arrested men could have dissuaded the veterans from organizing a march on 21 June. What is clear, is that Winnipeg could not. After the arrests the Strike Committee drifted, stunned and leaderless, incapable of decisive action. Once the march had been broken on the day known to history as Bloody Saturday, the strike could no longer continue. It had become more than apparent that victory was an illusion and this loss of faith made the other discomforts of the six-week strike intolerable. The decision to return to work was an anticlimax.

The Winnipeg general strike was not an attempted revolution. There has never been a shred of evidence to prove that claim—the issue was manufactured from the start. Was it, however, fought for the purposes so often repeated by the Strike Committee and historians sympathetic to it: collective bargaining and the right to organize industrial unions? The evidence suggests that these issues may have been oversimplified.

One of the most persuasive arguments used by general strike advocates was that such action was necessary to win collective bargaining as a universal principle and put an end to attacks on the system by employers such as those who owned the contract shops. Many of the approximately twelve thousand trade unions members who struck on 15 May were already bargaining with their employers, and any man who worked in one of the city's railway repair shops was represented in negotiations with management by Division 4 (where collective bargaining had reached a highly sophisticated level of practice). Therefore, the strike was actually fought to win a particular type of collective bargaining in one particular industry and this very specific demand was turned into a call for legislation of collective bargaining on a provincewide basis. The strike leaders converted the walkout into a campaign to give union recognition and collective bargaining a status in law so that employees would no longer have to depend on the whims of their employers for decent wages and job security.

Industrial unionism had little or nothing to do with the strike. The bargaining system demanded by the contract shop workers was actually committee representation of the type used by the railway shop craft unions; the Metal Trades Council did not seek to form an industrial union. It is possible that industrial unionism in the contract shops was something to try for after the achievement of committee representation, but this was not emphasized by the strikers. Many historians have attempted to use the issue both ways but they cannot; either the Metal Trades Council was patterned after the OBU's proposed form of organization, as Robertson and Meighen charged, and was a type of nascent industrial union, or it was not—and the evidence points to the latter.

The Winnipeg general strike was not, however, fought merely to win collective bargaining. To the contrary, everything suggests it was a modern version of the Children's Crusade and was marked by the same lack of planning, religious zeal, and plethora of causes that characterized the original. The presence of religious figures such as Rev. William Ivens and J.S. Woodsworth, and the popularity of the Labor Church are only the most obvious manifestations of this. The whole manner in which workers answered the call, the unshakeable belief in ultimate victory, the lack of thorough planning, the pacifism which marked the appeals of the strike leaders are also evidence of the strike's character. Russell, Johns, and other dedicated socialists probably had no religious convictions at all but replaced Christianity with Marxism. But a crusade it was, and, like the originals, one with a distinct purpose.

The one element which united moderates and radicals in their thinking and planning was the desire to achieve control over their industrial lives. For too long the labour movement in Winnipeg had lived in a vacuum divorced from the centres of decision making. Workers were in the majority in the city but could not capture city council. Their representation in the provincial legislature was small and attempts to elect a federal member to Parliament in 1917 were singularly unsuccessful. Workers felt themselves cut off and treated like social outcasts. They meant to gain dignity and respect and were determined to break through the barriers that separated them from those who governed. The general strike was one battle in a long campaign to achieve that measure of power necessary to sit and be recognized as equals with employers and government. In some manner never fully defined, victory would give them that power, at one stroke, in a way that would never be challenged.

The Winnipeg general strike was a manifestation of the continuing class division that has marked the history of the city for over half a century. The events of May and June 1919, were preceded and followed by growing splits in society and were largely products of those divisions. The strike was the most traumatic of events which contributed to class memory and polarization, but it did not initiate these psychological attitudes. Class consciousness was a strong factor in Winnipeg prior to the strike, laid the foundation for labour's political successes of the 1920s, and was largely responsible for the continuing division of Winnipeg into those whose parents or grandparents were strikers, and those whose forebearers were members of the Citizens' Committee.

Early polarization developed in Winnipeg, stimulated by the same conditions which created division elsewhere—workers were those who received a wage, employers were those who paid it. Industrial workers in Winnipeg, however, felt a particularly close community of interest. They were the vanguard of the industrial working class on the prairies and often the vanguard of trade unionism as well. They lived in a closely defined geographic area and were isolated from the great centres of working-class power in Ontario and the United States. From the very beginning of the emergence of trade unionism in Winnipeg there were articulate critics who pointed out the horrors of the new industrial society and continually harped on the precariousness of life for workers. The worker could be killed on a job, displaced by unskilled immigrants who were willing to work for less, lose his job in winter, or see his small savings wiped out in one of the periodic economic fluctuations.

To combat these conditions workers turned increasingly to trade unionism. In the days before the closed or union shop and automatic checkoff this very process further increased his awareness of himself as a member of a group with a special interest in society and very particular desires and ambitions. Union members began to believe that they were a special group, should be recognized and accepted as such, and should be given a share of power and responsibility with other groups.

These aspirations clashed with the interests of Winnipeg's owner-managerial class which was supported, before 1915, by civic and provincial governments. The tightly knit elite of brokers, merchants, lawyers, and manufacturers who ruled the business world refused to concede anything to labour because they refused to recognize that industrial workers or trade unions were entitled to any special considerations in the plants or halls of government. They saw labour as a resource, a commodity, and had no intention of relinquishing any of their power in the community to it. When labour threw out its first tentative challenges early in the century they were met by intransigent employers who used every weapon at their disposal to crush the budding power of trade unions. This process tended to increase class polarization and undermined the influence of any labour leader who dared assert, in the face of injunctions, strike-breakers, yellow dog contracts and hostile or apathetic governments, that capital and labour shared a basic community of interest.

Immigration, depression, and war further stimulated the development of class polarization in Winnipeg. The influx of large numbers of new settlers tended to underline the wide gulf that separated workers from employers, rich from poor, while the decision of many middle- and upper-class citizens to settle in the southern part of the city added the factor of geographic identification to the process. In the years prior to the First World War the north end and Wellington Crescent became attitudes as well as places; the rich grew richer but the poor remained mired in poverty.

When the depression struck in 1913 the skilled British and Canadian workers were hit harder perhaps than any other group. Machinists waited outside factory gates for long hours and construction workers looked in vain for new building sites, but wherever they turned for help they were rebuffed. All Trades Council suggestions to the civic and provincial administrations for dealing with depression and unemployment were ignored, except for pious pleas to the federal government to end immigration. Workers were forced to dig ditches where they could or listened to government officials discussing resettlement of urban wage earners on empty lands. Workers, therefore, came face to face with their helplessness and powerlessness in the community and this strengthened the feelings of class separateness.

War put the finishing touches to a process already well under way. Workers believed they were being forced to suffer low wages and rising prices while the wealthy raked in fat war profits. They saw that without men to fire the guns or run the lathes there would be no war effort. They heard stirring pronouncements from their national leaders and flowery statements from local, "part-time" patriots; but when they asked government for concessions in the form of fair wage clauses in war-supply contracts they were turned back. Once again it appeared as though those in power would not recognize the special desires or necessities of workers and they became more convinced than ever that they had little or nothing in common with employers or governments composed of and supported by the wealthy.

These processes were evident throughout Canada in the first decades of the twentieth century but were particularly pronounced in Winnipeg. Here the owner-managerial class was newer, fewer in number, and more tightly knit than in many other industrial centres. All frequented the same clubs and associations and lived in the same areas. Some, such as A.M. Nanton, T.R. Deacon, and the Barretts were *nouveaux riches*, recently arrived at the pinnacle of power and not yet mellowed by the passage of time or the self-assuredness that generations of wealth sometimes brings. This class deeply believed they would be the elite of a new industrial centre that might, with luck, ambition, and intelligence, soon rival Chicago as the western capital of the continent. Winnipeg had the raw manpower, the large pool of immigrants, the railways, the geographic location at the entrance to the prairies and, by the First World War, the financial and industrial strength, to enable it to fulfil its great promise. There was no room here for a powerful trade union movement, especially one that contained so many socialists among its leadership and held so many radical ideas. It was imperative, therefore, to challenge the rising power of the unions and sap the strength of the industrial working class. There might be room for paternalistic regulation, but not for recognition of an equal status for trade unions. When labour resisted these impulses class polarization was strengthened further.

Winnipeg's entrepreneurs were constantly trying to lower the costs of their operations by holding down wages. Almost every business engaged in manufacturing or distribution of consumer or capital goods was at a certain disadvantage in comparison with companies in eastern Canada or the United States because of the great distances to sources of raw materials or wholesale distributors. Deacon frequently complained that he had great difficulty trying to compete with eastern or American companies, and the unimportance of Winnipeg to national war production is ample evidence of the truth of his assertions. The Shell Committee and the Imperial Munitions Board had to make special provision for western shell manufacturers because greater shipping distances and, consequently, higher freight costs would have made the granting of contracts unfeasible. There was, thus, little difference in the approaches of local corporations to their labour problems. Vulcan and Manitoba Bridge, owned in Winnipeg, were allied to and supported by Dominion Bridge, a branch operation. All attempted to keep the one great variable, labour costs, as low as possible.

The war increased cost pressures on local businessmen and at the same time put workers under an additional strain. Manufacturers and suppliers were under even greater pressure to keep labour costs as low as possible because they were forced to pay more for raw materials while workers were pressured by rising retail prices to demand higher wages. The squeeze was particularly felt by workers in industries not essential to the war effort who had little bargaining leverage; those who were essential to war industry—machinists, for example—were more able to keep ahead of the inflationary trend. Winnipeg did not have many war workers because it was awarded so few contracts. Thus, a large number of workers hardly improved their position at all during the war or else saw their wages eaten away by inflation. They were determined to make up for lost time with peace and the normalization of economic conditions and industrial production.

The main exception to the cost-squeeze situation was the transportation industry. The railways had built their yards and repair shops at Winnipeg and it was precisely here that their costs were lowest. They did not need to compete with eastern or American corporations and did not have to import capital or consumer goods for wholesale or retail distribution. The need for their services was constant and the pressure of competition on them was less than on other corporations in the city. In this industry management and ownership had been divorced early, unions in the running trades had been accepted by the turn of the century, and those men responsible for the operation of the systems saw that unions were essential to the stabilization of the daily relationship between an employer and his men. Railway shop craft unions were therefore the most fortunate of organizations, with the exception of the running trades. Here, however, militancy and radicalism—class consciousness—was particularly strong, even though it did not develop from intense pressures placed on the unions. In fact, the opposite was the case: workers here turned increasingly to radicalism because they had tasted power and influence in this one industry, but were denied it elsewhere. The shop craft unions were determined to rectify this situation, raise the standard of living of workers in general, and enhance their own positions in the process.

Class polarization can be seen at work in Winnipeg in the street railway and contract shop disputes of 1906, in the Great West Saddlery lockout of 1911, and the debates over unemployment and depression in the months preceding the war. As time passed without any change in the existing social order or alterations in the thought patterns of the business and governing classes, the effectiveness of moderate thinking waned; attitudes began to gel into dogmas and doctrines. Many workers began to believe in the idea that there were only two classes of consequence in society, those who produced and those who lived off the producers. The eventual acceptance of this philosophy allowed workers to think in terms of general strikes or the creation of a single union of all wage earners. The belief, expressed in the actions of the Strike Committee, that they could allow just so much water pressure in the pipes, enough to service single-story dwellings, and thus easily separate owners from workers, followed naturally. This same mode of thought had contributed to the intense industrial struggles of 1917, 1918, and 1919 and the feverish labour political activity before and after the general strike. It led to the refusal to believe in the good will of a provincial government that had passed much favourable labour legislation, enforced measures on the books, introduced a comprehensive compensation scheme, regulated working conditions in the construction industry, and fixed minimum wages for women.

By the spring of 1919 the process of class polarization had gone so far that Winnipeg had been divided into two camps with little communication between them. Along the way moderates were discarded, as the most radical on one side and the most intransigent on the other emerged as ideological leaders. This is why labour spurned Norris's Industrial Conditions Act and ridiculed Parnell's belief that labour and capital had much in common. It also explains why the Builders Exchange reversed their earlier position and declared that they would not deal with the Building Trades Council. Labour's frame of mind allowed a general strike because workers had arrived at the conclusion that there was no such thing as a neutral citizenry. The middle class had aided the wealthy in their campaign against unions by their silence, and were thus almost as guilty. Under these circumstances the defeat of the strike did not reverse class polarization but rather aided it further.

It has often been observed that workers in Winnipeg turned to politics after the strike; but in fact they were engaged in steadily increasing political activity for over a decade before the war. Political activity had always been looked upon as complementary to industrial action, and the working class in the city had been more successful in electing its own candidates with each successive year. By the spring of 1919 they had representation in the halls of civic government and had elected MLAs to the provincial legislature. After the general strike they continued their political activity but were more successful because of the increased class consciousness which the strike and the methods used to defeat it generated. The great success of labour candidates in the 1920 provincial voting and the election of J.S. Woodsworth to the House of Commons in 1921 were actually manifestations of the same class polarization which had enabled so complete a general strike to take place and has been so strong a factor in the fortunes of the city for at least five decades. Fifty years after the general strike there were still bitter debates over its causes and meaning, and there continued to be a north end in attitude as well as geographic fact.

The Winnipeg general strike has been the key event in the collective memories of both groups who fought it. The strike provided the original mythology and martyrology that strengthened division within the community. The CPR tracks separated north from south physically, but the strike has separated them socially and historically. In both areas generations grew to maturity who continued to refight the battle of 1919 in almost every arena of social conflict, from school sports to the street battles of excitement-seeking juveniles to civic and provincial politics. In time, the class division symbolized by the strike was joined by ethnic and religious differences which further polarized society in the city. The lethargy which began to affect the community in the 1920s, holding development back and forcing some of Winnipeg's talented and ambitious sons and daughters to seek greener fields elsewhere was, at least in part, a result of these chronic divisions. The south end became the bastion of the English Establishment and those sons of immigrants who achieved financial and social success rarely moved there.

The victory of the New Democratic Party in the Manitoba election of 1969, fifty years after the defeat of the general strike, was in large measure a victory for attitudes and beliefs rooted in the old north end. Finally, seventy years after Sifton's immigrants began to arrive in Canada and labour began its long and frustrating campaign for political power, a government came to office which represented the sons and daughters of both groups. Perhaps this success of a social democratic government dominated by non-Anglo-Saxon members of society will finally heal the polarization within the city, and Winnipeg can once again become as unified in the spiritual sense as it now is in the physical.

Notes

1. Rigg/Rees Papers, Varley to ? (T. Moore or P.M. Draper), 12 July 1919.
2. Author's interview with Alex Shepherd, 6 May 1969.
3. *Labour Gazette*, May 1919, 577–81.
4. Rigg/Rees Papers, Varley to ? (T. Moore or P.M. Draper), 12 July 1919.
5. See City of Winnipeg employment application form in Manning Papers, File 47.
6. Borden Papers, OC 564, Ketchen to Elmsley, 26 June 1919.
7. See Borden Papers, OC 564, and Post Office Records Vol. 124, for correspondence and documents relating to the efforts of postal employees to regain employment.
8. *Labour Gazette*, February 1921, 165–89.
9. Rigg/Rees Papers, Rigg to Moore, 9 August 1919.

The Social Gospel as the Religion of the Agrarian Revolt

RICHARD ALLEN

Reprinted from C. Berger and R. Cook, eds., *The West and the Nation: Essays in Honour of W.L. Morton* (Toronto: McClelland and Stewart, 1976), 174–186, by permission of the author.

Between 1916 and 1926 Ontario and prairie farmers mounted a concerted attack upon the political and economic structure of the nation. Known to history as the agrarian revolt, it toppled three provincial governments, strengthened the agrarian hold on one other, routed one federal party and government and made the life of its successor a tenuous one. Provincially and federally the farmers secured legislation affecting freight rate, tariffs, credit, and marketing. They secured a modicum of electoral and social legislation, and were instrumental in ending federal control of the natural resources of Saskatchewan and Alberta. In the upshot, the agrarian revolt achieved a greater measure of equity for the farmer, and for the prairies in particular, but the balance of its program—indeed the Progressive Party itself—died a lingering death after 1923 amid the crosscurrents within the party and the legislatures of the nation.

The agrarian revolt in the West, like its predecessors and successors, had obvious political, social, and economic roots. Politically, the farmers had been underrepresented in Parliament. The West had been the stepping stone of nation-building, and stood on the sidelines of the federal power structure. Socially, the older agrarian regions were experiencing a march for the city, and to the newer ones immigration from Europe, Britain, and the United States had brought a new fare of reform ideas to feed discontent. Economically, the farmer in the West was disadvantaged by policies of industrialization which forced him to buy in a protected market and sell in an open one, far from the site of production and through agencies entirely unaccountable to him. It was a debtor region. The varied phenomena of the agrarian revolt can be and have been largely accounted for in such terms. However, all of those conditions were perceived and evaluated in terms both explicitly and implicitly religious. It was under the impress of religion that the farmers were rallied to the cause, chose their tactics, and explained their purpose. And religious considerations played a notable role in both their success and their failure.

No man lives by bread—or wheat—alone, and movements with ostensible economic beginnings invariably find themselves clothed with ideas and hopes which provide frameworks for action not reducible to economics or even politics. Patterns of behaviour, individually and collectively, emerge which sometimes owe more to religious concerns of alienation and reconciliation, of guilt, justification, redemption, and ultimate hope than to the cold rationalities of economic interest. The two impulses meet in a framework of ideas, or an ideology, combining self-interest and ultimate aspirations by which a group, class, section, or nation explains to itself and to the world, what its problems are, how it is approaching them, where it is going and why. To a remarkable degree, the Social Gospel and the ideology of the agrarian revolt coincided.

The identification of western agrarianism with religious motives was even closer than the foregoing implies, for both the leadership and the membership generally espoused religion with a will. Henry Wise Wood, the great Alberta agrarian leader of the time, though not an active churchman in his Alberta days, was a very religious man who viewed the United Farmers of Alberta as a religious movement.[1] The Regina *Leader* described the Saskatchewan Grain Growers' Association as "a religious, social, educational, political and commercial organization all in one, and in the truest and deepest meaning of these several terms."[2] W.R. Wood, secretary of the Manitoba Grain Growers, wrote that "we are practically seeking to inaugurate the Kingdom of God and its righteousness . . ."[3] and Norman Lambert, secretary of the Canadian Council of Agriculture, suggested that the aim of the Progressive Party was "to give 'politics' a new meaning in Canada," and "hand in hand with the organized farmers movement on the prairies has gone religion and social work."[4]

Such remarks were in the first instance a consequence of the formative influence of the churches in the years of prairie settlement. Even allowing for the ease with which members were lost in those vast expanses of plain and parkland, the church had been a major educative influence. The leaders of the Grain Growers were often (though not always) churchmen of note and even clergy; and most of the participants were church members who could sing "Onward Christian Soldiers" with great vigour and conviction.[5] Furthermore, many with aspirations to the ministry, others with some theological training, religious workers, and clergy took up positions of influence in one or another of the farmers' organizations: Henry Wise Wood, Percival Baker, Norman Smith, William Irvine, Louise McKinney, G.W. Robertson, R.C. Henders, W.R. Wood, R.A. Hoey. Not infrequently, clergy joined their laymen as members and officers of Grain Growers' locals. The Rev. P. McLeod, Presbyterian minister of Baldur, Manitoba, at the 1916 convention tried to move the organization from political independence to support for a farmer-labour party.[6] The Rev. W. Kelly was vice-president of the Wellwood local in Manitoba in 1919, and had experience in Australian farmers' movements. The Revs. A.C. Burley, Harold Wildings, and J. Griffiths were delegates to the Saskatchewan Grain Growers' Convention in 1920,[7] and in 1921 Rev. Hugh Dobson, western field secretary for Methodist Evangelism and Social Service, was a member of the inner policy group of the Regina constituency organization of the Progressive Party. In addition, a number of ministers dared to take unto themselves the controversy of running for political office as independent or Progressive candidates with farmer support.[8] The church was not, however, exactly of one mind about such clerical involvement. None of the denominational hierarchies discouraged such social action, but locally it was sometimes a different matter, as one young Presbyterian minister wrote: "Several of the old party men have left the church because of my active association with the Grain Growers' Movement."[9]

This interpretation of agrarian and church leadership, especially in the period of the agrarian revolt, was not of itself, however, only a consequence of the past services of the church in the settlement process. It was still more a reflection of the impact of the Social Gospel in prairie Protestantism and the farm movements themselves. As the prairie farmer faced the gargantuan task of marketing his ever-growing grain crop in the complex, impersonal international market, the agrarian myth of the virtuous individual yeoman, wresting his due from the soil by his own skill, broke down. Only in combination and cooperation could he cope with the forces arrayed before him: elevator companies, railroads, grain exchanges, even political parties and governments. He was in need not only of new organizations and techniques, but also of a new social faith. The Social Gospel supplied it.

The Social Gospel had been rising to the surface of Canadian Protestantism in the decade previous to the founding of the great prairie agrarian organizations. To one degree or another all the Protestant church colleges in the West—Wesley College, Manitoba College, Brandon College, Regina College, Alberta College—became disseminators of the Social Gospel. Wesley College was chief among them with men like W.F. Osborne and Salem Bland on its faculty, and was the first prairie institution to offer a course in Sociology to its students. As teachers, preachers, and laymen, the college students carried the message back to the communities of the West. The flow of the Social Gospel into the West was multiplied by the migration of British and American midwestern farmers, and then multiplied again when the churches were forced to turn to British recruits for the ministry. Many of them had already been influenced by both the labour movement and the social movement in the British churches, and readily confessed that they were already primed for the message of a professor like Salem Bland at Wesley College.[10]

Bland himself was probably the most vigorous exponent of the Social Gospel in the West. A cripple, an avid reader, an engaging teacher, and a powerful preacher and platform personality, he typified the many connections of the Social Gospel with prairie reform movements. He had been an ardent prohibitionist. He was on the executive of the Free Trade League, was honorary president of the Single Tax and direct Legislation Association. He was a representative of the Ministerial Association on the Winnipeg Trade and Labor Council. He was a favourite guest speaker at Grain Growers' conventions in Saskatchewan and Manitoba. On his first appearance before the former in 1913 he proved to be rather in advance of the leadership, though not of all the members, when he proposed the establishment of a third party led by the farmers. When he was dismissed from Wesley College under controversial circumstances the *Grain Growers' Guide* secured his services as a regular columnist, proclaiming: "There is no abler champion of the principles for which the organized farmers stand . . . " His column "The Deeper Life" related resources of Christianity and in particular the Social Gospel to a broad spectrum of agrarian needs and aspirations. The Chautauqua movement employed him (as well as Henry Wise Wood) in 1918 for its second summer of educational and entertaining programs in prairie communities. In 1919 the Saskatchewan Grain Growers' Association used him to spearhead the call to political action which the association leadership now considered unavoidable. And the next year, when the *Saskatoon Star Phoenix* reviewed his book *The New Christianity*, it pronounced it to be "a concentrated form of the message which ministers are sending forth from pulpits today," and "just what (one) has thought all his life but lacked the power of expression to put it into words."[11]

But it was not through the formal agency of Canadian Protestantism alone in the West that the Social Gospel reached its place of eminence in the agrarian revolt.

Agrarian leaders had minds of their own; many of them read widely; and the agencies of press, journal, and book brought the world to their doorsteps. The *Grain Growers' Guide's* book section publicized and sold many of the books like Henry George's *Progress and Poverty* and Edward Bellamy's *Looking Backward* that had made such an impact on the nascent social gospellers of the previous generation. The *Guide* occasionally leaned on the American Social Gospel, reprinting articles like Lyman Abbot's "My Democracy."[12] In 1916 it used articles by Washington Gladden to provoke discussion of the role of the church in prairie communities.[13] The prairie press at large carried news of notable developments in social Christianity elsewhere. The *Regina Leader* commented favourably upon the proposal of R.J. Campbell, English author of *The New Theology*, that it was the business of the church to profess the religion of Jesus which "was in its inception a social gospel" and by helping erect a socialist Christian state "sweep way those existing conditions which throw a pall over the lives of the larger proportion of our people." And when in 1912 and 1913 the "Men and Religion Forward Movement" was underway in the United States, the *Leader* carried a weekly column entitled "Religion and Social Service."

Primary farm leaders manifested the Social Gospel early. E.A. Partridge, the greatest agrarian radical of the early 1900s and the most innovative farm leader of the period, came to the West in 1883 with a Ruskinian socialist outlook already formed. It was not necessary to go much further than Partridge in looking for a definition of the Social Gospel. In 1909 he wrote, as editor of the *Grain Growers' Guide:* "Christ wasn't trying to save his soul for the next world . . . but was trying to serve humanity by showing men the truth about the proper relations to set up between themselves and God and themselves and others."[14] Therefore, he said, it was necessary to "take your love of God, which in its practical form is love of your neighbour, into politics. Practical religion is for every day, but more especially for Convention day, Nomination day, Election day until our legislative halls are purged of those who represent the most heartless and selfish instincts of the race . . . "[15] Such applications of Christianity were of ultimate significance, because the emphasis on wealth and competition in the present system "checks the march of civilization and indefinitely delays the coming of the Kingdom for which Christ so earnestly laboured."[16]

Henry Wise Wood was not a member of any church in Canada, but brought a liberal-leaning religious outlook from an upbringing and training under the Campbellite church in Missouri.[17] Wood was an assiduous reader, both of the Bible and works in social theory, and produced, out of elements of cooperative and socialist thought, social Darwinism, and Scripture, a comprehensive social philosophy for the agrarian movement which can only be categorized as Social Gospel. Wood held that over the centuries mankind had been held in subjugation by the spirit of animal selfishness, expressing itself in autocratic regimes of government or industry, competition between individuals, businesses, and states, and a quest for profit which was nothing less than a worship of mammon. Scripture, the Prophets, and Christ taught another way of social unselfishness which expressed itself in the alternatives of service, cooperation, and democracy. The fulfilment of the social spirit was synonymous for Wood with the achievement of the Kingdom of Heaven.

Tactically, Wood considered that the social spirit was best nurtured in those realms of life where men were closest to each other, namely in the economic realm of occupational groups. In this light, the UFA and the Wheat Pool were as much religious institutions as the church. The primary task of the time, therefore, was to organize those groups on a cooperative democratic basis, and once so organized, to maintain them in the true way. Government might then be built upon the self-government of the groups, and second, upon a legislature and executive representative of all occupational groups. These tactics entailed serious problems in the transitional period when not all groups were organized on a democratic basis, but Wood must have looked hopefully upon the widespread advocacy of industrial democracy after the Great War, when he was advancing his theories.

Because so much was hanging in the balance, not just economically or politically, but religiously, Wood was insistent that farmer politics must be UFA politics, and that UFA politics must not aim primarily at winning elections, but at developing principles. Hence his radical emphasis upon group politics. But he had no doubts about the outcome. How would God who had allowed the perfection of lesser creatures in the natural order, allow his supreme creation to fail? The Supreme Power had this work in hand.[18]

It was possible, then, for the agrarian leadership to appropriate the Social Gospel and give it forceful expression without a sustained contact with the prairie pulpit although few were without its influence at some stage in their careers. Either way, they sought the support—and sometimes rehabilitation—of the pulpits of the West; and in 1917 created UFA and Grain Growers' Sundays as formal occasions on which to celebrate the Social Gospel. Not all ministers and locals took up the opportunity, but the farm leaders left little to chance. The SGGA asked ministers to preach on the principles of the association, in the belief, as George Langley put it, that "bringing into prominence . . . our human interdependence will lift us into closer relationship with the Divinity that is the centre of our common brotherhood."[19] Henry Wise Wood was even more explicit in two forceful circulars on the subject. He advised the ministers of the province not to preach on "orthodox things," personal resistance to temptation, or an outdated Biblical view of farming. Rather "tell them that the only thing Jesus ever taught us to pray for, was this re-organized, regenerated perfect civilization. Tell them that this regeneration deals with every element of civilization . . . and that all that cannot pass through the refining fire . . . must be consumed by it." To the UFA members, Wood wrote that, if the church in the past had only offered them a personal saviour, it was because they had asked for nothing more. Now, however, the church was beginning to recognize Christ as a leader who offered the great social deliverance for which men were seeking. Only on these lines could the farmers and the church find a path through their perplexity. "Is Christ to develop the individuals and Carl [sic] Marx mobilize and lead them? Is Christ to hew the stones and Henry George build them into the finished edifice?"[20] Wood's advice was followed, and in 1920 the *Edmonton Free Press* observed that these Sundays had become established institutions providing an occasion to examine Christ's social teachings, and other press reports of the services convey a similar conclusion.[21]

The more traditional holy days were also occasions for the *Guide* and the agrarian leadership to put their activities in religious perspective, or to call on a sympathetic cleric to rehearse the Social Gospel. For example, J.B. Mussleman's Christmas message in 1918, as secretary of the SGGA, observed that "'Peace on Earth and Goodwill toward men' must ever remain a myth while men think of Christ and His teachings only as the means of their personal salvation."[22]

Although at one level, the adoption of the Social Gospel by the farm leaders brought the agrarian organizations and the church closer together, their heightened religious sense equally provided a severe critique of traditional organized religion. That message could also be read in Wood's circulars in Alberta, in Mussleman's deliverances in Saskatchewan, and W.R. Wood's articles in Manitoba.[23] William Irvine, who was later to become the chief systematizer of Henry Wise Wood's political ideas, urged with respect to the UFA Sundays that there might be more point in "Church Sundays" on which the true spirit and expression of Christianity might be communicated by the UFA to the churches of Alberta.[24] When only one of the ministerial delegates of the SGGA convention in 1919 turned up for a discussion of church union (the others no doubt sick of the subject and eager to discuss headier matters of farmer politics), it was suggested that it was up to the farmers to form a Grain Growers' Church of their own along union lines.[25] Even in the ranks, it would seem, an increasing number were viewing their movements as peculiar sources of social, even religious, regeneration, and expressing in practice what William Irvine was shortly to write in *The Farmers in Politics*: "The line between the sacred and the secular is being rubbed out" and "everything is becoming sacred." First and foremost in that process was the organized farmers' movement.

The Social Gospel, then, was a power to be reckoned with as the western farmer figuratively took up arms against the national system. But for all that the Social Gospel could be described as a new development in the religious culture of the agrarian West, once the farm organizations were baptized by the Social Gospel with the holy spirit, it was possible to make even the resources of the older evangelicalism do service in the agrarian revolt. Were not the farm organizations themselves now the centre of revival, calling the nation to repentance and conversion? Mussleman's reaction to the astonishing electoral victories of the fall of 1919 in Ontario and at Cochrane, Alberta, was to quote a hymn that had echoed from revival and camp meeting:

> Lo, the promise of a shower,
> Drops already from above;
> And the Lord will shortly pour
> All the pleasure of His love.[26]

And so it seemed as the following three years saw a remarkable harvest of constituencies, legislatures, and governments.

Insofar as the western farmer was in need of a social faith for the new commercial age that was upon him, he found it in the Social Gospel, and for him it provided not only a great manifesto of social justice but also the promise of a great deliverance and the coming of a new time. To say so much, however, and to document it, is not to exhaust the significance of that development. It is necessary as well to ask certain questions: How did the Social Gospel relate to the enduring ideology of the agrarian myth? What role did it play in the internal problems of the Progressive Party, and how did it affect its political tactics? Finally, how much was the Social Gospel of the agrarian revolt a part of the rampant English Protestantism of the second decade which won prohibition in the West with one hand, while it virtually wiped out foreign language instruction in the schools with the other? Definitive answers to these questions still await substantial research and interpretation, but at least some suggestive inferences can and ought to be drawn from what is already known.

Richard Hofstadter has made much of the inappropriateness of the agrarian myth of the virtuous yeoman to the situation of the western American farmer, whom he views rather as a large scale producer and land speculator, given to an indulgent identification with the common man in times of depression but assuming his entrepreneurial mantle when the going was good. Depending on the season, he ran with the hare *or* the hounds. Without going into all aspects of the applicability of this image to the prairie farmer, it is evident that in season and out, the Social Gospel sought to strip away the individualism of the agrarian myth—and did so with some success. Nevertheless, what was lost for the individual was gained for the group; and one might almost say, for the region. While the cartoons of the *Guide* still appealed to the beleaguered individual farmer, they nevertheless taught just that, that the farmer as an individual was no match for the world. In stressing the virtues of association and the common humanity of the farmer, however, the Social Gospel was far from detracting from the commercial realities confronting him. Each new triumph of organization from 1901 to 1923 was at one and the same time a celebration of the progressive march of Christian social ethics, the arrival of a new breed of virtuous cooperators, *and* an advance in the farmers' commercial sophistication. This enduring sense of his common humanity and the moral superiority of the farmer's response to his word could hardly do other than compound his sense of alienation in the nation in the political and economic crisis of 1918–21.

At the same time, in an apparent contradiction to the Social Gospel's emphasis upon the brotherhood of man, the overwhelming bulk of the agrarian leadership and a majority of their following were obviously deeply committed to the continuing surge of Anglo-Protestant culture religion, expressed in campaigns for "national schools" with English-language instruction only, prohibition, and church union; the Social Gospel of the agrarian revolt was closely associated with all that, as can be demonstrated in a number of ways. UFA support in Alberta was strongest—almost unshakeable—in the older settled region of the province south of Red Deer, populated largely by those of British, American, German, or Scandinavian extraction, and devoted to commodity production. This was where those campaigns on behalf of moral righteousness, which the UFA embraced—prohibition, social reform, direct democracy, and smashing the "interests"—had their strongest support. By contrast, these causes—and the UFA—were much less popular in the more recently settled northern area with its heavier concentrations of French Canadians and Ukrainians.[27] In Saskatchewan, in 1919 the provincial legislators among the ranks of the Grain Growers' Association were with one exception Protestant: half were Presbyterian, a fifth Methodist.[28] And in a study of the Progressive Party's middle leadership in 1921 in Saskatchewan all of those on whom significant data could be found were Protestant.[29] In Manitoba, using still another measure, Salem Bland was most frequently called to speak and preach in English Protestant regions west and south of Winnipeg, which was most constant in its support of prohibition.[30] Perhaps, on the one hand, what the association pointed to is obvious. It is not possible to link all social gospellers of the agrarian revolt equally to the status politics of Anglo-Protestantism in the West, but it is not surprising to read of the rousing reception given by the SGGA in convention in 1918 to the call for English only in the schools by Dr. J.G. Shearer, head of the Social Service Council of Canada and the preeminent Presbyterian social gospeller in the land.

What then does one say about the virtuous cooperator of the Social Gospel of the agrarian revolt? Simply that one man's redemption is another man's alienation? That is not an uncommon pattern with ideologies as the identities of self-interest within them became clearer, and it is evident in the dynamics of the agrarian revolt as well. But that its character can be entirely ascribed to status politics and nativism in the face of new urban—and even rural—groups and classes occasioned by a combination of industrialism and immigration, is not entirely fair or accurate. At a time when it is recognized that there was not, after all, that much to be feared from the maintenance of immigrant cultures, the western agrarian Protestant ought not to be belaboured too heavily for wanting to maintain *his* culture. One might assume that the immigrant was seeking a better country—as were the social gospellers and the agrarians—and were not they offering him its best? In the catalogue of responses to immigration, it cannot be ignored that it was the UFA which provided the House of Commons with its first MP of Ukrainian descent in 1926, or that the Saskatchewan Grain Growers' Association early began using immigrant languages in its publicity and developed a Foreign Organization Department whose staff were able to utilize languages other than English, or that the Women's Section of the SGGA showed a considerable and continuous concern for the welfare of immigrant families in prairie communities.[31] The culture religion underlying the Social Gospel did not speak an unequivocal word in response to immigration. If in the upshot that response was a mixture of inclusiveness and exclusiveness, it cannot be put down to simple negativism and nativism. Certainly that would not do justice to the literature which Protestant agrarians read on the subject—whether church papers, novels like *The Foreigner*, or texts like *Strangers Within Our Gates*—all of which were marked by a complex ambivalence.

If the agrarian's response to immigration was somewhat paradoxical, there was also an irony in his appropriation of the Social Gospel. Clearly, the Social Gospel of the agrarian revolt first derived from urban rather than agrarian responses to industrialism. Its framework of thought derived from urban universities, urban civil servants, and urban pastors, and it was popularized by urban-based presses and urban-trained preachers. It could be described as a metropolitan concoction which the hinterland came to share. It provided common ground for farm leaders and urban professionals, whether journalist, cleric, or social worker—and to a lesser degree and in the right season—labourer. It is not surprising, then, that when the Social Gospel came to prescribe for the countryside, its proposals were extensions of the amenities and social features of urban life.[32] The Social Gospel had no criticism of the agrarian drive after the turn of the century for the businesslike practice of agriculture. The problem was not with business *per se* but with the misuse of corporate wealth and power. What the Social Gospel of the agrarian revolt proclaimed was that the agrarians had found a way of handling business, wealth, and power, consistent with democracy and Christian social ethics.

Inevitably, the religious dimensions of the agrarian revolt made it more difficult for the movement to function in the given world of Canadian politics. The Progressive Party refused to function as an opposition party on behalf of all Canadians—which exposed how far it was after all an agency of group interest. Progressives who alone voted overwhelmingly in the federal House against race track gambling and for church union could hardly be expected to make up their minds between Conservative high tariff iniquity and liquor-corrupted Liberal administration in 1925-26. The one affronted their group economic interest and the other their Anglo-Protestant culture religion, both of which were incorporated in the Social Gospel of the agrarian revolt, even while they were in some measure transformed by it.

The inner problems of the party were likewise an expression of religious sensitivities. From the beginning the UFA representatives had been the bearers of the pure doctrine. They had refused to concede formal organization as a party; they had early separated out, constituting the majority of the "Ginger Group," associating themselves with the Labor "group," Woodsworth and Irvine; and they survived the debacle of 1926 almost intact. In religious terms of all the Progressives, they had, under Wood's tutorship, come closest to forming a new cult. It should come as no surprise that where postmillennial politics had been most intense, but had failed to avert the disasters and dispel the demons of the 1930s, a virulent premillennial politics of the second coming should take its place. The fundamentalist reaction of the 1920s, of course, had intervened and helped that process along.

In embracing the Social Gospel, the agrarian movement wedded a universal religious perspective to the particular problems of its own condition. The tensions inherent in that marriage were difficult to resolve and revealed themselves most clearly in the crisis of 1925-26. The tension, however, was a sign of the creative, transforming process of true religion at work. The depths of human alienation from the source of being, underlay the experience of agrarian alienation from the national sources of well-being. The enduring human urge for ultimate reconciliation hovered over the desire to be more fully a part of the national community. The perception of alienation and the identification of hope in the particular circumstances of the West in turn victimized some and excluded others, but in the process, the West became a new, mature society, notable for its cooperative structures of business and for what were almost nonpartisan service state governments, within a federal system committed to equal opportunity for all regions (however difficult that has been to realize in practice). The universal perspectives of the agrarian revolt helped move Canadian society to a greater measure of justice. The Social Gospel of the agrarian revolt had done its work.

Notes

1. W.L. Morton, "The Social Philosophy of Henry Wise Wood," *Agricultural History* (April 1948), 116.
2. 22 February 1919.
3. United Church Archives, Salem G. Bland Papers, letter, 17 April 1919, in Wood to Bland, 18 April 1914.
4. *Presbyterian Witness*, 23 June 1921, 10-11.
5. *Leader* (Regina), 22 February 1919.
6. *Grain Growers' Guide*, 12 January 1916.
7. *Christian Guardian*, 17 March 1920, 25.
8. For example, Rev. J.M. Douglas, the Independent Liberal who won the federal seat of Assiniboia in 1896 with Patron backing, followed later by R.C. Henders and W.R. Wood, Thomas Beveridge, the editor of *The Melita New Era* in Melita, Manitoba.
9. *Presbyterian and Westminster*, 8 May 1919, 457-58.
10. Interviews, F. Passmore, 13 December 1960; W. Irvine, 14, 15 May 1961.
11. 19 June 1920.
12. 8 January 1913.
13. 7 June 1916.
14. 28 August 1909.
15. Ibid., 14 August 1909.
16. Ibid., 30 September, 6 October 1919.
17. W.K. Rolph, *Henry Wise Wood* (Toronto, 1950), 9-10.
18. See "Organization for Democracy," *Grain Growers' Guide*, 4 December 1918, 39; "The Prince of Peace," ibid., 23; "Mr. Pepys in the West," ibid., 8 January 1919, 47; UFA convention address, ibid., 29 January 1919; also W.L. Morton, op. cit., and Rolph, *Henry Wise Wood*, 9-10, 63-66.
19. Minutes, Board of Directors, SGGA, 30 March 1917, Saskatchewan Archives; *Grain Growers' Guide*, 6 June 1917, 10.

20. UFA Circulars Nos. 9 and 10, 14, 18 April 1917.

21. 22 May 1920, 6; also *Grain Growers' Guide,* 6 June 1917.

22. *Grain Growers' Guide,* 4 December 1918, 41.

23. *Grain Growers' Guide,* 5 November 1919, 8.

24. *Nutcracker,* 10 May 1917.

25. *Leader* (Regina), 21 February 1919.

26. *Grain Growers' Guide,* 5 November 1919.

27. See Thomas Flanagan, "Political Geography and the United Farmers of Alberta," *The Twenties In Western Canada,* ed. S. Trofimenkoff (Ottawa: National Museums of Canada, 1972), 138-47.

28. *Morning Leader* (Regina), 19 February 1919.

29. Leo Courville, "The Saskatchewan Progressives" (unpublished M.A. Thesis, University of Saskatchewan, Regina Campus, 1971), 59.

30. J.K. Thompson, "The Prohibition Question in Manitoba, 1892-1928" (unpublished M.A. Thesis, University of Manitoba, 1969).

31. Guy J. Cyrenne, "The Saskatchewan Grain Growers' Association: Their Educational and Social Aspects" (Honours Paper, University of Saskatchewan, Regina Campus, 1973), 20, 25-26; "First Ukrainian M.P. Dies," *Leader-Post* (Regina), 23 April 1973, 41 (Michael Luchkovich).

32. John MacDougall, *Rural Life in Canada: Its Trends and Tasks* (Toronto, 1913).

4

THIRD PARTY PROTEST (1919–1945)

Introduction

The limited results of economic struggle in the period up to and including World War I made the political option inevitable. During World War I the Non-Partisan League, a movement originating in the Dakotas, began to make inroads into the Canadian West, but it was not until after the war that two indigenous political parties made their mark. The United Farmers of Alberta were victorious in the 1921 provincial election, the same year that the Progressives elected sixty-five representatives to the House of Commons.

W. L. Morton describes the Progressive movement in the West, which was an early expression of the postwar trend to indigenous political parties that eventually peaked during the Depression. He discusses its antiestablishment ideology, indicates the flaws that marred Progressivism, and analyses the reasons for its rapid demise.

Carl Betke's essay shows how a dominant rural population in Alberta (75 percent of the total population) was able to transform an economic lobby group, the United Farmers of Alberta, into a provincial government that remained in power from 1921 to 1935. He also points out how modest were the results of this tenure in terms of economic and social change.

It was in the 1930s, when the region was ravaged by the Great Depression and drought, that the West finally created political movements that have survived, in one form or another, to this day. Social Credit stands on the right, while the Co-operative Commonwealth Federation (CCF), and its successor the NDP, stand on the left.

Thomas Flanagan and Martha Lee trace the fortunes of Social Credit from 1935, when it swept Alberta under the charismatic leadership of William Aberhart, until its dying days in the late 1960s. They argue that populist mass movements, like Social Credit, often begin with a radical platform but end with a conservative agenda because their millenarian hopes are unattainable. They demonstrate how this particular utopian protest movement became a pillar of the right.

Peter Sinclair continues the theme of populism and its right- and left-wing manifestations in "Class Structure and Populist Protest." He explains why Alberta gave rise to a right-wing movement like Social Credit, while Saskatchewan gave birth to the first and only CCF government. He sees the agrarian population as leaning in two directions simultaneously—one radical and the other conservative.

The West is often characterized as a region that gives birth to new political parties. This characterization is rooted in the 1921 to 1945 period when the political economy of agrarianism was at its peak. But the region did not give birth to any other new political parties until a spate of fringe groups appeared in the 1970s under the banner of western alienation, an important forty-year hiatus, which raises the question of whether third party protest is a permanent western phenomenon.

The Western Progressive Movement, 1919-1921

W.L. MORTON

Reprinted from A.B. McKillop, ed., *Contexts of Canada's Past: Selected Essays of W.L. Morton* (Toronto: Macmillan of Canada, 1980), 113–130, by permission of Mrs. G. Margaret Morton.

The Progressive movement in the West was dual in origin and nature. In one aspect it was an economic protest; in another it was a political revolt. A phase of agrarian resistance to the National Policy of 1878, it was also, and equally, an attempt to destroy the old national parties. The two aspects unite in the belief of all Progressives, both moderate and extreme, that the old parties were equally committed to maintaining the National Policy and indifferent to the ways in which the "big interests" of protection and monopoly used government for their own ends.

At the root of the sectional conflict, from which the Progressive movement in part sprang, was the National Policy of 1878. Such conflict is partly the result of the hardships and imperfect adaptations of the frontier, but it also arises from the incidence of national policies.[1] The sectional corn develops where the national shoe pinches. The National Policy, that brilliant improvisation of Sir John A. Macdonald, had grown under the master politician's hand, under the stimulus of depression and under the promptings of political appetite, until it had become a veritable Canadian system Henry Clay might have envied. Explicit in it was the promise that everybody should have something from its operation; implicit in it—its inarticulate major premise indeed—was the promise that when the infant industries it fostered had reached maturity, protection would be needed no more.

This, however, was but a graceful tribute to the *laissez faire* doctrine of the day. This same doctrine it was which prevented the western wheat grower from demanding that he, too, should benefit directly from the operation of the National Policy. That he did benefit from the system as a whole, a complex of land settlement, railway construction, and moderate tariff protection, is not to be denied. But the wheat grower, building the wheat economy from homestead to terminal elevator in a few swift years, was caught in a complex of production and marketing costs, land values, railway rates, elevator charges, and interest rates. He fought to lower all these costs by economic organization and by political pressure. He saw them all as parts of a system which exploited him. He was prevented, by his direct experience of it, and by the prevailing doctrine of *laissez faire*, from perceiving that the system might confer reciprocal benefits on him. Accordingly, he hated and fought it as a whole. Of the National Policy, however, the tariff was politically the most conspicuous element. Hence the political battle was fought around the tariff; it became the symbol of the wheat growers' exploitation and frustration, alleged and actual. Like all symbols, it oversimplified the complexities it symbolized.

This clash of interest had, of course, to be taken into account by the national political parties. The Liberal-Conservatives, as creators of the National Policy, had little choice but to extol its merits even in regions where they seemed somewhat dim. They could stress its promise that a good time was coming for all, they could add that meanwhile the Yankees must be held at bay. When the Liberals quietly appropriated the National Policy after attaining national power in 1896, the task of the Conservatives became much easier. Not only could the Liberals be accused of having abandoned their principles; they could even be accused of unduly prolonging the adolescence of infant industries. A western Conservative, Mr. Arthur Meighen, could indict the Laurier administration on the charge of being maintained in power "behind ramparts of gold"[2] erected by the "interests." This echo of the "cross of gold" was not ineffective in the West, where the charge that there was no real difference between the parties on the tariff not only promoted the growth of third-party sentiment, but also prolonged the life of western Conservatism.

The Liberals, for their part, had not only abandoned "continentalism" in the convention of 1893, but with the possession of power had developed that moderation without which a nation-wide majority may not be won or kept in a country of sectional interests.[3] Liberal speakers might proclaim that the party was the low-tariff party; Fielding might make the master stroke of the British preferential tariff; certain items might be put on the free list here, the rates might be lowered on certain others there; but the Liberal Party had become a national party, with all the powers and responsibilities of government, among them the maintenance and elaboration of the now historic National Policy. In consequence each national party began to appear more and more in the eyes of the wheat grower as an "organized hypocrisy dedicated to getting and holding office,"[4] and the conditions were created for a third-party movement in the West.

The tariff, then, was a major predisposing cause of a third-party movement in the West. Down to 1906 the British preference and other concessions of the Fielding tariff, together with reiterated promises of further reductions, kept the western Liberals within the fold. The completion in that year, however, of the three-decker tariff marked the beginning of more serious discontent. It grew with the offer of reciprocity in the Payne-Aldrich tariff of 1909. With the increase of agricultural indebtedness, concomitant with the settlement of the West, and the disappearance of the advantageous price differential between agricultural prices and those of manufactured goods, on which the wheat boom had taken its rise, the discontent deepened. It found expression through the grain growers' organizations, those "impressive foci of progressive ideas."[5] In 1909 came the organization of the Canadian Council of Agriculture, in 1910 Laurier's tour of the West,[6] and the Siege of Ottawa by the organized farmers. Plainly, the West was demanding its due at last. The Liberal Party, which had lost support in Ontario in every election since 1896, which saw its hold in Quebec threatened by the Nationalists under Bourassa, could not afford to lose the support of a new and rapidly growing section. In 1911 the helm was put hard over for reciprocity, and Liberal prospects brightened in the West.[7] But this partial return to continentalism in economic policy was too severe a strain for a party which had become committed as deeply as its rival to the National Policy. The "Eighteen Liberals" of Toronto, among them Sir Clifford Sifton, broke with the party, and it went down to defeat under a Nationalist and a National Policy crossfire. At the same time the Conservative Party in the West, particularly in Saskatchewan and Alberta, suffered strains and defections which were to show in a lowered vitality in succeeding elections. But the offer of reciprocity remained on the statute books of the United States for another decade, and year by year the grain growers in convention demanded that the offer be taken up.

The demand of the western agrarians for the lowering of the tariff, however, was by no means an only factor in the rise of the third party. Into the West after 1896 poured immigrants from the United States and Great Britain. Most of the Americans came from the middle west and the trans-Mississippi region. Many brought with them the experience and the political philosophy of the farmers' organizations and the third parties of those regions. Perhaps the clearest manifestation of their influence on the political development of the West was the demand for direct legislation which found expression in those forums of agrarian opinions, the grain growers' conventions, and which also found its way to the statute books of the three western provinces. From the British Isles came labour and socialist influences, felt rather in labour and urban circles, but not without effect among the farmers. These populist and socialist influences were mild; their exponents were in a minority. Nonetheless, they did much to give western discontent a vocabulary of grievance. Above all, they combined to repudiate the politics of expediency practised by the national parties, to denounce those parties as being indifferently the tools of the "big interests," and to demand that the farmer free himself from the toils of the old parties and set up a third party, democratic, doctrinaire, and occupational.[8]

In the Canadian West this teaching fell on a soil made favourable not only by a growing disbelief in the likelihood of either of the national parties lowering the tariff, but also by a political temper different from that of eastern Canada. (One exception must be made to this statement, namely, the old Canadian West in peninsular Ontario, from which, indeed, the original settlement of the West had been largely drawn.) This difference may be broadly expressed by saying that the political temper of the eastern provinces, both French and English, is Whiggish. Government there rests on compact, the vested and legal rights of provinces, of minorities, of corporations.[9] The political temper of the West, on the other hand, is democratic; government there rests on the will of the sovereign people, a will direct, simple, and no respector of rights except those demonstrably and momentarily popular. Of this Jacksonian, Clear-Grit democracy, reinforced by American populism and English radicalism, the Progressive movement was an authentic expression.

No better example of this difference of temper exists, of course, than the Manitoba school question. Manitoba was founded on a balance of French and English elements; this balance was expressed in the compact of the original Manitoba Act, the essential point in which was the guarantee of the educational privileges of the two language and religious groups. The balance was destroyed by the Ontario immigration of the 1870s and 1880s; in 1890 Manitoba liberalism swept away the educational privileges of the French minority and introduced the "national" school, the chief agency of equalitarian democracy. This set in train a series of repercussions which, through the struggle over the Autonomy Bills in 1905, the introduction of compulsory education by the Liberal Party in Manitoba in 1916, and the friction caused by Regulation 17 in Ontario, led up to the split in the Liberal Party between the western and the Quebec Liberals on the Lapointe resolution in the federal Parliament in 1916. This split not only foreshadowed

151

and prepared the way for that on conscription; it also contributed to the breakup of the old parties which opened the way to the rise of the Progressive Party after 1919.[10] The western Liberals, that is to say, were turning against Laurier because they feared Nationalist domination of the party.

Thus it was that the ground was prepared for the West to throw its weight behind Union government, first suggested as a war measure, then persisted in to prevent a Liberal victory under Laurier. Western Liberals and radicals did so with much reluctance and many misgivings. An independent movement was already taking root.[11] For the Liberal Party, an electoral victory was in sight, following a succession of provincial victories and the discontent with the Borden government's conduct of the war.[12]

This probable Liberal victory, to be based on anticonscription sentiment in Quebec and low tariff sentiment in the West, was averted by the formation of the Union government. The issue in that political transformation was whether the three western Liberal governments could be detached from the federal party. But the attempt made at the Winnipeg convention in August 1917 to prepare the way for this change was defeated by the official Liberals.[13] The insurgents refused to accept the verdict of the convention; and by negotiations, the course of which is by no means clear, the support of the three western administrations and of the farmers' organizations was won for Union government. Thus the leadership of the West was captured, and assurance was made doubly sure by the *Wartime Elections Act*. At the same time, the nascent third-party movement was absorbed by the Union government, and the Liberal Party in the West was wrecked by the issue of conscription, as the Conservative Party had been mortally wounded by reciprocity.

Though the Union government was constituted as a "win the war" administration, which should still partisan and sectional strife, other hopes had gone to its making. It was thought that a nonpartisan administration might also be an opportunity to carry certain reforms, such as that of civil-service recruitment, that it would be difficult, if not impossible, for a partisan government to carry. There was also, and inevitably, the tariff. The Union government was not publicly pledged to tariff reform, but there can be no doubt that western sentiment had forced Unionist candidates to declare themselves on the tariff; indeed many western Unionists were low-tariff Liberals, or even outright independents. The eastern industrialists, on the other hand, were alert to see that the weighty western wing of the cabinet should not induce the government to make concessions to the West. Thus there was an uneasy truce on the tariff question during the remainder of the war, the issue lying dormant but menacing for the unity of the government and its majority once the pressure of war should be removed. The test was to come with the first peace budget, that of 1919.

These, then, were the underlying causes of the rise of the western Progressive movement. In 1919 they came to the surface, unchanged in themselves but now operating in a heated and surcharged atmosphere. That there would have been a Progressive movement in any event is not to be doubted; the war and the events of the postwar years served to give it explosive force.

Certain elements in this surcharged atmosphere were general, others peculiar to the farmer, in effect. Chief of the general elements was the fact that the war of 1914–18 had been fought without economic controls of any significance. The result was inflation, with all the stresses and strains inflation sets up in the body economic and social. The high cost of living, as it was called, was an invariable theme of speakers of the day, particularly of spokesmen of labour and the farmer. The farmer was quite prepared to believe that he, as usual, was especially the victim of these circumstances, and would point to the "pork profiteers," to clinch his contention. Inflation was at the root of the general unrest of the day, and the influence of the Russian Revolution, the radical tone of many organizations and individuals, the Winnipeg strike, and the growth of the labour movement are to be ascribed to inflation rather than to any native predisposition to radical courses.

Among the farmers' special grievances was the conscription of farmers' sons in 1918. The farming population of English Canada, on the whole, had supported conscription, but with two qualifications. One was that there should also be "conscription of wealth," by which a progressive income tax was meant. The other was that the farms should not be stripped of their supply of labour, a not unreasonable condition in view of the urgent need to produce food. But the military situation in the spring of 1918 led to the revocation of the Order in Council exempting farmers' sons from military service. The result was a bitter outcry from the farmers, the great delegation to Ottawa in May 1918, and an abiding resentment against the Union government and all its works, especially in Ontario.

In the West itself, drought, especially in southern Alberta, had come to harass a farm population already sorely tried. Suffice it to indicate that in the Lethbridge area of southern Alberta the average yield of wheat between 1908 and 1921 ranged from sixty-three bushels to the acre in 1915 to two in 1918, and eight in 1921.[14] This was the extreme, but the whole West in varying degrees suffered a similar fluctuation in yield. It was a rehearsal of the disaster of the 1930s.

To the hazards of nature were to be added the hazards of the market. In 1917 the government had fixed the price of wheat to keep it from going higher, and had established a Wheat Board to market the crops of the war years. Now that peace had come, was wheat once more to be sold on the open market, or would the government fix the price and continue to market the crops through the Wheat Board, at least until the transition from war to peace was accomplished? Here was a chance to make the National Policy a matter of immediate benefit and concern to the western farmer, a chance not undiscerned by shrewd defenders of the National Policy.[15] Here also, under the stimulus of war, was the beginning of the transition from the old Jeffersonian and *laissez faire* tradition of the frontier West, to the new West of wheat pools, floor prices, and the Co-operative Commonwealth Federation. The point of principle was clearly grasped by the farmers, but their response was confused. The Manitoba Grain Growers and the United Farmers of Alberta declined in annual convention to ask the government to continue the Wheat Board, but this decision was severely criticized, one might almost say, was repudiated, by the rank and file of the membership. The Saskatchewan Grain Growers, who met later, emphatically demanded that the Wheat Board be continued. In the upshot it was, but only for the crop yield of 1919, and in 1920 it was liquidated. From this action came much of the drive, indeed the final impetus, of the Progressive movement.[16] Thereafter the western farmer was caught between fixed debt charges and high costs on one hand and falling prices on the other; his position seemed to him desperate. From his despair came first the Progressive electoral sweep in the West and then the economic action which created the wheat pools.

Finally, there was the question of tariff revision. It was, however, no longer the simple clash of sectional interests it had been. The custom tariff had been increased to help finance the war. Any revision now would affect governmental financing of the war debt, and also the financial resources of private individuals and corporations in the postwar period. In short, the question had now become, what place should tariff revision have in reconstruction?

It was to this question that the Union government had to address itself, while preparing the budget of 1919 under the vigilant eyes of the farmers' organizations on the one side and of the Canadian Manufacturers' Association on the other. The decision was, in effect, to postpone the issue, on the ground that 1919 was, to all intents and purposes, a war year and that only a very moderate revision should be attempted. The decision was not unreasonable, and was clearly intended to be a compromise between eastern and western views on the tariff.[17] But western supporters of the Union government were in a very vulnerable position, as the McMaster amendment to the motion to go into Committee of Supply was to show.[18] The pressure from the West for a major lowering of the tariff was mounting and becoming intense. In the outcome, the Honourable Thomas A. Crerar, minister of agriculture, resigned on the ground that the revision undertaken in the budget was insufficient. In the vote on the budget he was joined by nine western Unionists. This was the beginning of the parliamentary Progressive Party.

The position of the remaining western Unionists became increasingly difficult, though also their pressure contributed to the moderate revision of 1919.[19] The fate of R.C. Henders is very much in point. Henders had been, as president of the Manitoba Grain Growers, an ardent and outspoken agrarian. In 1916 he had been nominated as an independent candidate for Macdonald. In 1917 he accepted nomination as Unionist candidate and was elected. In 1919 he voted with the government on the budget, on the ground that this was in effect a war budget and the time premature for a revision of the tariff. In 1920 the United Farmers of Manitoba, following the action of their executive, "repudiated his stand, accepted his resignation, and reaffirmed [their] confidence in the principles of the Farmers' Platform."[20] In 1921 he vanished from political ken. An honest man had taken a politically mistaken line and was mercilessly held to account. Such was the fate of western Unionists who did not cross the floor or find refuge in the Senate. Western low-tariff sentiment would admit of no equivocation.

The third-party movement, stirring in the West before 1917 but absorbed and overridden by the Unionist government, was now free to resume its course with a favourable wind fanned by inflation, short crops, and postwar discontent. A chart had already been provided. The Canadian Council of Agriculture had in 1916 taken cognizance of the mounting demand that political action be taken by the farmers. Without committing the council itself, it prepared the Farmers' Platform as a program which the farmers' organizations might endorse and which they might press upon the government. The events of 1917 diverted attention from it, but in 1918 it was revised and enlarged, and in 1919 was adopted by the farmers' organizations. In substance, the platform called for a League of Nations; Dominion autonomy; free trade with Great Britain; reciprocity with the United States; a lowering of the general tariff; graduated income, inheritance, and corporation taxes; public ownership of a wide range of utilities; and certain reforms designed to bring about a great measure of democracy, such as reform of the Senate, abolition of titles, and the institution of direct legislation and proportional representation.[21] The platform gave the incoherent western discontent a rallying point and a program, and was the occasion for the organized farmers entering federal politics. Its title, "The New National Policy," was a gage of battle thrown down before the defenders of the old National Policy, a challenge, direct and explicit, to make that policy national indeed.

This decision to enter federal politics was opportune beyond the dream of seasoned politicians. The prairie was afire in a rising wind, and soon the flames were flaring from one end of the country to the other. In October 1919, the United Farmers of Ontario carried 46 seats in a house of 111, and formed an administration. Later in the same month O.R. Gould, farmers' candidate in the federal seat of Assiniboia, defeated W.R. Motherwell, Liberal stalwart and a founder of the Grain Growers' Association, by a majority of 5,224.[22] A few days later Alex Moore carried Cochrane in a provincial by-election for the United Farmers of Alberta. In 1920 the organized farmers carried nine seats in Manitoba, seven in Nova Scotia, and ten in New Brunswick.[23] By-election after by-election went against the government, usually to farmer candidates, until the smashing climax of the Medicine Hat by-election of June 1921, when Robert Gardiner of the UFA defeated a popular Unionist candidate by a majority of 9,764.[24] Even the Liberals' tariff plank of 1919 did little to check the sweep of the flames. The political prophets were estimating that, of the 43 seats west of the lakes, the Progressives would carry from 35 to 40.[25]

All was propitious, then, for the entry of the Progressives into federal politics. There they might hope to hold the balance of power, or even emerge as the largest group. The work of organization was pushed steadily. In December 1920 the Canadian Council of Agriculture recognized the third party in the House of Commons as the exponent of the new national policy and endorsed the members' choice of the Honourable T.A. Crerar as leader.[26] During 1920 and 1921 Progressive candidates were nominated by local conventions in all federal constituencies in the West.

Two major difficulties, however, were arising to embarrass the Progressives in their bid for national power. The first was the charge that they were a class party. The second was the demand that political action be taken in the provincial as well as the federal field.[27] These embarrassments were eventually to split the movement, defeat its bid for national power, and reduce it to the status of a sectional party.

The origin of these divisions in the movement may best be examined by turning to provincial politics in the West. That the entrance into federal politics could not be kept separate from a demand that political action be taken in the provinces arose in part from the federal composition of national parties. Any federal political movement is driven to attempt the capture of provincial governments, in order to acquire the means, that is to say, the patronage, whereby to build an effective political organization. It is not to be supposed that this political maxim was unknown to the leaders of the Progressive movement. They hoped, however, that national success would be followed by a voluntary adherence of the western governments, which would render capture by storm unnecessary.

The Progressive movement, at the same time, was a genuine attempt to destroy machine politics, and there was in its leadership a sincere reluctance to accept the facts of political life. They hoped to lead a popular movement, to which the farmers' economic organizations would furnish whatever direction was necessary. It was the zeal of their followers, eager to destroy the old parties wherever they existed, that carried the Progressive movement into provincial politics.

Province by province, the leaders were compelled to bow to the pressure of the rank and file, and allow the organized farmers to enter the provincial arenas. The methods and the results, however, were by no means identical, for they were conditioned by the different political histories of the three provinces.

In Manitoba the dominating fact was that from 1899 until 1915 the province had been governed by the Conservative Roblin administration. The sheer power and efficiency of the Roblin-Rogers organization, perhaps the classic example of the political machine in Canadian history, accounts in great part for the victory of the antireciprocity campaign in Manitoba in 1911. Its spectacular demise in the odour of scandal in 1915 left the provincial Conservative Party badly shattered. Henceforth there were many loose Conservative votes in the most Conservative of the prairie provinces, a province a whole generation older than the other two, and during that generation the very image and transcript of Ontario. But the succeeding Liberal government, that of the Honourable T.C. Norris, was reformist and progressive. There was little the Grain Growers could ask of the provincial administration that it was not prepared to grant. Why then should the organized farmers oppose the Norris government? The answer was that the Progressive movement was, for many Progressives, a revolt against the old party system, and the provincial Liberal organization had been affiliated with the federal Liberals. It might, indeed, become a major buttress of Liberalism as the breach between the Laurier and the Unionist Liberals closed. If the old parties were to be defeated at Ottawa, they must be rooted out at the source of their strength in the provinces. Out of this conflict, largely one between leaders and rank and file, came the decision of the new United Farmers of Manitoba in 1920 that the organization as such should not enter provincial politics, but that in the constituencies the locals might hold conventions, nominate candidates, and organize. If a majority of constituencies should prove to be in favour of political action, then the executive of the United Farmers would call a provincial convention to draft a platform.[28] As a result, political action was taken locally, and nine farmer representatives were elected to the Manitoba legislature in 1920.[29] As a result of this success, the UFM placed the resources of the organization behind the farmers' political action,[30] and in the election of 1922 the farmers won a plurality of seats in the legislature. The suspected *rapprochement* of the Norris government with the federal Liberals may have contributed to its defeat.[31]

In Saskatchewan and Alberta the dominating factor was that at the creation of the two provinces in 1905 the federal Liberal government used its influence to establish Liberal administrations. In Canada the possession of power is all but decisive. Governments fall not so much by the assaults of their enemies as through their own internal decay. From 1905 until 1921 the Liberals ruled in Alberta; from 1905 until 1929 they were in power in Saskatchewan. Moreover, in both, the Conservative Party was cut off from patronage and unnaturally compelled to be a party of provincial rights. Both provincial Conservative parties declined from 1911 on, and rapidly after the provincial elections of 1917. In these provinces too, the administrations were careful to govern in harmony with the wishes of the organized farmers. Why then should the farmers enter provincial politics against the Liberal government? Again the answer is that the provincial Liberal parties were affiliated with the federal party, and were examples of the machine politics which Progressives hoped to destroy, politics rendered noisome by the corruption arising from the scramble for the resources of the West, and the political ruthlessness of the professional politicians of the day.

Down to 1917 the political developments of the two provinces were alike, but a remarkable diversion occurs thereafter. In Saskatchewan the Liberal Party enjoyed shrewd leadership, considerable administrative ability, and a fine political organization. Threatened by scandal in 1917, it made a remarkable recovery under Premier William Martin. In that almost wholly rural province, the Liberal government was a government of the grain growers. Leadership, as in the instance of the Honourable Charles A.

Dunning, graduated from the association to the government. The slightest wish of the Saskatchewan Grain Growers became law with as much dispatch as the conventions of government allow.[32] When the demand for provincial political action arose, Premier Martin met it, in the Preeceville speech of May 1920, by dissociating the provincial from the federal party. At the same time the weight of the executive of the Grain Growers was thrown against intervention as a separate party in provincial politics. As in Manitoba, when the demand, partly under pressure from the Non-Partisan League, became irresistible, it was referred to the locals.[33] The locals gave little response during 1920–21, and an attempt by third-party men in 1921 to commit the central organization to political action was foiled.[34] As a result, the provincial Progressive movement in Saskatchewan became largely an attempt at organization by independents, under the leadership of Harris Turner of Saskatoon.[35] Before organization could be well begun, Premier Martin dissolved the legislature and headed off the movement by a snap election. This was decisive. Only thirteen independents were returned, to a great extent, it would seem, by Conservative votes, for the provincial Conservative Party simply did not contest the election. Thus the Liberal administration in Saskatchewan survived the Progressive rising, but at the price of severing temporarily its ties with the federal party.

In Alberta the same story was to have a very different outcome. Not only was the Liberal Party of that province less fortunate in its leadership, though no less realistic in its tactics, not only did it suffer division by the quarrel over the Alberta Great Waterways Railway scandal, which created a weakness in the party that the division into Laurier and Unionist Liberals did nothing to mend,[36] but the farmer organization of that province was separate in its leadership from the government, and that leadership was from 1915 the leadership of Henry Wise Wood. In Alberta, the forceful personalities were outside the government; in Saskatchewan, they were, on the whole, in the government or close to it. Alberta lost the brilliant A.L. Sifton to the Union government in 1917, and Alberta alone possessed a Henry Wise Wood. Wood and the executive of the United Farmers of Alberta were no more anxious than other leaders of the farm organizations to go into provincial politics. He, indeed, was on principle opposed to going into politics at all. The drive for a third, independent, farmer party, however, developed much greater force in Alberta than elsewhere. This was partly because the decline of the Conservative Party was even more pronounced in Alberta than in Saskatchewan. It was also because the Non-Partisan League became more powerful in that province than in Saskatchewan. American populism and British radicalism had freer play in frontier Alberta than in older Saskatchewan. The Non-Partisan League, for example, captured two provincial seats in Alberta in 1917, whereas it had captured only one in Saskatchewan in the same year, and that by a fluke. The League went on to threaten to capture the locals of the UFA by conversion and infiltration. This was a threat that could not be ignored, because it was in and through the locals that the farmers' organizations lived. Wood and the UFA leaderships were therefore caught on the horns of a dilemma. They knew that political action had invariably ruined farm organizations in the past, as the Farmers' Alliance in the United States had gone to wreck in the Populist Party. They knew also that they might lose control of the UFA if the Non-Partisan League obtained control of a majority of locals and assumed leadership of the drive for political action. Wood solved the dilemma by his concept of "group government," and in doing so crystallized the strong tendency of the Progressive movement, a tendency which owed much to the Non-Partisan League, to become a class movement, deeply averse to lawyers, bankers, and politicians. The UFA would take political action, but it would take it as an organization. It would admit only farmers to its ranks; it would nominate only farmers for election; its representation in the legislature would constitute a separate group, cooperating with other groups but not combining with any to constitute a political party. Guided by this concept, the UFA in 1919 entered politics, both federal and provincial.[37] In 1921 it won a majority of the seats in the Alberta legislature.

These varying fortunes of the Progressive movement in the three provinces were significant for the character of the federal Progressive Party. Broadly speaking, two concepts of the character and future of the party prevailed among its members. One, which may be termed the Manitoba view, was that the Progressive movement was one of insurgent Liberalism, which might have the happy result of recapturing the federal Liberal party from the control of the Conservative and protectionist Liberals of the East. This was the view, for example, of J.W. Dafoe, a mentor of Progressivism. It aimed at building up a national, popular movement by "broadening out," by "opening the door" to all sympathizers. The Saskatchewan federal Progressives also accepted this view, the more so as the provincial movement had been headed off for a decade. The other concept may be called the Alberta concept. It was that the Progressive movement was an occupational or class movement, capable of extension by group organization to other economic classes, but not itself concerned with bringing about such extension. Farmer must represent farmer, the group must act as a group.

It may be noted in passing that neither view of the Progressive movement demands an explicit farmer-labour alliance. Why Progressivism did not develop this characteristic of the earlier Populist Party and the later Co-operative Commonwealth Federation cannot be explained here, but it may be said that the leadership of both wings of the movement was averse to an open alliance with labour.

Here again is the two-fold character of the Progressive movement postulated in the opening paragraph. Progressivism which was an economic protest, seeking a natural remedy by political action little more unconventional than a revolt from caucus rule, is here termed Manitoban. Progressivism which was doctrinaire, class conscious, and heterodox is here called Albertan. The former assumed that exploitation would cease in a society made competitive by the abolition of protection; the latter proposed to produce a harmony of interests by putting an end to competition by means of the cooperation of organized groups. Both tendencies, of course, existed all across the movement. Each was personified and the respective protagonists were the Honourable T.A. Crerar and Henry Wise Wood.

The extremes, however, were fundamental and irreconcilable. Manitoban Progressivism sought economic ends through conventional political means and admitted of compromise with the old parties. Albertan Progressivism sought much the same economic ends, but also sought to transform the conditions of politics. In this it was closer to the essential nature of Progressivism, with its innate distrust of elected representatives and of party organization.[38] Its pledging of candidates, its frequent use of the signed recall, its levy on members for campaign funds, its predilection for direct legislation and for proportional representation, establish its fundamental character. That in so conducting itself it was to give rise to forms of political organization which oldline politicians were to envy is one of those little ironies which delight the sardonic observer.

An examination of the course of the general election of 1921 adds little to the exposition of the theme. As revealed in the campaign literature, it turned on the issues of protection and of the class doctrines of Henry Wise Wood. Prime Minister Meighen, first of those western men with eastern principles to be called to head the Conservative Party, put on the full armour of protection, and fought the western revolt in defence of the National Policy. It was courageous, it was magnificent, but it was not successful. His party attacked the Progressives as free traders seeking to destroy the National Policy for selfish class advantage. Mr. W.L. Mackenzie King stood firmly on the Liberal platform of 1919, which, marvellously contrived, faced squarely all points of the political compass at once. Liberal strategy was to avoid a sharp stand, to pose as the farmers' friend—"There never was a Farmers' Party while the Liberals were in power"[39] —to denounce the class character of Progressivism. Mr. Crerar was in the embarrassing position of a leader whose followers persist in treading on his heels, but he fought the good fight with dignity and moderation, protesting that his was not a class movement.

In the upshot, the Progressives carried sixty-five seats, and emerged as the second-largest group in the House. Coalition with the Liberals was seriously considered and was rejected only at the last moment, presumably because Messrs. Crerar and Drury could not obtain from Mr. King those pledges which would have ensured the identity of the group and the curbing of the protectionist elements in the Liberal cabinet. This decision marked the beginning of the disintegration of the movement, for the Progressives neither imposed their policies on the Liberals nor definitely became a parliamentary party seeking office. With that fatal tendency of third parties to avoid responsibility, of which George Langley had warned a decade before,[40] they declined to become even the official opposition.

Thereafter Manitoban Progressivism lost its bright speed amid the sands and shallows of official Liberalism. Albertan Progressivism, represented by the Ginger Group, the federal UFA members, and a few others, alone survived the decay of Progressive zeal, and remained for fourteen years to lend distinction to the national councils, and to bear in its organization the seeds at once of Social Credit and the Co-operative Commonwealth Federation.

Notes

1. Cf. Frederick Jackson Turner, *The Significance of Sections in American History* (New York, 1932), 314.

2. *Hansard*, 1910–11, Vol. I, 1918.

3. Wilfred E. Binkley, *American Political Parties* (New York, 1944)—" ... Madison's principle that a nation wide majority can agree only on a moderate program," 87; also 17–18.

4. Dafoe Library of the *Winnipeg Free Press*, Dafoe Papers, Dafoe to Sir Clifford Sifton, 21 July 1919, on the prospects of reorganizing the Liberal Party.

5. *Manitoba Free Press*, 10 April 1917, 9.

6. *Grain Growers' Guide*, 14 September 1910, 13. Fred Kirkham, advocate of a third party, wrote to the editor from Saltcoats, Saskatchewan: "If the memorials presented to Sir Wilfrid Laurier have failed to imbue him with the determination to battle with the vested interests of the East to grant our just requests, we have no alternative but to become democratic insurgents, and form a new party and find a new general to fight under. We must be courageous in politics before Laurier will treat with us as a big community of votes to be reckoned with."

7. Public Archives of Canada, *Laurier Papers*, 3089, J.W. Dafoe to Laurier, 28 April 1911. "In my judgment reciprocity has changed the whole political situation in the West. Until it was announced the drift out West was undoubtedly against the government; but now it is just the other way about."

8. United Farmers of Alberta, *Annual Report*, 1910, 43.

Moved by the Vermilion Union: Resolved, that ten farmers, as members of Parliament with votes would have more weight in shaping the laws and influencing government than one thousand delegates as petitioners:

Therefore be it further resolved that the farmers, to secure this end, should vote for farmers only to represent them in Parliament and vote as a unit and cease dividing their voting power. Carried.

9. I am indebted to Professor J.R. Mallory of Brandon College, now of McGill, for a discussion clarifying this point.

10. *Manitoba Free Press*, 13 May 1916, Editorial, "Consequences." "Whatever may be the political consequences of this blunder to Liberalism in Canada at large, Western Liberalism will not suffer if it adheres to the independence which its representatives have displayed at Ottawa this week. These developments at the capital must tend to strengthen the feeling which has been growing steadily for years that Western Liberals need not look to the East, at present, for effective and progressive leadership ... Canadian public life will thus be given what it sorely needs, ... a group of convinced radicals ... To your tents, O Israel!"

11. Ibid., 28 June 1917, 9, "The Saskatchewan Victory." "The Canadian West is in the mood to break away from past affiliations and traditions and inaugurate a new political era of sturdy support for an advanced and radical programme. The break-up of parties has given the West its opportunity; and there is no doubt it will take advantage of it." At least four independent candidates had been nominated in the West before June 1917 in provincial and federal seats. In December 1916 the Canadian Council of Agriculture had issued the first Farmers' Platform.

12. Henry Borden, ed., *Robert Laird Borden: His Memoirs* Vol. II (Toronto, 1938), 749–50, J.W. Dafoe to Borden, 29 September 1917.

13. Dafoe Papers, Dafoe to Augustus Bridle, 14 June 1921. "The Western Liberal Convention was a bomb which went off in the hands of its makers. It was decided upon at Ottawa by a group of conscription Liberals; the intention was to bring into existence a Western Liberal group free from Laurier's control who would be prepared to consider coalition with Borden on its merits, but the Liberal machine in the West went out and captured the delegates with the result that the convention was strongly pro-Laurier."

14. *Report of the Survey Board for Southern Alberta*, January 1922.

15. *Hansard*, 1919, Vol. I, 558. Colonel J.A. Currie (Simcoe). "I am quite in agreement with the hon. member for Maple Creek (J.A. Maharg) when he says we should fix a price for the wheat of the West. That is in line with the National Policy." See also the Right Honourable Arthur Meighen's proposal for a modified Wheat Board in his speech at Portage la Prairie during the campaign of 1921. *Canadian Annual Review*, 1921, 449–50.

16. Cf. Vernon C. Fowke, *Canadian Agricultural Policy* (Toronto, 1946), 268.

17. The changes were as follows: The 7.5 percent increase for war purposes was removed from agricultural implements and certain necessities of life; the 5 percent war duty was modified; an income tax was levied.

18. Fourteen western Unionists voted for the amendment. *Hansard*, 1919, Vol. IV, 3678.

19. *Hansard*, 1919, Vol. IV, 3475. W.D. Cowan, Unionist (Regina). "I believe that the changes which have been made in the tariff have been made entirely because of the agitation which has been carried on by the West. We have had, for the first time, I fancy, in the history of Parliament, a western caucus and in that we have been united. Old time Liberals united with old time Conservatives. On the one point that they should try to get substantial reductions in the tariffs ... "

20. *Canadian Annual Review*, 1920, 741.

21. See ibid., 1919, for text, 365–68.

22. *Parliamentary Companion*, 1921, 196.

23. *Manitoba Free Press*, 25 February 1921; *Grain Growers' Guide*, 4 August 1920, 4, and 27 October 1920, 5.

24. *Parliamentary Companion*, 1922, 247.

25. Dafoe Papers, Dafoe to Sir Clifford Sifton, 20 January 1920.
26. *Grain Growers' Guide*, 15 December 1920, 3. Resolution of executive of the Canadian Council of Agriculture in meeting of 7–9 December 1920.
27. Dafoe Papers, Dafoe to Sir Clifford Sifton, 26 January 1921. "Crerar's only troubles out here arise from the ardor with which certain elements in his following insist upon organizing a purely class movement against the three local governments, thereby tending to antagonize the very elements which Crerar is trying, by broadening its basis, to add to his party."
28. *United Farmers of Manitoba Yearbook*, 1920, 67.
29. *Grain Growers' Guide*, 7 July 1920, 6, Editorial, "The Manitoba Election." "The United Farmers of Manitoba, as an organization, took no part in the election, and each constituency where farmer candidates were nominated and elected acted entirely on its own initiative."
30. Ibid., 19 January 1921, 3.
31. *Manitoba Free Press*, 28 April 1922. Dafoe Papers, Dafoe to Sir Clifford Sifton, 7 July 1922.
32. *Minutes of the Annual Convention of the Saskatchewan Grain Growers' Association*, 18–21 February 1919, 4, report of Premier Wm. Martin's address. "There are questions now coming before you affecting the welfare of the whole community of the Province. It is the policy of the present government and will continue to be the policy of the present government to carry out these suggestions."
33. Ibid., 9–13 February 1920, 114–19.
34. Ibid., 31 January–4 February 1921. The debate on provincial political action was involved; a motion to enter provincial politics as an organization was defeated (118) and a motion to support action by constituencies was, it would seem, shelved (93).
35. *Saskatoon Daily Star*, 1 June 1921. Report of the convention of independents at Saskatoon, 31 May 1921.
36. John Blue, *Alberta Past and Present* (Chicago, 1924), 125. "The session of 1910 witnessed a perturbation and upheaval that split the Liberal party into two factions, which more than a decade afterwards regarded each other with some jealousy and distrust."
37. *United Farmers of Alberta, Annual Report,* 1919, 52–53.
38. *Grain Growers' Guide*, 5 March 1919, 26, article by Roderick McKenzie on "Political Action." "The purpose of the movement inaugurated by the farmers is that whenever the time comes to make a choice of representation to parliament, the electors get together to make their selection."
39. P.A.C., Pamphlet No. 5081, *Group Government Compared with Responsible Government.*
40. *Grain Growers' Guide*, 2 September 1910, 13–14. "It may be urged that a separate farmers' party might influence the government even if it did not become strong enough to take on itself the actual work of governing. The answer to that is this. The legitimate objective of a political party is to control the legislative and administrative functions. Without [that] objective it cannot exist for any length of time . . . "

The United Farmers of Alberta, 1921-1935

CARL F. BETKE

Reprinted from Carlo Caldarola, ed., *Society and Politics in Alberta*
(Agincourt, Ont.: Metheun, 1979), 14-32, by permission of the author.

In the history of Alberta provincial politics, the 1920s and early 1930s are known as the period of farmer ascendancy. I propose to turn this around, to state that, in the history of Alberta farmer organization, the 1920s and early 1930s are known as a brief period of political ascendancy. To shift the emphasis allows one to perceive the passing political activity of the period against the much richer complexity of the efforts made by Alberta farmers to cope with their collective problems, which they consistently described in economic terms. Their economic place in society was the concern which underlay the creation of the United Farmers of Alberta (UFA) in the first place. Chronologies written by farm group spokesmen themselves retain the perspective I am choosing. While outsiders may be fascinated by the political phase of Alberta farmers' group endeavours, the farmers themselves understood it to have less significance than the formation of the UFA organization, for example, or the long-term experiments with produce pool marketing.[1]

Besides, giving attention to the farmers' own preoccupations permits one to notice a relatively ignored but nevertheless important theme: the development among Alberta farmers of the same kind of cohesive attack on impediments to their economic advancement which would for educated groups such as lawyers or doctors be termed "professionalization," or for factory and trade workers be known as "unionization." Henry Wise Wood, the president of the UFA from 1916 to 1931, did not come to his views of modern community development in an environmental vacuum, nor was his social theory unrealistic in terms of Alberta farmer experience. The consolidation within economic groups to define their socioeconomic space was most obvious to him in the example of the Canadian Manufacturers' Association, but his own Alberta farmer followers had a history of organizational effort stretching back to the 1880s.[2]

Of course, the experiences of the Alberta farmers with prairie farming changed over the years. Their situation after World War I was not comparable with their situation in, say, 1900. For one thing, the people had changed. There were eight times as many people in Alberta in 1921 as in 1901, and three-quarters of them lived and worked in a rural and agricultural environment. Most had been there long enough to have seen that their original homestead quarter-sections had to be supplemented by further acquisitions, and boom conditions, especially during wartime, had encouraged them to go into debt. Most had been in North America, if not in Alberta, for quite some time, becoming seasoned in North American and prairie farming ways. Many who could not adjust could and did leave; those who remained, added to the young prairie-born, were presumably committed to Alberta farm life. They had discovered that the best cash crop was wheat and the next best oats, but that the costs of transportation, equipment, feed for work animals, land, and labour were high and sometimes as unpredictable as the size or market value of their crops.

It was small wonder that farmers got together to complain about the Canadian protective tariffs on farm machinery, to pressure governments to regulate marketing practices at grain elevators and to regulate railway freight rates, and to cooperate in running their own elevator companies and grain marketing agencies.[3] While they may have seemed political novices, they were not organizational novices. By the time the UFA began to consider active political intervention both federally and provincially, they had, in common with other prairie farm groups, a considerable tradition of concerted collective effort to cope with their economic circumstances. And when politics proved not to be the answer, they were not particularly slow to move on to other measures.

The Electoral Success of the UFA

The political alternative arose towards the end of World War I, coinciding with the election of Henry Wise Wood to the UFA presidency in 1916. With a knack for expressing traditional UFA aims and methods within the framework of portentous social theory, Wood at first resisted the novel and exciting idea of direct farmer participation in federal and provincial politics. Its effect, argued Wood, would be to jeopardize the advances the UFA had made in establishing collective solidarity and lobby pressure on governments, by diverting farmer energies to an activity which involved premature attention to outside interests.[4]

Wood was no Marxist. He saw society in terms of brotherhood and community; but, with a goodly dose of realism, he thought that end likely only if each economic group—and it was a community of economic specialty groups that he envisioned—represented its own interests as powerfully (but fairly) as possible. His was not a vision of antagonism, of victory over an enemy. It was not, as C.B. Macpherson[5] would have it, for Wood a contest between producing and nonproducing (parasitic) groups, the one side to vanquish the other. Rather, farmers ought to *emulate* successful groups such as the Canadian Manufacturers' Association or doctors' and lawyers' professional associations, the end result to be a healthy, cooperative tension among a community of distinct groups.

When Alberta farmers showed enthusiasm, therefore, for the "New National Policy" issued by the Canadian Council of Agriculture in 1918, with its impetus to direct political action, Wood was stimulated to ensure that the organized Alberta farmers would not lose their unanimity in the process of the transition to politics. In speeches, interviews, and articles through 1919, 1920, and 1921, Wood sustained the UFA tradition of solidarity by preaching the doctrine of "group government," on the principle of instructed delegation, with successful political candidates representing the local branches of the economic organization that had supported their candidature. Farmers went into politics in Alberta in 1921 in exactly the same way they had undertaken other projects: as an isolated group, slightly apart even from those Labour candidates in urban centres who were eager to associate themselves with a burgeoning political movement.[6]

Practical obstacles to the fair implementation of such a scheme were raised repeatedly during the 1921 provincial election campaign in the Liberal and Conservative rhetoric and in most of the province's newspapers. Those arguments did not deter rural voter enthusiasm for the UFA program. Over 62 percent of the vote in the rural ridings propelled thirty-eight successful UFA candidates into control of the sixty-one-seat Legislative Assembly. This unforeseen result immediately revealed the glaring impossibility of "group government" in the new legislature. In Wood's formula, the legislative representative of various economic groups, once elected, should go on to administer the province's affairs on the basis of the consensus reached on each issue, eliminating cabinet government. But the dominance of the representatives of the organized farmers, coupled with the normal partisan tactics of the opposition, made a mockery of the whole scheme.

Not that all UFA legislators perceived the situation on the spot. The highlights of the first session of the Legislative Assembly after the election were the revolts of certain UFA backbenchers against unanimity imposed after caucus deliberations. A pair of UFA members embarrassed the government by proposing an alternate nominee for the Speaker's chair after the government choice had been indicated. The controversy over that had hardly died away before a motion was proposed which would make legislative defeat of a government bill insufficient reason for the resignation of the government, a motion designed to undermine cabinet and caucus control. Later a Dairyman's Bill, which had been introduced by Minister of Agriculture George Hoadley, appeared to have passed third reading when some UFA members challenged the Speaker to call a vote, in which the government was barely sustained with the help of a few Labour and Independent members. But these and other disruptions were soon ended by arguments of parliamentary reason—within the very caucus meetings the minority of members sought to eliminate.

The cabinet minister most responsible for settling down rebellious UFA members to the system of government by cabinet and caucus solidarity was Attorney General John Edward Brownlee, the only lawyer on the government side of the legislature, whose candidature as a farm representative had been judged legitimate on the basis of his former positions as solicitor for the UFA and the United Grain Growers (UGG). He had declined, however, to be considered for the position of premier on the grounds that a UFA premier should be a farmer. But the farmer premier, Herbert Greenfield, was gradually superseded in the Legislative Assembly debates by Brownlee. By 1925 Greenfield's frequent absences due to illness, coupled with Brownlee's organizational efficiency and dominance of legislative debate, caused UFA representatives to prefer Brownlee's leadership to Greenfield's, despite the latter's continuing personal popularity. In November 1925, Brownlee replaced Greenfield as premier of Alberta. It was a timely change, for Brownlee epitomized the administrative competence which was the foundation of the next two UFA provincial election campaigns.

In Brownlee, the UFA had a leader who knew how to organize a busy short session of government legislation, provoking the *Edmonton Bulletin* more than once in 1926 to attack the "U.F.A. steamroller." In an auspicious first session for Brownlee as premier, the government was able to announce, for the first time since before the war, a budget surplus for the previous year. This important coup seemed at first about to be joined by others, as negotiations for the transfer of natural resources to provincial jurisdiction came near completion and conferences were held in Ottawa to arrange for the sale of the costly northern Alberta railways to either the Canadian Pacific Railway (CPR) or the Canadian National Railway (CNR). Unfortunately, in April Brownlee had to announce that the CPR, previous manager of the Edmonton, Dunvegan, and British Columbia Railway, was unwilling to purchase on government terms and that neither the offer from the CNR nor the CPR for lease of the line was satisfactory to the Alberta government. Then, in May, government uneasiness about a clause in the Dominion natural resources bill indicating that a system of separate schools for Alberta would be included in the transfer resulted in a telegram to Prime Minister King advocating the elimination of any such wording which would affect Alberta's constitution under the 1905 Alberta Act.[7] These two pieces of unfinished business had to be postponed until after the mandatory election. Just how badly the government wanted to have the natural resources transfer completed in time for the election is indicated by the premature inclusion in an election campaign pamphlet of the January agreement between the province and the Dominion.[8]

The election campaign in 1926 was a rather different affair from that of 1921. Some of the best UFA organizers in some areas had become marketing pool officials, and provincial constituency associations were relatively weak. Local interest had shifted from the UFA organization to the pools, particularly because farmers now had political farmer representatives at both the federal and provincial levels. Many locals active in 1921 had ceased to exist or were conducting infrequent token meetings. For a government with no campaign funds of its own, this was potential disaster.[9] Accordingly, Brownlee pressed Wood in January for an early meeting with the UFA executive to discuss "ways and means of perfecting plans for the organization drive and the campaign for the election" in order to have the necessary preliminary work well taken care of. The following UFA campaign for the election of 28 June was based primarily on the government record rather than on a set of UFA principles.[10] The important campaign speakers were cabinet ministers, defending the achievements of the previous five years.

As soon as the election date was announced, Brownlee outlined the government's strategy:

> On our record for the past five years, and that alone, we are going to the people. Rather than make promises I may be unable to fulfill, I would rather go down to defeat at the polls. We contend that the record of the present administration is the answer to the charges of the leaders of the old-line parties . . . whatever government goes into power after that vote is taken, it will inherit a balanced budget and other big public problems either solved or well on the way toward solution.

The cabinet ministers would follow this formula, emphasizing economical administration and constructive policies to focus attention on the government rather than on the UFA. The principal UFA campaign pamphlet was entitled *Five Years of Progress* and featured a front full-page picture of Brownlee. In this summary of government activities of the past five years, all provincial problems were held to have been inherited from the previous regime and either to have been or to be in the process of being cleared away by the current administration. Lower freight rates and better Vancouver harbour facilities for grain marketing were the result of pressure by the provincial government on the federal government. Problems of debt adjustment and rural credit unsolved by the provincial government were actually matters of purely federal concern. Efficiency was held to characterize the operation of Alberta Government Telephones and of the Lacombe and North Western and the Alberta and Great Waterways Railways, as well as of all government departments. Partisan patronage in government appointments had been replaced by the principle of merit.[11]

The UFA faced a larger number of candidates than they had in 1921, but on the whole these were less experienced and under the leadership of newcomers. Liberal leader Captain J.T. Shaw and Conservative leader A.A. McGillivray, supported by almost full slates of candidates, both attacked the government for permitting annual accumulations of debt, even though in the last year the deficit, they claimed, had been disguised as a surplus. Both leaders emphasized the inefficiency of a government which was unable to complete either the natural resources transfer or dispensation of the northern railways.[12] Neither was able to remove his campaign from the very battleground confidently marked out by the government. Neither presented a spectacular new program for the future.

The main effect of the campaign activities of the UFA organization (as distinct from the government) was to identify the successful Wheat, Dairy, Poultry, and Livestock Pools which had been integrated since 1923 with the UFA organization and, therefore, with the UFA government. Upon a united UFA, *The U.F.A.* implied, depended all the benefits accruing to the farmers of Alberta. In this case too, the opposition leaders unwittingly aided the government. There were repeated charges that UFA candidates were unfairly referring to the Wheat Pool as though it had been secured by the UFA government alone and did not have the approval of the Conservatives or the Liberals. The Conservative leader pointed out the names of several prominent Conservatives actively involved in the creation of the Wheat Pool but in the same breath urged separation of the UFA from politics. He encouraged the development of even greater UFA membership, "but along the lines that it was originally intended, an organization where the farmers and their wives may meet socially and to discuss matters pertaining to the farm." Evidently unaware that he was condemning one of the most successful UFA enterprises, he went on to state that the UFA "was never intended to be a political organization."[13]

The force of the opposition attack, feeble to begin with, was further blunted by repeated reports from all over Alberta that crops were away to a splendid start. Then too, during the final two weeks of the campaign, press coverage of campaign activities was overshadowed by stories of the fascinating disappearance and return of American evangelist Aimee Semple McPherson and by the threat of a Liberal government collapse in the House of Commons occasioned by withdrawal of support by a few rebellious UFA members. In the cities there was noticeably less enthusiasm for the 1926 campaign than there had been in 1921. Only J.F. Lymburn was able to arouse a measure of interest. Chosen by Brownlee to be the new attorney general at the outset of the campaign, Lymburn was to be offered a rural seat but chose, as an Edmontonian, to test urban opinion. Branded by the *Edmonton Bulletin* as the "handpicked Attorney-General" of the "present H.W. Wood Premier," Lymburn nevertheless campaigned as "Edmonton's Cabinet Minister" and based his appeal on the elimination of "partyism" in Alberta, claiming that neither established party in Alberta was founded on any great principle.[14]

When the votes were counted, Lymburn was at the top of the list in Edmonton, and the UFA government found itself with greater support in the legislature than it had had during the previous term. Of sixty seats, forty-three would be filled by successful UFA candidates. Liberal representation dropped from sixteen to seven, who, with the four new Conservatives, would form the only consistent opposition, since the six Labour members could be counted upon to support many UFA policies. Alex Ross, former minister of public works and only a hesitant candidate for reelection in Calgary, was one casualty, but that result did not appear to disturb Brownlee unduly. He declined to invite a Labour member into his cabinet, preferring instead former Speaker

O.L. McPherson to take the Public Works portfolio.[15] The total turnout of voters had been down some 40 percent from the nearly full turnout of 1921, but, with whatever degree of enthusiasm, the electorate had presented the Brownlee administration with a generous mandate to carry on with the policies initiated in the preceding term.

During the 1926 election campaign, Brownlee indicated his awareness of two unsolved problems inherited from the Liberal administration which should be settled as quickly as possible. The first of these concerned the administration of several northern railway lines and the second the transfer of Alberta's natural resources from federal to provincial jurisdiction.[16] Both these issues involved intensive negotiations by the government and almost no participation by the UFA, but both were subjects of interest to UFA adherents. The solution of both was extremely significant to the outcome of the 1930 provincial election.

The farmers of the Peace River district made the strongest representations, on behalf of reduction of their formidable freight costs as well as suitable additions to the Edmonton, Dunvegan, and British Columbia and the Central Canada Railways, their two railroad outlets. The government's dilemma was its financial commitment to those two lines as well as to the Alberta and Great Waterways Railway, which, by a 1920 agreement, the Alberta government had been compelled to take over according to the terms of a guarantee to the former owner, J.D. McArthur.[17]

The government was operating the Alberta and Great Waterways Railway itself, so when the Canadian Pacific Railway operational lease of the first two Peace River lines ran out in November 1926, the government gambled on running them as well, until either the CPR or the CNR should make a suitable offer to purchase the railways and extend their ranges. The gamble paid off exceedingly well, for the subsequent two-and-one-half years of negotiation were carried on against the background of unexpectedly prosperous railway operations by the government. When in February 1929 the final agreement was drawn up, relinquishing to the CPR and the CNR jointly the Edmonton, Dunvegan, and British Columbia Railway, the Central Canada Railway, the Central Canada Express Company, the Alberta and Great Waterways Railway, and the Pembina Valley Railway, the purchasers agreed to complete the extensions initiated by the Alberta government, as well as to add not less than sixty miles within five years to the Edmonton, Dunvegan, and British Columbia and the Central Canada Railways in the Peace River district. A great burden was removed from the UFA government, and congratulations were received from all sides.

The transfer of natural resources to the jurisdiction of the province was accomplished after rather sporadic communications between Edmonton and Ottawa. The first breakthrough did not come until late 1928, when the Dominion government finally agreed to extend proposed subsidies, to be paid to the provinces for years of alienation of resources, past a three-year limit into perpetuity. Another year later, it was agreed to follow Saskatchewan Premier Gardiner's proposal to escalate the subsidies as provincial populations increased. Not until December 1929 did the final meetings take place which resulted in the agreement for the transfer.[18] The success and timing of the negotiations depended rather less on Brownlee than on the initiative of Premiers Gardiner and Bracken and the procrastination of Mackenzie King. Nevertheless, it was politically fortunate for the UFA government that 1930, a good year for an election, featured the legislative session in which the transfer was ratified.

Speculators early began to predict an election, pointing out that an administration with sale of the railways and transfer of natural resources to its credit stood "about as 'ace-high' as any government could hope to stand after nine years of office." The government announced in April that an election would take place on 19 June. The formal notice was accompanied by the statement that the government confidently expected the imminent ratification in the Dominion House of the natural resources transfer agreement. "This agreement, following the completion last year of the sale of the Northern Alberta Railways, brings to a close the last of the major problems facing the province in the last nine years." The people would now be allowed to decide which government should administer the newly acquired natural resources, and an election at this time would permit whatever group triumphed a decent interval to organize the new department before implementation.[19]

It was a strange campaign. There could be no doubt that the premier was popular, particularly for his part in the solution of Peace River railway administration. The Peace River UFA Federal Constituency Association had introduced a resolution at the UFA annual convention in January which put the UFA on record as so appreciating Brownlee's services in selling Peace River railways on good terms and securing provincial control of natural resources that they were willing to see his salary increased! The UFA member for Peace River, Hugh Allen, attributed his election by acclamation in 1930 to the railway deal.[20] The UFA generally capitalized on the prevalent mood. Brownlee's message was the core of the UFA campaign. A tireless traveller, his campaign journeys well publicized, he emphasized the government's action to eliminate two of the province's most traditional troubles. His was an experienced administration, he reminded his listeners, and there had been little opposition directed against government policies in recent years.[21]

Notwithstanding that the economy of the province was experiencing a downwards swing, the UFA's opposition in the election failed to present effective alternatives. Once again, both the Liberals and the Conservatives changed leadership just before the contest. J.W. McDonald succeeded J.T. Shaw, and D.M. Duggan took over from A.A. McGillivray. Neither was supported by an enthusiastic organization. The Liberals fielded only thirty-seven candidates and the Conservatives just eighteen. Their effect was so tenuous that Attorney General Lymburn, campaigning in Edmonton, was able to argue that, as it was important for Edmonton to have cabinet representation, the voters' course was clear: they had better elect Lymburn, for neither of the old-line parties had enough candidates in the field to hope to form a government![22]

The urban press, even the generally outspoken *Edmonton Bulletin*, was much more subdued than during other elections, although the *Calgary Herald* seemed to put some effort into supporting Conservatives within the city of Calgary.[23] Part of the reason for this was that greater attention was reserved for the federal election, due 28 June. In that contest, both Conservatives and Liberals would have to be particularly active. The national Conservative leader was an Alberta MP, Calgary's R.B. Bennett, and urban Liberals at least would face a stiffer challenge than usual in opposing his party. In any case, it seemed that Brownlee was much more often in the news than either McDonald or Duggan. The most prominent opposition candidate appeared to be Edmonton's W.R. Howson, a Liberal, who would go on to become provincial Liberal leader in time to oppose Aberhart for 1935 election honours.

The election changed little. The UFA lost a few seats, but, with thirty-nine representatives out of sixty-three, they seemed unlikely to be unduly challenged. Perhaps the most startling aspect of the election was the strong showing of twenty-nine Independent candidates, eighteen of them in rural ridings, who secured close to 15 percent of the vote and won three rural seats.[24] Perhaps deteriorating economic conditions on the farms were beginning to disillusion rural voters. The "resting period" for the UFA, as Henry Wise Wood put it, was drawing to a close. A prolonged economic depression would create increasing rural disenchantment with the expertise of the government.

Recurring Agrarian Priorities: Debt and Marketing

This short review of the electoral success of the UFA government clearly shows how little this success depended upon actual satisfaction of basic farming requirements. The organized farmers of Alberta had, in fact, with some government assistance, turned to solutions of their own, some of which had for a time seemed to be successful, quite apart from the operations of the provincial government. It is against the background of these developments, rather than the provincial electoral history of the UFA, that the UFA political disaster of 1935 must be seen in order to be understood.

Starting immediately after the 1921 election, farmers had poured letters and resolutions into Premier Greenfield's office, at an only slightly diminishing rate through 1923.[25] The favourite solutions demanded were all financial. Foremost among them initially was a "moratorium" on debts, especially to prevent foreclosure by mortgage companies or land forfeiture by tax sale proceedings. Government leaders saw, however, that such drastic intervention would jeopardize all rural credit. They preferred to send Minister of Agriculture Hoadley, Attorney General Brownlee, and Provincial Treasurer R.G. Reid to Calgary in the fall of 1921 to meet with representatives of banks and mortgage companies to urge leniency in debt adjustments, trusting financiers' understanding that the eventual success of their farmer clients was their only redeemable asset.

Almost as popular as debt moratorium were "monetary reform" propositions, which arose regularly at UFA conventions as a result of resolutions sent in from UFA locals. Before 1921, these generally called on the federal government to establish a national central bank, but at the 1922 to 1924 UFA conventions, the UFA Committee on Banking and Credit, and particularly its chief spokesman, George Bevington, tried unsuccessfully to convince their provincial administration of the merits and viability of a provincial bank. Nor was that the only monetary reform entertained by UFA rank and file; it was merely the choice of each UFA convention from a welter of local suggestions. At the same time, The U.F.A. published reviews of books describing the unorthodox system of "Social Credit" proposed by English economic theorist C.H. Douglas.

What the farmers wished to avoid by debt moratorium or monetary reform was the demeaning but necessary relief program in household provisions and seed grain instituted by the preceding Liberal administration and carried on by its UFA successor. Extensive crop failures in 1921 and 1922, especially in southern Alberta, ensured the program's continuation for the time being, but the government hoped to find some way around the drain this caused on the treasury. Despite the expressed desire of the 1923 UFA convention for continued provincial relief measures to aid farmers afflicted by one agricultural disaster or another, the government was obviously pleased during the 1923 legislative session to announce the termination of the policy of seed grain advances inherited from the Liberal administration.

Programs of relief, monetary reform, and postponement of debt repayments would not seriously be demanded again until the Depression of the 1930s, but not altogether because all farm problems had disappeared. Instead, the attention of organized farmers was diverted to a new panacea, the concept of marketing pools.

Wheat producers felt they had benefited from the marketing policies of the Board of Grain Supervisors during the war and of the Canadian Wheat Board in 1919 and 1920 and were not happy about the return to an open market in the summer of 1920. Since the federal government refused to restore the Wheat Board, the Canadian Council of Agriculture began to entertain the idea of a voluntary cooperative pool which could judiciously deliver members' wheat to foreign markets. President Wood became an enthusiastic advocate of this plan, and at the 1921 UFA annual convention successfully encouraged adoption of a resolution in favour of establishing a wheat pool organization. Agrarian leaders in the other prairie provinces, however, had serious doubts about the feasibility of such an organization, and the wheat pool idea became more remote as farmer energies were turned towards the 1921 provincial and federal elections.[26]

As 1922 wheat prices steadily dropped, farmer organizations returned to pressuring the federal government for a wheat board. Finally, after months of discussion, the Canadian Wheat Board Act received royal assent on 28 June. To become effective, it required the enactment of enabling legislation by at least two provinces. A steady stream of petitions to Edmonton from UFA locals confirmed that most UFA members desired the services such a compulsory board would provide. The coordination of the efforts of the Saskatchewan and Alberta governments resulted in closely similar acts passed in each province at the end of July, after debate in special sessions of the legislature.[27] A flurry of correspondence and meetings took place in late July and early August, as Greenfield, Dunning, and W.C. Kennedy, acting federal minister of trade and commerce, attempted to secure the appointment of capable men prominent in the grain trade as chairman and vice-chairman of the proposed board. Prominent executives of the regular grain trade were, however, unavailable because they disagreed with the concept of a wheat board, while those who did not had no wish to become involved because the unfavourable attitude of the grain trade would cast doubt on the possibility of the wheat board securing necessary facilities controlled by those engaged in the trade.[28] A wheat board to handle the 1922 crop therefore was an impossibility.

Nothing daunted, the UFA annual convention of 1923 unanimously passed a resolution in favour of a national wheat board or, failing that, a provincial wheat board. In April the Alberta government prepared to restore its enabling act of the previous year, and Greenfield and Dunning renewed their efforts to find a board of directors. Once more the project failed, but by this time the UFA had been immersed in negotiations with the UGG to arrange a livestock pool in cooperation with them.[29] If a livestock pool was feasible, why not a voluntary wheat pool?

In early July, Attorney General Brownlee assured the UFA board of directors of the assistance of the government in such an undertaking, both to pass a suitable cooperative associations act and to cooperate in the planning. Although Wood was pessimistic about the possibility of beginning operations early enough to handle the 1923 crop, the board decided simply to work quickly and be prepared if possible.[30] Brownlee became chairman of the Cabinet Cooperative Committee, which immediately initiated a study of American examples of cooperative marketing. In late July, Brownlee left for the western United States. From San Francisco he wired Greenfield that a government invitation to Aaron Sapiro, solicitor for the California Fruit Growers' Association, to tour the rural areas of Alberta would be instrumental in securing support for a voluntary wheat pool, although Brownlee disagreed with Sapiro's conviction that the pool could be organized in time for the marketing of the 1923 crop.

170

By this time, representatives of farmers' organizations in the three prairie provinces had decided that an interprovincial pool to handle the 1923 crop was impossible.[31] Edmonton's Macdonald Hotel was the scene for the inspirational meeting of 4 August, at which plans were initiated which were to result in the Alberta Wheat Pool. Sapiro, who had in 1919 provided the advice on which to establish the first contract wheat pool in Washington and Idaho, dominated this meeting of cabinet and UFA directors with the general message: "What's the use of getting crops if you cannot sell them intelligently?" He outlined the steps necessary for an effective and immediate sign-up drive among the farmers. As a result of Sapiro's confidence, the sign-up goal of 50 percent of Alberta wheat acreage had pretty well been reached by mid-September, and the first general meeting of Alberta Wheat Pool delegates was set for 13 November. Brownlee, on behalf of the government, negotiated the terms of a government guarantee to the banks, upon which they agreed to extend a line of credit to the new organization.[32] The Alberta Wheat Pool was a solid reality.

In 1924 a Livestock Pool, Dairy Pool, and Egg and Poultry Pool were also operating in Alberta. In 1928 some thirty-six thousand farmers were signed to Wheat Pool contracts, while UFA membership languished around twelve thousand.[33] The government roles were to assist in the coordination of the efforts of cooperative marketing and purchasing agencies in Alberta and to guarantee bank advances to cooperative organizations.[34] Thus, it might be said that in the late 1920s the UFA and the UFA government committed themselves philosophically and financially to cooperative economic organization.

In 1930, unfortunately, market values of grain sank, so that while crops in general were much better than in 1929, their value to farmers represented only a fraction of the farmers' 1929 incomes. Wheat yields averaged 18.6 bushels per acre in 1930, compared with a 12-bushel average in 1929, but the average price per bushel shrank from $1.14 in 1929 to 39 cents in 1930. Field crop receipts, Alberta's principal farm income, were halved between the 1929 and 1930 harvests. In 1931, while field crop prices declined further, livestock market prices finally ceased to hold up, dropping to 60 percent of their 1930 levels. If there were in subsequent years slight price recoveries, these were more than eclipsed by a succession of climatic disasters, which hit Alberta farm regions unevenly but thoroughly.[35] Although there were fractional market price recoveries for most farm products between the beginning of 1933 and 1935, diminished crop production and accumulated debts reduced the actual benefit of these increases.

The general pattern for the majority of Alberta farmers was one of sudden disastrous decline in fortunes between 1929 and 1931, with little or no chance to redeem themselves in the years immediately following. For those who took a load of debts into the Depression years, the experience was a grim one indeed. The alternative open to thousands of disillusioned farmers of the dry areas in the early 1920s—to leave Alberta—apparently was either not possible or not especially inviting in the early 1930s. In the five-year period 1921 to 1925 inclusive, approximately eighty-five thousand people emigrated from Alberta, a figure far in excess of the number of immigrants. Between early 1930 and 1935, only about twelve thousand five hundred departed, despite the greatly intensified severity of the average farmer's problems. On the other hand, few entered Alberta after 1931.[36] The people who supported a UFA government in 1930 were essentially the same group of people, sadder and more desperate, who had voted Social Credit in 1935.

The triumphant solution of the 1920s to Alberta's earlier marketing difficulties had been the cooperative marketing pool. Struggling to stem the tide of the economic depression after 1929, the Alberta Wheat Pool soon got into trouble guaranteeing prices which never returned. All Canadian Wheat Pools coordinated their marketing at the time in the Central Selling Agency. This agency engaged in holding tactics in 1928 in order to secure higher prices after other world supplies were exhausted, therefore bringing a record carry-over of wheat to the 1929 market. Consequently, after world markets were closed by high tariff policies in late 1929, the initial price of $1.00 per bushel set by the Selling Agency was far in excess of plunging market rates.

Before prices hit bottom, the prairie provincial governments guaranteed the Wheat Pools' banks against losses on their advances made to pay the initial price. As wheat prices continued to fall, the provinces guaranteed a 60-cents-per-bushel initial price on the 1930 crop, which had, however, to be revised downwards as winter neared and Russia unexpectedly entered the world market for the first time in sixteen years with large supplies of wheat. In order to keep the banks from foreclosing, the Central Selling Agency was forced to dissolve its executive in favour of the general managership of John McFarland, former head of the Alberta Pacific Grain Company and a man more dedicated to the system of marketing wheat through the Winnipeg Grain Exchange than to direct sales on the world market. McFarland, with the aid of a federal guarantee, was able eventually to achieve a substantial profit on the 1930 crop, but the disintegration of the old marketing system resulted in the withdrawal of the Alberta Wheat Pool from the Central Selling Agency in mid-1931. With world markets as they were, the Alberta Wheat Pool concentrated on efficient handling of grain through its elevator system.[37]

The Wheat Pool now faced, in trying financial times, a debt to the provincial government of about $5,500,000, which could be said to represent the unexpected legacy of their confident operations of the 1920s. The agreement with the government provided for payments until 1952; in the next few difficult years, the necessity to make good on the pool losses to its banks proved most bothersome to the government.[38] While the federal government in subsequent years followed a policy of granting bonuses on wheat produced, a measure unsatisfactory to those farmers annually experiencing total crop failure, interest in the concept of a national wheat marketing board similar to that of 1919 soon revived. In the pressure for a wheat board exerted on the federal government after 1931, the Alberta government again played a leading role, with the help of UFA members of the House of Commons.[39] For years their efforts were futile, while the effects of the Depression on many farmers were intensified annually. Clearly, the supposed salvation of farmers in the 1920s—voluntary cooperative marketing—was not to suffice in alleviating the problems of the 1930s.

The problems of the Wheat Pool were the problems of individual farmers writ large: debts mounted once again, until loans became almost impossible to secure.[40] Farmers (and not only UFA members) began petitioning the provincial government once again for financial relief. At first the government tried to avoid reinstating all the old abandoned policies of feed and seed grain relief. In late 1929 and 1930, the government restricted itself to arrangements with railway companies to eliminate freight charges on seed moving to certain dry districts, to the guarantee of advances of seed grain in only the most extreme hardship cases, and to advisory assistance to those wishing to purchase livestock to feed low-grade grain.[41] Only in early 1931 did Premier Brownlee petition Canadian Prime Minister R.B. Bennett for a federally underwritten general relief program on behalf of farmers stricken by three successive seasons of climatic disaster and debt accumulation.[42]

In May 1931 the federal and provincial governments reached agreements to guarantee needy farmers the annual acquisition of seed grain, which afterwards would mire them in an ever-deepening debt load.[43] The provincial government was particularly burdened, as the Dominion government alternately agreed and declined as time went on to accept some of the costs of seed grain advances to farmers which were repeatedly not repaid.[44] The Alberta Department of Agriculture's "Relief Division" incurred staggering costs. For example, the provincial share of the cost of transporting farmers' effects from dry areas to more promising parts of Alberta drained the provincial treasury of better than $500,000 a year.[45] Under extreme pressure, the Alberta government in August 1931 agreed to guarantee farmer loans to purchase essential binder twine. A year later, forced to make good on nearly $40,000 still outstanding on binder twine loans, the government regretted the policy; another year later, the government could no longer be induced by the central UFA Cooperative Committee to renew such guarantees.[46] The government simply was faced with more expenses than could be financed.

In contrast to the steps hesitatingly undertaken and often revised by the governments to assist farmers in continuing their operations, the farmers' favourite solution was amazingly simple. As in the early 1920s, the government was subjected to a barrage of resolutions demanding a moratorium on debt and tax payments. The Debt Adjustment Act included a clause exempting debtors from foreclosure for one year after debts came due. The storm of protest against foreclosure did not begin, therefore, until the fall of 1930. In one typical case, wrote MLA Donald Cameron to Brownlee, a farmer's exemption from foreclosures had nearly expired, but he had no chance of repaying his $2,000 debt because of frost damage to his 1929 crop and a crop failure in 1930. "This is a problem that ... is applicable in thousands of similar cases in the drought area of our province this year and applies more particularly to men who are not elligible [sic] to take advantage of the Farm Loans Act." Not only Cameron but also MLAs A.M. Matheson and John Buckley endorsed the farmers' desire to have at least a one-year extension of the exemption on foreclosure.[47] At this stage, optimism still prevailed that the following year's crop would set the farmers back on the road to prosperity.

Government efforts to "compromise" individual debts without declaring the preferred general moratorium on debt collection proved futile. Resolutions forwarded from the UFA and large mass farmer meetings during the winter advocated complete suspension of debt and tax collection. At the UFA convention in Calgary in January 1931, all manners of radical solutions to the debt problem were submitted, including a call for the cost of necessary government services to be borne by funds drawn from the profits and reserves of commercial institutions. All the alternatives were eventually set aside in favour of a resolution urging upon the provincial government "a policy of consolidation of all arrears of taxes to be paid over a period of years with provision for a rebate or remission of penalties."[48] The government responded with an act enabling municipal councils to pass a bylaw providing for agreements with farm land owners until the end of 1931 for the consolidation and payment in installments of tax arrears, in temporary suspension of the Tax Recovery Act. In addition, the legislature established the Alberta Rural Credit Corporation to coordinate and consolidate the financial affairs of all cooperative credit societies.[49] Substantial efforts were also made by the government in negotiations with banks to reduce stringency in responding to individual loan applications.

By this time, government action was designed to provide assistance only insofar as the credit of the provincial treasury would not be unduly damaged. Brownlee was impatient with the growing feeling that the financial state of individual farmers should take precedence over the credit of the province.

> In the first place, it is only in certain districts of the Province where the credit of the people has been lost, but it is vitally important in times like these that the Province should be solid otherwise we would be quite helpless in attempting to give the relief we are giving in the Province at the moment to the various localities which are in need of assistance.[50]

Delegates attended the 1932 UFA convention in a desperate state of mind. It took all of Brownlee's persuasive powers to turn aside a convention resolution favouring a moratorium on debt collection. He was aware that, despite his unbridled opposition, the idea of a moratorium gained strength with each successive poor and unmarketable harvest and could not be ignored.[51] Legislative backbenchers such as Donald Cameron of Innisfail were rising to condemn the "despotic sway" of the "money kings of our day." Witness after witness heard by the Agriculture Committee advocated debt relief for farmers in dry belts of the south by cancelling interest on loans and mortgages and penalties for late payment of taxes. On the same day on which Brownlee strenuously opposed a resolution introduced in the assembly to declare a moratorium on debt collection, Donald Cameron pronounced himself in favour of the same measure.[52]

The government elected to introduce a bill fixing a quarter share of the crop as the maximum to be collected under a crop lease, but declined to have the resultant act brought immediately into effect. The strategy, explained Brownlee to the UFA executive, was to avoid causing resentment among mortgage companies. His deal with the mortgage companies was that they would not foreclose this year to collect the principal but would be satisfied with the equivalent of a year's interest and payment of taxes, and that they would give the director of Debt Adjustment three weeks before foreclosure to attempt an adjustment. In mid-July the crop situation would again be discussed, with a view to agreeing on a voluntary zoning system by which the maximum amount to be collected on crop leases would depend upon the crop yield in the zone.[53]

This approach evidently was not satisfactory to all UFA adherents. UFA director John Sutherland, noting that the government would not accept a moratorium policy, submitted a plan embodying a temporary moratorium to be in effect in each case until a satisfactory readjustment of debts was negotiated. Perhaps as much of the debt as possible should first be retired by payment in grain at a fixed price. Such a procedure would, argued Sutherland, not only reduce indebtedness and force creditors to take an interest in the problems of deflation but also "give some hope to the debt ridden people of this Province that we are trying to do something for them." Large numbers of farmers, UFA Vice-President Priestley agreed, were "looking to us for leadership in what perhaps constitutes the greatest crisis of their lives."[54] Brownlee seemed to capitulate in September, warning the Edmonton Board of Trade that unless creditors eased their demands on farmers a moratorium might become necessary. He remained nevertheless ambivalent about that possibility, observing ruefully that the situation had deteriorated to the point where it was now a matter of "giving as much assistance as possible while at the same time making conditions unfortunately worse in the Province by destroying all forms of credit both in the rural and urban centres."[55]

The government began a sceptical investigation of its legal power to enforce such

174

an action, "in order," as Brownlee informed Priestley, "to meet the demand in different parts of the Province." Government legal advisers suspected that this sort of law would conflict with the Dominion Bankruptcy Act, and, in any case, Brownlee was sure the Dominion government would disallow it as "contrary to the well-being of Canada as a whole so that the total effect would be to destroy the credit of the Province by such legislation without being able to enforce same because of it being ultra vires." He personally opposed a moratorium because it would protect everyone, including those who would not require it. It would, furthermore, put everyone on a cash basis in transactions, and he failed to see how many farmers would manage. Finally, it would eliminate the province's power to borrow and thus to provide normal public services and special relief.[56]

Winter conditions, however, stimulated a flood of letters and petitions to the premier's office pleading for debt relief. Uneasy about the effects of a moratorium, the government was pleased to discover an alternative partial remedy, as a result of November meetings with representatives of the other prairie provinces. All three provinces would adopt legislation reversing former procedure by requiring the creditor to apply to the Debt Adjustment Board for permission to foreclose. In addition, a bill would be introduced to combine consolidation of taxes for six years and easy payments for the first two years, with measures for relief of penalties that had accumulated and encouragement for the payment of current taxes. Appropriate legislation was passed during the 1933 legislative session, amidst general congratulations that the new Debt Adjustment Act was superior to a moratorium because it provided for negotiations to adjust interest and debt burdens downwards.[57]

Farmer representations to Edmonton decreased and in the main referred to alleged lack of sympathy displayed for farmers by officials of the Debt Adjustment Board. Still, accumulations of debt remained, moving UFA MLA Matheson in 1934 to renew, though unsuccessfully, the proposal for declaring a moratorium on debts and causing the UFA executive in early 1935 to submit a confidential letter to R.G. Reid about possible measures to reduce farmer debt.[58] After that, perhaps all the energies previously expended by individual farmers in attempts to gain a moratorium were by mid-1935 channelled into Social Credit study groups.

While the agitation for a moratorium on debt repayments represents one of the factors within the UFA which formed the background to the rise of Social Credit in Alberta, monetary reform schemes illustrate another. From 1924 until 1932, muted UFA interest in monetary reform was deflected towards Ottawa. In March 1932, however, the Alberta Legislature's Agricultural Committee listened once more to George Bevington, whose evidence only renewed their conviction that the sorts of solutions he offered, involving the issue of Dominion currency to equalize the availability of credit with the need for credit, were beyond provincial jurisdiction.[59] Premier Brownlee was compelled, though, to make it clear to representatives of both the UFA and the Farmers' Unity League (FUL, a new rival and more radical farmers' group which had been spreading since late 1930 from its Saskatoon headquarters) that with no legislative control over finance the provincial government could raise money for relief purposes only in exactly the same way as a private individual might—by borrowing to the limit of the credit available. It would be ludicrously impossible, therefore, to issue monthly cash subsidies to needy families, as one local FUL group demanded. Throughout 1932, the government considered creating a nonlegislative committee on monetary policy to clarify the roles a central bank of discount and the issue of "scrip" could play in obtaining easier credit for agriculture. The committee eventually included MP George Coote and UFA director John Sutherland,[60] but did not reveal to the provincial government any possible new provincial monetary policy.

In the spring of 1933, agitation on behalf of the Douglas Social Credit system increased. To Brownlee, it was unfortunate that "in times like these, all kinds of proposals are made, the majority of which are not thought out to any conclusion" but received supporters "on the theory that a drowning man will grasp at a straw." Although he received letters from all over the province in favour of Douglas's scheme applied at the provincial level, he considered it to be in practice utterly inapplicable, because currency and credit were the jurisdiction of the federal government and because any specially created legal tender would be virtually useless if not recognized outside the country. Consequently, even "scrip" issued by the provincial government would apply only to the payment of taxes, and even then only if it obtained the approval of the local businessmen, which was doubtful.[61]

On 18 August, the five-man Royal Commission on Banking and Finance, of which Brownlee was the only western member, conducted a hearing at Calgary. The UFA submission remained totally on the national level, arguing that money was not properly used in Canada but was failing to act as a satisfactory medium of exchange, measure of value, or standard for deferred payments. The standard for the amount of money in circulation should not be gold, it was contended, but rather the volume of goods and services produced, which could best be consistently determined within a nationalized system of currency controlled by a nationally owned government bank. Even at that, the ultimate solution would be a step further in extensive centralized economic planning by the government. Later, after the commission submitted its report, Brownlee was congratulated by the UFA president as the only commissioner to recommend public ownership of a national central bank.[62]

The Fall of the UFA Government

By the time of the Royal Commission Report, however, Brownlee's immense influence had been undermined by a hugely publicized controversy over his personal affairs. On 3 August 1933 he was served notice of a legal action to be taken against him by a secretary in the attorney general's department and her father, claiming damages as a result of an alleged seduction. The public's first concrete knowledge of this came on 22 September, when the newspapers featured the sensational story of the writ entered in the Supreme Court of Alberta. Brownlee promptly issued a statement of denial and indicated that a countercharge of conspiracy would be laid. The UFA executive immediately sent a nightwire to Brownlee (who was in Ottawa) expressing the executive's complete confidence in his integrity and personal honour, but the public revelation could scarcely have come at a more inopportune time.[63]

Not only were Alberta farmers in the depths of a confusing depression, but the Brownlee scandal story of 22 September followed a week of headlines devoted to incidents from the legal proceedings involving Minister of Public Works O.L. McPherson's divorce, a spectacular affair which had been going on sporadically since October 1932. While McPherson's private life had thus been constantly in the news, Liberal leader W.R. Howson managed in March 1933 to imply corruption in the administration of McPherson's Department of Public Works, charging that some forty highway contracts had been let without calling tenders and that gross overpayments had been made to these contractors. The eventual exoneration of McPherson and his department by the Public Accounts Committee of the legislature did not, of course, satisfy Howson. McPherson was inclined, with considerable support in his constituency, to attribute both the personal and the public attacks to a concerted, politically motivated campaign to discredit the UFA government through him. "Was it not intended as a knockout for the whole Farmer Movement?" he suggested to a June convention of the Little Bow Provincial Constituency Association.[64]

Public attention now was turned unfavourably on the most important member of the UFA government, and it remained there until the verdict was delivered at the end of June 1934. The jury found Brownlee guilty of seduction and awarded the plaintiffs a total of $15,000. That Judge W.C. Ives disagreed with the award and dismissed the action 2 July only enabled the editor of the *Edmonton Bulletin* to question his judgment in light of the considered opinions of the jury. Brownlee, feeling the pressure, had wanted to resign earlier, but had been persuaded to continue as premier and in fact received expressions of support from various UFA organizations and the annual convention in January 1934. When the verdict was announced, Brownlee could no longer retain his position, despite the encouragement of the UFA executive.[65]

So was lost whatever remained of the Alberta government's influence against doubtful monetary solutions to the Depression difficulties of Alberta's farmers. Since World War I, Alberta's farmers had collectively investigated through the United Farmers of Alberta and related organizations the merits of five major provincial antidotes for their special problems: direct political participation as a group, government relief to the destitute, voluntary cooperative produce-marketing pools, a moratorium on debt repayments, and provincial banking with monetary manipulation. They either had not worked or had not been proven workable.

Flexibility and strenuous effort had characterized organized attacks by farmers on obstacles to their economic security. No single solution had claimed their entire enthusiasm. But only one of the five here outlined—monetary reform—by the mid-1930s retained a vociferous champion in William Aberhart. All others had been discredited on the provincial level. A new UFA executive and remaining UFA members of Parliament brought from their national perspective a second, somewhat alien possibility: a commitment to the socialist Co-operative Commonwealth Federation (CCF). The choice in the immediate future would once again be made in the realm of politics, between the advocates of Social Credit and those of the CCF.[66]

Notes

1. N.F. Priestley and E.B. Swindlehurst, *Furrows, Faith and Fellowship* (Edmonton: Co-op Press, 1967); and L.D. Nesbitt, *Tides in the West* (Saskatoon: Modern Press, n.d., ca. 1962).

2. David G. Embree, "The Rise of the United Farmers of Alberta" (unpublished M.A. thesis, University of Alberta, 1956).

3. These developments are outlined in more detail in C.F. Betke, "The United Farmers of Alberta, 1911–1935" (unpublished M.A. thesis, University of Alberta, 1971), 1–18.

4. On Wood's social and political philosophy, see also: W.K. Rolph, *Henry Wise Wood of Alberta* (Toronto: University of Toronto Press, 1950); W.L. Morton, "The Social Philosophy of Henry Wise Wood," *Agricultural History* 22 (1948): 114–23; and C.B. Macpherson, *Democracy in Alberta* (Toronto: University of Toronto Press, 1962 [1953]), 28–61.

5. Macpherson, *Democracy*, 54–61. There is, of course, animosity evident in Wood's rhetoric about apparent malpractices as he saw them in the conduct of financiers and manufacturing businessmen, but his theory did not dismiss them as unnatural or nonessential to the economic order.

6. The next several paragraphs are amplified in C.F. Betke, "Farm Politics in an Urban Age: The Decline of the United Farmers of Alberta after 1921," in L.H. Thomas, ed., *Essays on Western History* (Edmonton: University of Alberta Press, 1976), 175–89, 214–17.

7. *Edmonton Bulletin*, 8 March, 2 April, and 22 and 25 May 1926.

8. "Five Years of Progress," a 1926 UFA provincial election campaign pamphlet, Glenbow-Alberta Institute Archives (GAIA), U.F.A. Papers, File 47.

9. Taped interview with J.E. Brownlee by Una Maclean, 1961, GAIA. See also: Minute Book, Edgerton U.F.A. Local, Provincial Archives of Alberta (PAA); Minute Books, Devon and Carolside U.F.A. Locals, GAIA; Minute Books, several Peace River U.F.A. Locals, GAIA, microfilm; and Minute Book, Chinook U.F.A. Local, GAIA, Lorne Proudfoot Papers.

10. Letter, Brownlee to Wood, 26 January 1926, PAA, Premiers' Papers, File 1-600-0; and *Edmonton Bulletin*, 22 May 1926.

11. Reports of a speech by Brownlee in Cardston and of information from Minister of Public Works Alex Ross in *Edmonton Journal*, 27 and 28 May 1926; "Five Years of Progress," GAIA; and "The U.F.A. Viewpoint," manuscript of an article distributed by the UFA to Alberta weeklies, GAIA, U.F.A. Papers, File 17.

12. *Edmonton Bulletin*, 27 and 29 May and 17 June 1926; *Calgary Albertan*, 18 June 1926; and *Edmonton Journal*, 7 June 1926.

13. *The U.F.A.*, 17 June 1926; speech by J.T. Shaw in Red Deer, 3 June 1926, reported in the *Calgary Albertan*, 4 June 1926; and speech by A.A. McGillivray in Lloydminster, 12 June 1926, reported in the *Edmonton Journal*, 14 June 1926.

14. *Edmonton Journal*, 14 June 1926; *Edmonton Bulletin*, 21 June 1926; and *Calgary Herald*, 23 June 1926.

15. Statistical summary of Alberta provincial electoral returns, 1905-1963, GAIA, George Cloakey Collection; *Calgary Albertan*, 4 June 1926; and *The U.F.A.*, 15 January 1927.

16. *Edmonton Journal*, 27 May 1926.

17. See: Betke, *The United Farmers*, 94–99, for a more detailed and documented account of the resolution of this issue; and J.D. Williams, "A History of the E.D. and B.C. Railway, 1907-1929" (unpublished M.A. thesis, University of Alberta, 1956).

18. *Statutes of Alberta*, 1930, Chap. 21, "The Alberta Natural Resources Act"; and H.B. Neatby, *William Lyon Mackenzie King*, The Lonely Heights, Vol. 2 (Toronto: University of Toronto Press, 1963), 294-99.

19. *Edmonton Journal*, 4 February 1930; and *Calgary Albertan*, 25 April 1930.

20. Priestley and Swindlehurst, *Furrows*, 101-102; and transcript of interview with Hugh Wright Allen by Una Maclean, 1961, GAIA.

21. *The U.F.A.*, 15 May 1930.

22. *Canadian Annual Review*, 1929-30, 503; *Edmonton Bulletin*, 17 June 1930; and statistical summary, George Cloakey Collection.

23. See, for example, editorials, *Calgary Herald*, 23 May and 18 June 1930.

24. Statistical summary, George Cloakey Collection.

25. The next few paragraphs are expanded in Betke, "Farm Politics," 182-87.

26. Rolph, *Henry Wise Wood*, 120-30.

27. Ibid., 130-32; *Statutes of Canada*, 12-13 George V, 1922, Chap. 14, "The Canadian Wheat Board Act, 1922"; letters, UFA local unions to Greenfield, April-July 1922, PAA, Premiers' Papers, File 1-100-45(a); *Edmonton Journal*, 25 July 1922; and *Journal of the Legislative Assembly of the Province of Alberta*, 1922 (second session), 13.

28. Correspondence about a Wheat Board, late July to 14 August 1922, PAA, Premiers' Papers, File 1-100-45(b); and *The U.F.A.*, 15 August 1922, 1.

29. *The U.F.A.*, 15 December 1922, 6, and 15 February 1923, 12; *U.F.A. Convention Minutes*, Minutes, U.F.A. Annual Convention, Calgary, 16-19 January 1923, microfilm, GAIA; *U.F.A. Executive and Board Minutes*, Minutes, U.F.A. Board Meeting, Calgary, 20-23 January 1923, microfilm, GAIA; and 7 April 1923 draft of an Order in Council which was never implemented;

transcript of telephone conversation, Dunning to Crerar, 5 June 1923; telegram, Crerar to Dunning, 5 June 1923; minutes, meeting of boards of directors of the UGG and the SCEC, 12 June 1923; and press statement, Premiers Greenfield and Dunning, 22 June 1923; all to be found in PAA, Premiers' Papers, File 1-100-45(b).

30. *U.F.A. Executive and Board Minutes*, Minutes, U.F.A. Board Meeting, Calgary, 3-6 July 1923, microfilm, GAIA.

31. Telegrams between Greenfield, Brownlee, and Sapiro, July 1923, PAA, Premiers' Papers, File 1-100-46; and *The U.F.A.*, 1 August 1923, 1.

32. Rolph, *Henry Wise Wood*, 143; *The U.F.A.*, 15 September 1923, 1; and minutes, meeting of Aaron Sapiro with the Alberta cabinet and UFA board of directors, Edmonton, 4 August 1923; form letter, Alberta Wheat Pool Provisional Committee to "President and Secretary of Each U.F.A. Local Union," 8 August 1923; form letter, W.J. Jackman to Wheat Pool members, 16 October 1923; and correspondence between Brownlee and Greenfield, September-October 1923; all in PAA, Premiers' Papers, File 1-100-46.

33. *U.F.A. Convention Minutes*, Report of the Central Board and Minutes, U.F.A. Annual Convention, Calgary, 17-21 January 1928, microfilm, GAIA; *The U.F.A.*, 1 February 1928; and copy, presidential address of H.W. Wood to the 1929 UFA convention, PAA, Premiers' Papers, File 1-600-9.

34. See Betke, *The United Farmers*, 92-94.

35. *Canada Year Book*, of 1930, 215-16; of 1931, 224-25; of 1932, 1036-37; of 1933, 238-39; of 1934-35, 265-66 and 290; of 1936, 238-39; and Report of the Alberta Department of Agriculture for 1931, 7; for 1932, 7; for 1933, 7, 8, 25; for 1934, 7, 23; for 1935, 7.

36. These figures are obtained by subtracting the actual population increase during the time period specified from the total of natural increase (births minus deaths) plus immigration. All initial figures are to be found in the appropriate editions of *Canada Year Book*. For an estimation of the total private debt in Alberta see The Province of Alberta, *The Case for Alberta* (Edmonton: King's Printer, 1938), Part 1, 114-41. See also David McGinnis, "Farm Labour in Transition: Occupational Structure and Economic Dependency in Alberta, 1921-1951," in Howard Palmer, ed., *The Settlement of the West* (Calgary: University of Calgary/Comprint Publishing Company, 1977), 174-86, 266-67.

37. Rolph, *Henry Wise Wood*, 200-207.

38. Copy, indenture between Alberta Wheat Pool, Alberta Wheat Pool Elevators, and the Government of Alberta, 23 October 1931; and correspondence between Brownlee and bank managers, December 1932 to August 1933: PAA, Premiers' Papers, File 1-600-61; and *Statutes of Alberta*, 1932, Chap. 7.

39. Telegrams, Brownlee to H.E. Spencer, Ottawa, 1 June 1931, and Brownlee to Manitoba Premier Bracken, 16 and 18 June 1931, PAA, Premiers' Papers, File 1-600-98; letter, E.A. Hanson, secretary, Stettler U.F.A. Provincial Constituency Association, 12 June 1931, PAA, Premiers' Papers, File 1-100-61; and *The U.F.A.*, 1 August 1933, 26.

40. In early 1931, the UFA circulated among its locals questionnaires designed to disclose the possibilities of credit for farmers from the local banks. In April, information about 134 community banks revealed that in only sixteen cases were the UFA farmers reasonably satisfied. See letter enclosing statistical summary of questionnaire results, N.F. Priestley, UFA vice-president, to Brownlee, 28 April 1931, PAA, Premiers' Papers, File 1-1600-10.

41. Copy, memorandum, W. Holdsworth, Livestock Branch, to Deputy Minister of Agriculture H.A. Craig, 21 November 1929; memorandums, Brownlee to Hoadley, 9 January 1930, Brownlee to A. Wakelyn, Calgary, 23 April 1930 and Brownlee to Hoadley, 22 April 1930, PAA, Premiers' Papers, File 1-100-6(b); memorandum, H.A. Craig to Hoadley, 13 October 1930, and government statement to the press on feed and livestock policy, n.d. (probably October 1930), PAA, Premiers' Papers, File 1-100-61.

42. Correspondence between Bennett and Brownlee, 6-24 February 1931, PAA, Premiers' Papers, File 1-100-61.

43. *Statutes of Alberta*, 1931, Chap. 58, "The Temporary Seed Grain Advances Act, 1931"; and copy, confidential letter, R. Weir, federal minister of agriculture, to provincial ministers of agriculture, 28 February 1931, PAA, Premiers' Papers, File 1-100-61.

44. Correspondence among Alberta Department of Agriculture officials and federal UFA MPs Brownlee and Weir, March and April 1932; letter, Brownlee to Ben Ferguson, Heathdale, secretary, Collholme U.F.A. Local, 12 March 1932; copy of agreement between the Government of Canada, represented by Wesley A. Gordon, minister of labour, and the Province of Alberta, represented by Brownlee, under the Dominion Relief Act of 1932, 20 June 1932; all in PAA, Premiers' Papers, File 1-100-61.

45. *Journal of the Legislative Assembly of the Province of Alberta*, 1933, Sessional Paper No. 1, Public Accounts of the Province of Alberta for the Year Ended March 31, 1933, 105-106.

46. Telegram, Hoadley to Brownlee, 4 August 1931; memorandum, Brownlee to Hoadley, 4 June 1932; copies, letters, bank officials to R.B. Bennett, 25 and 26 May 1932; letter, Brownlee to Hazleton, Pincher Creek Cooperative Association Ltd., 5 July 1932; and letters, Brownlee to bank managers, Alberta, 12 August 1932, Brownlee to J.C. Warden, Reid Hill, 13 August 1932, and N.F. Priestley to Brownlee, 3 August 1933: all in PAA, Premiers' Papers, File 1-100-61.

47. Cameron, Elnora, to Brownlee, 8 October 1930, PAA, Premiers' Papers, File 1-200-9; and Buckley and Matheson to Brownlee, 5 and 8 September 1930, PAA, Premiers' Papers, File 1-100-6.

48. Brownlee to MLA M.J. Conner, Vulcan, 16 September 1931, PAA, Premiers' Papers, File 1-200-9; and *UFA Convention Minutes*, Minutes, U.F.A. Annual Convention, Calgary, 20-23 January 1931, microfilm, GAIA.

49. *Statutes of Alberta*, 1931, Chap. 54, "The Local Tax Arrears Consolidation Act," and Chap. 66, "The Alberta Cooperative Rural Credit Act."

50. Letter, Brownlee to B.C. Lees, Edgerton, 12 March 1931, PAA, Premiers' Papers, File 1-100-61.

51. *U.F.A. Convention Minutes*, Minutes, U.F.A. Annual Convention, Edmonton, 19-22 January 1932, microfilm, GAIA. The convention resolution for a moratorium on debt collection was defeated by only ninety-nine to ninety-five. Hence Brownlee's acknowledgement of the prevailing sentiment in an address to the Legislative Assembly and a capacity audience, 11 February 1932, reported in the *Edmonton Journal*, 12 February 1932.

52. *Edmonton Journal*, 13 February, 12 March, and 2 April 1932.

53. Letter, Brownlee to N.F. Priestley, 17 June 1932, PAA, Premiers' Papers, File 1-600-9.

54. Letters, J.K. Sutherland to Brownlee, 4 July 1932, and N.F. Priestley to Brownlee, 28 September 1932, PAA, Premiers' Papers, File 1-200-9.

55. Correspondence between C. Frederickson, secretary, Castor U.F.A. Local, and Brownlee, 27 and 30 September 1932, PAA, Premiers' Papers, File 1-100-61.

56. Letter, Brownlee to Priestley, 5 October 1932, PAA, Premiers' Papers, File 1-600-9; and letter, Brownlee to R.B. Manly, secretary, Kerndale U.F.A. Local, 29 October 1932, PAA, Premiers' Papers, File 1-200-9.

57. Letter, Brownlee to W.M. Wallace, Viking, 9 November 1932, PAA, Premiers' Papers, File 1-200-9; *The U.F.A.*, 2 January and 1 February 1933, the latter especially for Brownlee's analysis of the proposed legislation in his written statement to the UFA convention, 1933; and *Statutes of Alberta*, Chaps. 13 and 28.

58. *Edmonton Journal*, 15 March 1934; and *U.F.A. Executive and Board Minutes*, Minutes, U.F.A. Executive Meeting, 19-20 March 1935, microfilm, GAIA.

59. Copy of "Summary of Evidence of Mr. George Bevington on Canadian Finance," as presented to the Agriculture Committee of the Alberta Legislature, 10 March 1932, PAA, Premiers' Papers, File 1-1600-10.

60. Letter, Brownlee to Priestley, 4 April 1932, PAA, Premiers' Papers, File 1-600-9; letter, Brownlee to Sam Oleskey, secretary, Farmers' Unity League Myrnam, 30 August 1932, PAA, Premiers' Papers, File 1-100-61; letter, Robert Gardiner to Brownlee, 12 May 1932; and

memorandum, Brownlee to Hoadley, 5 October 1932, PAA, Premiers' Papers, File 1-1600-22. On the origins of the Farmers' Unity League, see: Duff Spafford, "The 'Left Wing' 1921-1931," in N. Ward and D. Spafford, eds., *Politics in Saskatchewan* (Don Mills, Ontario: Longmans Canada Ltd., 1968), 44-58; and Ivan Avakumovic, "The Communist Party of Canada and the Prairie Farmers: The Interwar Years," in D.J. Bercuson, ed., *Western Perspective I* (Toronto/Montreal: Holt, Rinehart and Winston of Canada, 1974), 78-87.

61. Letter, Brownlee to A.S. Roberts, Barons, 12 April 1932, PAA, Premiers' Papers, File 1-600-104; letters, Brownlee to Stanley Stasel and Huxley to Grainger U.F.A. District Association, 18 April 1932, PAA, Premiers' Papers, File 1-600-9.

62. *The U.F.A.*, 1 September 1933, 8ff., and 1 February 1934, the latter for a report of the presidential address of Robert Gardiner to the 1934 UFA annual convention, 16 January 1934.

63. Microfilm account of the John E. Brownlee case as presented for appeal to the Privy Council, London, 1938, GAIA; and *Edmonton Bulletin*, 22 September 1933.

64. *The U.F.A.*, 3 July 1933, 8ff., including a reprint of an article in the *Vulcan Advocate*, 28 June 1933; and *Edmonton Journal*, 15 March and 7 April 1933.

65. "The John E. Brownlee Case," *Edmonton Bulletin*, 5 July 1934; taped interview with R.G. Reid by Una Maclean Evans, 1962, GAIA; *U.F.A. Convention Minutes*, Minutes, U.F.A. Annual Convention, Edmonton, 16-19 January 1934, microfilm, GAIA; and *U.F.A. Executive and Board Minutes*, Minutes, U.F.A. Executive Meeting with U.F.A. MLAs, Edmonton, 4-5 July 1934, microfilm, GAIA.

66. For two assessments of the lesser known UFA roots of the CCF, see Carl Betke, "The UFA: Visions of a Cooperative Commonwealth," *Alberta History*, Vol. 27, No. 3 (Summer 1979), 7-14; and M. Johnson, "The Failure of the CCF in Alberta: An Accident of History," in Carlo Caldarola, ed., *Society and Politics in Alberta* (Toronto: Methuen, 1979), 87-107.

From Social Credit to Social Conservatism: The Evolution of an Ideology

THOMAS FLANAGAN AND MARTHA LEE

Reprinted from *Prairie Forum,* Vol. 16, No. 2 (Fall 1991), 205–223,
by permission of the Canadian Plains Research Center, University of Regina.

Alberta Social Credit underwent remarkable changes from 1935 to 1967. Beginning as a populist mass movement espousing radical changes in the financial system, it ended as a conservative political party defending free market economics against socialist centralization. This ideological evolution will be analysed from a new perspective utilizing the literature on millenarian movements and the failure of prophecy. Fifty hours of interviews with Ernest Manning recorded in the years 1979–1982 (hereafter cited as MI)[1] were used extensively as source material.

Earlier interpretations emphasizing pressures on third parties (Mallory, 1976), Alberta's peculiar class structure (Macpherson, 1962), or the leadership transition from William Aberhart to Ernest Manning (Finkel, 1989) are not challenged. While recognizing the value of earlier views, this article will consider aspects of Social Credit history inherent in the situation of radical parties coming to power. Because Social Credit is seen as a secular millenarian movement, the failure of prophecy literature that pertains to the study of millenarianism is relied upon; however, the logic of failed expectations and cognitive dissonance applies to radical parties generally, so readers who may be sceptical about the millenarian character of Social Credit should still be able to follow the evolutionary aspects of the analysis.

Yonina Talmon defined millenarianism as the hope for "imminent, total, ultimate, this-worldly, and collective" salvation (Talmon, 1968: 349). This definition applied in the first instance to religious movements, but it is now recognized that the secular ideologies of political movements can also be millenarian in character (Barkun, 1974). That Alberta Social Credit was indeed a secular millenarian movement has been argued elsewhere at length (Flanagan, 1973).

Social Credit viewed all history up to the present as the "Age of Scarcity," in which human existence had been dominated by the need to work; but technical progress had brought mankind to the verge of the "Age of Potential Plenty," in which individualism could flower as the necessity of labour was relaxed (Colbourne, 1935). Only an irrational financial system stood in the way, making it impossible to purchase all that could be produced. Taking credit out of the hands of the financiers and putting it into the hands of the public would produce a new age without significant social conflict—the hallmark of all millenarian visions, whether religious or secular.

The "Age of Potential Plenty" was a this-worldly form of secular salvation, to be achieved through political means rather than divine intervention. As the ultimate stage of social evolution, it would resolve all serious social problems. It was collective in the sense that it had to be implemented for society as a whole; individuals could not obtain Social Credit for themselves. And it was imminent to the extent that the system could be adopted almost immediately; there was no need to wait for ages of further evolution.

Social Credit not only conformed to the formal definition of millenarianism, it exhibited many characteristics frequently found in such movements. It depended upon an esoteric ideology invented by an autodidact—Major Clifford Hugh Douglas, a Scottish engineer—operating outside the intellectual establishment. It combined intellectual monism, in which all explanations referred to the financial system, with moral dualism. Douglas divided the world into financial exploiters, particularly Jews, and the exploited masses.

Aberhart transformed the esoteric ideology of Douglas into a mass movement by simplifying it and linking it to the hardship of the Depression. He presented to the people of Alberta a "wondrously simple plan"—the main points were the payment of dividends to all citizens, the continuous flow of credit, and price controls (Aberhart, 1933, 1935). He estimated it would take fifteen to eighteen months after electoral victory to put this plan into effect, including the payment of dividends estimated at $25 per month for adults. A monthly divided of $25 was close to a minimum standard of living at the time (MI, 1: 26), but eighteen months was a pure guess taken "out of the air" (MI, 5: 8). Aberhart committed himself to a provincial strategy for implementing his plan, despite section 91 of the BNA Act, which gave the federal government control over financial matters (Aberhart, 1934). He argued that, if legal barriers arose, popular pressure would force the federal government to amend the Constitution, or at least refrain from enforcing it.[2]

Aberhart thus put himself in a position where his predictions about the future could be tested. His promise to implement his "wondrously simple plan" within eighteen months makes it possible to deploy the literature on disappointed expectations in millenarian movements.

The Failure of Prophecy

Reluctance to renounce basic convictions is always pronounced in politics and religion, where theories are loose, predictions vague, and evidence inconclusive. Adherents of emotionally charged mass movements do not give up their beliefs at the first sign that the universe is not "unfolding as it should." Believers cling to their hopes and discover reasons to justify their adherence—at least up to some point of overwhelming negative evidence.

In their seminal work, Festinger, Riecken, and Schachter (1956) studied a small cult known as the Seekers, led by a woman announcing revelations from extraterrestrial beings. They informed her that the earth would soon be destroyed in a great flood, but that she and her followers would be rescued by a flying saucer and transported to a paradisiacal world. She set a specific date for these events, but they never came to pass. While some followers left the group in disappointment, others began to proselytize energetically to attract further adherents to their cult. The researchers' explanation drew on the theory of cognitive dissonance. The disconfirmation of the prophecy had resulted in psychological stress, exposing the Seekers to internal doubt and external ridicule. One way to relieve the tension was to leave the cult, another was to become a missionary. Recruiting followers willing to accept the Seekers' rationalization that God had postponed the catastrophe because of their faith would effectively eliminate the cognitive dissonance.

Hardyck and Braden showed in another case study that increased proselytism was not a necessary outcome of the failure of prophecy, even when all the conditions of the Festinger study were present (Hardyck and Braden, 1962: 136-41). An outburst of evangelism was one, but not the only, possible response.

Joseph Zygmunt's analysis of the Jehovah's Witnesses demonstrated that they did not make a decisive commitment to worldwide proselytism until after suffering no less than five failures of millennial prophecy—1878, 1881, 1914, 1918, 1925 (Zygmunt, 1970). He found a typical cycle of "disappointment," "watchful waiting," "conjectures," reinterpretation of prophecy, and "issuance of redated predictions." In each instance of reinterpretation, the Witnesses asserted that their prophecies had been partially fulfilled, or that some event of prophetic significance had transpired on the date in question. Each failure was "thus redefined in retrospect in a manner which provided non-empirical confirmation for the group's chiliastic outlook" (Zygmunt, 1970: 933-34).

A separate line of work by German theologians on the delay of the Second Coming in early Christianity highlighted a special kind of eschatological reinterpretation, for which Ernst Benz has created the awkward but useful concept of "de-eschatologizing." It may be considered a special case of Weber's "routinization of charisma" (Gerth and Mills, 1958: 297). For Benz, de-eschatologizing is "the removal of the original basic attitude toward the end of time in the gospel message" (Benz, 1968: 28). The early Christians, in his account, were forced to deal with persistent delay in the return of Jesus to earth. The problem was finally given a definitive solution by St. Augustine, according to whom the Kingdom of God was not a future event to be expected, but a present condition in which the faithful participated. The church, as the visible aspect of the City of God, could mediate salvation to its members; one did not have to wait for the Parousia. Augustine retained the gospel symbols of eschatological redemption but transformed them from objects of imminent expectation into theological dogmas without pressing temporal significance.

Converging with this line of theological investigation is a new generation of scriptural studies drawing on cognitive dissonance theory and focusing on the disciples' reaction to the Crucifixion. These works interpret Christological dogmas, such as the Resurrection, as the disciples' reaction to the disappointment of their hopes that Jesus would be revealed in His lifetime as the Messiah (Wernik, 1975; Jackson, 1975).

The literature identifies several typical responses to prophetic failure: postponement of the date; reinterpretation of the events suggesting that the prophecy has actually been fulfilled but in an invisible or supernatural manner not subject to empirical testing, or that the faithful have somehow misunderstood God's plan and further fulfilment will occur in the future; membership purges in the belief that the failure of the end to come is God's punishment for the group's moral weakness or lack of faith (Zygmunt, 1972: 261); proselytism, especially if a suitable reinterpretation can be achieved and if adherents are able to encourage each other; de-eschatologizing, a specific form of reinterpretation, suggesting that the fulfilment has occurred spiritually, and that orientation to the future is no longer appropriate; resurgence of millenarian expectations, as adherents rediscover the original meaning of the de-eschatologized message; and falling away, especially if the disconfirmation is so severe that no reinterpretation seems to work, and if adherents are relatively isolated from one another.

Although this collective portrait is based on the study of religious movements, it is assumed that the adherents of secular millenarian movements will respond in parallel fashion when confronted with failed expectations of social change, for they face a similar situation of cognitive dissonance. Evidence was found of all seven typical responses outlined above; but in this article stress is placed on the de-eschatologizing of Social Credit ideology carried out tentatively by Aberhart and definitively by Manning. While preserving the symbols and vocabulary of Social Credit doctrine, the leaders reoriented the ideology away from futuristic expectation of sweeping economic change towards the conservative goal of defending the free market.

Aberhart in Power

During the election campaign of 1935, Aberhart had emphasized that "all you have to do about Social Credit is to cast your ballot for it, and we'll get the experts to put the system in" (Barr, 1974: 84). So it was logical for him to telegraph Major Douglas, who already had a contract with the Alberta government as economic reconstruction adviser: "Victorious when could you come?" (Douglas, 1937: 125).

Douglas, however, disapproved of Aberhart's appointment of the Newfoundland banker Robert J. Magor as financial adviser, foreseeing that Magor would steer the Alberta government towards orthodox attempts to balance the budget and refinance the provincial debt. Aberhart, on the other hand, refused to enact the confiscatory measures proposed by Douglas, such as exacting an interest-free loan from the banks, and encouraging Alberta residents to exchange their stocks and bonds for provincial securities. Such measures, wrote Aberhart, would "alarm our citizens to a very grave degree, and would give the opponents a splendid opportunity to attack viciously the whole method of procedure" (Douglas, 1937: 142). Douglas offered to resign as early as 29 October and cabled in blunt language on 5 December: "Will you announce resignation or shall I?" (Douglas, 1937: 158). Aberhart knew by December of 1935 that his expectation of receiving a fully detailed plan from Douglas would not be fulfilled. Douglas seemed to be "so intent on protecting the purity of this theory so it wouldn't be discredited, that he almost seemed to shy away from any all-out attempt at implementation" (MI, 1: 34–35).

Aberhart then turned to a plan for a dated stamp scrip proposed in caucus by Lucien Maynard. This idea, invented by the German economist Silvio Gesell, was remote from Social Credit theory, but was at least an attempt at monetary reform. Maynard's proposal was to use provincial scrip to pay the dividends promised to all Alberta citizens (Coe, 1938: 62–63). But the cautious Aberhart preferred a much smaller experiment. He used about $240,000 of provincial scrip, depreciating at the rate of 1 percent per week, to pay unemployed men for highway work in the summer of 1936. Aberhart saw it as a test of whether Albertans would accept a medium other than legal tender and presented it to the public as a step toward Social Credit (MI, 1: 70).

The results were discouraging because recipients of scrip converted it into dollars as soon as the government would allow. The government had impaled itself on the horns of a dilemma. Promising to redeem all scrip for dollars had preserved its credibility with the public but had also ensured that "prosperity certificates" would not stay in circulation and thus would not add to the community's purchasing power. The source of the dilemma was the province's constitutional inability to issue legal tender.

The scrip scheme was authorized by Orders in Council pursuant to the Social Credit Measures Act. The preamble of this act was grandiose, but its provisions were modest. It authorized cabinet to appoint persons to investigate ways of implementing a system of monetary reform based on Social Credit, as long as such measures were within the jurisdiction of the Legislative Assembly of Alberta.

In August, the government began a drive to get Albertans to sign "registration covenants." In order to receive dividends, citizens had to promise "to work whenever possible, and to accept my remuneration in Alberta Credit as far as I can reasonably do so." In return, the government promised "to redeem, when possible, Alberta Credit with Canadian Currency for the purpose of allowing the member to take up residence outside the Province or for other essential requirements" (Elliott and Miller, 1987: 242). It seemed an attempt would be made to issue a provincial currency, an impression strengthened by the Alberta Credit House Act of 1 September 1936. The Alberta Credit House would have been a virtual provincial bank dealing in Alberta Credit and exchanging it for other forms of money. As these preparations went forward, Aberhart heightened hopes for early dividends by telling a Calgary crowd: "In spite of the fact that I told you that it would be 18 months after we were in power that the first dividend would be paid, we are making a systematic effort to pay it at an earlier date" (Elliott and Miller, 1987: 245).

Aberhart, however, was realistic enough to perceive the basic difficulty in all these schemes. When he met John Hargrave, leader of the British Social Credit Party, in December, he repeatedly asked: "If I issue a dividend, how do I get the money back?" (Social Credit Party of Great Britain and Ireland, 1937: 2). The province might issue any amount of Alberta Credit but, without the constitutional power to create legal tender, it would have to back its credit with real money.

In January 1937, Aberhart asked the public for more time; and, when the legislative session opened in February, he admitted his government's inability to issue dividends and said he would consult those who had signed registration covenants (Elliott and Miller, 1987: 255). His provincial treasurer introduced another orthodox budget, including an increase in the income tax and the introduction of a retail sales tax.

According to Manning, the cabinet's dedication to the ultimate goal of implementing Social Credit had not wavered, but they considered it irresponsible to bring in legislation before they had solved the practical difficulties. They were still trying to square the circle by issuing Alberta Credit that would be convertible into legal tender, would continue to circulate and thus increase purchasing power, and yet would not encroach upon federal jurisdiction. They were "nowhere near the end of all the exploratory work" (MI, 5: 9–23).

The impatience of many caucus members led to the famous "backbenchers' insurgency," which finally forced Aberhart's hand. When it appeared that rebels in his own caucus might combine with the opposition to defeat him in the legislature, he capitulated to their demands for immediate action. The first result was the Alberta Social Credit Act, which set up a Social Credit Board composed of five backbenchers. The board had the power to appoint technical experts in Social Credit policy to examine the legislation and make recommendations for legislative action to implement the program. The act also contained elaborate provisions for an Alberta Credit House with headquarters and branch offices. Although more detailed than previous legislation, it was still an attempt to mobilize Alberta's constitutional powers within its own sphere and did not trench directly under federal jurisdiction.

Major Douglas complied with the Social Credit Board's request for expert advice by sending G.F. Powell and L.D. Byrne, who helped draft the truly radical legislation passed in the special session of 3–6 August 1937. The Credit of Alberta Regulation Act required all banks to obtain a provincial operating licence and put them under the control of local directorates. Companion legislation cut off the banks' access to the courts.

However much Aberhart may have hesitated before, he backed this move to the hilt. He fired his attorney general when the latter recommended that the lieutenant-governor reserve royal assent, took responsibility for the act itself, and bullied the lieutenant-governor into signing. But it was in vain, as the federal cabinet quickly disallowed the legislation.

Aberhart then arranged for another session of the legislature. The essential features of the Credit of Alberta Regulation Act reappeared in another bill—Bill 8. A provincial tax was levied on the capital of banks (Bill 1), which would have raised more than $2 million a year, solving many of the provincial government's financial difficulties (MI, 6: 5). According to Social Credit theory, however, the real purpose of the tax was to encourage the banks to increase the quantity of their loans, thus expanding purchasing power to finance consumption (MI, 6: 7). For good measure, the chairman of the Social Credit Board was empowered to compel newspapers to "correct" their reporting (Bill 9). The lieutenant-governor reserved royal assent, and the federal cabinet referred the package of three bills to the Supreme Court of Canada. On 4 March 1938, the court held unconstitutional all three bills, as well as the Alberta Social Credit Act, which the former three were supposed to implement (Mallory, 1976: 87–90).

This sequence of disallowance, reservation, and judicial review amounted to a strong disconfirmation of the Social Credit program. It was now obvious that no legal means existed to put a provincial Social Credit plan into practice. The disconfirmation, however, was only political and constitutional. One could still plausibly claim that Social Credit economic theory had never been put to the test.

Up to this point, the main failure-of-prophecy reactions had been hesitation and delay by the leaders, punctuated by outbursts of fundamentalism among the followers, but the behavioural repertoire became richer after the setback of 4 March 1938. Rather than admit the whole thing had been a mistake from the start, Social Crediters went off in several directions as is characteristic according to the literature on the failure of prophecy. As Aberhart put it shortly after the Supreme Court's ruling: "a vessel has sometimes to sail against the very wind that is its only means of propulsion. To do this, the vessel pursues, you know, a zigzag course from side to side. It is called 'tacking in the wind'" (Schultz, 1964: 201).

The government immediately reaffirmed its faith in Social Credit ideology by passing the Alberta Social Credit Realization Act to reestablish the Social Credit Board. The reconstituted board had neither regulatory authority over the banks nor the ability to issue Alberta Credit, but it became a tireless source of Social Credit propaganda.

Aberhart also tried to widen the struggle to the national arena. Social Credit entered forty-five candidates in the federal election of 1935 and won all but two of the Alberta seats plus two in western Saskatchewan.

Ten days after the Supreme Court's verdict Aberhart announced, apparently without having consulted anyone in Saskatchewan, that Social Credit would put up candidates in the impending provincial election. He campaigned vigorously, making forty appearances in three weeks (Andrews, 1982: 59–66). Although the results in Saskatchewan were disappointing—only 16 percent of the popular vote and two seats—Aberhart continued to widen the struggle. In June 1938, he wrote a congratulatory letter to W.D. Herridge, who had broached the subject of monetary reform at a

Conservative convention (Hallett, 1966: 302). Although he and Herridge differed on many issues, he supported the latter's New Democracy movement in the federal election of 1940, and for a time the Social Credit caucus in Ottawa claimed to be members of the New Democracy.

After this episode, Aberhart organized another national vehicle, the Democratic Monetary Reform Organization (DMRO). He remained leader of the organization from its founding in Winnipeg in October 1941 until his death in 1943. In spite of his duties as premier of Alberta, he devoted a good deal of effort to the DMRO. He even studied French in the hope of expanding Social Credit's influence in Quebec (Elliott and Miller, 1987: 302-304).

Although none of these efforts was particularly successful, Aberhart's desire to launch a national movement was a logical response to the federal government veto of the provincial Social Credit program. If the government of Alberta could not obtain control of the credit system, it would be up to Parliament to enact "national monetary reform" and to "[conscript] the money system in the service of the nation" (Aberhart, 1941: 23). Moreover, the national strategy helped justify the continued presence of a Social Credit government in Alberta despite its admitted inability to carry out its provincial program.

Another way of rationalizing Social Credit's failure in Alberta was to evoke the world financial conspiracy, a theme present in the thought of Douglas from the outset. The spurious *Protocols of the Elders of Zion* first appeared in English translation in January or February 1920 (Cohn, 1969: 152), just as Douglas was beginning to publish. In his book *Credit-Power and Democracy* (1921), Douglas mentioned the possible existence of "an active, conscious conspiracy to enslave the world" (145). The next year he was more explicit about "the great financial groups, many of which are purely Jewish" (Elliott, 1985: 80); and in *Social Credit* (1924), he remarked about the *Protocols*: "The authenticity of this document is a matter of little importance; what is interesting about it, is the fidelity with which the methods by which such enslavements might be brought about, can be reflected in the facts of everyday experience" (Elliott, 1985: 80).

With the passing years, Douglas became more paranoid and anti-Semitic. He saw the Jewish financial power everywhere, conspiring to erect a totalitarian world slave state. World War II and the ostensible persecution of the Jews were merely a diversion. "I am convinced," he wrote, "that the Jewish High Command desires the ultimate victory of Germany, and will fight tooth-and-nail, *not to end the war*, but to see that Germany is not defeated in the peace" (Elliott, 1985: 82).

With the outbreak of World War II, the Social Credit Board began to import this demonological anti-Semitism into Alberta.[3] The board reprinted Douglas's publications and incorporated his thinking into their own. A fair example is *The Battle for Freedom* (1943), written by L.D. Byrne, one of the "technicians" sent by Douglas in 1937. In this pamphlet, Byrne refrained from mentioning the word "Jew," but he wrote of

a deliberate conspiracy by a group of internationalists (comprised for the most part of non-Christian Germans), to poison and pervert the reservoirs of human knowledge, to attack and weaken Christianity, and to discredit and destroy democracy for the purpose of enslaving mankind under a world totalitarian system (Byrne, 1943: 9-10).

Aberhart publicly and privately criticized "this foolish spirit of anti-Semitism" and questioned the authenticity of the "notorious *Protocols of Zion*" (Elliott, 1985: 83-84).

Manning also rejected the *Protocols* (MI, 17: 36). But both seemed to accept the conspiracy theory in all relevant details except for the Jewish identity of the conspirators. Aberhart told a radio audience shortly before his death:

> The task of defeating the war machine of the Axis powers—that is our first and greatest duty. The second, an equally important task, is that of defeating the machinations of the money powers who would impose upon us an evil totalitarian dictatorship by intrigue and cunning (Aberhart, 1943: broadcast 22, p. 11).

Like the national campaign for Social Credit, the conspiracy theory justified the continuance of the Social Credit government in Alberta. Even if it could not implement a Social Credit plan in one province, it could expose and struggle against the "machinations of the money powers." The emphasis had now shifted from creation of a secular millennium to defence against a diabolical enemy—an implicit step towards de-eschatologizing the ideology.

As the Social Credit millennium receded over the horizon, Aberhart announced an Interim Program. Central to it were the Treasury Branches, authorized by Order in Council 29 August 1938, with an initial capital of $200,000. These branches of the provincial treasury were never called banks, so as to avoid conflict with the federal Bank Act; but they functioned much like retail banks, taking deposits, paying interest, and making small loans. They also issued non-negotiable "transfer vouchers," somewhat like bank cheques, as a means by which depositors could make payments to merchants who participated in the scheme. A "consumer bonus" coupled the transfer vouchers to the government's "Buy Alberta" campaign. The Treasury Branch granted a 3 percent bonus to the depositor computed on three times the amount spent on made-in-Alberta goods purchased with transfer vouchers. Complementing the Treasury Branches were the provincial marketing boards, which retailed items made in Alberta (MI, 13: 26). The Treasury Branches also participated in a scheme to assist farmers to pay off their tax arrears through work on the highways (Nichols, 1963: 85–88). These measures loosely resembled monetary reform and lent a Social Credit flavour to a provincial exercise in mercantilist economics.

Although Aberhart would not have liked the comparison, the Interim Program stood to Social Credit as socialism stands to communism in Soviet ideology—not the ultimate goal but a step towards it, the best that can be done under present circumstances:

> The Alberta Interim Program was an extremely restricted effort to demonstrate what could be done in a minor way, within the limitations imposed by monopoly finance. It was a pointer to the vastly greater achievement that could follow in due course: the re-assumption of control over their own financial credit by the people of all Canada, as well as the Province of Alberta (Nichols, 1963: 96).

To Social Credit believers, the Interim Program demonstrated that goods could circulate without using legal tender, and that Alberta could eventually emancipate itself from the federal financial system:

> It was called an 'Interim' program because there were still high hopes at that time that we would be able to acquire in legislation the power to actually pay dividends and have the credit recognized as a medium of exchange within Alberta (MI, 13: 26).

As time went on, Aberhart naturally became involved in many aspects of provincial government that had little to do with Social Credit ideology, and he came to see competent execution of these tasks as a political *raison d'être*. In the provincial election of 1940, the Social Credit platform had twelve headings, only two of which, "True Democracy" and "Finance and Monetary Reform," had much to do with Social Credit. The other items, such as "Education," "Public Works," and "Municipal Administration," represented concerns that would have been addressed by a government of any stripe (Thomas, 1977: 146–50). The general themes of the Social Credit campaign were "good government" and "Honest Abe" (Schultz, 1962: 17). Thereafter, Social Credit presented itself as the party of honest and competent administration, further justifying its existence while waiting for the millennium.

By choosing a "zigzag course" and "tacking in the wind," Aberhart arrived at a halfway house of temporary ideological legitimacy. Although he still acknowledged implementation of Social Credit as his long-term goal, he put off the attainment of that end into an indefinite future. To reach the goal would require political struggle in a widened arena, with little prospect of immediate success. He loaded the blame for the delay onto the shadowy conspiracy of the international "money powers." In the meantime, the Alberta government justified itself with the Interim Program and general "good government." Social Credit had been de-eschatologized in practice but not yet in theory.

The Manning Years

When Ernest Manning became premier in May 1943, the CCF, riding high in the Gallup poll, looked like a credible contender for power. Social Credit responded to the challenge with a shift of emphasis in the conspiracy theory. Aberhart, following Douglas, had regarded socialism and communism as part of the international conspiracy; but he had reserved his main fire for the "money powers" and the Nazis. On occasion, the Social Credit League had cooperated with the CCF and even the Communists against the "old line" parties. In the mid-1940s, however, Manning began to emphasize

> that the socialistic doctrines of a supreme State are, in principle, identical with the doctrines of financial dictatorship which the rank and file of many socialistic parties claim to be fighting . . . the socialistic move is, if anything, a greater threat today to true democracy than the actions of those who continue to champion the already established financial dictatorship (Finkel, 1989: 86).

A.V. Bourcier, chairman of the Social Credit Board, said in the legislature, "the Socialist movement and the CCF were connected with a group of men behind the scenes, 'who never are seen in the full light of day,' who control international finance" (Finkel, 1989: 87).

Reformulation of the conspiracy theory gave Social Credit an effective weapon against the CCF. It remained a staple of propaganda thereafter, except that socialism gradually became more important in the conspiracy, while international finance became less so.[4]

The success of Social Credit's antisocialist campaign of 1944, together with the end of World War II, set the stage for a revival of fundamentalism. At the annual convention of December 1945, Social Credit activists expressed fear that the return to peace would let Alberta slip under the control of the financial and socialistic dictatorship of the United Nations, International Monetary Fund, and similar organizations. A resolution to make one more try for Social Credit passed unanimously (Macpherson, 1962: 207–208).

The result was the Alberta Bill of Rights Act, passed in March 1946. "We decided," said Manning many years later, "to make one last, sincere, concerted attempt to implement Social Credit monetary proposals and institute a system that would use what we called Alberta Credit within the Province for the distribution of goods and services in Alberta" (MI, 19: 25). The bill required the province to guarantee education, medical care, and the "necessities of life" to those under nineteen years of age; the opportunity to work, or a social security pension, to those between nineteen and sixty; and a retirement pension plus medical benefits to those over sixty. Changes in the monetary system would finance this cornucopia of welfare. A Board of Credit Commissioners, empowered to license all banks, would monitor the supply of credit in the province. It would issue Alberta Credit certificates to serve as reserves for the banks to generate new loans, both to private customers and to the government of Alberta. In this way the province could fund the proposed pensions and other benefits for the residents of Alberta. The Board of Credit Commissioners would have functioned much like the central bank of a sovereign state, regulating the money supply and financing the government's deficits when necessary.

At Manning's insistence, the act itself provided that it would not be proclaimed until its validity had been tested by reference to the Supreme Court of Alberta. Not surprisingly, both that court and the Judicial Committee of the Privy Council found it to be *ultra vires*.

Invalidation of the Alberta Bill of Rights Act became the prelude to Manning's purge of the "little faction of 'Douglasites' who think they have some special monopoly on the basic principles of Social Credit" (Macpherson, 1962: 211–12). The occasion was the extravagant language of the Social Credit Board's Annual Report for 1946:

> In previous Reports we have drawn attention to the existence of a deliberate conspiracy to establish a World slave State to be maintained by overwhelming force concentrated in the hands of a ruthless and closely knit international junta . . . The events of the past year provide further evidence of a rapidly developing and preconceived plan for world domination (Palmer, 1989: 18).

Publicly condemning all forms of anti-Semitism, Manning dissolved the Social Credit Board and fired several influential defenders of the Jewish conspiracy thesis, including L.D. Byrne, deputy minister of Economic Affairs; A.V. Bourcier, Social Credit whip and chairman of the Social Credit Board; and John Patrick Gillese, editor of *The Canadian Social Crediter*. Other Douglasite ministers and MLAs were either forced out of the caucus or resigned in protest (Macpherson, 1962: 211–12; Barr, 1974: 128–30). Such purges are familiar from the history of radical regimes in power. They are a sign of the millenarian movement's increasing entanglement in the evil reality it is supposed to transform.

Most writers have held that, from this point forward, Social Credit in Alberta became a "synonym for right of centre pragmatism" (Young, 1978: 108). According to this view, oil revenues allowed the government the luxury of embracing the social welfare policies fashionable throughout the Western world in the postwar period. The "end of ideology" supposedly marked Social Credit in Alberta as much as it did less exotic ideologies in other jurisdictions.

While there is some truth in this account, the story is more complicated. Premier Manning continued to espouse monetary reform as well as other policies not found in most models of conservatism.

In spite of, or perhaps because of, his inability to implement a robust version of Social Credit, Manning continued to preach the necessity of monetary reform at the federal level, as seen in this sample statement from around 1954:

> What Social Credit proposes (and this is what they call "funny money") is that we should see to it that the purchasing power available for the purchase of goods always approximates the value, or the total amount of the prices of the goods produced (Manning, ca. 1954: 7).

While this may have been little different from Keynesianism, it was rare for a conservative politician to be an avowed Keynesian in the early 1950s.

Another distinguishing mark of Social Credit ideology in these years was its great emphasis on the individual. All ideological pronouncements began with a statement like this: "We believe the individual is the most important unit in organized society" (Manning, ca. 1954: 3). Stress on individualism was the other side of the Social Credit doctrine; there was a financial-socialist conspiracy to erect a totalitarian "supreme state." Individualism led Social Crediters to an enthusiastic embrace of "free enterprise," as they called the market system.

The movement, however, never gave up its original "humanitarian" intention of assuring a decent standard of living to all. The result was a demand for the state to supplement, but not supplant, the market:

> A major objective of organized society should be to assist each citizen to attain through his own enterprise sufficient financial resources to enable him to obtain for himself and his dependents an acceptable standard of social welfare without dependence on State Welfare services. To the extent this is impossible, society collectively must assume the cost of an acceptable standard of social services, to bring such services within the financial reach of each individual citizen (Manning, n.d.).

This view inclined Social Credit governments towards putting a floor under the living standard of the poor, but not towards equalization for its own sake.

Government policy never arises solely from ideology, but the record of the Manning years seems largely congruent with the ideology described above. In the financial sphere, Manning continued Aberhart's "pay as you go" approach. After defaulting on the provincial debt, the province had been unable to borrow money through normal channels and had had to balance its annual budget. After the war, Manning settled with the province's creditors and ran an annual budgetary surplus, which he used to reduce the provincial debt (Hanson, 1952: 326), thus seeking to ensure Alberta's independence from the "money powers." Fiscal responsibility did not stem merely from the good fortune of having found oil; the "pay as you go" policy had originated long before the discovery of oil at Leduc.

Social Credit individualism had other interesting consequences. Labour legislation was generally restrictive, because Social Credit saw unions as collectivistic cartels, at least potentially linked by the CCF and the Communist Party to the "supreme state" conspiracy, and strikes as virtual sabotage of the productive power of the community (Finkel, 1989: 108–15). For different but parallel reasons, Manning opposed the bilingual initiatives of the 1960s and criticized the legal entrenchment of collective differences of language and culture (Finkel, 1989: 153). Throughout his time in government, Manning also pushed Alberta's cities to exercise their responsibilities and raise their revenues independently. He resisted paying the full cost of municipally administered programs, fearing to encourage fiscal irresponsibility on the part of the cities (Finkel, 1989: 123). This was also part of his philosophy of decentralization in opposition to the "supreme state."

Under Manning's leadership, Social Credit adherence to free enterprise was more principled than usual in conservative parties. He consistently opposed public ownership of utilities, and managed to avoid nationalization of Calgary Power when that issue arose (Finkel, 1989: 149). He opposed federal regional development subsidies, even when the money might have gone to northern Alberta (Finkel, 1989: 151–52). His government spent more lavishly than any other province on services, such as transportation, health care, and education, that were intended to provide opportunities for self-improvement to all members of the public; but it resisted policies whose rationale was egalitarian or redistributive. Welfare payments were means-tested, and health benefits were tied to user fees or co-insurance payments (Finkel, 1989: 144, 149–50, 155). Deterrent fees encouraged "recognition by the individual that he had a personal responsibility for these things" (MI, 30: 11). Except for the Canada Pension Plan, Manning opposed the universal compulsory welfare programs introduced by the federal government under Lester Pearson. The Social Credit welfare state in Alberta was expensive, but it was based on more individualistic principles than the Canadian welfare state.

After the nullification of the Alberta Bill of Rights Act, Social Credit strategy amounted to pursuing federal monetary reform through the national party, defending individualism and free enterprise in Alberta, and using the provincial government as a humanitarian supplement to a market economy. While this strategy was perhaps formally consistent with Social Credit ideology, it became unsatisfactory to Manning in his later years. By 1965, he was speaking openly about the need to rethink ideological and partisan alignments in Canada (Manning, 1965). He revealed the full extent of his rethinking in 1967 when he published *A White Paper on Human Resources Development*, directed to Alberta, and *Political Realignment: A Challenge to Thoughtful Canadians*, a short book aimed at the whole country.

The *White Paper* outlined the tasks to be played by the provincial government in future years. The reference to "human resources" emphasized the coming transition from reliance on physical resources, so important in Alberta's past, to a knowledge-based "society of free and creative individuals" (MI, 38: 2). Traditional Social Credit principles of individualism, free enterprise, and humanitarian concern figured prominently in their formulation. "The Government of Alberta," wrote Manning,

> is resolved to destroy, once and for all, the fallacious notion that those who believe in freedom of economic activity, private ownership of property, and individual enterprise and responsibility, are incapable of "social concern" devoid of humanitarian sentiments (Manning, 1967a: 97).

Conspicuously absent from the *White Paper* was any mention of monetary reform. The closest reference was a criticism of federal tight money policies for slowing growth in the less well developed peripheral regions of the country (Manning, 1967a: 64).

In *Political Realignment,* Manning called upon Canadian federal parties to become less opportunistic and more principled, both in their appeals to voters and in their formulation of policy. He advocated a "social conservative" position to "weld the humanitarian concerns of those with awakened social consciences to the economic persuasions of those with a firm conviction in the value of freedom of economic activity and enlightened private enterprise" (Manning, 1967b: 63). He offered to merge the national Social Credit Party with the Progressive Conservatives, hoping also to attract some free-enterprise elements from the Liberals.

Manning rushed to get his book into print before the upcoming Conservative leadership convention (MI, 38: 20–21). While he did not actively pursue the Conservative leadership, he would have welcomed a draft. His underlying hope was that the united Conservative and Social Credit parties would become a new "populist movement" against the opportunistic politics of the welfare state (MI, 38: 47).

Manning admitted that his party had originally been elected to pursue monetary reform, but did not mention the many unsuccessful attempts in that direction, except to object to "the long and persistent practice of certain news media to consistently misrepresent Social Credit as a party advocating printing press money." He emphasized that for over thirty years Social Credit had governed Alberta in a way "generally compatible with the Social Conservative position." Since the national Social Credit Party faced "almost insurmountable difficulties in becoming a vehicle for national reconstruction in the foreseeable future," merger with the Progressive Conservatives was the most sensible alternative (Manning, 1967b: 73–75).

Without repudiating Social Credit ideology, Manning, first in practice and then in theory, had de-eschatologized it into social conservatism. The transformation took place through rearrangement of elements that had always been present. Monetary reform was reduced to Keynesian dimensions, while the international conspiracy theory lingered in the background as part of the indictment of socialism. Individualism and free enterprise expanded to fill the vacant ideological space, while humanitarianism provided a noncollectivist, noninterventionist rationale for government services.

Manning and Social Credit had moved a long way from Aberhart's "wondrously simple plan." Success as a millenarian movement had brought control of a government, but the millenarian vision had proved impossible to implement. Bearing the practical responsibility of government had changed Social Credit from a millenarian protest movement to a mainstream political party.

The ultimate irony is that the final rapprochement with reality was the prelude to political collapse. Social Credit had presided over the economic and political modernization of the province. Encouragement of the oil industry had brought unimagined prosperity, and with it a new urban population, largely managerial and professional, to whom the Social Credit style seemed anachronistic. Peter Lougheed was able to renew the provincial fortunes of the Progressive Conservatives by appealing to this class created by the success of Social Credit policies.

Conclusion

Over the years, the leaders of Alberta Social Credit displayed a variety of responses to the failure of their expectations about the future. Their main frustrations were the refusal of Major Douglas to come to Alberta and present the government with a ready-made plan; the exercise by the federal government of its powers of disallowance, reservation, and judicial review to nullify Social Credit legislation; the failure of Social Credit to gain much ground outside Alberta, either at the federal level or in other provinces; and the judicial rejection of the Alberta Bill of Rights Act of 1946. In connection with these disappointments, the following responses emerged, approximately in the order listed, but with some chronological overlap: procrastination and experimentation with marginally related initiatives, such as prosperity certificates; an outbreak of fundamentalism and acute expectation, followed by an attempt to create the millennium by legislation; proselytizing outside Alberta as a response to stalemate within the province; creation of the Interim Program to fill the ideological void; preoccupation with other activities of "good government"; elaboration of a conspiracy theory to explain the difficulties of implementing the ideology; a second flare-up of fundamentalism and a second attempt to create the millennium by legislation; a purge of the fundamentalists by the pragmatic leadership; a long period of dissonance between the announced long-term goals of the movement and the perceived short-term possibilities of action; and, a final reinterpretation to de-eschatologize the ideology, accompanied by a desire to reenter Canadian politics as a mainstream party.

All these actions can be seen as responses to the cognitive dissonance arising from the inability to remake the world as demanded by Social Credit ideology. As Carroll (1979:104) has argued, cognitive dissonance presents an opportunity for creative response, for transcending an apparent stalemate. Alberta Social Credit conformed to this model by transforming itself from a utopian protest movement into a responsible governing party with a distinctive, practical ideology.

General knowledge of millenarian movements helps to illuminate the special case of Alberta Social Credit by rendering its history intelligible; but the special case is also of wider significance because the twentieth century is the epoch *par excellence* of millenarian politics. The Fascist, National Socialist, and Khmer Rouge regimes were short-lived; but the longer-lived Communist regimes of the Soviet Union and its satellites, as well as of Yugoslavia, China, North Korea, Vietnam, and Cuba, are now confronting the failure of their particular prophecies. Numerous radical regimes of the Third World, such as Nicaragua, Mozambique, Angola, Iran, and Libya, also find themselves in varying degrees of the same dialectic. Millenarian theory does not prescribe an invariant course of development, but it predicts the appearance of particular responses as part of an evolutionary tendency towards de-eschatologizing. Alberta Social Credit is an important point of reference for the study of these trends precisely because its ideology was *sui generis*. That patterns found in the history of Alberta Social Credit can be discovered in other radical regimes of the left and right suggest that the logic of failed expectations is a powerful influence on millenarian regimes in power.

Notes

The authors would like to thank the Social Sciences and Humanities Research Council of Canada for financially supporting the research upon which this paper is based.

1. University of Alberta Archives, E.C. Manning Interviews, 81–32. We are grateful to Senator Manning for permission to consult the transcripts.

2. William Aberhart, lecture in Edmonton, 23 May 1935. Glenbow Alberta Institute, W.J. Bowen Papers.

3. The Social Credit Board's annual reports are in the Sessional Papers of the Alberta Legislative

Assembly, Provincial Archives of Alberta, 70–414. The first mention of an international conspiracy is in the report for 1939 (no. 1936).

4. In the interviews conducted around 1980, Manning's adherence to conspiracy theories seemed highly attenuated. While acknowledging that Communists were dedicated and purposive, he said: "I've never gone along with those people that find a Communist under every bed. I think that's a gross exaggeration" (MI, 33: 37). Regarding international finance, he said: "When you carry it to the place where you see a financier hiding under every bed, this is a little extreme! It doesn't work that way. But this doesn't detract from the fact that there's a real problem there" (MI, 17: 18–20).

References

[Aberhart, William]. [1933]. *The Douglas System of Economics*. n.p.

[Aberhart, William]. [1934]. *The BNA Act and Social Credit*. Calgary: Social Credit League of Alberta.

Aberhart, William. 1935. *Social Credit Manual*. Calgary: Social Credit League of Alberta.

Aberhart, William. 1941. *National Monetary Reform: Canada's Urgent Need*. Edmonton: Today and Tomorrow.

Aberhart, William. [1943]. *Post-War Reconstruction*. Edmonton: Today and Tomorrow.

Andrews, Ken. 1982. "'Progressive' Counterparts of the CCF: Social Credit and the Conservative Party in Saskatchewan, 1935–38." *Journal of Canadian Studies* 17:58–74.

Barkun, Michael. 1974. *Disaster and the Millennium*. New Haven: Yale University Press.

Barr, John J. 1974. *The Dynasty: The Rise and Fall of Social Credit in Alberta*. Toronto: McClelland and Stewart.

Benz, Ernst. 1968. *Evolution and Christian Hope*. Garden City: Anchor Books.

Byrne, L.D. 1943. *The Battle for Freedom*. Edmonton: Social Credit Board.

Carroll, Robert P. 1979. *When Prophecy Failed: Reactions and Responses to Failure in the Old Testament Prophetic Traditions*. London: SCM Press.

Coe, V.F. 1938. "Dated Stamp Scrip in Alberta." *Canadian Journal of Economics and Political Science* 4:60–91.

Cohn, Norman. 1969. *Warrant for Genocide: The Myth of the Jewish World-Conspiracy and the Protocols of the Elders of Zion*. New York: Harper.

Colbourne, Maurice. 1935. *The Meaning of Social Credit: Revised Edition of "Economic Nationalism."* 4th ed. Edmonton: Social Credit Board.

Douglas, C.H. 1921. *Credit-Power and Democracy*. London: Cecil Palmer.

Douglas, C.H. 1937. *The Alberta Experiment: An Interim Survey*. London: Eyre and Spottiswoode.

Elliott, David R. 1985. "Anti-Semitism and the Social Credit Movement: The Intellectual Roots of the Keegstra Affair." *Canadian Ethnic Studies* 17:78–89.

Elliott, David R., and Iris Miller. 1987. *Bible Bill: A Biography of William Aberhart*. Edmonton: Reidmore Books.

Festinger, Leon, Henry W. Riecken, and Stanley Schachter. 1956. *When Prophecy Fails: A Social and Psychological Study of a Modern Group that Predicted the Destruction of the World*. Minneapolis: University of Minnesota Press.

Finkel, Alvin. 1989. *The Social Credit Phenomenon*. Toronto: University of Toronto Press.

Flanagan, Thomas. 1972. "Social Credit in Alberta: A Canadian 'Cargo Cult'?" *Archives de Sociologie des Religions* 34:39–48.

Gerth, H.H., and C. Wright Mills. 1958. *From Max Weber: Essays in Sociology*. New York: Oxford.

Hallet, Mary. 1966. "The Social Credit Party and the New Democracy Movement." *Canadian Historical Review* 47:301–25.

Hanson, E.J. 1952. "Public Finance in Alberta Since 1935." *Canadian Journal of Economics and Political Science* 18:322–35.

Hardyck, Jane Allyn, and Marcia Braden. 1962. "Prophecy Fails Again: A Report of a Failure to Replicate." *Journal of Abnormal and Social Psychology* 65:136–41.

Jackson, Hugh. 1975. "The Resurrection Belief of the Earliest Church: A Response to the Failure of Prophecy?" *Journal of Religion* 5:415–25.

Macpherson, C.B. 1962. *Democracy in Alberta: Social Credit and the Party System.* 2nd ed. Toronto: University of Toronto Press.

Mallory, J.R. 1976. *Social Credit and the Federal Power in Canada.* Toronto: University of Toronto Press.

Manning, E.C. [n.d.] *The Social Credit Yardstick.* Edmonton: Alberta Social Credit League.

Manning, E.C. ca. 1954. *Social Credit in a Nutshell.* Edmonton: Alberta Social Credit League.

Manning, E.C. 1965. "Key Manning Address." *Canadian Social Crediter,* December 1965, 4, 5, 7.

Manning, E.C. 1967a. *A White Paper on Human Resources Development.* Edmonton: Queen's Printer.

Manning, E.C. 1967b. *Political Realignment: A Challenge to Thoughtful Canadians.* Toronto: McClelland and Stewart.

Nichols, H.E. 1963. *Alberta's Fight for Freedom.* Edmonton, n.p.

Palmer, Howard. 1989. "Politics, Religion and Anti-Semitism in Alberta: 1880–1950." Unpublished manuscript.

Schultz, Harold J. 1962. "A Second Term: 1940." *Alberta Historical Review* 10(1):17–26.

Schultz, Harold J. 1964. "Portrait of a Premier." *Canadian Historical Review* 45:185–211.

Social Credit Party of Great Britain and Ireland. 1937. *Official Report: Alberta. A Documented Record of Mr. John Hargrave's Visit to the Province of Alberta, Canada December 8, 1938 to January 25, 1937.* London: Social Credit Party of Great Britain and Ireland.

Talmon, Yonina. 1968. "Millenarism." *International Encyclopedia of the Social Sciences.* New York: Macmillan.

Thomas, Lewis H. 1977. *William Aberhart and Social Credit in Alberta.* Toronto: Copp Clark.

Wernik, Uri. 1975. "Frustrated Beliefs and Early Christianity." *Numen* 22:96–130.

Young, Walter D. 1978. *Democracy and Discontent: Progressivism, Socialism and Social Credit in the Canadian West.* 2nd ed. Toronto: McGraw-Hill Ryerson.

Zygmunt, Joseph F. 1970. "Prophetic Failure and Chiliastic Identity: The Case of Jehovah's Witnesses." *American Journal of Sociology* 75:926–48.

Zygmunt, Joseph F. 1972. "When Prophecies Fail." *American Behavioral Scientist* 16:245–68.

Class Structure and Populist Protest:
The Case of Western Canada

Reprinted from the *Canadian Journal of Sociology* 1 (1975), 1–15,
by permission of the *Canadian Journal of Sociology*.

The emergence of Social Credit and the Co-operative Commonwealth Federation (CCF) from similar social conditions in Alberta and Saskatchewan is best explained by stressing how the populist elements in each were consistent with the *petit-bourgeois* character of the most numerous class in each province. Differences in the historical development of each province prior to the Depression explain the acceptance of separate expressions of populism in Alberta and Saskatchewan. This is the thesis to be elaborated and defended in this paper.

In 1968 S.M. Lipset concluded that there had been no "adequate explanation, or even a detailed descriptive account of the factors involved that resulted in such different reactions from two quite similar social units."[1] Shortly afterwards David Smith[2] proposed that the federal system of government was a key explanatory factor. This did indeed make separate political development possible, but in itself is no explanation of the nature of that development. Walter Young[3] reconstructed the history of the Progressives, the CCF (which he treated as a national movement), and Social Credit. However, each political movement was treated in isolation, with no attempt to present an explicit comparison. More recently Naylor has stressed the similarity of Social Credit and the CCF as answers to the problems faced by the agrarian *petite bourgeoisie*:

> As to the contradiction between Social Credit and the CCF emerging from identical conditions, it ceases to exist once these movements are viewed in terms of objective class standards rather than the subjective standards of the leaders. The two movements are indistinguishable. For the farm constituency, the policy proposals of both groups were identical.[4]

In this paper the similar class base of Social Credit and the CCF is also emphasized, but these movements are certainly not "indistinguishable." There is still a need to account for their separate development in neighbouring provinces.

What Is Populism?

My contention is that *both* Social Credit and the Saskatchewan CCF developed as populist protest parties. But what are the salient characteristics of populism? The concept has certainly been among the most difficult to pin down in the sociology of politics because it has been applied indiscriminately to such disparate groups as North American cash-crop farmers and the *narodniki* of nineteenth-century Russia, as well as twentieth-century rural and urban movements in Africa, Asia, and South America. Proposed definitions vary from those which are so general in their emphasis on popular participation as to be equivalent to many definitions of democracy to those which tend to emphasize the characteristics of the particular movement which the author has studied in depth.[5] In part, the failure to agree on a definition reflects the difficulty of trying to include in one concept a large number of political movements which developed separately on different continents and with no influence on each other.

If we are to develop an adequate concept of populism, it is necessary to investigate what the "examples" have in common. Yet, when this is attempted, similarities are found only at a highly abstract or general level. Attempts to be very specific seem doomed, as in the work of Peter Wiles, to whom populism is:

> any creed or movement based on the following major premise: *virtue resides in the simple people, who are the overwhelming majority, and in their collective traditions.* I hold that this premise causes a political syndrome of surprising constancy, albeit with now more, now fewer, socialist overtones.[6]

Wiles's syndrome lists twenty-four characteristics of populism, and he recognizes that no single case will have all of them. While this is to be expected in all ideal-type constructions, it is less acceptable that for most hypotheses in the list we can find examples of political movements which have been classified as populist and which contradict Wiles's assertions. The point is that statements which attempt to be specific about populism's ideology and organization must be qualified by exceptions. This does not mean that the category should be abandoned, but we must recognize that populism is a highly general category which must be qualified when looking at specific cases, just as categories such as socialism, communism, and capitalism must be qualified when applied to particular examples. It is still valuable to know what disparate events and situations have in common.

I shall now attempt to establish several general populist characteristics and indicate the correspondence of Social Credit and the CCF to them.

First, populist ideology stresses the worth of the common people and advocates their political supremacy. Reports of how William Aberhart, the Social Credit leader, stirred the people of Alberta in the thirties suggest his emotional commitment to their plight. For example, a small-town businessman claimed that "above all, he had an absolutely great love for the suffering of the common people," and a farmer reported that "he took up our problems and made them his own. That's why I worked for him."[7] By explaining to the unemployed how the Depression was not a consequence of their personal failings, Aberhart restored a lost dignity. In more abstract terms, Social Credit theory proclaimed that the general will of the people must be realized, and this could be done through the inspired leadership of William Aberhart. The Social Credit League was to represent the will of all the people in one organization, which would be morally superior to the corrupt and socially divisive parties of the old political system.

Within the CCF, a close identification with the common people also existed. For example, Tommy Douglas[8] stated that "this is more than a political movement, it is a people's movement, a movement of men and women who have dedicated their lives to making the brotherhood of man a living reality." However, whereas in Social Credit populist emphasis on the worth of the people was shown mostly in the paternalistic concern of the leadership for the suffering of the people, in the Saskatchewan CCF it was most evident in the ideological commitment to popular control of the political organization.

This leads to the second characteristic of populism, that is, the rejection of intermediate associations between the mass and leaders. Of course, political organizations do develop, but their structure is influenced by the populist desire for direct democracy. In this respect, the Saskatchewan CCF followed the common practice of North American populism by requiring that organization leaders be controlled from the mass base. Therefore, the CCF developed a form of delegate democracy, which provided institutional means for the mass membership to retain control over its representatives. For example, the party leader was subject to election by convention each year, and policy resolutions, which might originate at any level of the organization, were not considered binding until passed by the annual convention. Whether such attempts to avoid the problem of oligarchical control in the CCF were successful is a disputed matter, but I am only concerned here to show the influence of democratic populist ideals on the formal organization.

In the case of Social Credit, the commitment to direct democracy took an authoritarian form. William Aberhart, claiming to represent the general will, was charismatically legitimated and had personal control of decision making. In matters of policy, candidate selection, and administration, general conventions had given Aberhart the final say. Party conventions became no more than convenient locations for the leaders to distribute information and give inspirational addresses. Aberhart retained his "direct" relationship with the people through his frequent public meetings and his regular radio broadcasts. This kind of authoritarian populism is rare in North America and develops, as we shall see, when the more democratic form is discredited. Although more extreme and less popular than Social Credit, the American movements led by Coughlin, Long, Winrod, and Pelly were similar cases of authoritarian populism.[9]

A third characteristic of populism, closely linked with its emphasis on the common people, is the tendency for populist protest to be directed against some group which lies outside the local society. When deprivations are experienced, the stress on the homogeneity and virtue of the people means that external causes must be sought. This is the basis of the nationalist and isolationist sentiment of much populism. Among the most common scapegoats have been colonial capitalist states, monopoly industry and finance, industrial labour unions, Jews, and other ethnic minorities. In their frustration, supporters of both Social Credit and the CCF turned against the "Big Interests" from the metropolitan East and against their representatives in the West. In attacking the eastern-controlled corporations, they were continuing a long tradition of protest by western Canadian farmers. The thrust of Social Credit was against financial institutions, leading in its most extreme development to a theory that there was a world Jewish conspiracy to dominate the common people. (This minority group was disowned by the Social Credit leadership.) There was no evidence of such scapegoat theorizing in the CCF, but there was certainly a recognition that monopoly capitalism lay at the root of the farmers' problem and that the Saskatchewan party stood for the West against the East.

A fourth and critical quality of populism is that it demands the reform of capitalist structure rather than social revolution. Several writers refer to the Janus quality of populism, looking forward and backward at the same time.[10] Innovation is accepted provided the aim is to modify the existing order by making it more bearable for the common people. Occasionally such innovation has taken on a socialist façade (for example, the setting up of state-owned grain elevators in some parts of North America), but in populist programs there is never any commitment to a fundamental change in property relations as they pertain to the small producer. Populist ideology reflects a desire to shore up what exists, or even to revert to some imagined golden age.

The debate about the ideological nature of American populism in the late nineteenth century has considerable theoretical relevance for an understanding of the Canadian cases. I shall not enter here the dispute about the rationality, nativist, or anti-Semitic character of American populism; rather I shall limit my comment to the economic ideology. Norman Pollack's[11] provocative work argued that populism had strong support from and close ties with eastern labour, but Goldschmidt[12] has presented evidence that New York workers looked on populism as a movement of agrarian class interests that had little to offer as a solution to the labourers' problems. Whether popular with labour or not, populism was not socialist. For example, Durden[13] records that H.D. Lloyd joined the populists in order to advance socialism, but his collectivist proposals were rejected.[14] Most convincing is Nugent's[15] study of Kansas, in which populism is shown as a practical reform movement aiming to solve problems of land control, monopoly in transportation, and, especially, money supply. Similarly, the Non-Partisan League of North Dakota advocated policies of state intervention to prop up the position of the farmer.[16] It had a direct influence on Canadian populism, particularly on the United Farmers of Alberta.

Populism in Western Canada

In western Canada, similar reformist solutions were presented, as both Social Credit and the CCF claimed to solve the class problems of the *petite bourgeoisie* within the framework of capitalism. Social Crediters emphasized that they did not threaten private property, savings, or the principle of free enterprise but they did claim that the freedom and prosperity of the people could be restored by reforming the monetary system of capitalism. The cause of poverty, they said, was a lack of purchasing power, which could be resolved by controlling financial institutions and issuing dividends of social credit to each member of society.[17] Having accepted the panacea of monetary reform, there was less emphasis on other favoured techniques of populist defence. Therefore, in the Social Credit program we find little attention to promotion of cooperatives, state control of monopolies, and state-welfare provisions, all of which were part of CCF policy. These solutions would be unnecessary after the financial system had been reformed.

By 1934 the Saskatchewan CCF was in the process of dropping its socialist program for the state ownership of land and was becoming a party of populist reform.[18] The elements of socialism in the CCF's program did not challenge the dominant form of the organization of production in Saskatchewan (small-scale private enterprise in the form of the family farm), but rather provided for its continuation. That such a policy might involve government control, or even ownership, of the forces which were affecting the farmer was consistent with populist ideology. The CCF leaders rejected Social Credit monetary reform, although there was considerable pressure in the thirties for some cooperation with Aberhart,[19] and so they fell back on the staples of North American agrarian populism—support for the cooperatives, control of the banks and industrial monopolies, state medicine, etc. The Saskatchewan CCF was also influenced by the urban labour background of some of its leaders and by its association with the national party, which was not farmer-dominated. Therefore, the party proposed and later enacted legislation which was more favourable to the rights of labour than that found anywhere else in the country. Yet, as Lipset[20] recognized, this was a trade-union program, not a socialist one. Even in the CCF's state enterprises, there was no commitment to workers' participation in management.

In assessing the CCF's ideology as populism, it is necessary to come to terms with the evidence that many leaders of the CCF saw it as a socialist party in opposition to capitalism. But when we understand the meaning of capitalism and socialism in Saskatchewan, there is no longer any reason to withdraw the populist label. When CCF leaders attacked capitalism, they were not attacking the idea of private ownership of productive property or the private accumulation of profit, which is essential for a long-term commitment to socialism. (Using this criterion, many of Europe's social-democratic parties could not be considered socialist either.) As evidence of the CCF position on profits, we may take a speech by party leader George Williams, who argued that small businessmen had nothing to fear from a supposed attack on profits because:

> From an economic point of view, a profit is something over and above a fair and just reward for a service rendered . . . But the small margin our retail merchants receive is not in that class at all.[21]

To be against capitalism in Saskatchewan meant to be against monopoly exploitation; it did not mean to be against small-scale private enterprise, because this would have meant challenging the whole way of life of prairie farmers. The meaning of capitalism is made clear in a statement by T.C. Douglas, replying to a charge that his new government's proposals to help private enterprise were in contradiction to the official CCF policy of eradicating capitalism:

> Premier Douglas said "private enterprise" and "capitalism" were not synonymous terms. The reference to capitalism meant monopoly capitalism where a small group of men were able to control the whole economy of a community . . . The government recognized three types of enterprise, public, co-operative and private, and all had a place in the province's economy. It was the government's intention to encourage private enterprise wherever it did not interfere with the welfare of the people.[22]

In the late thirties, public reference to socialism was usually avoided in CCF speeches and literature. When Douglas replaced Williams as party leader, the concept of socialism reappeared, but it now meant either opposition to monopolies or extension of the cooperative movement. In this, the CCF continued the tradition of pragmatic agrarian populism under another label. The cooperative commonwealth is still based on capitalist property relations. Thus, it is true that:

> the co-operative movement does not advocate a basic change in capitalist institutional structure. It accepts profits and private entrepreneurship; indeed, it seeks to extend the benefits of these institutions to a larger number.[23]

Therefore, we should question the CCF's own statement about the relationship between cooperatives and socialism—that "their fundamental principles and objectives are the same."[24] This could only be true if socialism can be defined to exclude a social revolution. In 1945, enabling legislation was passed to allow the establishment of collective farms in Saskatchewan, but only twenty-nine were actually set up. This was the limit of the socialization of agriculture.

The preceding paragraphs have tried to establish the populist character of Social Credit and the Saskatchewan CCF, but why did populism develop in western Canada? The explanation to be presented here stresses the influence of a person's class position on his political action. While this is hardly a novel idea, the concept of class has been used in such varied ways in the sociological literature that it is not clear what is intended by this statement. For example, with reference to the emergence of agrarian class-consciousness, Lipset employs a concept of economic class in which a class is defined in terms of relationship to the market. Such an approach to class is realist in the sense that "it considers social class as a real ensemble defined at one and the same time by material facts and by the collective consciousness which individuals form of it."[25] It is possible to conceive of such a group as an acting unit. However, in his analysis of the social base of CCF support, Lipset changes his use of class. Now the status-group categories favoured by many American sociologists appear. These categories describe aggregates of individuals and do not carry the implication that the groups are acting units. This would only be possible if they formed communities. Here class will be used consistently in the former sense.

The best attempt to analyse the class basis of prairie politics is C.B. Macpherson's *Democracy in Alberta*, in which he argues that the most useful way of categorizing people in order to understand political action is based on their relationship to the productive process—in particular, "how much freedom they retain over the disposal of their own labour, and how much control they exercise over the disposal of others' labour."[26] Those who occupy similar positions in these respects are liable to develop similar assumptions and outlooks as a result of their common life experience.[27] From this perspective, the farmers of western Canada form part of the *petite bourgeoisie*, a concept which denotes a class of small-scale entrepreneurs who are self-employed and employ little or no labour from outside the family. In twentieth-century Canada, as the scale of organized production constantly increases, they form the transitional marginal remnants of a past era.[28] The various sections of the class are united by their insecurity and their belief that they are *independent*. As Macpherson noted, the belief in independence, although it is an important determinant of their action, is an illusion, because the *petit-bourgeois* class is subordinate to large-scale, labour-utilizing capitalists, who control the price system. The small producer is independent, perhaps, in that he may still be able to decide for himself when and how to use his own labour.

Before commenting on the divisions within the *petite bourgeoisie*, the *petit-bourgeois* character of agricultural production in both Alberta and Saskatchewan until mid-century will be documented. Using census data, Macpherson[29] was able to show that small independent commodity producers formed the largest class in Alberta during the period of concern here. From table 1, it is clear that the dominance of agricultural occupations has been even greater in Saskatchewan than in Alberta. Neither white-collar nor blue-collar occupations approached the agricultural in size. There is some indication in the table that agriculture is declining in importance, and later census reports show an acceleration of this trend.

Table 2 has been constructed to show that agriculture has been conducted largely by the *petite bourgeoisie*. Farming in the West has been overwhelmingly conducted by family units of commodity producers employing little or no hired labour. Normally, wage-earners account for less than 20 percent of the agricultural labour force and are employed largely on a seasonal basis. Since 1936, less than 40 percent of farms have used any hired labour at all, and there has been a continual decline in the number of weeks for which this labour has been employed. Thus, the trend towards larger farms has not resulted in greater dependence on wage labour; rather, increased mechanization has created the conditions which are summarized in table 2.

Table 1. Occupational Distribution of the Labour Force, 1911–15

(In Percentages)

	1911	1921	1931	1941	1951
Alberta					
Professional managerial	7.9	10.5	9.9	10.6	14.0
Other white-collar	6.4	9.6	9.3	9.4	14.7
Agricultural	49.9	52.8	50.9	49.0	32.5
Blue-collar	29.6	20.0	22.4	22.1	28.3
Service	6.3	6.6	7.7	9.0	10.0
Not stated		0.1		0.1	0.6
Saskatchewan					
Professional managerial	6.0	9.7	9.2	9.8	12.9
Other white-collar	5.2	8.0	7.6	7.7	11.7
Agricultural	63.9	65.2	60.3	59.3	48.8
Blue-collar	19.7	11.3	15.9	14.4	18.6
Service	5.3	5.6	7.1	8.8	7.7
Not stated				0.2	0.5

SOURCE Calculated from data in Dominion Bureau of Statistics. Census of Canada, 1961. Bulletin 3.1–2.
NOTE The Canadian census uses occupational categories which are not suitable for conventional sociological analysis. This table has been constructed by collapsing census categories. While the result is far from ideal, it is the best that can be achieved with the available data. Percentages may not add to 100 owing to rounding error.

Table 2. Employment in Agriculture, 1921–51

(In Percentages)

	1921	1931	1936	1941	1946	1951
Farmers as Percentage of Labour Force						
Alberta	37.9	32.2	31.3	29.5	28.2	23.2
Saskatchewan	43.5	36.2	36.6	36.4	37.9	36.0
Farmers plus Unpaid Family Labour as Percentage of Labour Force						
Alberta		41.6	42.1	37.9		27.0
Saskatchewan	NA[b]	49.1	50.7	46.9	NA	42.7

Wage Earners as Percentage of
Agricultural Labour Force

Alberta	14.7	18.0	20.1	16.3	12.3	16.6
Saskatchewan	18.0	18.5	18.9	14.7	10.7	12.6

Farms Having Hired Labour as
Percentage of All Farms[a]

Alberta		40.5	43.2	36.4	31.4	39.2
Saskatchewan	NA	41.8	43.2	34.0	29.6	38.7

Average Weeks of Hired Labour per
Farm Having Any Hired Labour

Alberta		26.3	28.4	27.9	23.8	
Saskatchewan	NA	27.1	24.5	23.9	20.4	NA

SOURCE Calculated from data available in Dominion Bureau of Statistics, Census of Canada,
1921 to 1951; Census of the Prairie Provinces, 1936 and 1946.
[a] The figures here refer to the year preceding that of the census.
[b] NA=relevant statistic not available.

Table 3. Farm Tenure, 1921–51

(In Percentages)

	1921	1931	1941	1951
Alberta				
Owner-operated	79.5	72.6	62.5	62.7
Tenant-operated	9.7	12.2	17.1	11.6
Part owner-operated[a]	9.9	14.9	19.8	25.0
Manager-operated	0.9	0.3	0.6	0.7
Total	100.0	100.0	100.0	100.0
Saskatchewan				
Owner-operated	76.7	66.1	52.6	54.6
Tenant-operated	10.8	15.4	24.6	14.7
Part owner-operated	11.6	18.2	22.4	30.2
Manager-operated	0.9	0.3	0.4	0.5
Total	100.0	100.0	100.0	100.0

SOURCE Dominion Bureau of Statistics, Census of Canada, 1961, Bulletin 5.3.
[a] "Part owner-operated farms" refers to those farms which are composed of land which is owned
by the operator and additional land which he has rented.

Finally, from table 3 we see that the class position of some farmers is complicated
by the fact that there is a trend for them to become both owners and tenants, because
this is the easiest way to expand as the price of land rises. Only about 1 percent of farms
were being operated by managers. Considering all the census data available, there can
be little doubt that farming in both provinces was mainly a *petit-bourgeois* occupation.

It is now appropriate to turn to the problem of the unity of the *petite bourgeoisie* as a class. When a large number of people occupy a similar class position it does not follow that all of them will be conscious of their class identity and act in terms of it. The *petite bourgeoisie* has seldom done so. Indeed, different strata of the class have frequently been in conflict with each other. For a class to exist as an active force, there must be a communal sentiment and an organization to bring people in similar circumstances together. This has rarely been the case in western Canada. For example, there have been important differences in political alignment between small business-men and farmers, because their common problem of insecurity in a state of economic oligarchy has seldom been sufficient to compensate for the antagonistic relations between them in other respects. The *petit-bourgeois* businessman in the towns and villages of Alberta and Saskatchewan is an artisan or merchant capitalist, who derives profit from providing a service. Perhaps the retail merchant is most interesting. In order to survive, he must dispose of the products of capitalist enterprise at a price which leaves him a surplus. The alternative of being a wage-earning distributor of goods conflicts with his image of self-independence. For these reasons the retailer becomes a supporter of liberal capitalist ideology, particularly when he is threatened by agrarian cooperatives. During depressions, the merchant is often defined by the farmer as a nonproductive parasite on his labour, and consumer cooperatives have been estab-lished to bypass the merchant.[30] In this situation, we would expect the village *petite bourgeoisie* to be susceptible to appeals from Liberals and Conservatives to support the old parties, thus saving the West from socialism. However, when the small businessmen recognize their dependence on trade with farmers, they may be attracted to reformist groups at times when the price system is operating to reduce farm income. Then, platforms which propose monetary reform in order to restore purchasing power to the consumer can make a significant impact on this stratum. This is probably why Social Credit was able to get its initial support and much of its leadership from the urban *petite bourgeoisie*, to whom the CCF appeared too radical. Also, the Reconstruc-tion Party, which flourished briefly in 1935, proposed an investigation of monetary problems as well as a series of mild economic reforms and drew most of its support from small businessmen who had previously been Conservatives.

United *petit-bourgeois* action is rare, even when attention is restricted to the agrarian sector of the *petite bourgeoisie*. In Alberta and Saskatchewan, the "vigorous consciousness of common interests" to which Macpherson[31] refers was not experienced by all farmers, and it is doubtful whether "agrarian class unity was emerging out of economic conflict"[32] to the extent that we can talk about united class action. Of course, this is not to deny that large numbers of farmers did periodically act together for common political and economic ends. We must now consider the conditions on the Canadian prairies which contributed to or hindered the development of class-conscious political protest.

It may safely be assumed that for organized class protest to develop there must be some widespread experience of deprivation. For prairie farmers this has always been related to the problems of income insecurity. Given this, there must also be adequate means of communication among those who are subject to deprivation or exploitation in order that they develop some feeling of common identity. Although interaction in Alberta and Saskatchewan was limited by geographical factors until telephones, radios, and cars became numerous, agrarian problems were constantly aired in widely circulated farm journals, such as the *Grain Growers' Guide*. Political ideas were also promoted through the cooperative associations and grain growers' associations which emerged after the turn of the century.[33] These organizations were the training ground for protest leaders among the farmers; the roots of CCF and Social Credit populism lie there; it was the Depression of the thirties which stimulated a more radical expression of populism than was found in the Progressive movement[34] or in the provincial Liberal parties.

Class-conscious organization develops only when people feel more united by their common interests than they are divided on other grounds. In western Canada, those in a common class position have often been divided by differences of social status. Thus, the *petit-bourgeois* farmers have been internally stratified by wealth, by type of agriculture, by ethnic origin, and religion. This disunity was shown in Saskatchewan elections between 1934 and 1944 when the CCF received less than average support in French, German, and Mennonite districts. The highest level of CCF support was in municipalities dominated by Anglo-Saxons, which casts doubt on Milnor's[35] thesis that the CCF was more a party of ethnic protest than a class movement. Differences based on type of agriculture were pointed out by John Bennett,[36] who found that ranchers in southwest Saskatchewan enjoyed greater economic security than grain growers and were also more inclined to oppose government intervention in economic affairs. Such differences within the agrarian stratum of the *petite bourgeoisie* have often gone unnoticed, because enough farmers have combined with urban labour (in Saskatchewan) or with other *petit-bourgeois* strata (in Alberta) to elect populist governments to the provincial legislatures.

I have argued that class-conscious *petit-bourgeois* action is likely to take a populist form. Put another way, the mass support of populism is typically *petit-bourgeois*. Although the CCF began as a socialist party and the Social Credit League was eventually transformed into a conventional conservative party, the conclusion is warranted that from 1934 to 1944 both were populist parties, advocating reform wherever necessary to protect or restore the way of life of the *petite bourgeoisie*. Yet the two parties did differ considerably in organizational structure and the nature of the reforms for which they pressed. Therefore, it becomes necessary to account for the development of different forms of populism in Alberta and Saskatchewan. Here the sociologist must pay close attention to the historical background of each province.[37]

Different Historical Backgrounds

What is crucial to our understanding of why an authoritarian populism emerged in Alberta is that Social Credit sprouted from the failure of an earlier democratic populism, the United Farmers of Alberta (UFA), to control the effects of the Depression. The UFA was dominated by Henry Wise Wood, whose political beliefs on group government owed much to his knowledge of the populist tradition of the American mid-west. According to Wood, social life in industrial society is a history of conflict between a plutocracy and the masses. In this competitive society, only the plutocracy was organized. This enabled industrial producers to exploit others, who participated in the market as disorganized individuals. Farmers were especially exploited. Wood's solution lay in cooperative production and class organization; the organized strength of each class would then prevent the exploitation of any one class. Morton quotes Wood as follows:

> When you get class and class equally efficient in competition, as the less developed classes develop higher, I don't think the conflict in the last analysis will be very destructive. I think before it reaches the acute stage the better judgment of all will prevail.[38]

This approach assumes either common interests or the inability of one organized group to dominate others, both of which are unlikely. However, in a province where farmers were so numerous, it proved popular, especially when coupled with a denunciation of the party system. Instead of parties, Wood supported a system of political representation by democratically organized occupational groups, each nominating its delegates to the legislature and instructing them about what to support. Failure to comply would lead to the recall of the member. The organization of a new party was rejected because it was felt that parties led inevitably to corruption. Rather, a new cooperative government would be formed by elected representatives of class organizations. This was a Canadian corporatist theory.

Nevertheless the UFA proceeded to act much like a conventional party, winning the election of 1921 and governing the province for the next years by traditional means. It was thus the misfortune of the UFA to be in power during the early thirties. Crop failures, coupled with declining prices, generated a severe depression in rural areas. Like other governments in similar circumstances, the UFA proved incapable of producing legislation to protect the interests of the *petit-bourgeois* population. Urban dwellers were already alienated from the government because they were barred from membership in the UFA. Now the farmers also found themselves rejecting their own populist organization, whose leaders had grown distant from the rank and file. Yet they could not turn to the Liberal and Conservative parties, since these were both associated with the forces of exploitation. The UFA had been directly involved with the founding of the CCF and was stigmatized by its association with the early CCF socialism. Therefore, with all existing political associations discredited for some reason, there was a political vacuum in Alberta. It could not be filled by a revolutionary movement because of the *petit-bourgeois* commitment to existing property institutions; any new mass movement would have to be consistent with this commitment. The situation of Alberta in the thirties made possible the development of a kind of populism in which allegiance is given to an authoritarian leader, who claims divine inspiration for his simple plan to solve the unsolvable—in this case, William Aberhart and Social Credit. From the conjunction of economic crisis and the failure of democratic populism, Social Credit was able to develop as a powerful authoritarian populism.

Saskatchewan history was such that the development of authoritarian populism was unlikely. In 1921, a year of much discontent, the Liberal government called an election before the Grain Growers' Association met, thereby eliminating the possibility of a farmers' government like that of the UFA in Alberta. When the first Depression election was held in 1934, however, the Liberals were out of office and were not tarnished by the economic disaster. Although the Liberals were linked by many people to the monopolies of eastern Canada, the provincial party had absorbed many of the most able farm leaders and had been receptive to the demands of agrarian spokesmen to some extent. Therefore, the Liberals were returned to power in 1934 with a large majority over the new CCF, which suffered mainly from a lack of funds and from popular opposition to its socialist land policy.

Although populism had not been discredited in Saskatchewan by failure to control the effects of Depression, the CCF had to wait ten more years before winning power. Meanwhile, Aberhart tried to expand Social Credit into Saskatchewan in the 1938 election, but by this time he was suffering a crisis of legitimation in Alberta, having failed to introduce Social Credit monetary reforms. The CCF emerged from this test as the only plausible alternative to the Liberals, despite falling far behind the Liberal total

of elected representatives. At this time, portions of the Palliser Triangle in Saskatchewan were so chronically depressed that neither populist party made much headway. An
apathetic, suffering people had neither the economic nor psychological resources to
build an effective protest party. As economic conditions improved, the CCF was more
successful in organizing support in these areas, until in 1944 a block of constituencies
in the centre of the Triangle was in the top quartile of CCF support. Similarly, the
poorest areas of Regina and Saskatoon were now among the strongest areas of CCF
support.[39]

If this analysis of the emergence of Social Credit and the CCF is to be adequate,
the failure of the New Democracy and National Reform movements must be accounted
for, since they had similar populist ideologies. The answer lies in the interrelationship
among these movements. Basically, National Reform and New Democracy developed
when Social Credit and the CCF were already well established, with the result that the
leaders of each had a vested interest in retaining their independence.

In the 1938 Saskatchewan election, two Social Credit and two United Reform
candidates were victorious. Three of them had won with informal support from the CCF,
and the CCF had hopes of forming a united opposition in Regina. However, when J.F.
Herman accepted a position as Social Credit house leader, his invitation to join the CCF
caucus was withdrawn.[40] Having failed to link up with the CCF, the four other
opposition members formed a new National Reform group with a populist program
including low tariffs, development of cooperatives, and the enforcement of anti-
monopoly legislation.[41] The new group tried to encourage cooperation with the CCF by
suggesting that they avoid fighting each other at any future election, but this was
rejected by the CCF's annual convention, which marked the end of National Reform as
a provincial force.

A greater threat to both the CCF and Social Credit was New Democracy, a national
movement organized by William Herridge. Until 1938, he worked inside the Conservative Party but could not persuade that organization to adopt his policies. Herridge's
frequent references to the need for monetary reform and more purchasing power
attracted several Social Crediters, whose support was instrumental in leading him to
announce, at the beginning of March 1939, that he would lead a drive to unite all
progressive people under the banner of New Democracy.[42]

The national CCF reacted ambiguously to New Democracy. A circular instructed
every section of the CCF not to attack it, yet there was to be no collaboration either.
Wherever possible, all public discussion was to be avoided and the door left ajar for
interested people to come to the CCF.[43] However, some weeks later, George Williams
publicly rejected cooperation with New Democracy on the grounds that it was a
capitalist reform organization, backed by the Communist Party[44] and out to destroy the
CCF.[45] Despite the efforts of M.J. Coldwell, it was no longer possible for New Democracy
to succeed in Saskatchewan. A few months later, New Democrats approached the CCF
to join them in order to implement a reform program which was very similar to the
CCF's. Unspecified economic and monetary reforms were proposed to promote
maximum production and consumer purchasing. Government intervention was called
for to promote cooperatives, improve collective-bargaining laws, establish minimum
prices for farmers, set minimum wages, control monopolies, and increase social
services.[46] However, the united-front approach was rejected by the CCF's convention.
Now the national office felt safe in putting out a statement rejecting Herridge as just
another reformer.[47]

For a time Herridge was more successful with Social Credit. Aberhart was quick to express "encouragement and inspiration" from the announcement of New Democracy.[48] He was keen for Herridge to adopt Social Credit as his official policy, but Herridge preferred an umbrella movement. The alliance was successful to the point where federal Social Credit MPs called themselves New Democrats, and it held up until the 1940 federal election. However, the relationship deteriorated in the fall over the issue of conscription. Subsequently, Social Credit members simply produced their own program and called it New Democracy over the strong objections of Herridge.[49]

From this brief history, we can see that New Democracy and National Reform had a populist orientation but could not be successful in the West because the CCF and Social Credit, already well established, refused to integrate with them.

Conclusion

The thrust of this paper has been to demonstrate that the development of Social Credit and the CCF in Alberta and Saskatchewan can be explained by the appeal of their populist ideologies to the *petit-bourgeois* population. The class has been divided and its members have seldom agreed on their main interests, being, as Macpherson demonstrated, both committed to and exploited by capitalist relations. However, a sufficient number became convinced of the need to *reform* society that they could bring to power two parties, which we may describe as populist, while recognizing the different means by which each tried to protect the *petite bourgeoisie*. Today this is no longer the largest class in western Canada; the era of agrarian populism is disappearing with the decline of the class which promoted it.

Suggestions for Further Reading

John A. Irving, *The Social Credit Movement in Alberta* (Toronto, 1959).
Seymour M. Lipset, *Agrarian Socialism* (New York, 1968).
Walter D. Young, *Democracy and Discontent: Progressivism, Socialism and Social Credit in the Canadian West* (Toronto, 1969).

Notes

1. S.M. Lipset, *Agrarian Socialism* (New York, 1968), xxii.
2. David E. Smith, "A Comparison of Prairie Political Developments in Saskatchewan and Alberta," *Journal of Canadian Studies* 4 (1969), 17-26.
3. Walter D. Young, *Democracy and Discontent* (Toronto, 1969).
4. R.T. Naylor, "The Ideological Foundations of Social Democracy and Social Credit," Gary Teeple, ed., *Capitalism and the National Question in Canada* (Toronto, 1972), 251-56.
5. For reviews of the concept see J.B. Allcock, "Populism: A Brief Biography," *Sociology* 5 (1971), 371-87. See also G. Ionescu and E. Gellner, eds., *Populism: Its Meaning and National Characteristics* (London, 1969).
6. Peter Wiles, "A Syndrome, Not a Doctrine: Some Elementary Theses on Populism," in G. Ionescu and E. Gellner, eds., *Populism*, 166.
7. John A. Irving, *The Social Credit Movement in Alberta* (Toronto, 1959), 266.
8. T.C. Douglas, speech reported in CCF Minutes, Eighth Annual Convention, Archives of Saskatchewan (1943).
9. See Victor C. Ferkiss, "Populist Influences on American Fascism," *Western Political Quarterly* 10 (1957), 350-73. See also S.M. Lipset and Earl Raab, *The Politics of Unreason: Right Wing Extremism in America* (New York, 1970).
10. See, for example, Angus Stewart, "The Social Roots," in G. Ionescu and E. Gellner, eds., *Populism*, 186-91. See also A. Walicki, *The Controversy over Capitalism: Studies in the Social*

Philosophy of the Russian Populists (London, 1969), 22.

11. Norman Pollack, *The Populist Response to Industrial America* (Cambridge, Mass., 1962).

12. Eli Goldschmidt, "Labor and Populism: New York City, 1891-1896," *Labor History* 13 (1972), 520-32.

13. Robert F. Durden, *The Climax of Populism* (Lexington, 1965), 3-5.

14. One might object here that socialists often try to advance their ideas by playing on the same deprivations as populists. It might be argued that the Russian "populists," although they looked backward to a revival of the peasant *mir* community, also looked forward to a decentralized socialist society. (See Franco Venturi, *The Roots of Revolution: A History of the Populist and Socialist Movements in Nineteenth Century Russia*, London, 1960). However, Russian populism, while anti-intellectual in its pronouncements, was largely a movement of intellectuals who did not have a mass appeal for the peasantry. They were usually treated with great suspicion. My argument is, essentially, that the socialist revolution is too radical for the *petite bourgeoisie* to accept. It is true, nevertheless, that Russian populism creates the biggest obstacle for the concept of populism presented here. Perhaps it would be best to agree with Walicki (*The Controversy over Capitalism*, 93) that the distinctive features of the Russian intellectuals are best captured if the Russian term *narodnichestvo* is retained.

15. Walter T.K. Nugent, *The Tolerant Populists: Kansas Populism and Nativism* (Chicago, 1963).

16. See Robert L. Morian, *Political Prairie Fire: The Nonpartisan League 1915-1922* (Minneapolis, 1955). See also: Theodore Saloutos, "The Rise of the Nonpartisan League in North Dakota, 1915-1917," *Agricultural History* 20 (1946), 43-61; and Paul F. Sharp, *The Agrarian Revolt in Western Canada* (Minneapolis, 1948).

17. See Caldarola's paper, "The Social Credit in Alberta, 1935-1971," in C. Caldarola, ed., *Society and Politics in Alberta: Research Papers* (Agincourt, 1979).

18. Peter R. Sinclair, "The Saskatchewan CCF: Ascent to Power and the Decline of Socialism," *Canadian Historical Review* 54 (1973), 419-33.

19. Ibid., 426-30.

20. S.M. Lipset, *Agrarian Socialism*, 180.

21. George Williams, "Problems Confronting the Retail Merchants of Western Canada," transcript of Radio Broadcast, CCF Papers, pamphlet collection, Archives of Saskatchewan, 1939.

22. *Regina Leader-Post*, 1 April 1947.

23. John W. Bennett and Cynthia Krueger, "Agrarian Pragmatism and Radical Politics," in S.M. Lipset, *Agrarian Socialism*, 351.

24. CCF Papers, "Socialism and Cooperatives," Archives of Saskatchewan, 1944. Even E.C. Manning, who hardly qualifies as a socialist, felt able on several occasions to give strong support to cooperatives and credit unions. See, for example, E.C. Manning, Budget Speech, Edmonton, Government of Alberta, 1945.

25. Raymond Aron, "Two Definitions of Class," in A. Beteille, ed., *Social Inequality* (London, 1969), 76.

26. C.B. Macpherson, *Democracy in Alberta* (Toronto, 2nd ed, 1962), 225.

27. For a similar interpretation of the class position of the farmer, see James McCroirie, "Changes and Paradox in Agrarian Social Movements," in R.J. Ossenberg, ed., *Canadian Society: Pluralism, Change and Conflict* (Scarborough, 1971), 36-51.

28. On the decline of the *petite bourgeoisie* in Canada as a whole, see Leo Johnson, "The Development of Class in Canada in the Twentieth Century," in Gary Teeple, ed., *Capitalism and the National Question in Canada*, 141-83.

29. C.B. Macpherson, *Democracy in Alberta*, 10-20.

30. Jim F.C. Wright, *Prairie Progress: Consumer Cooperation in Saskatchewan* (Saskatoon, 1956).

31. C.B. Macpherson, *Democracy in Alberta*, 226.

32. S.M. Lipset, *Agrarian Socialism*, 69.

33. See the following studies: Hugh Boyd, *New Breaking: An Outline of Cooperation among the Farmers of Western Canada* (Toronto, 1938); S.M. Lipset, *Agrarian Socialism*, 1968; W.A. Mackintosh, *Agricultural Cooperation in Western Canada* (Toronto, 1924); Harold S. Patton, *Grain Growers' Cooperation in Western Canada* (Cambridge, Mass., 1928); and Paul F. Sharp, *The Agrarian Revolt in Western Canada*, 1948.

34. See W.L. Morton, *The Progressive Party in Canada* (Toronto, 1950).

35. Andrew J. Milnor, "Agrarian Protest in Saskatchewan, 1929–1948: A Study in Ethnic Politics" (unpublished Ph.D. thesis, Duke University, Durham, 1962).

36. John Bennett, *Northern Plainsmen* (Chicago, 1969).

37. For a more detailed analysis of the historical background of Alberta and Saskatchewan, see Johnson's paper, "The Failure of the CCF in Alberta: An Accident of History," in C. Caldarola, ed., *Society and Politics in Alberta*.

38. W.L. Morton, "The Social Philosophy of Henry Wise Wood, Canadian Agrarian Leader," *Agricultural History* 22 (1948), 118. See also: William K. Rolph, *Henry Wise Wood of Alberta* (Toronto, 1950); W.L. Morton, *The Progressive Party in Canada;* and C.B. Macpherson, *Democracy in Alberta.*

39. For a more complete account of the rise of the CCF, see Peter R. Sinclair, "The Saskatchewan CCF."

40. George Williams, Williams to J.F. Herman, 25 October 1938, CCF Papers, file no. 163, Archives of Saskatchewan.

41. J.F. Herman *et al.*, press statement, CCF Papers, file no. 239, Archives of Saskatchewan (no date, but probably 1939).

42. Mary Hallett, "The Social Credit Party and the New Democracy Movement: 1939–1940," *Canadian Historical Review* 47 (1966), 302–304.

43. CCF National Office, National Office to National Council Members, 12 March 1939, CCF Papers, file no. 240, Archives of Saskatchewan.

44. The Communists appeared much more delighted with the new political development. In Regina, Tim Buck announced Communist backing for the New Democracy group, although it was not as socialist as he would have liked (*Regina Leader-Post*, 27 April 1939). However, this was an endorsement which New Democrats did not want. When a Communist official was nominated as the New Democracy candidate in Maple Creek, he was not recognized by party officials (*Regina Leader-Post*, 6 September 1939); the New Democracy was Christian, Canadian, and British, opposed to fascism and communism, and committed to reforming and modernizing the present system. (See G.H. Barr, Barr to G. Williams, 4 November 1939, CCF Papers, file no. 240, Archives of Saskatchewan.)

45. *Regina Leader-Post*, 27 April 1939.

46. Ibid., 4 July 1939.

47. Ibid., 25 July 1939.

48. Ibid., 6 March 1939.

49. Ibid., 21 October 1939.

5

PROTEST REORIENTED (1945-1971)

Introduction

The period from 1945 to 1971 was a time of reorientation for western protest. During these years western Canada moved from being an agrarian society to an economy based on new resource extraction industries such as oil and potash.

Political scientist Roger Gibbins of the University of Calgary has produced a major study of this transition. In his 1980 book, *Prairie Politics and Society: Regionalism in Decline*, he argues that the unified political economy of the prairie West started to disintegrate as the importance of agriculture declined after World War II. Farmers, once a powerful social class, began to lose influence as mechanization of agriculture and the increase in average farm size resulted in an ever-diminishing rural population, and the West's urban centres became home to more and more westerners. This gradual change in the agricultural sector and the resulting shift in the regional economy as it moved in different directions meant that common regional interests declined. Gibbins concluded that the "regional homogeneity of the past is rapidly disintegrating" and yet, in a later book, *Regionalism: Territorial Politics in Canada and the United States* (1982) he pointed out that the West remained a source of territorial conflict in Confederation. Even with the demise of a single regional economy, protest continued. Of course, it may be argued that western protest was always a multifaceted phenomenon that embraced division and disagreement as well as unity.

John Richards and Larry Pratt heralded the "New West" that replaced agrarian society in their contemporary classic *Prairie Capitalism: Power and Influence in the New West* (1979). The excerpt from their book, "Oil and Social Class: The Making of the New West," deals with the impact of the oil economy, the creation of a new entrepreneurial class in Alberta, and the rise of Peter Lougheed's Progressive Conservative Party as a manifestation of this class.

Although Alberta was the preeminent example of a new society and a new economy in the West, the other prairie provinces were undergoing similar, if less spectacular changes, based on their smaller populations and specific natural resources. From uranium development in northern Saskatchewan to export-oriented hydroelectric power development in Manitoba, the move was away from agriculture to new export commodities.

The postagrarian society that was formed after the Second World War remains dominant today, yet the region's economy continues to rely on the export of resources, as it did during the agrarian period when wheat was the major product. And after a decade of low resource and commodity prices in the 1980s the power of what was once the "New West" has dissipated. Nonetheless, the heyday of resurgent regional power, discussed in the next chapter, was a significant moment for western protest that came after a long hiatus associated with the transition to a postagrarian society.

Regionalism in Decline: 1940 to the Present

ROGER GIBBINS

Reprinted with deletions from Roger Gibbins, *Prairie Politics and Society:*
Regionalism in Decline (Toronto: Butterworths, 1980), 65–82,
by permission of the author and the publisher.

Since the Second World War the character of the prairie society has been dramatically transformed. While the contemporary prairie society has deeply embedded roots in the agrarian frontier of the past the resemblances between the two are becoming fewer and fewer. Moreover, the tide of social change has eroded the social and economic homogeneity of the past and in so doing has eroded the regional distinctiveness of the prairies. As R.M. Burns has stated, the concept of a homogeneous prairie region is more " . . . a heritage of the past than a statement of the present."[1]

The change in the prairie society is analogous in degree to the process of metamorphosis; although the butterfly develops directly from the caterpillar larva the change is of such magnitude that the two seem of different species. The direction of change has moved the prairie society closer and closer to the English-Canadian norm so that in a social and economic sense the prairie provinces have been losing both their regional distinctiveness and, to a lesser extent, their intraregional homogeneity. As the regionally distinctive social and economic underpinnings of political behaviour have disintegrated, the political regionalism that characterized prairie politics in the past has also waned. This can be demonstrated through an examination of postwar federal electoral behaviour on the prairies.

Pillars of Regionalism

Population Change

The 1931 census marked the peak of the prairies' share of the national population. The percentage of the Canadian population residing on the prairies has fallen steadily since the onset of the Depression all but ended immigration to the Canadian West. In absolute terms the prairie population continued to inch upwards during the 1930s and 1940s, but growth was largely restricted to the province of Alberta. Even there the growth rate was less than what the natural population increase alone should have produced. From 1931 to 1941 the region experienced a net migration loss of 248,000 people; from 1941 to 1951 the net loss was 268,000 before a modest net gain of 45,000 was achieved during the 1950s.[2] The outflow was particularly severe in Saskatchewan where the net emigration was 158,000 between 1931 and 1941, 199,000 between 1941 and 1951, and 79,000 between 1951 and 1961. The initial onslaught of the Depression, coupled with a process of rural depopulation that has continued unabated through the

1970s, cut Saskatchewan's share of the total prairie population from 39.2 percent in 1931 to only 24.4 percent in 1976.

Population growth in the prairies has been largely confined to Alberta. There the debilitating impact of the Depression was less evident; Alberta's population actually increased by 8.8 percent in the decade between 1931 and 1941 and then increased again by 18.0 percent between 1941 and 1951. Since 1951 Alberta's oil-rich economy has fired a rate of population growth that has been rapid relative to Canada as a whole (with only British Columbia experiencing more rapid growth) and even more rapid relative to the other prairie provinces. From 1951 to 1961 Alberta's population increased by 41.8 percent; in the same period Canada's population increased by 30.2 percent while the populations of Manitoba and Saskatchewan increased by only 18.7 percent and 11.2 percent respectively. From 1961 to 1976 Alberta's population increased by 38.0 percent compared to an increase of 26.1 percent for Canada as a whole. By 1976 Albertans made up 48.6 percent of the prairie population compared to 31 percent in 1931. By the end of the 1970s one out of two prairie residents lived in Alberta.

To summarize briefly, the population picture on the Canadian prairies has changed substantially during this century. The early decades were marked by explosive population growth. There was a dramatic westward shift in the distribution of the Canadian population. However, since 1931 the proportion of the Canadian population residing on the prairies has declined steadily and the gap between the prairie and Ontario populations has progressively widened. Within the prairie region the bulk of growth is occurring within a single province, Alberta. These demographic shifts are charged with political implications, two of which must be touched upon here. The first is that today the prairie population packs less electoral punch in national politics than it did during the peak years of political radicalism. In 1935 22.4 percent of the federal seats came from the prairie provinces; by 1979 that proportion had shrunk to 17.4 percent. If the population gap between Ontario and the prairies continues to widen, and as the Canadian electoral system imperfectly translates population shifts into political power through representation in the House of Commons, the political imbalance between the prairies and Ontario will continue to grow. The second implication is that the electoral power of Alberta within the prairie region will slowly eclipse that of the other two provinces. In 1979 Alberta had twenty-one seats while Saskatchewan and Manitoba had fourteen each. This enhanced electoral power, coupled with Alberta's economic pre-eminence, will further unbalance the political character of the prairie region.

Urban-Rural Redistribution

The shift in the bulk of the prairie population from first Manitoba and then Saskatchewan to Alberta is not the only demographic change that has occurred. An even more dramatic shift has occurred with the urbanization of the prairie population. The prairie provinces, along with Ontario and Canada, underwent rapid urbanization following the Second World War.[3] Given Ontario's lead going into the war urbanization across the prairies still falls well short of that in Ontario; in 1971 the prairies approximated the Ontario situation in 1941. Nevertheless the distinction between Ontario and the prairies with respect to urbanization is being steadily eroded. By 1971 over 67 percent of the prairie population was classified as urban. In the next few decades the rate of urbanization in Ontario can only slacken as the proportion of the population living in urban areas edges closer to 100 percent. On the prairies the limit to urbanization has yet to be approached. As a consequence the next few decades should witness a continued erosion of the gap between Ontario and western Canada.

At present the degree of urbanization is far from uniform across the three prairie provinces. The 1971 census classified 73.5 percent of the Alberta population as urban, with 55 percent of the provincial population living in Edmonton and Calgary alone. In Manitoba 69.5 percent of the 1971 population was classified as urban while in Saskatchewan the proportion was only 53.0 percent, 1971 marking the first census in which urban dwellers formed a majority. Considerable intraregional variation in the degree of urbanization thus exists although all three provinces have been undergoing roughly similar rates of urbanization. Between 1961 and 1971 the proportion of the provincial population that was urban increased by 10.2 percent in Alberta, 10.0 percent in Saskatchewan, and 5.6 percent in Manitoba.

To a considerable extent the prairie population is being not only urbanized but "metropolitanized." Winnipeg, the slowest-growing major centre on the prairies, contained 54.7 percent of Manitoba's population in 1971 compared to 46.0 percent two decades earlier. Regina and Saskatoon have increased their joint share of the Saskatchewan population from 15.4 percent in 1951 to 28.8 percent in 1971. In Alberta, Calgary and Edmonton together claimed 55.3 percent of the 1971 provincial population, a substantial increase from 35.7 percent in 1951. Calgary, Edmonton, and Winnipeg, it should be stressed, are not only metropolitan centres relative to the surrounding countryside; they are also metropolitan relative to the nation as a whole. The three are the fourth, fifth, and sixth largest cities in Canada with their relative rankings being a matter of hot dispute among the competing Chambers of Commerce.

Not surprisingly there is considerable competition among the metropolitan centres for regional dominance, as evidenced particularly by the competition for regional head offices. In the past Winnipeg was the metropolis to the prairie hinterland, the gateway to, and the financial and service centre of, western Canada. Today economic power is shifting further westward. Modern air transportation and telecommunications links between Alberta and central Canada have removed much of the traffic from the Winnipeg gateway. With the development of the oil industry in Alberta the regional financial and head office hegemony of Winnipeg is being strongly challenged by Edmonton and, in particular, by Calgary. The latter city is now claimed by local residents to be "the financial centre of western Canada," a claim that reflects more than civic pride. In June 1979 the Bank of Montreal announced that it was moving its Chairman of the Board to Calgary and would consolidate its operations in a new office tower, the building to be the tallest structure between Toronto and Hong Kong. The symbolic importance of this move, given the role that financial dependency upon eastern financial operations has traditionally played in western alienation, is difficult to exaggerate.

In bringing this discussion to a close it should be noted that the farm population on the prairies—the bedrock of the earlier agrarian society—has declined in absolute as well as relative terms. The decline in the prairie, Ontario, and Canadian farm populations has been almost precipitous. The prairie farm population declined from 50.4 percent of the regional population in 1931 to only 16.9 percent in 1971, during which period the actual number of farm residents fell by 587,000. The absolute decline has made it very difficult for rural communities to sustain many of the basic services offered in the past. The decline in population coupled with the increased ease of travel into urban areas has crippled the viability of many local schools, stores, services, and recreational facilities.

As most prairie residents adopt an urban lifestyle little different from that experienced by the residents of Toronto, Vancouver or Hamilton, the West is rapidly losing its regionally distinctive rural character. As a consequence the likelihood of a regionally distinctive political culture being maintained is diminished. As George F.G. Stanley writes:

> It may be argued ... that the Western scene is changing: that an urban population is taking over from the rural ... and second—that *an urban population is not exposed to the full impact of the prairie environment.* This, of course, is true ... In time, the osmotic action that carried the spirit of independence from the countryside to the urban communities may cease and *we will become as the others are.* (emphasis added).[4]

In short, the experiential conditions for a regionally distinctive political subculture are being eroded by the process of urbanization.[5]

Table 3:1

Farm Population of Canada, Ontario, and the Prairies

Census Year	Farm Population		
	Canada	Ontario	Prairies
1931	3,223,400	785,600	1,186,600
1941	3,116,900	694,700	1,142,700
1951	2,827,700	678,000	952,700
1956	2,631,600	632,200	890,000
1961	2,072,800	505,700	762,000
1966	1,913,700	481,700	717,100
1971	1,419,800	363,600	599,800

Source: *1971 Census of Canada,* Vol. V—Part 1 (Bulletin 5.1-2), 18.

Ethnic Composition

While earlier in this century the Canadian West had been a land rich with opportunity and optimism, conditions had changed drastically by the end of the Second World War. Open land was by then scarce, expensive, and generally located in the less hospitable north. The opening of a new farm or the acquisition of an existing one required a large capital investment that was beyond the means of most immigrants and indeed most Canadians. The manpower needs of prairie agriculture were being trimmed by extensive mechanization with the consequence that there were insufficient jobs to sustain the existing rural population much less attract immigrants. Moreover as industrial employment opportunities were scarce in the West, employment prospects outside the agricultural sector were little better than within. Finally, years of depression and drought had stripped the prairie residents of their earlier confidence and optimism. Many pre-Depression immigrants abandoned the economic collapse that gripped the prairies and moved on; others were deported as Canadian governments sought to reduce the costs of relief payments.[6] Small wonder that new immigrants looked askance at the prospect of starting a new life in the West.

It was Ontario that became the magnet for postwar immigration to Canada. Of the new immigrants arriving in Canada between 1941 and 1951, 50 percent named Ontario as their intended destination compared to 17 percent naming the prairies.[7] The prairie proportions fell to 13.5 percent in the 1950s and 10 percent in the early 1960s with the Ontario proportion holding at 53 percent throughout the period. At the time of the 1961 census more than 55 percent of all postwar immigrants lived in Ontario while only 14 percent lived on the prairies. Ontario offered an urban environment and industrial employment opportunities which better suited the skills, talents, and inclinations of postwar immigrants than did agricultural pursuits on the prairies.

The fact that postwar immigration largely by-passed the prairie provinces has had some important consequences. The first is that the prairie population, while built upon an immigrant base, is now largely native-born. The native-born component of the prairie population was by 1961 proportionately larger than in the province of Ontario; by 1971 it had reached the overall Canadian average and had surpassed the Ontario proportion by nearly 8 percent. The upshot of this change in immigration patterns is that today the prairie population is one of the most indigenous in Canada. Therefore one might speculate that the contemporary prairie population is less open to the allure of radical politics than was the prairie population of the past. At present there is no sizeable immigrant population which, lacking in traditional attachments to Canadian political institutions and actors, can be mobilized behind radical alternatives. To the extent that the immigrant character of the prairie population facilitated radicalism in the past and thereby helped produce a regionally distinctive style of political behaviour, that support for regional distinctiveness has been erased from the contemporary political landscape of the Canadian prairies.

. . .

Changes in the Nature of Prairie Agriculture

Although the Prairies experienced an absolute decline in the number of farms, farm operators, and farm employees since 1941, the number of acres occupied by farms actually increased from 120,129,000 acres in 1941 to 133,571,000 in 1971, an increase of over 11 percent.[26] The size of the average prairie farm increased from 221 acres in 1941 to 502 acres in 1971,[27] an increase that was accompanied by a tremendous surge in mechanization. Mechanization made the growth in farm size not only possible but necessary as small-scale farming operations simply could not carry the heavy costs of the new agricultural equipment that was becoming available. Advancements in mechanization had been occurring steadily since settlement began—in the 1880s portable steam engines were introduced for threshing, gas farm tractors appeared around 1910, and combines were introduced in 1925. The pace of mechanization then increased noticeably with the manpower shortages encountered during World War II. At the war's end the surge of mechanization continued. While the number of farms decreased from 1941 to 1971 the number of trucks increased from 43,363 to 251,377, the number of tractors from 112,624 to 308,475, and the number of combines from 18,081 to 127,509.[28] During the same period rural electrification was being carried out across the prairies which allowed the introduction of countless labour-saving devices, both domestic and agricultural. Steady advances had also been made in agricultural productivity with the introduction of new crop varieties, pesticides, herbicides, and fertilizers. All of these changes, but particularly those relating to mechanization and farm size, led to a sharp increase in the capital value of prairie farms. The average capital value rose from $6,565 in 1941 to $72,805 in 1971, an increase that far outstrips any inflationary devaluation of the Canadian dollar over the same time interval. The increase in capital value has been particularly steep in recent years; between 1971 and 1975 the average capital value of prairie farms increased to $136,537, a rise of 88 percent in only four years.[29]

In 1976 the *Financial Post* described a farming operation in Manitoba that illustrates, although undoubtedly does not typify, the changes that have taken place. The farmer described in the article had started with half a section of land purchased for $2,500 in 1942. Now he and his four sons run an incorporated business with eight sections of land worth $750,000 and farm machinery worth another $500,000. There are four tractors which are worth $43,000 each, more than the $37,000 Mercedes driven by the father. The yearly operating costs of the farm top $300,000 including $25,000 for weed killer alone. This is indeed a large-scale operation.[30]

Mechanization and a growing reliance on fertilizers, pesticides, and herbicides have made Canadian agriculture increasingly dependent upon petroleum products that are rapidly escalating in price. Although prairie agriculture is much more energy-efficient than that in Ontario the prairie region still consumes about two-thirds of all agricultural fuel used in Canada.[31]

Another agricultural change that has occurred both nationally and on the prairies has been the growth of corporate farming. Large corporations have entered the production of food-crops in both a direct and indirect fashion. Apart from corporate-owned farms, "the agricultural system now includes the large food conglomerates who often sell the farm inputs to the farmer through one subsidiary and buy the farm products through another."[32] Although "agri-business" may be more omnipresent in eastern Canada than it is in the prairies, corporate inroads have been made in western agriculture. The result is that the individualistic and competitive nature of farming has been somewhat diminished.

The expansion of corporate farming highlights a very basic transformation of agrarian life in western Canada. Farming used to be more than a business; it was a different way of life with its own mores, patterns of community organization, and institutional forms. Mutual aid and cooperation were fundamental ingredients of the agrarian frontier and were inevitably extended beyond the local community through the creation of countless cooperative organizations. Donald Willmott has identified five factors which underlay the formation of cooperative organizations: common economic problems; ecological conditions requiring collective labour such as threshing parties, barn-raisings, and snow plowing; ecological conditions, such as the large distances between homesteads, that encouraged organized recreation and sociability in place of over-the-back-fence socializing; ecological conditions which required small units of local government; and emergent cultural values which encouraged collective action at the local level.[33] With respect to this last factor Willmott points out that "the nostalgic accounts which oldtimers gave to pioneer times makes it clear that mutual aid and cooperation were not merely for convenience or necessity alone: they involved an ideology which grew out of, and in turn reinforced, the loyalty and solidarity which the early farmers developed among themselves."[34]

Most of these factors have disappeared or are disappearing from the prairie scene.

Collective labour and multitudinous small units of local government are no longer needed while radio, television, and vastly more convenient means of transportation and communication have eroded the need for organized recreation and sociability. Willmott also suggests, although the evidence here is inconclusive, that the ideological tenets of mutual aid and cooperation are fading in the prairie community. Agricultural diversification has undercut the degree to which western farmers share a common set of problems or economic conditions. Thus the ecological and economic conditions that in the past fostered cooperative endeavours and a rich infrastructure of formal organizations have been eroded. As a consequence Morton's comment upon an earlier era seems particularly germane to the prairies today:

> With the Progressive revolt, farming ceased to be a way of life and became simply another occupation. Countryman and city dweller no longer inhabited separate social orders; the city had prevailed over the country ... [35]

Changes have also occurred in the crops and products of prairie agriculture. In the early decades of prairie settlement wheat was unquestionably the dominant crop. Its dominance can be attributed to a variety of factors perhaps the most important being the absolute and comparative economic advantage that Canadian grain growers have enjoyed over other major wheat producers.[36] On the world market Canadian wheat has a well-won reputation for its superior baking characteristics, high protein content, and low sedimentation. Thus while alternate crop possibilities existed for the prairie farmer none matched the potential profitability of wheat. Thus while prairie agriculture was never a one-crop system, wheat was the export staple; "prosperity and stimulus came through wheat, as did depression and discouragement."[37]

During the 1970s the dominance of wheat was still apparent. Nevertheless there has been a noticeable trend in prairie agriculture towards crop diversification which has reduced the region's dependence upon a single crop and thereby helped to stabilize the regional economy. The precise extent of crop diversification is difficult to determine as the composition of the prairie grain crop will fluctuate with the price and supply conditions for both wheat and alternative crops. The acreage yield for different grain crops will also fluctuate substantially from year to year in response to climatic variability. Although the acreage seeded in wheat seldom varies more than 10 percent from year to year, price-determined fluctuations can at times be of considerably greater magnitude.[38] For example in 1970 wheat sold at $1.44 a bushel and comprised 34.6 percent of the total grain crop. By 1973 the price had risen to $4.47 a bushel and, as a consequence, wheat's share of the following year's grain crop rose to 51.9 percent.[39]

Despite the fluctuating composition of the prairie grain crop it is possible to illustrate at least the rough character of crop diversification by relying on five-year averages. Table 3:5 presents the average composition of the prairie grain crop for two five-year periods; 1935 to 1939 and 1971 to 1975. While wheat, oats, and barley were the dominant crops in both periods their relative shares of the total crop changed considerably. Barley and oats, it should be pointed out, are the most common substitutes for wheat and their acreage tends to vary inversely with the acreage planted in wheat. In the 1971 to 1975 period, when the total prairie grain production was over twice that of 1935-1939, the production of flaxseed, rapeseed, and mixed grains began to reach significant proportions. Although their total output came nowhere near that of the three major grain crops a trend towards diversification is clearly apparent. Prairie grain farmers will continue to increase their crop diversification in order to be more responsive to changing market conditions and to achieve a degree of economic stability that a reliance upon a single crop prohibited.

Table 3:5

Diversification of the Prairie Grain Crop

Crop	1935/39 Average		1971/75 Average	
	Bushels (000's)	%	Bushels (000's)	%
Wheat	290,579	51.3	520,400	38.3
Oats for grain	197,325	34.9	245,400	18.1
Barley	67,772	12.0	458,800	33.8
Rye	7,780	1.4	16,247	1.2
Flaxseed	1,424	.3	18,120	1.3
Mixed Grain	1,291	.2	36,940	2.7
Rapeseed	–	–	63,380	4.7
Total	566,171	100.0%	1,359,287	100.0%

Source: R. Daviault, *Selected Agricultural Statistics for Canada*, Ottawa Economics Branch, Agriculture Canada, June 1976, 78.

Another aspect of agricultural diversification has been the expansion of the cattle industry. During the Second World War foreign grain sales declined as the market for Canadian grain was limited to Great Britain. At the same time there was a substantial increase in both the domestic and American demand for beef cattle, and the production of cattle and feedgrains on the prairies has increased steadily ever since.[40] The number of beef cattle has increased from a 1935-1939 average of 439,000 to a 1971-1975 average of 3,014,400.[41] While Alberta retains the lead in the cattle business, the rate of growth has been more rapid in Saskatchewan and Manitoba.

The diversification of prairie agriculture has followed different paths in the three provinces with the result that it is becoming increasingly difficult to discuss agriculture in *regional* terms. The monolithic regional wheat economy of the past is no more. Today the wheat economy is strongest in Saskatchewan where the acreage in wheat is approximately five times that in Manitoba and three times that in Alberta.[42] While Saskatchewan farmers derive most of their income from wheat, livestock is predominant in Alberta along with barley, tame hay, honey, forage seeds, sheep, and sugar beets.[43] In Manitoba flaxseed, buckwheat, peas, and sunflowers are the top crops. This variability among the prairie provinces throws the utility of regional agricultural statistics into question and reinforces the argument that the regional homogeneity of the past is rapidly disintegrating ...

222

Notes

1. R.M. Burns, "Prairie Union–Implications for Canadian Federalism," in David K. Elton, ed., *One Prairie Province?* Lethbridge Herald, 1970, 66.

2. Warren E. Kalbach and Wayne W. McVey, *The Demographic Bases of Canadian Society,* Toronto, McGraw-Hill, 1971, 86.

3. It should be noted that census definitions of "rural" and "urban" have changed substantially over time. For a discussion see *1971 Census of Canada,* Vol. V, Part 1 (Bulletin 5.1–2).

4. George F.G. Stanley, "The Western Canadian Mystique," in David P. Gagan, ed., *Prairie Perspectives,* Toronto, Holt, Rinehart, and Winston, 1970, 25.

5. For a counterargument see J.M.S. Careless who argues that metropolitan growth within provinces and the devolution of major government functions onto provincial governments may have increased provincial struggles with the federal government and hence regional cleavages. "Limited Identities in Canada," *Canadian Historical Review,* L, No. 1 (March 1969), 1–10.

6. James Gray notes that nearly ten thousand people were deported between 1932 and 1933 alone. *The Winter Years: The Depression on the Prairies,* Toronto, Macmillan, 1966, 131.

7. Kalbach and McVey, *Demographic Bases,* 93.

[Notes 8–25 of deleted section omitted.]

26. Daviault, *Selected Agricultural Statistics,* 9. During the same period in Ontario the number of acres *decreased* by 28.7 percent.

27. Ibid., 14.

28. Ibid., 40.

29. Ibid., 51.

30. *Financial Post,* 17 July 1976, 6. The article points out that this is not a typical Manitoba farm; 72 percent of Manitoba's thirty-five thousand farmers earned less than $3,000 in 1971.

31. Barbara J. Genno and Larry M. Genno, *Food Production in the Canadian Environment,* Ottawa, Science Council of Canada, 1976, 27.

32. Ibid., 53.

33. Donald E. Willmott, "The Formal Organizations of Saskatchewan Farmers, 1900–65," in Anthony W. Rasporich, ed., *Western Canada Past and Present,* Calgary, McClelland & Stewart West, 1975, 39.

34. Ibid., 39.

35. W.L. Morton, *The Progressive Party of Canada,* Toronto, University of Toronto Press, 1950, 293.

36. Gerald I. Trant, David L. MacFarlane, and Lewis A. Fischer, *Trade Liberalization and Canadian Agriculture,* Toronto, University of Toronto Press, 1968, 8.

37. W.A. MacKintosh, *Economic Problems of the Prairies,* Toronto, Macmillan, 1935, 7–8.

38. Trant, *Trade Liberalization,* 12.

39. *Canada Year Book,* Ottawa, Information Canada, 1975, 471.

40. Robert W. Crown and Earl O. Hardy, *Policy Integration in Canadian Agriculture,* Ames, Iowa, Iowa State University Press, 1972, 13.

41. Daviault, *Selected Agricultural Statistics,* 83–85.

42. Bruce Proudfoot, "Agriculture," in P.J. Smith, ed., *Studies in Canadian Geography: The Prairies,* Toronto, University of Toronto Press, 1972, 61.

43. *Calgary Herald,* 18 January 1977, 27.

[Notes 44–97 of deleted section omitted.]

Oil and Social Class:
The Making of the New West

JOHN RICHARDS AND LARRY PRATT

Reprinted from John Richards and Larry Pratt, *Prairie Capitalism:
Power and Influence in the New West* (Toronto: McClelland & Stewart, 1979),
148–176, by permission of the Canadian Publishers, McClelland & Stewart.

Alberta's large and growing urban middle classes, nurtured by twenty-five years of oil and gas development, acceded to political power in the provincial election of 30 August 1971. That election, which saw Peter Lougheed's revived Progressive Conservatives win forty-nine seats to Social Credit's twenty-five and the NDP's one, was one of critical realignment—the political consolidation of major economic, demographic, and social changes which had occurred in Alberta in the generation of growth after Leduc. With the considerable advantage of hindsight, Lougheed's victory and the abrupt termination of the Social Credit dynasty represented an inevitable, albeit considerably delayed, response of the electoral system to rapid population growth, urbanization, and secularization—trends underway during and after World War II, but greatly accelerated by the oil boom. The meaning of Lougheed's victory was this: the political centre of gravity within Alberta had shifted in favour of metropolitan interests. The city, represented by an alliance of business and professional elites and led by a descendant of one of Alberta's ruling families, now dominated the towns and farms. Power had passed into the outstretched hands of Alberta's new bourgeoisie.

To understand the changes that helped bring Peter Lougheed to power, we require some historical perspective on the development of social class in Alberta and the other prairie provinces. Our primary concern is to sketch the rise to prominence of a new urban middle class in postwar Alberta, but the initial task must be to debunk the historical myth of prairie society as homogeneous and lacking most of the antagonistic relations that grow out of a modern capitalist economy.

Class in Alberta: Macpherson Revisited

Writing about Alberta's rural, small-town *petite bourgeoisie* and Social Credit, C.B. Macpherson, in his influential *Democracy in Alberta* (a book which has had a powerful impact on the left's understanding of the Canadian West), described "a society that is politically and economically a subordinate part of a mature capitalist economy, and whose people, at the same time, have preponderantly the outlook and assumptions of small-propertied independent commodity producers." The introduction of the party system to the prairies had been discouraged, Macpherson argued, by the West's "relatively homogeneous class composition" and its "quasi-colonial" relationship to the rest of Canada. The "absence of any serious opposition of class interests within the province meant that alternate parties were not needed to express or to moderate a perennial conflict of interests." For Macpherson, the outstanding features of the class composition of Alberta, as compared with the more industrialized provinces, were "(1) that independent commodity producers... have been from 1921 until 1941 about 48 per cent of the whole gainfully occupied population while in Ontario they have been from 20 to 25 per cent, and in Canada about 30 per cent; (2) in Alberta the industrial wage and salary earners... have been 41 per cent of the whole, in Ontario about 70 per cent, in Canada about 60 per cent."[1]

The preponderance of independent commodity producers ensured that class tensions within Alberta were muted: "the peculiarity of a society which is at once quasi-colonial and mainly petit-bourgeois is that the conflict of class interests is not so much within the society as between that society and the forces of outside capital." Alberta was not a classless society, but through Macpherson's eyes it approximated a one-class society. And the hegemony of commodity producers determined the limits of Social Credit's hinterland revolt. It was merely a regional revolt against eastern domination, not an attack on capital and the property system. Social Credit's *petit-bourgeois* radicalism was inherently conservative. "Aberhart, from his first day in office, preferred to placate the established outside interests... his economic radicalism was very limited... nothing that he did was in conflict with a basic acceptance of the established order."[2]

Democracy in Alberta has been described as "the best political analysis in the Marxist tradition undertaken in Canada."[3] This is a rather uncritical endorsement. Macpherson is a political theorist and his discussions of the ideas and thought of Social Credit are undeniably brilliant. In other respects, notably its elucidation of the class structure of Alberta and prairie society generally, the work is flawed and seriously misleading.[4] Macpherson makes no attempt, for example, to analyse different variants of agrarian populism or to differentiate between what we have called left and right populism—the CCF in Saskatchewan, Social Credit in Alberta. He is unconvincing in his casual dismissal of Social Credit's controversial financial and debt adjustment legislation of the late 1930s. The assertion that such laws were not "in conflict with a basic acceptance of the established order" is clearly incorrect, unless we exclude Canada's banks, trust companies, insurance and financial houses, business press, and the Supreme Court and federal Liberal Party from our conception of the established order. In 1938 the *Montreal Gazette* charged that Social Credit "has now run amok through a field of radical legislation that is without precedent in any country. It has legalized theft."[5] This implied at the very least that the bitter war between the province and its creditors was not merely rhetorical. That Aberhart did not intend to bring down the property system is true, but what is more interesting is that Social Credit's efforts to free the province's producers from the grip of external finance capital were close enough to the mark to provoke an unprecedented response by an overwhelming alliance of capital and federal political power.

The central flaw in Macpherson's study of Alberta society and politics—and it is an unusual failing in an avowedly Marxist work—is its consistent tendency towards single-class analysis. Alberta has never been as homogeneous or free of internal class conflict as is argued by Macpherson; nor has Manitoba or Saskatchewan. In Alberta tensions among rival metropolitan centres, between urban and agrarian interests, between ranchers and farmers, mine-owners and coalminers, between indigenous and external capital, and between capital and labour are recurring, not occasional, themes in the various stages of the province's development; and they can be ignored only at the risk of distortion. It is one thing to assert that Social Credit's base was mainly (though by no means exclusively) on the farms; that the independent commodity producer was numerically and politically dominant on the prairies between the wars; and that agriculture accounted for a majority of the West's income prior to Leduc, thus exposing the region to the vicissitudes and instabilities which overtook the wheat economy after 1928. It is quite another to argue that this society had been relatively homogeneous since its settlement, and that any serious opposition of class interests was absent in the prairie West between the wars. In the first place, by no means all of the farming population of Alberta or the other prairie provinces was engaged in the production of a single commodity, wheat; the farm economy also comprised ranching and mixed farming and was considerably less monolithic than Macpherson suggests. Second, the class structure of Alberta and the other prairie provinces also included urban labour, a professional middle class, small independent businessmen in the cities and towns, and the remnants of the bourgeoisie of Winnipeg and Calgary. Neither regional capital nor urbanized labour, each of which has played significant roles in the evolution of the Canadian West, feature at all in Macpherson's study. Thus he passes over in silence such developments as the radicalization of western labour during and after World War I, the considerable influence of the Communist Party on the prairies, especially among East European and Ukrainian immigrants, the movement for a One Big Union, the Winnipeg General Strike, and the bitter and prolonged strikes in the coal mines of Drumheller, Estevan, and the Crow's Nest Pass in the early 1930s—none of which is evidence of an insignificant working class or an absence of class divisions within prairie society.

Macpherson's emphasis on Alberta's dependence on metropolitan central Canadian capital is not misplaced for the early period of Social Credit. But his account ignores the presence of a significant Alberta-based bourgeoisie in an earlier stage (1885 to 1925) of the province's economic development, and he thus exaggerates the influence of metropolitan factors. Alberta's economic base, like Manitoba's, has always been a good deal more diversified than that of Saskatchewan. To wheatlands, Alberta added large-scale ranching, stock-raising and meat-packing, vast coal deposits, conventional oil and gas, tar sands, mixed farming, and a substantial business and financial community. Compared with Saskatchewan, Alberta has been considerably more urban since its settlement, and rivalries and conflicts among its urban business and political elites (notably the historic rivalry between Calgary and Edmonton) have shaped its growth. Alberta has had "more business and industry and hence a larger and stronger business oriented bourgeoisie"[6] than its neighbour, and while this class was originally an offshoot of eastern and British capital, it developed strong roots, particularly in the prairie southwest.

Sixty years before the oil boom of the 1950s, Calgary was an important regional centre of entrepreneurial and financial activity, thanks in large part to the establishment of the big ranching companies in southern Alberta following the critical decision of the Canadian Pacific in the early 1880s to take a southerly route across the prairies and through the Rockies. Induced by federal land grants and access to the railroad, and capitalized by British and central Canadian finance, the ranching interests of the South were the founding members of a vigorous Alberta business elite—complete with exclusive men's clubs, polo grounds, and private boys' schools. An alliance of ranchers and urban businessmen and professionals, notable among whom were Senator James A. Lougheed and his law partner, R.B. Bennett, owned and developed Calgary's waterworks, light, telephone, and street-car utilities; raised the capital to develop the natural gas utilities of the cities of Medicine Hat, Calgary, and Edmonton; opened up the coal mines of Lethbridge and the foothills; and organized the syndicate which discovered oil in the Turner Valley in 1914, triggering Calgary's first bout of oil delirium. Nurtured in a context of metropolitanism by eastern and English capital and Tory patronage, by the turn of the century the ranching-landowning-urban business bourgeoisie of Alberta was a significant, albeit regional fraction of Canada's capitalist class.[7]

By contrast Saskatchewan, although it ranked as the third most populous province in Canada in the four censuses from 1911 to 1941, ahead of Alberta, offered fewer opportunities for regional capital accumulation. Lacking a diversified economic base, it actually corresponded better than did Alberta to the stereotype of a one-class society of independent commodity producers, although even in Saskatchewan there was sufficient diversity of interest between farmers and the local business community, composed largely of merchants, to create serious internal class tensions.

In his economic and class analysis Marx concentrated upon England, the society in which industrialization and capitalist class relations were the most fully developed by the mid-nineteenth century. But after the Chartist revolts of the 1840s English society failed to fulfil Marx's revolutionary political predictions, and he turned his political analysis increasingly to continental Europe where revolutions did occur. In an analogous fashion Macpherson's class analysis better fits Saskatchewan, but perhaps because that province has generated more internal class-based struggle than its neighbours, he uses Alberta to illustrate his thesis that a society of *petit-bourgeois* farmers can produce only a critique of the terms of trade between themselves and the rest of society, not a full-blown critique of capitalist property relations. By ignoring the complexity of class relations within the prairie hinterland and assuming its social homogeneity, Macpherson overlooks substantial differences between Social Credit and the CCF—the same error committed by many contemporary Marxists eager to prove the CCF was merely a manifestation of *petit-bourgeois* social democracy.

The Age of Prairie Elegance—Its Rise and Fall

Edgar Peter Lougheed was born in Calgary on 26 July 1928, the son of the late Edgar Donald and Edna Alexandria (Bauld) Lougheed, and the grandson of Senator Sir James A. Lougheed, one of Alberta's pioneering capitalists and among its most powerful political spokesmen in the formative years of the modern prairie West. The early successes, rapid decline, and subsequent rehabilitation of the Lougheed family across three generations and nearly a century of Alberta history cannot be chronicled here in any detail, but some background is essential to an understanding of the motivations and behaviour of the dominant political figure of the contemporary West.[8]

Like so many of the ruling members of his generation, James A. Lougheed was a lawyer by profession who shrewdly combined Conservative politics with railways and a sharp eye for real estate values. His life was devoted to the accumulation of property and capital and to the arts of political manipulation, and his place in the nation's history texts was therefore assured. He traded in land, patronage, and votes, and rose accordingly among the eminent to the highest reaches of Canadian politics and business. Born in Brampton, Ontario, the son of an Irish carpenter, he studied law in Toronto, then moved west, arriving in Fort Calgary on retainer to the CPR in 1883, shortly before the arrival of the railroad itself.

The Calgary townsite was then located on the east bank of the Elbow River near its confluence with the Bow, and most of its community of speculators, keenly anticipating the coming of the railroad, were trading in east bank properties. But Lougheed bought up large blocks of property on the west side of the Elbow, and when the CPR subsequently announced its decision to bypass the existing townsite and to build its station on the west bank, thereby outraging the businessmen and speculators of east Calgary, the young solicitor was in the enviable position of owning much of what is today downtown Calgary. He purchased more property, built a number of office blocks, and in one year reportedly paid half the city's tax bill. In 1884 he married Belle Hardisty, niece of Senator Richard Hardisty, whom he succeeded in the Senate in 1889 at the unlikely age of thirty-five. Later he built an imposing mansion on fashionable Mount Royal hill to entertain royalty, importing marble cutters from Italy to build the fireplaces to heat this ostentatious symbol of the new prairie wealth.

Lougheed also recruited from the Maritimes as a junior partner in his law firm the future prime minister, R.B. Bennett. Thus began a highly profitable alliance of political influence and property. The most prestigious law firm in Alberta, Lougheed and Bennett represented the CPR, the Bank of Montreal, the Hudson's Bay Company, and other leading corporate interests. They invested heavily in land and mineral developments, were part owners of both the *Calgary Herald* and *Albertan*, and founded companies such as Calgary Power, Canada Cement, and the drilling company which opened up the Turner Valley in 1914 (it was later acquired by Imperial Oil). Lougheed was also a director of the Canada Life Assurance Company, Canadian General Electric, and Canada Security Assurance, and reportedly left an estate worth some $12 million on his death in 1925. The senator was also a powerful figure in the national Conservative Party, although unlike his junior partner, Bennett, he died without attaining his life-long ambition, the prime minister's office. He was passed over for Arthur Meighen, it is said, because his wife's half-Native ancestry was too exotic for the Tory hierarchy. He did however assume the Conservative leadership in the Senate, that august institution of the propertied which he once described as a necessary "bulwark against the clamour and caprice of the mob," and held ministerial posts in the Borden and Meighen governments. His senatorial orations were notable for their passionate attacks on democracy and their equally fervent promotion of Alberta's mineral wealth.

The age of prairie elegance did not long outlive Sir James Lougheed. Like many other members of the old mansion set of Winnipeg, Edmonton, and Calgary, the Lougheed family did not fare well during the Depression. Indeed, it very nearly wiped them out. The Lougheed estate, like the prairie economy itself, was overextended and exposed. The Depression severely trimmed the values of the family properties, and the city of Calgary increased its levy on the Lougheed holdings. Following the death of the senator's widow, the Royal Trust Company, which held the mortgages on the Lougheed properties, ordered the family mansion auctioned off (it is today the headquarters of the Red Cross in Calgary). The executor of the senator's estate was Edgar Lougheed, one of four sons and the father of Peter. Edgar reportedly had many of the typical problems of the offspring of the privileged and powerful. An alcoholic who shared the senator's taste for fine living but lacked his gifts of accumulation, he presided over the steady dissipation of the family fortune during the Depression. "I wouldn't call him a weak man, but he sure as hell wasn't a strong one, and you soon learn that one of Peter's main drives is to restore the family name," a family friend says.[9] Peter's mother also suffered a nervous breakdown during the Depression and spent some time in an asylum. These traumatic events all occurred before Peter Lougheed was a teenager, and their combined impact cannot have been a happy one. Without delving into the relationships between childhood experience and later political behaviour, we can speculate that at least some of Lougheed's better known traits—his driving ambition, his competitiveness, and his well-known sensitivity to criticism—may be symptomatic of an insecurity and fear of failure and weakness which stem from his boyhood experience. Is it too fanciful to speculate that his family's sudden decline during the Depression explains something of his near obsession with prairie economic diversification?

The decline of Alberta's original business class awaits its historian. The ranching-Conservative elite of southern Alberta was overwhelmed by the rapid influx of immigrants and settlement of the north by Clifford Sifton's "men in sheepskin coats." Edmonton was chosen over Calgary as the seat of political power, and after 1905 the Liberals dominated the provincial legislature. The Tories ceased to be a significant force in provincial Alberta politics until the 1960s. Alberta capitalists handed over the control of Turner Valley and the important gas utilities of Calgary and Edmonton to American interests during the 1920s, and the Depression wiped out or severely trimmed many of the great prairie fortunes. Incomes declined less in Alberta than in Saskatchewan, thanks to the somewhat more diversified economy of the former, but the impact of the great collapse was traumatic across the West. The main lesson drawn from that experience, it cannot be too strongly emphasized, was the danger of economic specialization and the need to diversify away from an agriculture-dependent economy as swiftly as possible—even if such a transition implied a very great reliance on foreign capital. Indeed, given the indifference of eastern Canadian capital and the relatively undercapitalized state of Alberta business after World War II, rapid development of new export staples would have been impossible without heavy foreign investment.

Instead of producing a resurgence of entrepreneurial activity (as it appears to have done in the 1970s) the push towards economic diversification in the late 1940s after Leduc encouraged the growth of a rentier mentality and an accommodation with American resource capital. The new export staple happened to be oil, and the fact that the oil industry was highly capital-intensive and traditionally dominated by a few integrated international firms further helped discourage domestic entrepreneurship in Alberta. We have seen how Imperial Oil early obtained a dominant foothold in the province's major producing field, Turner Valley, and how it consolidated its dominance over the province's oil industry in spite of an often bitter resistance from the independents. This set the pattern for the remarkable domination of the Alberta oil and gas economy by foreign capital after Leduc. "Development over the subsequent decades was dependent on a steady and plentiful supply of risk capital and while the persistent formation of Calgary-based exploration companies bears witness to the continued generation of capital in the Calgary area, it was never sufficient. This, with the general aloofness of eastern Canadian investors towards western Canadian oil ventures, accelerated the process of foreign acquisition of capital-starved enterprises."[10]

The striking failure of the post-Leduc resource boom to replicate the historical conditions of turn-of-the-century Texas and to nurture a powerful class of Alberta entrepreneurs united with populist farmers in hostility to a takeover by external corporate and political interests is one of the great puzzles of modern prairie development. It is easier to document the effects than to explain the failure itself. The absence of a vigorous entrepreneurial-populist reaction within the province permitted Social Credit to pursue its entente with American capital without fear of the political consequences. No single factor adequately explains the phenomenon of the absent entrepreneur and the different responses of Texans and Albertans to the arrival of oil. Government policies certainly played their part, but this does not explain why the policies themselves met with such broad measure of popular support or acquiescence. The historian James H. Gray recalls in his autobiographical *Troublemaker!* how as the editor of the *Farm and Ranch Review* he had campaigned, indeed crusaded, on behalf of Alberta farmers in the late 1940s to have the province turn back its Crown-owned mineral rights to the farmers. "The natural resources beneath the farmlands of Alberta had to be restored to the farmers on the land, to put them on a par with the farmers in Manitoba and in most of Saskatchewan who had received mineral rights with the title to their farms. Then it would be the farmers who got rich and, like the American farmers, they would plough their riches back into the development of the country." The central question facing Albertans, according to the Calgarians backing the *Farm and Ranch Review,* was whether they wanted a province of poor people with a rich government, or a province of rich people with a poor government. "A government that had to come to the people every year for every dollar it spent would be responsive to the wishes of the people. A government that, through oil income, could get along without taxing authority would be unresponsive to the people and might ultimately become completely dictatorial." But such noble populist sentiments notwithstanding, the *Farm and Ranch Review's* crusade over mineral rights not only failed to change provincial policy, it met with little support from the farmers themselves. Whereas Texan farmers and ranchers had driven wildcatters from their land at the point of a gun, and then forced the state legislature to turn mineral rights over to the surface owners,

> Albertans, however, were more Caspar Milquetoast than Texan when it came to asserting their rights. Instead of fighting for the oil under their land, they were content to accept the law as it stood and haggle with the oil companies for an increase in the pittances they were offered for the use of ten-acre well sites, and later for the running of gathering lines and pipelines across their land ... In some areas, the farmers barricaded access to their land until compensation claims were settled. The government then sided with the oil companies and passed the Right-of-Entry Act, which made it a criminal offence for farmers to bar their land to drilling rigs or seismic crews. The farmers accepted that order without even a whimper.[11]

Federal and provincial economic policies in the years immediately following the Leduc discovery tended to promote the external takeover of Alberta's oil and gas, and, with but a few exceptions, precluded the rapid expansion of the numerous Calgary-based independents formed in the 1940s and early 1950s. Under the guidance of C.D. Howe, successive postwar Liberal administrations in Ottawa pursued a strategy of rapid economic expansion and an open door to foreign investment. Resource industries such as oil and gas, developed for continental markets with large infusions of U.S. capital, would spearhead this expansion, while offsetting the balance-of-payments effects of Canada's manufacturing imports. In spite of his later support for an all-Canadian route for the Trans-Canada natural gas pipeline, Howe remained unsympathetic to, and unmoved by, the arguments of Canadian nationalists that his policies were fraught with dangerous long-term implications for Canada's political sovereignty and economic structure. Unapologetically centralist in design, his grand strategy for postwar development left little room for provincial economic autonomy, and, accordingly, he moved swiftly to pressure the Manning government to permit removals of natural gas on grounds of continental military strategy when protectionist sentiments began to build in Alberta in the early 1950s. Howe and his federal Liberal colleagues evidently viewed Alberta's new energy resources as potentially critical assets in, first, North America's international struggles with the Communist bloc, and, second, the industrial growth of the central Canadian heartland. Howe's impatience with Alberta protectionists and Canadian nationalists alike derived from his fear that parochialism would impede the country's rapid economic advance by discouraging the inward flow of foreign capital. When the owners of the small Alberta independents pleaded for changes in federal tax legislation to place them in a stronger position vis-à-vis the major American oil companies (after 1950 U.S. oil companies were permitted to write off substantial portions of their foreign exploration expenses against their American income tax), Ottawa's response was one of indifference. "I don't give a damn who owns this country, as you put it," James Gray recalls being told by the federal assistant deputy minister in the Department of Finance, "as long as we have the power to tax, because whoever has the power to tax calls the tune."[12]

Provincial development policies similarly had the effect of strengthening the market power of the integrated firms and discouraging the entry into the industry of companies capitalized locally. The risk-averse allocation structure adopted by the Manning government on the basis of American experience guaranteed an immediate cash flow to the provincial treasury from the auction of Crown lands, but it also favoured large companies with good financial reserves over small independents with limited access to capital. Alternative allocation structures would have required the provincial government to share, in varying degrees, in the uncertainty of development. Their rejection constituted implicitly a decision in favour of rentier development.

In such a political environment, with both the federal and provincial governments favouring foreign over local capital, yet another Texan precedent was precluded in Alberta. In Texas the economics and politics of oil have typically been dominated by the independents. At the end of the nineteenth century the populist movement in Texas successfully fought off domination of the state's infant oil industry by Rockefeller's Standard Oil trust, thereby creating the necessary conditions for expansion of the independents. By contrast, Alberta's independents were too small and lacking in capital to do much more than enter into unequal arrangements with the integrated companies and thereby ensure themselves a stable share of the province's crude oil markets. In conditions of surplus and soft markets, however, the independent producers typically do badly, and such were the conditions prevailing in Alberta's oil industry throughout much of the 1950s and the 1960s. At times the industry was operating at 30 percent capacity. The province's system of prorationing oil to market demand attempted to strike a compromise between the interests of the integrated majors and the independents, sacrificing efficiency in order to guarantee the latter group a share of production, but the prolonged conditions of surplus capacity inevitably took their toll. The independents fought a lengthy political battle in the late 1950s to expand the domestic oil market by pushing the Interprovincial Pipeline into the Montreal area—supplied by the international companies from offshore sources—but they failed, and in the early 1960s a number of the larger independent producers passed into foreign ownership.

The presence or absence of entrepreneurship—the perception and rational pursuit of new market opportunities under conditions of uncertainty and risk—within a region can be an important factor in determining the degree of economic development and diversification obtained from any new export staple such as petroleum. Its absence may mean economic rents are foregone and investment is precluded in closely linked industries. This can lead to an overconcentration of resources in the export sector, thereby giving rise to a "staple trap."[13] An adequate supply of domestic entrepreneurship, whether private or governmental, is therefore crucial if the export staple is to be used to generate strong linkage effects and thus enable the economy to grow and diversify. Where the entrepreneurial function is left in the hands of foreigners and a passive rentier mentality exists among the dominant domestic groups, then the growth of a new staple is unlikely to generate a pattern of diversified development. In that event, the fate of the economy will depend in large part on the fortunes of its export markets, and any available domestic entrepreneurship is likely to be channelled into the conservative task of protecting these markets instead of creating new opportunities and "carrying out new combinations"—the true role of the entrepreneur in the classical literature on capitalist economic development.

The Impact of Oil

Local entrepreneurial decision making, public as well as private, was largely absent during the development of Alberta's oil industry after 1947. But how much economic diversification actually did occur? Did the rapid exploitation of the province's major oil and gas fields provide the stimulus for sustained economic development?

The answers to these questions are complex. At best we can arrive at a qualified negative. In the initial stages of petroleum development linkages were generated, but the pattern of diversification was not sufficient to enable the economy of Alberta to transcend its dependence on export staple industries—oil and gas essentially became a second export staple in addition to agriculture. Oil did not provide the spur to industrialization.

Under the heavy investment of the oil and gas industry in the years of rapid growth after Leduc, Alberta's economic base shifted dramatically from its prewar dependence on agriculture to a new reliance on the industrial staples of petroleum and natural gas. Between 1935 and 1971, agriculture's share of the total value added in goods-producing industries in the province declined from 54 to 14 percent, while mining (essentially oil and gas extraction) increased its share from 11 to 39 percent, manufacturing from 16 to 20 percent, and construction from 14 to 23 percent.[14] Professor J.C. Stabler has summarized the extent to which early oil and gas development did generate linkage effects:

> Once the importance of the oil fields had been ascertained, the building of storage facilities, pipelines, and refineries created a significant increase in demand for construction services and materials. A second round of induced investment came with the creation of petro-chemical and natural gas processing facilities. The increased activity directly stimulated the trade and transportation sectors as well as the construction industry. The local production of some manufactured inputs was begun or expanded, and legal, technical, managerial, maintenance, and other service activities directly serving the petroleum industry came into existence. The royalties collected by the province made it possible to expand government services and employment. The new jobs thus created further stimulated the population oriented trade and service activities as

well as some manufacturing sectors. The end result of this expansion was the creation of jobs at a faster rate than they could be filled by the natural increase in the province's labour force even taking into account the release of surplus workers from agriculture. Labour, and population, was therefore attracted from outside the province.[15]

E.H. Shaffer, however, has argued persuasively that the early patterns of induced investment in backward- and forward-linked industries were insufficient to enable Alberta to make a transition from an oil-dependent economy.[16] (Backward linkages refer to additional income generated in industries that expand to provide inputs to the oil industry; forward linkages refer to additional income in industries that, using oil as an input, transform it further.) Backward-linked industries providing professional services slowly expanded, and the petroleum industry itself increased the number of its specialized employees trained within Alberta. But the backward linkages within Alberta for manufactured inputs (e.g., drilling equipment) were not substantial because the capital-intensive oil industry imported a very large percentage of its heavy equipment, engineering, and design technology. Nor, except for a brief spate of petrochemical development in the 1950s, the gradual transfer of prairie refining capacity of Alberta, and local pipeline construction, was there significant investment in forward-linked industries. Much of the early opposition to removals of gas from the province, we may recall, had its rationale in the fear that exports would have a negative impact on Alberta's chances for industrialization. But the real barriers to petroleum-linked industrial development appear to have been the traditional regional disadvantages of the prairies: the West's geographical isolation and distance from markets, high transportation costs, and the absence of developed infrastructure. The problem lay in "being small and isolated rather than with discriminatory treatment."[17]

Oil did not initiate the process of prairie industrialization many Albertans anticipated after Leduc, and in retrospect such anticipations were decidedly unrealistic. Consequently, as late as 1970, Alberta's manufacturing industries (by far the most important of which is the food and beverage group) employed merely 11 percent of the province's nonagricultural labour force.[18] The political upshot was Social Credit's vulnerability to Conservative attacks that the province was too dependent on agriculture and oil and gas extraction, and that a "third phase" of development was necessary.

The greatest impact of oil occurred via final demand linkages. Oil called into being a large service economy, public as well as private, through the direct expenditures of income earned by those employed in the petroleum industry, and through the government's discretionary spending of resource rents—which have accounted for 40 to 50 percent of Alberta government revenue since the late 1940s, a higher percentage than for any other province. Oil, according to Shaffer's estimates, accounted for over half of the new jobs created in Alberta during the 1960s. Of his estimated eighty-seven thousand oil-related new positions, more than half were in noncommercial services (e.g., teachers and hospital employees), commercial services (e.g., lawyers and hairdressers), wholesale and retail trade. Growth of a new urban and professional labour force, much of it in the public and para-public sectors, enlarged the ranks of a new middle class, but it also diminished the relative importance of Social Credit's rural base.

The demographic impact of the new mineral staples has been particularly striking. Rapid urbanization is not, of course, unique to Alberta, but in no other Canadian province has the domination of the city over the countryside been accomplished so abruptly. Dramatic population growth commenced in the late 1940s and continued through the 1950s, much of it caused by the in-migration of workers and their families from provinces such as Saskatchewan, Manitoba, and Ontario. Alberta's annual population growth rate exceeded the national average consistently until 1965, levelled off until the early 1970s, and then resurged under the impact of the energy crisis. Between 1946 and 1971 Alberta doubled its population, from roughly eight hundred thousand to 1.6 million, and an overwhelming proportion of the growth was concentrated in the two major urban centres of Calgary and Edmonton, and to a lesser extent in Lethbridge, Medicine Hat, and Red Deer. The postwar growth rates of Alberta's two large cities have considerably outdistanced those of Canada's other principal metropolitan regions: between 1951 and 1971 Calgary and Edmonton increased their populations by 158 and 135 percent respectively. Between 1911 and 1941 Alberta's rural-urban population distribution changed little (urban population grew from 29 to 32 percent of the province's total) but in the next three decades, from 1941 to 1971, the demographic balance tilted decisively in favour of the cities (the urban percentage of the population escalated from 32 to 73 percent). In 1941 approximately half of Alberta's population still lived on census farms and less than a quarter in Calgary and Edmonton; three decades later when Peter Lougheed's Conservatives swept to power, less than 20 percent of the population was still on the farms while better than half of Alberta's citizens were concentrated in the big urban centres.[19]

The Rebirth of the Alberta Tories

The Lougheed family recovered some lost ground during the postwar oil boom—Edgar reportedly left some $3 million on his death in 1951. Peter, encouraged by his ambitious and highly competitive mother ("She was the one who gave me goals and objectives"), studied law at the University of Alberta, briefly ran back punts for the Edmonton Eskimos, and then went on to the Harvard Business School to study business administration. He spent a summer in the early 1950s working with the petroleum industry in Tulsa, Oklahoma, then in steep decline as an oil-producing state. Today he uses Tulsa as the model of what Alberta must avoid: "If you want to see what happens when the oil industry moves on, go to Tulsa. It's a dead city."[20] He returned to Alberta and did a brief stint of legal practice; then in 1956 he joined the family-owned Mannix group, the large Calgary-based construction and engineering conglomerate that is today known as Loram (an acronym for "Long Range Mannix") Company Limited. Lougheed was a great success at Mannix, moving up the corporate escalator from secretary to general counsel, vice-president, and director in five short years.

The Mannix connection is an intriguing one, and not merely because of Lougheed's close personal relationship with the family patriarch, Frederick C. Mannix, the second-generation head of the group.[21] The Mannixes, like the Lougheeds, are an Alberta dynasty—rich, politically influential, and dedicated to the concept of a strong conservative West. The group was founded by Frederick S. Mannix in the early years of this century. Mannix specialized in heavy earth moving and the construction of hydroelectric dams for Calgary Power, the province's big privately owned electrical utility. Recognizing that the utility would need to move into thermal power generation, Mannix bought up coal properties, then sold the strip mines to Calgary Power but retained the contracts to operate them. Mannix has since built most of Calgary Power's hydro dams and operates its strip mines. During the 1940s majority control of Mannix passed into the hands of Morrison-Knudsen Company of Boise, Idaho, one of the major U.S. construction groups, and it was through this connection that Mannix was able to break into the large postwar Canadian projects engineered and constructed by American companies: the St. Lawrence Seaway, Interprovincial Pipe Line, the Trans Mountain Pipe Line, and the Mid-Canada radar line.

In 1951, through a complicated financial arrangement, F.C. Mannix bought back control of the company and began to diversify. Mannix won Social Credit's approval to build and operate one of Alberta's largest oil-gathering systems, Pembina Pipe Lines, over the opposition of the major oil companies who controlled the big Pembina field. One of the few instances of entrepreneurial instincts displayed by the Manning administration, this proved to be of lasting benefit to the Mannixes. Today, in addition to its construction, engineering, and pipeline interests, the Loram-Mannix group of operating companies control a major coal producer, Manalta Coal, an oil and gas producer, Western Decalta, and land and ranching holdings. Loram is among the most important and influential Alberta-owned companies in western Canada.

Described as "rich, private, dynastic and inaccessible," the Mannix family is staunchly rightwing and fiercely dedicated to western regionalism. Fred C. Mannix, a close friend of both Ernest Manning and Peter Lougheed, has been called a "rabid Albertan" by the former, and the family foundation has been a major backer of the Canada West Foundation—an organization founded by a group of prominent Albertans and British Columbians dedicated to fostering the cultural and political identity of the West. Several former Mannix executives (including the present head of the Canadian Petroleum Association, Harold Millican) were recruited by Peter Lougheed to key positions in his first government, and there is little doubt that Lougheed's own managerial and quasi-corporatist style of government, as well as his penchant for strong executive government, were forged in the Mannix boardroom. More to the point, the Mannix group is among the handful of home-grown Alberta-based corporations which can successfully compete in national and world markets. It has been a model for the new capitalist West and an obvious training ground for Alberta's rising business class.

Peter Lougheed left Mannix in 1962 for law and politics. He considered running for the federal Tories, then opted to rebuild the nearly defunct provincial party. Why the Conservatives? In part because of family traditions and, according to one friend, "Once you accept that vaguely rightist position, it doesn't matter whether you're a Conservative or a Socred, but the Socreds were dominated by all those old guys . . . by going Conservative, Peter was able to call his own shots."[22] He began by organizing a Lougheed Club (annual membership was $100) among his close friends, and planning strategy at weekly meetings in the Palliser Hotel in Calgary. In March 1965, he easily won the party's leadership.

When Peter Lougheed took over as leader, Alberta's provincial Conservatives were "a party only one step from outright decrepitude."[23] The Tories had been dormant in Alberta politics for decades and an attempt earlier in the 1960s to revitalize the party had collapsed. "The Conservatives have never been considered a threat to any government of Alberta," remarked the *Edmonton Journal* a year before Lougheed assumed the leadership. On the other hand, the NDP was relatively weak and the provincial Liberals, who had been a serious challenger in the late 1950s, had disintegrated because of internal leadership struggles. Lougheed and his small coterie of Calgary advisers sensed that Ernest Manning was close to retirement and that a more fluid political situation was opening up. The Tories were respectably conservative, but they differed from Social Credit in their emphasis upon political modernization and a more diversified economic base. The Conservatives, with their slogans "The future belongs to us" and "It's time for a change," "offered the electorate continued free-enterprise conservatism, but with the added bonuses of urban middle-class respectability, a comfortably vague social conscience and a little political excitement."[24]

The years 1965–67 were devoted to an intensive reorganization of the Conservatives at the grassroots level and to the mastery of television. Lougheed learned to use television as Aberhart had used radio in an earlier era–as a weapon of opposition politics. He attacked Social Credit as a "reactionary" government, but infuriated Manning by praising him personally. And he continued to hammer home his familiar critique of Alberta's economic policy. The province required a "third stage" of development, that of industrialization:

> We have been coasting on our petroleum revenues for the last decade–we have failed to use capital revenues from the petroleum industry–over one billion dollars–as an investment in the future by way of imaginative development, research and promotional programs . . . we have utilized this one billion dollars from the petroleum industry to establish a built-in level of provincial government spending–far larger than any other province on a per capita basis . . . we have been out-negotiated by the Federal Government and perhaps by other provinces . . .[25]

In the 1967 election Lougheed's revived Conservatives won 27 percent of the popular vote and six seats–five from the upper-income suburbs of Calgary and Edmonton–to become the official opposition. The next year Manning retired, having failed to stimulate interest in his proposal for a "realignment" of Canadian politics on the right (it was rumoured at the time that Manning was, in effect, making a bid for the national Tory leadership, and that Lougheed was seen as his natural heir to the provincial leadership). The Tories managed to win Manning's seat, and they added several more through defections and by-elections. Without the pious Manning at the helm, Social Credit began the rapid slide toward political oblivion that has been the fate of most North American populist movements. Its new leader, Harry Strom, proved quite incapable of adapting the party to the province's changed economic and social environment. Would another leader have managed to stem the Tory tide? Probably not. Material circumstances were ultimately more significant than personalities in reshaping Alberta's political system. The economic and social base of Social Credit had been eroded by a generation of petroleum development and urbanization. Wheat had created Social Credit. Oil tamed it, then displaced it in favour of Lougheed's Conservatives.

On 30 August 1971, six years after Peter Lougheed entered politics, the Tories won a stunning upset victory, electing forty-nine MLAs to the seventy-five-member Alberta legislature. The Conservatives swept both large cities (twenty-five of the twenty-nine seats), most of the smaller urban areas, and the disaffected north of the province, increasing their share of the popular vote from 27 to 46.5 percent. Much of this increased support came, interestingly, from Liberal and NDP supporters–the former party had captured 11 percent of the popular vote in 1967, but in 1971 it was reduced to barely 1 percent, while the NDP dropped from 16 to 11 percent. Social Credit's popular support declined from 45 to 41 percent, and the party managed to hold on to twenty-five seats–most of them from the traditional rural "heartland" of the south and south-central regions of the province. The Tories found their support among urbanites, new voters, and those of higher income, educational and occupational status–in brief, from the new middle class.

Some believed that the 1971 election had restored competitive party politics to Alberta, but this proved far from true. Demoralized and leaderless, Social Credit rapidly began to disintegrate as an effective political force. Internal leadership rivalries, between a fundamentalist "old guard" and reformers, spilled openly into public view, so that by 1975 the Social Credit corpse was in an advanced state of decomposition. In that year Alberta returned to its tradition of one-party rule, as Lougheed turned the election into a referendum on provincial rights and resources. Booming economic conditions and the Conservatives' mobilization of regional alienation decimated the ranks of the opposition parties. Lougheed's government won sixty-nine of the seventy-five seats and fully 63 percent of the popular vote; Social Credit returned four members; the NDP leader, Grant Notley, was narrowly reelected; and a single independent was returned. This massive Tory consolidation of power was clearly assisted by Ottawa's heavy-handed interventions in 1973 and 1974, but even without the factor of regional protest it seems probable that the result would have been broadly similar. As of the late 1970s, no serious threat to the Conservative hegemony is yet posed by any of the three Alberta opposition parties and, barring completely gross mismanagement or serious scandal, none appears likely for at least a generation.

Alberta's Arriviste Bourgeoisie

By the opening of the 1970s, then, Alberta's population was substantially urbanized and its expanding labour force was oriented to the service sector and the managerial, professional, and white-collar occupations of the new middle class. Oil had induced little investment in manufacturing and Alberta's industrial working class remained relatively small, in spite of prolonged economic expansion. The new middle class was urban and secular in its outlook and impatient with Social Credit's blend of religious fundamentalism and the remnants of its agrarian populist past. Social Credit, the Lougheed Conservatives were fond of saying, had grown isolationist and was outside the mainstream of North American culture, something which could never be said of Peter Lougheed. While the pious Manning was still delivering his weekly radio Back to the Bible Hour sermons ("in any unregenerate society, the will of the people is bound to come into conflict with the will of God" was the somewhat ominous theme of a typical 1966 broadcast), Lougheed was thumbing the pages of Theodore White's *The Making of the President 1960* and sharpening his television image in the Kennedy mould—the young, dynamic, and safely right-of-centre heir to a family dynasty.

A precondition for a movement away from the passive rentier behaviour which characterized provincial resource politics after the war was the development of domestic entrepreneurial ambitions and skills, private and governmental. In Saskatchewan a resurgence of Fabianism within the government bureaucracy and the leadership of the NDP in the 1970s has provided the requisite entrepreneurship, but it lacks a broad popular base and has antagonized local business elites. Its future is precarious. In Alberta, by contrast, local entrepreneurial energy is being generated by the province's upwardly mobile urban middle class—in effect, a rising urban bourgeoisie comprising leading indigenous entrepreneurs, managers, and upper-income professionals—linking private and public sectors in a quasi-corporatist alliance of interests. This arriviste bourgeoisie is led by the owners and managers of the few Alberta-based corporations large enough to compete on a national and international scale—notably such firms as Alberta Gas Trunk Line, the Mannix-Loram group, ATCO Industries, the Alberta Energy Company—as well as some of the more dynamic oil-related businesses which have their head offices in Calgary. In addition, it includes a large body of well-educated and upwardly mobile professionals, such as corporate lawyers, economic and financial consultants, engineers, geologists, and other scientists or technical experts providing services of a specialized nature to the petroleum industry and government. A third group, a state-administrative elite, occupies the top bureaucratic posts within the public sector, particularly, though not exclusively, in government departments and boards charged with the tasks of managing the province's resources, negotiating with other governments, investing the huge revenue surpluses of the 1970s and charting future economic directions. Confident of its own administrative competence and committed to a provincial strategy of development, this state-administrative elite sees Alberta as the logical arena for the advancement of its career opportunities and, like its private sector counterparts, is fiercely loyal to the province as a semi-sovereign political entity and deeply involved in the process of "province-building." As in Saskatchewan, bureaucracy in Alberta is an active and relatively autonomous participant in entrepreneurial debates and decisions concerning resource development. A good deal of the pressure to use Alberta's remaining energy supplies as bargaining leverage for economic diversification appears to originate, for example, within the provincial bureaucracy itself—which is hardly surprising, given its own heavy dependence on rents extracted from nonreplenishable resources.

It is no exaggeration to suggest that Alberta's new bourgeoisie has begun to make arrangements for its own future in preparation for the inevitable day when the international oil industry leaves the province. What motivates this alliance of private and public interests is a fear of economic stagnation and secular decline. It is driven by an ambivalent sense of dependency and vulnerability and an acute awareness of the degree to which its own prospects rise and fall with the petroleum industry and the world oil market. The provincial Conservative Party has been hammering at this theme since 1965, and not without success. "Since entering public life over nine years ago," Peter Lougheed told an audience of Calgary businessmen in 1974, "my theme has been that this province's economy is too *vulnerable*, it is too dependent upon the sale of depleting resources, particularly oil and gas for its continued prosperity ... Frankly, I despair of the short-term thinking of a few Albertans who believe we can coast on the sale of our depleting resources for our continued prosperity."[26]

Throughout most of the 1950s and 1960s the central problem of Alberta's oil industry was that of markets. In the late 1950s a number of external factors (the resolution of the Suez crisis and the reopening of the Suez Canal to tankers, a recession in the United States, and a new U.S. oil import quota system) combined to depress demand for Alberta's crude. The decline in exports led to a demand by independent domestic producers to push the domestic market into Montreal, which was supplied exclusively by foreign oil. That proposal was strongly opposed by the international oil companies, who wanted to retain the Montreal market for their unprorated offshore oil, and by the U.S. State Department, which feared the political repercussions in Venezuela of a loss of one of the latter's key markets. The upshot was the compromise known as the National Oil Policy (NOP). The U.S. agreed to exempt Canada from its import restrictions, if Canada agreed to reserve the area east of the Ottawa Valley for imports. Under the NOP the increase in Alberta production was to be absorbed by the expansion of exports to the U.S. Midwest and West Coast and by the displacement of foreign oil in Ontario west of the Ottawa Valley. While this compromise brought some measure of stability to the Alberta oil industry, it had the effect of tying the province into a continental oil policy. Alberta's economic prospects were intimately linked to U.S. quota politics.

The event which brought home to many Albertans the precariousness of their prosperity was the discovery of a major oil field at Prudhoe Bay on Alaska's North Slope in January 1968. Prudhoe Bay vividly emphasized the vulnerability of Alberta's oil-dependent economy to exogenous developments and, in particular, to the prospect that the Alaskan find might in the long run permit the United States to regain its self-sufficiency in oil and displace imports from western Canada. This fear caused Social Credit to delay approval of the Syncrude oil sands venture for another three years (because of marketing difficulties and pressure from conventional producers, Social Credit restricted oil sands development to one small-scale prototype plant, Sun Oil's Great Canadian Oil Sands). A more immediate concern was that Prudhoe Bay encouraged the major integrated companies to shift their exploratory activities out of Alberta to the northern Canadian frontier in search of new "elephant" pools. This movement out of the province, which had ominous implications for government revenues as well as for many small oil-service companies, was apparently based on a collective decision by the majors that the limits of Alberta's oil-producing potential had been reached and that new exploratory work would bring diminishing returns. While drilling activity in Alberta in the late 1960s was stable, the number of exploratory wells drilled by the majors fell off sharply between 1968 and 1970, while the smaller operators accounted for 75 to 80 percent of new exploratory work in the province. New field wildcat wells drilled in Alberta fell from 421 in 1969 to 256 in 1971. Alberta's share of total Canadian net cash exploratory expenditures declined from a 1966 peak of 74 percent to 54 percent in 1970, and this had a predictable impact on provincial government revenues. Industry expenditures for Crown reserves in Alberta dropped off abruptly. Revenues were becoming dependent to an ominous degree on royalties on production from declining reserves.[27]

The northward shift of the majors' exploration activities and the vulnerability of Alberta export markets in the U.S. after Prudhoe Bay were exploited by the Lougheed Conservative opposition in the late 1960s. Peter Lougheed attacked Social Credit for its "overdependence on the oil industry" and pressed for a "much higher priority to the field of industrial development. It's been kind of a lost cousin here in Alberta."[28] In his reply to the budget speech in 1969, Lougheed emphasized the weakness of the government's revenue position, "The dependence by Social Credit upon the continued prosperity of the oil industry has been evident for all to see for some time. In fact, they have established a framework of programmes and services as the largest spending province per capita in Canada—and it is dependent upon the ever-upward growth of petroleum revenue." With the oversupply then prevailing in North American oil markets, Lougheed, like Social Credit, at this point equated the maximization of production with optimal policy. But, unlike Social Credit, he intended the provincial government to "take the initiative":

> What role should the Alberta Government play in helping to develop new growth markets for Alberta oil? A fundamental question for the people and for this House. Social Credit policy seems to be ... to leave it to the Federal authority, be content to rely upon them to handle the negotiations and keep us informed. We disagree. We do not suggest at any time that any approach be taken directly by the Alberta Government with the United States Government ... without prior concurrence or co-operation and in joint

239

conjunction with the Federal authorities. But we do suggest that the Alberta Government is definitely in the oil marketing business. That it must take the initiative.[29]

Lougheed was in effect giving notice that any Conservative government would consider itself an entrepreneurial actor in provincial economic development.

The Spirit of Capitalism

Change at the political level was a necessary but not sufficient prerequisite for the emergence in Alberta of provincial entrepreneurship. The development of bureaucratic competence and expertise and the growth of province-building elites in the public sector (e.g., at the Energy Resources Conservation Board) complemented the transition from Social Credit to the Conservatives, giving the latter an administrative advantage in bargaining over such issues as new royalty terms, the pricing of resources, the creation of an Alberta-based petrochemical industry, or development of the Athabasca tar sands. Of at least equal significance, however, was the growth among Alberta's business classes of what, borrowing from Max Weber, we might call "the spirit of capitalism."

So long as Social Credit's rentier approach to resource development governed relations between the province and the large international oil companies, Alberta businessmen had to be content with a highly limited and dependent, if relatively prosperous, role in life: either working for one of the branch plants of the foreign-controlled companies, or running one of the many small independent producers or service companies which grew up in Calgary in the years after Leduc. As we have seen, Social Credit's development philosophy grew out of Manning's belief in the overriding necessity for an entente with American capital. Without such an entente, accompanied by highly favourable terms of development, Manning was convinced that Alberta would lack the capital, expertise, technology, and markets to exploit its energy resource potential: the province was bargaining from a position of weakness, and its terms must therefore be attractive. Recall that the accommodation negotiated between Social Credit and the major oil companies after Leduc was designed to provide the latter with a minimum of uncertainty over tenure, royalty charges, and property rights, and the assurance of long-term political stability. In return for their large capital investments in exploration and development after 1947, and sufficient royalties to enable the province to retire its debt and to expand government services without increasing personal taxes, Manning's "businesslike" administration abjured intervention without consultation, and followed a policy based upon the premise that the interests of the petroleum industry and the interests of Alberta were roughly the same. By tacit, if not explicit, agreement any entrepreneurial role by the province in the resource economy (e.g., through the creation of Crown exploration companies or a more innovative policy towards Crown reserves) would have violated the spirit of this broad entente.

In such a limited scheme of things, with both the province and an indifferent federal government encouraging external capital to take the leading role in development, Alberta business had to be satisfied to eke out an existence on the fringes of the industry. Local capitalists were far too small to compete with the integrated majors, and most settled for a frustrated marginal role, often within the large oil-service economy that developed in Calgary in the 1950s and 1960s. For the most part they did not even play an important "comprador" function, facilitating the takeover of Alberta's resources by foreign capital: that function was largely performed by the traditional institutions of central Canadian finance capital and their branch plants in Calgary. With a handful of notable exceptions, Alberta capitalists played a very limited and subordinate role in the post-Leduc development of the western Canadian sedimentary basin. In marked contrast to what had occurred in Texas half a century earlier, the arrival of the majors did not provoke a fierce defensive response by Alberta capital (although, as we have seen, there was considerable friction in the Turner Valley between Imperial Oil and the independents in the 1930s). Overwhelmed by the international petroleum industry and stifled by Social Credit's preferential policies towards external capital, for twenty-five years after Leduc indigenous Alberta capital settled for a marginal, dependent status in the shadows of Calgary's Americanized business environment. Calgary's gleaming new skyscrapers for the most part housed the branch offices of companies headquartered in New York, Houston, San Francisco, and Toronto. And since most of the economic surplus generated from the exploitation of Alberta's oil and gas was captured either by the provincial treasury or by multinational oil corporations, local capital had little prospect of growth. A less likely location for the emergence of a new regional bourgeoisie could scarcely be imagined.

A break with marginality and dependence has, however, occurred in the 1970s. While foreign capital continues to be preponderant within the provincial economy—indeed, measured on a percentage basis Alberta still leads the provinces in terms of foreign control of its industries—among Alberta's indigenous business elite there has been a definite awakening of expectations and ambitions in the past decade. A new consciousness, largely defined in regional imperatives, has emerged, a growing restlessness with the West's hinterland capitalist status and an awareness of the possibilities for accumulation. To an important extent this is being deliberately nurtured by the development strategy of the Lougheed government, but the origins of the strategy lie in the aspirations and anxieties of an arriviste bourgeoisie. The break with dependence has occurred because of the fear of economic stagnation and secular decline and because of the threat of encroachments by eastern Canadian interests, but it has been reinforced by the sudden stimulus of the world oil crisis and by the relative "overdevelopment" of the Albertan economy since 1973—an overdevelopment in sharp contrast to the conditions of recession and stagnation that have plagued the rest of Canada throughout the late 1970s. Once merely a hinterland service centre, Calgary is fast replacing Montreal as Canada's second largest financial centre (behind Toronto) and now ranks only behind Houston and London as a world capital for oil finance. It is the location of several hundred head offices, including those of postwar parvenus such as Alberta Gas Trunk Line, Ron Southern's ATCO Industries conglomerate, the Mannix-Loram group, Dome Petroleum (now under Canadian control) and many others. Much money is first or second generation wealth and the province still lacks large financial institutions which could compete with Bay or Wall Street, but it does have, as *Canadian Business* puts it, "the social energy and innovation that seem to have moved out of eastern Canada. Calgary's businessmen and their friends in the Alberta government are absolutely determined to make permanent capital out of the oil boom."[30]

The Shift of Power to Alberta

Powered by the shift in bargaining advantage from energy consumers to producers, Alberta's nascent bourgeoisie is in revolt against the uneven historical patterns of accumulation characteristic of Canadian capitalism. With interests in oil and gas, real estate, construction, petrochemicals, ranching and agribusiness, and the fast-growing sports and tourism industries, Calgary's business elite aims at nothing less than a transfer of wealth, industries, and decision making from central Canada to the western periphery—"a fundamental change in the economy of Canada," as Premier Lougheed puts it. And to an important extent, this is already occurring. Measured by almost any standard of regional income distribution, the traditional hegemony of the central Canadian heartland has been slipping for well over a decade. Alberta's ability to exact a major regional transfer of income from the heavily populated oil-importing provinces can be seen in the huge surpluses accumulating in its Heritage Fund. Western business interests, headed by Calgary-based Alberta Gas Trunk Line, in 1977 defeated the powerful Arctic Gas consortium, composed of eastern-based firms, Canadian and foreign owned, for the right to transport Arctic gas south. It was an important step in the growth of western Canadian regional power in the natural gas industry. Allied with international chemical giants such as Dow, Trunk Line and Dome have played a major role in putting together Alberta's new petrochemical complex. Corporate empire-building is *de rigueur* among Alberta businessmen.

There are interesting parallels here with the politics of sectionalism in other advanced capitalist societies. Tom Nairn, for example, has written of a tendential relative "over-development" which lies behind the neonationalist movement in Scotland. "Obviously linked to the discovery and exploitation of North Sea oil, this new awareness has proved particularly effective in the face of English decline and political immiseration ... It has awakened the Scottish bourgeoisie to a new consciousness of its historic separateness, and fostered a frank, restless discontent with the expiring British world."[31] The inability of the Scots to capture the rents from North Sea oil in the highly centralized British unitary state provides fuel for secession, as will Westminster's spending of the rents to delay the process of English secular decline, but for the time being at least the Scottish middle class is severely disadvantaged by the absence of a federal political framework. One need only recall the role of the Alberta government in opposing new federal taxes on oil after 1973 to appreciate the advantages of constitutional decentralization to an ascendant regional bourgeoisie.

A closer parallel is to be found south of the 49th parallel. There the American political agenda is increasingly defined by the sectional rivalries between "frostbelt" and "sunbelt" and the steady shift in power towards the latter—the so-called Southern Rim stretching from Virginia to California—since World War II. The traditional economic and political hegemony of the "Yankee" northeastern establishment has been undermined by the postwar military displacement of bases and defence industries to the sunbelt states, and by the rapid growth of the new technology, oil, agribusiness, real estate, and leisure industries.[32]

The process of regional decline, symbolized by the threatened bankruptcy of New York City, has advanced to the stage where embattled northeastern politicians led by Massachusetts Congressman Michael Harrington have launched a sixteen-state Northeastern-Midwest Economic Advancement Coalition to fight for "frostbelt" interests. Invoking memories of Franklin Roosevelt's attempts to assist the South in the 1930s, New York Senator Daniel P. Moynihan recently asked, "What happens to this tradition of national liberalism if it turns out, two generations later, that while the South was willing to accept the resources of the North to get it going, it has no intention to reciprocate now that the Northeast is in need?" Replying to his own question, he claimed there would be a "response in bitterness that would equal what the South expressed and endured after its defeat in the war between the states," adding that the bankruptcy of New York during a Carter Presidency "would be to the Northeast what Sherman's march was to the South."[33]

Conclusion

The rise of the Canadian West in the 1970s is a close parallel to the emergence of the American sunbelt, and the relative economic decline of the central Canadian heartland approximates the slipping hegemony of the American Northeast. The causes of regional decline are very similar: high energy costs, stagnating manufacturing industries, the outward flow of professionals and skilled labour to the periphery, a transfer of wealth and income via government policies (federal defence policies in the U.S., provincial resource policies in Canada). The shift in power is not as far advanced in Canada as it is below the 49th parallel—the periphery does not become the centre overnight—but it certainly has begun. That many observers in central Canada have not yet noticed it, let alone begun to mount a counterassault on the West, does not make it any less real. It merely confirms the ancient psychological tendency of individuals to ignore that which they prefer not to happen—until it has already happened.

Notes

1. C.B. Macpherson, *Democracy in Alberta: Social Credit and the Party System*, 2nd ed. (Toronto: University of Toronto Press, 1962), 21, 15-16.

2. Ibid., 219-20.

3. L. Panitch, "The Role and Nature of the Canadian State," in Panitch, ed., *The Canadian State: Political Economy and Political Power* (Toronto: University of Toronto Press, 1977), 10.

4. For an excellent critique, see A. Jackson, "Patterns of Hinterland Revolt: Alberta and Saskatchewan in the Inter-War Period," unpublished paper presented at the Canadian Political Science Association annual meetings, Fredericton, N.B., May 1977.

5. Quoted in J.R. Mallory, *Social Credit and the Federal Power* (Toronto: University of Toronto Press, 1954), 106.

6. Lorne Brown, as cited in Jackson, op. cit., 14.

7. D.H. Breen, "Calgary: The City and the Petroleum Industry since World War Two," *Urban History Review* (1978); L.G. Thomas, "The Rancher and the City: Calgary and the Cattlemen, 1883-1914," *Transactions of the Royal Society of Canada*, VI (June 1968); A.R. McCormack and I. Macpherson, eds., *Cities in the West* (Ottawa: National Museums of Canada, 1975).

8. The discussion of Lougheed's family and his career is substantially based on interviews; but see W. Stewart, "The Upwardly Mobile Mr. Lougheed," *Maclean's*, January 1972; *Edmonton Journal*, 17 May 1967; *Edmonton Journal*, 22 March 1965; R. Gwyn, "Impressions of Premier Lougheed," *Calgary Herald*, 11 February 1977; *Calgary Herald*, 3 August 1974.

9. Stewart, "The Upwardly Mobile Mr. Lougheed," op. cit.

10. Breen, op. cit., 68.

11. James H. Gray, *Troublemaker! A Personal History* (Toronto: Macmillan of Canada, 1978), 201-202 and 211.

12. Ibid., 232.

13. See M.H. Watkins, "A Staple Theory of Economic Growth," reprinted in W.T. Easterbrook and M.H. Watkins, eds., *Approaches to Canadian Economic History* (Toronto: McClelland and Stewart, 1967), 49-73.

14. *Survey of Production, 1975*, 61-202 (Ottawa: Statistics Canada).

15. J.C. Stabler, *Prairie Regional Development and Prospects* (Royal Commission on Consumer Problems and Inflation, 1968), 53. See also Hanson, *Dynamic Decade* (Toronto: McClelland and Stewart, 1958).

16. E.H. Shaffer, "The Employment Impact of Oil and Natural Gas on Alberta 1961-70," University of Alberta, Faculty of Business Administration, mimeo, 1976.

17. K.H. Norrie, "Some Comments on Prairie Economic Alienation," *Canadian Public Policy,* II, 2 (1976), 223.

18. *Estimates of Employees by Province and Industry,* 72-008 (Ottawa: Statistics Canada), February 1971.

19. D.M. Ray, et al., eds., *Canadian Urban Trends* (Toronto: Copp Clark, and Ottawa: Ministry of State for Urban Affairs, 1976), I, 18-19.

20. Gwyn, "Impressions of Peter Lougheed," op. cit.

21. On the Mannix family and Lougheed's period with the firm, see the *Edmonton Journal,* 7 December 1977; and the *Financial Post,* 26 November 1977.

22. Stewart, op. cit.

23. J. Barr, *The Dynasty* (Toronto: McClelland and Stewart, 1974), 216.

24. H. and T. Palmer, "The 1971 Election and the Fall of Social Credit," *Prairie Forum,* I, 2 (1976).

25. Cited in Barr, op. cit., 218-19.

26. P. Lougheed, "Alberta's Industrial Strategy," speech to the Calgary Chamber of Commerce, 6 September 1974.

27. Data from *Tentative "Natural Resource Revenue Plan" for the Government of the Province of Alberta,* April 1972.

28. Lougheed speech in the Alberta legislature, 12 March 1971. Text in Provincial Legislative Library, Edmonton.

29. Lougheed speech in Alberta legislature, 3 March 1969; also his address to the Empire Club, 7 May 1973: "Essentials for a New Canadian Industrial Policy."

30. *Canadian Business,* March 1978, 54 ff.

31. T. Nairn, *The Break-up of Britain: Crisis and Neo-Nationalism* (London: New Left Books, 1977), 72.

32. K. Sale, *Power Shift: The Rise of the Southern Rim and Its Challenge to the Eastern Establishment* (New York: Random House, 1975), 6.

33. H. Sutton, "Sunbelt vs. Frostbelt: A Second Civil War," *Saturday Review,* 15 April 1978, 36. See also Kevin Phillips, "The Balkanization of America," *Harper's,* May 1978.

6

AGE OF ALIENATION (1971-1991)

Introduction

After the Arab oil embargo of 1973 caused an upsurge in oil prices, a nouveau riche West developed a sense of power and influence that had not been experienced for half a century. This New West, led by provincial premiers such as Peter Lougheed of Alberta and Allan Blakeney of Saskatchewan, took on the federal government of Pierre Trudeau by emphasizing provincial rights based on provincial ownership of natural resources granted in the 1930s. The West felt its potential was being stifled.

This period was heralded by John Barr and Owen Anderson's provocative collection entitled *the unfinished revolt: Some Views on Western Independence*, which profiled the region's grievances. The themes of western alienation in the 1970s and 1980s were outlined in John Barr's contribution, "Beyond Bitterness: The New Western Radicalism," which talked about federal interference, the favouritism shown Quebec, and the legacy of economic and political inequality within Confederation. Barr contended that the new revolt was a continuation of Métis and agrarian protest. And he was not afraid to raise the spectre of western independence as a political solution.

On the other hand, an analysis of this new wave of western alienation of the 1970s by David Elton and Roger Gibbins concluded that it was not separatist in essence, but rather a search for a new federalism, in which the region would no longer be an unequal partner facing discrimination from a powerful centre. They discussed the tactics of the West's provincial premiers, whose then burgeoning economies provided an impetus for political readjustment.

The distinctive political culture of the prairies was revitalized by the new western alienation and its provincial exponents. Nelson Wiseman's essay, "The West as a Political Region," summarizes the entire history of western regionalism, examining its social and economic roots and the particular political parties and philosophies that have arisen in the West. Describing western regional discontent as "a chronic, not a temporary, condition," he concludes that it is not a danger to Canadian unity because the historic record and modern polls indicate that loyalty to Canada outweighs regional allegiance.

This does not mean that protest will not continue. In fact, one can conclude from the political observations in this chapter, that western protest is a basic feature of Canadian politics. Elton and Gibbins contend it will be with us as long as "the wheat shall grow," and Wiseman concludes that "neither a western political union within Canada nor a separatist West is on the agenda." Alienation and anger in the West have been and continue to be accepted political expressions and will most likely find political expression through one level of government or another in the future. In the 1970s protest was a provincial phenomenon. In the 1990s it may very well be channelled through a western-based federal party that seeks power in Ottawa.

Beyond Bitterness:
The New Western Radicalism

JOHN J. BARR

Reprinted from John J. Barr and Owen Anderson, eds., *the unfinished revolt: Some Views on Western Independence* (Toronto: McClelland & Stewart, 1971), 11-32, by permission of the Canadian Publishers, McClelland & Stewart, Toronto.

"Make a noise in the West and strike in the East."
—Sun Tzu, 600 B.C.

I can't really claim to come from a long line of western separatists nor does my hostility to the present role of the West in Confederation date back to when my family first lost their farm to an eastern mortgage company during the Depression—we were city people. My first involvement in "the Western question," in fact, was almost accidental.

It was several years ago, and a new Transportation Bill was before the House of Commons. The CBC called and asked if I would do something for *Viewpoint* on the West's attitudes toward the railways.

Without really thinking about it, I said yes. Then a sense of dismay began to creep in: what did I know about the railways, really? Apart from some vaguely remembered stories about discriminatory freight rates, a hoary part of western folklore, not much. So I did some reading.

What emerged from those old newspaper files activated some primordial memories. Referring to the fact that the railways held a colossal amount of downtown land in almost every major western city, a Vancouver alderman had called the CPR "the biggest slumlord in Canada." Referring to callous attempts by the CPR to abandon western passenger services—an attempt that goes on until this day, the most recent disclosure being that the CPR has forced western passengers to ride in baggage cars on old wooden benches—several public figures had reminded the CPR management of the enormous quantity of land and of the subsidies that were given to the company to enable it to build its facilities and to cover the cost of operating basic services in the public interest.

(Cleverly, the CPR spun these assets off into subsidiaries such as Cominco, Marathon Realty, and Canadian Pacific Investments, in order to claim that the railway itself was going broke trying to provide the passenger services which nobody wanted anymore. Cool.)

The CBC asked me to summarize how westerners had viewed the railways through our history. I did so, pointing out that westerners have tended to see the railways—particularly the CPR[1]—as an exploitative instrument of eastern Canadian control.

The morning after the broadcast the local CBC outlet received over a dozen wires and long distance calls requesting immediate transcripts of my talk. The requests came from a host of corporations and brokers in Toronto and Montreal as well as from federal government agencies. One query was from the CPR.

For two weeks I heard nothing more. Then one morning I received a call from the publisher of the newspaper where I then worked as an editorialist. Some gentlemen were there to see me, he said. When I came in I was introduced to five or six very beefy, red-faced, and stern-looking representatives of the Canadian Pacific Railway from Montreal. One of them, a vice-president, accompanied me to my office where he presented me with a well-documented brief, prepared by the CPR research department, which dissected my miserable talk line by line and commented on its inadequacies at some length, with suitable footnotes to this Royal Commission and that study by Professor so and so which showed conclusively in 1947 that... [2]

Hence my introduction to national discussion of one of our most cherished national institutions.

Consider, just for a moment, the paradoxes posed for a westerner by the existence of a corporation like Canadian Pacific. Here is a company, one of the largest in the world, which is both Canadian-owned and very much in the forefront of technological change—the kind of progressive, nationalistic corporation, in other words, that ought to warm the cockles of Walter Gordon's heart and produce a smile on the dour countenance of Jean-Jacques Servan-Schreiber. Canadian Pacific is "one of us." Canadian Pacific ought to make every westerner who believes in competition, technology, and Canadian control of our economy, feel warm inside. Instead, it breeds western socialists and separatists. Why?

It does this because, as anyone who has read Canadian history knows, Canadian Pacific is an eastern-controlled institution that regularly rides roughshod over western interests and western sensibilities.

It is a growing consciousness that we are powerless that lies at the heart of western unrest today. As one contributor to this book [*the unfinished revolt*] said at one of our earlier meetings—he is not a political person, and has never written anything political in his life until now—"It's beginning to dawn on me that one of the surest tests of being in a colonial relationship is that your own problems and concerns don't seem particularly important or even interesting."

And one of the surest tests of the development of an *anti* colonial movement is when people discover, as they are discovering today in the West, that their own problems *are* interesting, are certainly important to their exploiters, and are capable of being tackled.

The day I blundered into my accidental collision with the CPR, I began to realize that there are people in this country to whom it is very important that the world-view of westerners does not become more widespread—just possibly because it might endanger their interests. This book came into being because a number of westerners simultaneously agreed it was high time to draw up a manifesto of western discontents.

Not all of us agree on the nature of the problem or the solution. Everyone agrees, however, that the current status of the West in Canada is unacceptable. Perhaps the most interesting feature of our strange alliance—an alliance that stretches across many otherwise high ideological barriers—is that all of us feel there is a strong case to be made for the West, and westerners are more than capable of making it. The region's old sense of intellectual inferiority is sloughing off.

I hope the reader will now pardon me if I ramble somewhat. What I want to do is to sketch out the roots of the present discontent in the West and the factors which have brought about western alienation, and then offer a highly personal view of the alternatives that are before us.

My problem is that the growing movement of western protest is still in a relatively early phase, intellectually and developmentally. It is not a tough, mature movement with a well-defined canon of beliefs, myths, and martyrs—and perhaps this is a good thing. Those of us who are trying to pinpoint the still sometimes inchoate outline of western consciousness are in the position of a wader feeling with his toes for mussel shells on the bottom of a muddy prairie lake: the price of finding one is stirring up a lot of murk and, occasionally, slicing open your toe. But let us begin.

The Roots of the Present Discontent

Sometime in 1969 the media in this country began to awaken to the existence of "separatist" movements in western Canada. For westerners this discovery was a mixed blessing. Many of these analyses dealt exclusively with the existing western separatist movements, none of which are presently too impressive in either intellectual terms or in numbers. (In this sense, the existing western separatist organizations resemble their counterparts in Quebec in the late fifties and, like them, may well be replaced in time by quite different and more formidable movements.) Also, most of these analyses were journalistic crisis-pieces and therefore tended to look for simple single causes at the root of the agitation for change. The commonest theory at the time—and probably the theory that has gained the widest acceptance in central and eastern Canada—is the facile notion that if the western wheat surplus could simply be sold, "western bitching" would probably fade away.

Now, obviously, there is some force to this "wheat politics" interpretation of the West: western frustration at the mediocre record of federal government grain agencies in penetrating world markets is a continuing source of irritation, especially in rural areas. But the sense of western injustice transcends rural-urban categories. A sense of persecution fills the hearts of many westerners who feel the grain pinch little or not at all.

Many westerners in all four provinces feel that their legitimate economic needs and aspirations are not being looked after by the federal authorities. Wheat is only one chapter in this story. Others include the failure of the federal government to bring about a deeper penetration of the U.S. market for western oil and natural gas. Another chapter is the use by the federal government of fiscal devices, such as the change in capital cost allowances for construction of office buildings, which have had an uneven effect across the country and have worked their greatest hardship on western cities such as Vancouver, Edmonton, and Calgary.

Perhaps the most important evidence of economic callousness by the federal government towards the West was Mr. Benson's White Paper on Taxation. Certain proposed changes in the taxation system outlined in the White Paper would not only have damaged an already precarious agriculture but, more important, would have struck a serious blow at the oil industry, on which Alberta in particular depends. (In 1969, oil accounted for 30 percent of Alberta's net value of production by primary industries and 37 percent of Alberta's net government revenue.)

The thought that Mr. Benson was prepared to sabotage U.S. investment in western Canada as a part of a federal tax-reform scenario outraged westerners, not because they love Americans but because they know what the alternative to American investment is

248

for *them:* a return to economic stagnation. In the battle for tax reform, it seemed, Edgar Benson was prepared to fight to the last westerner.

In some ways, however, the federal government has injured our pride worse than our pocketbooks.

The ongoing economic problems of the West—problems such as the failure of the federal government to insure access to the Quebec and Maritime markets for Alberta oil—are the fuel on which western ire feeds. But from time to time the fires are fanned by policies and statements—sometimes patronizing, sometimes brutally callous—which remind westerners, all over again, that they do not matter much politically in this country.

These incidents are often fairly trivial, objectively speaking, but they have a hard psychological impact on a large number of people. To westerners they symbolize Canada's decision-making system. Albertans already have the federal government to thank for the fact that the vast Syncrude Ltd. project in the Athabasca oil sands has been stalled for months—a project on which the future development of Alberta's north, and the future of many Native people, depends.

One example was the creation of Channel 11 in Edmonton. For many years educational television authorities in Alberta lobbied for a VHF educational television station in Edmonton. This was possible in Edmonton, as in few other areas, because of our remoteness from American broadcast stations and a large open space on the VHF broadcast band.[3] The upshot of this lobbying was an eventual decision by federal authorities to permit a temporary half-day educational television outlet on a VHF band, operating in conjunction with a French language outlet. It was announced that at the end of a three-year period the great generosity of the federal government in allowing this educational broadcasting outlet on a VHF band would terminate, the entire station would become a French language outlet for the full broadcasting day, and the educational outlet would have to move to UHF or cablevision.

A small issue? Perhaps. But the creation of a French language television station in Edmonton—where fewer than 6 percent of the viewers list French as their mother tongue but almost 8 percent of the viewers list German and 8 percent Ukrainian as their mother tongue—says some interesting things about the determination of the federal government to push a bilingual policy on all parts of the country, regardless of local needs or circumstances. It also says some interesting things about who is influential in this country and who is not.

At about the same time, Edmontonians were reminded by the Canadian Radio-Television Commission that cablevision (CATV) was becoming a threat to Canadian content in our broadcasting industry. A combination of cablevision and close proximity to border U.S. television stations has long made it possible for residents of the heavily populated areas of Ontario, Quebec, parts of the Maritimes, and the southern mainland of British Columbia to receive a variety of American television programs. Cablevision would have made it possible for Edmonton, Saskatoon, and many of our northern and Maritime centres to receive the same variety of programs. The CRTC in its wisdom decided that this was not in the national interest and that applications for cable service to these centres would not be entertained. This was being done in order to safeguard Canadian content in broadcasting. Of course, it did nothing of the sort—inasmuch as it made no more than token noises about either reducing the American program content of *existing* CATV licences in eastern Canada or restricting the reception of U.S. channels in Canada. What it really did, in the eyes of westerners, was to sanctify and formalize into a policy the inequality that now exists in this form of broadcasting, and tell westerners that privileges long available to other Canadians would not be available to *them*.[4]

The list of minor irritations of this kind could be adumbrated at some length. But let us pass on to the largest irritant: the *stereotype* of the West propagated in the media in this country.

Now, we all know what this stereotype involves. And I do not really object to being portrayed as the Cousin Clem of Confederation—nobody is ever going to catch me with horse manure on *my* boots! But in an age when liberal scribes in Toronto and Montreal would leap in outrage at a derogatory generalization about a race or creed, it is puzzling to find them helping to perpetuate an insulting stereotype of "the average westerner" which blends equal parts of cloddishness, parochialism, and, most important, bigotry.

Let me just focus on the bigotry part: it is instructive. Everybody knows (I assume from reading *Maclean's*) that western Canada is the national home of anti-French bigotry in Canada. Western opposition to federal policy towards Quebec and French minorities outside Quebec during the 1960s was consistently taken by eastern opinion-makers to represent nothing more than western prejudice and insularity.

The facts are a little more complicated.

There unfortunately is a hard core of "pure" anti-French prejudice in parts of the West, particularly in some rural areas and among the less well-educated. This prejudice usually exists in an inverse relationship to the amount of actual contact these persons have had with French-speaking people. It is rooted in ignorance and fear of people who are different. There is this kind of prejudice in the West, but I do not know of any evidence to show that it is any more widespread in the West than in other parts of Canada.

The *major* opposition to the "pro-French" movement of national policy over the past decade came from westerners who had nothing in particular against the French—they simply resented Ottawa's imposition on their style of life and their habits when Pierre Trudeau suggested that at least a substantial minority of people outside the Ontario border should have special language facilities, special schools, and special language rights not available to other ethnic groups that were at least as numerically important in their communities as the French, if not more important. These westerners grasped a subtle sociological truth: a bilingual or multilingual society is only possible in a certain historical, social, and geographical setting. Such a setting would encourage a high degree of social and economic contact between different cultural groups; the children of all the people would be exposed to a wide range of languages in their educational setting and would be given actual rewards and encouragement to practise and develop their proficiency in these languages once outside of the school setting. These conditions are *not* present in the West, and there is no conceivable way in which they could be created, even given vast public expenditures and the largest amount of good will in the world on the part of everyone.[5]

For some reason this reality of the western position on Quebec is seldom treated in the national media; there is little inclination in the rest of Canada to ever view western motives as having any generosity in them. When Albertans propose something in a national forum it is "selfishness"; when Quebecers propose something it is "the legitimate aspirations of the people."

If some westerners are bitter about their treatment by the rest of this country they have understandable reasons for their bitterness.

But it is, in the final analysis, in the political arena that the roots of the present discontents in the West lie.

Consider the current frustration of politically conscious westerners faced with the dearth of real political choices in the current federal scene. On one side we have Pierre Trudeau—a man with an obvious "design for Canada" in his head.

Unfortunately, whether the issue has been selling western wheat, adjusting freight rates, listening to western grievances—or responding to the separatists or the FLQ—Trudeau has made it clear that he is marching to his own drummer and is not afraid of, or even particularly interested in, those who step to a different tempo. Pierre Trudeau can be respected by westerners but not supported.

And then there is Robert Stanfield, a man of fine, quiet, decent qualities—but obviously not a modern politician, and certainly not a man sufficiently sensitive to western vibrations to realize something is drastically out of whack in our federal system.

Real Caouette is an interesting regional figure, unfortunately too tied to a peculiarly Quebec protest movement, and the New Democratic Party is currently riding a wave of nationalist hysteria which has quite blinded it to the growing regionalization of the country.

This lack of real and viable political choices is a factor that deepens the discontent of westerners. For us, there do not seem to be very many channels left for legitimate political change at the national level.[6]

This feeling of bitter helplessness is deepened somewhat by the growing power of economic nationalism in our politics.

National control of our economy, we are told, is absolutely essential to control of our own political destiny as a people, and we must agree: it is very good. But, unfortunately for westerners, economic nationalism has a wealth of vivid mental associations, few of them good.

Until the Second World War, westerners had fairly broad control of the "instruments of production" in the western economy: the land and the forests. We were poor, of course, but that was because agriculture and forestry are not industries that produce broad affluence. We chafed because outside forces, particularly eastern and foreign capital, controlled our systems of credit and finance and set the market rules under which we sold the production from our lands and forests. But, far more than today, westerners owned their "industries" and they were poor, both in dollar terms and also in terms of the ability of western governments to provide the kind of services to people that make it possible for them to be fully free, i.e., educated, healthy, and mobile.

Came the war, Leduc, the prosperity of the BC lumber industry, and the discovery and production of Saskatchewan potash. Today foreigners own far more of our dollar-producing industry than before the war, agriculture has shrunk somewhat in importance, and many of the big economic decisions that affect our welfare are being made by outsiders. (Many of them always were.) Yet while we may be, theoretically, more under the thumb of outside decision makers than we were thirty years ago, we are far better off—and this translates itself not only into the kind of idle consumer luxuries social critics love to ridicule but also into the kinds of services governments must provide to help people realize their potential: education, health, income maintenance.

We may be less "free" to make collective economic decisions. In another sense we are *more* free to become educated, healthy, and mobile to realize our potential as individuals. Obviously there are several kinds of freedom, and undifferentiated attacks upon imperialist economic control of the western economy only deal with the first kind.

The average westerner is not inclined to accept all the arguments of the economic nationalists at face value, because he knows from hard experience that too often in our history economic nationalism has been used by eastern interests to maintain their control over the rest of the country. Consider Canadian Pacific. If the issue is involvement of people in every region in the decisions that affect their lives, it is no guarantee of this kind of involvement simply to assure that the governing heights of the economy are controlled by "Canadians." Would westerners have been worse off in any meaningful way to have been served by Northern Pacific rather than Canadian Pacific?

What the country must learn to understand is that, because of unique historical and geographic conditions, the West developed an economy heavily dependent upon, and vulnerable to, fluctuations in the movement of foreign capital. To start meddling with this movement without exercising the greatest possible care and consultation could spell economic disaster for western Canadians. Quite apart from the nationwide economic reverberations that such a policy would trigger, are Canadians prepared to carry this on their conscience?

The Catalysts of Change

All the factors I have described above add up to irritation and unrest, but not necessarily to that rare state of mind in which a people resolve to embrace radical change. And yet, clearly, more and more westerners are beginning to "think about the unthinkable" and examine western independence as a serious question. What has caused them to take this fateful step?

The first factor, I would suggest, is a change over the past thirty years in the way westerners live, make their livings, and interrelate with each other. The stereotyped West of grain elevators and the pleasantries of small town life is rapidly disappearing from the landscape. In terms of demographic patterns the western provinces are either urban or moving rapidly in that direction. In both Manitoba and British Columbia the vast preponderance of the population lives in one large metropolitan urban aggregation. In Alberta, Edmonton and Calgary are steadily increasing their dominance over the life of the province. Saskatchewan is also moving in this direction, albeit more slowly. The most interesting fact about urbanization in Alberta is that most of it is resulting from the internal movement of the people: the astonishing growth of Edmonton and Calgary, especially in recent years, has come more from the emigration from declining farm and small town areas within the province than it has from outside the province. The wheat crisis in Saskatchewan over the past two years has brought thousands of Saskatchewan people to Alberta and British Columbia. They too have contributed to this urban growth.

As the West has become more urban there has been an incredible proliferation and expansion of higher education facilities. All the western provinces are now generating trained and educated people to meet their internal needs. Thus we have a growing intelligentsia that has been exposed to the social sciences, to social criticism. Not for a moment would I argue that all or even most of these people, even the young people, are necessarily independentists. They are, however, increasingly sophisticated and feel that they need give nothing away to their counterparts in the rest of Canada. They want to control their own destiny, they know they are capable of controlling their own destiny, and such discontent with Confederation as they feel relates not only to economic grievances—a growing number are underemployed—but also to the contrast between their ambition and training on one hand and the role they have been assigned to play in Canada on the other. These people are not weighed down with the traditional sense of intellectual and cultural inferiority that has plagued westerners for so many generations. And, like younger and better-educated people everywhere in the Western world, they are not particularly respectful of their betters, nor patient about solutions to old grievances.

These new westerners are awakening to some heretofore unappreciated good things about western life—the clean air and water, the more civilized tempo of life, the courtesies, the absence of sham. This awakening has reduced their sense of inferiority.

⟶ Another factor that has tended to deepen western alienation is a growing realization that many of the traditional channels of communication are closed to westerners and that we have made, over the past thirty years, precious little progress in obtaining solutions for some of the West's oldest problems. The fact that excellent western artists are still unable to gain sufficient recognition from the Canadian Broadcasting Corporation programing department to reach a regular national audience has its counterpart in the political world in the fact that it is very difficult to get more than a brief and patronizing hearing for the "Case for the West" in the national newspaper chains, television networks, and—perhaps most importantly—the liberal-radical-intellectual magazines of politics and protest.[7]

But the most interesting result of all of this change and ferment is that the currents of western protest thought are starting to mature intellectually and emotionally.

This came to me in a strange way. I was reading a lengthy interview with Genevieve Bujold in *Time* and my eye stopped at the point where the interviewer asked her if she was a separatist and she replied, as if nothing in the world would be more natural, "of course."

My first reaction was resentment. Then I realized I was being silly. My first reaction told me something: close beneath the skin of every angry westerner today you will find a one-time naive Canadian nationalist who felt betrayed by the events of the 1950s and 1960s.

These westerners (their number is legion) supported John Diefenbaker for many reasons, one of the chief of which was his vision of nationalism. But the quiet revolution in Quebec and the growth of separatism confronted them with the fact that the "united Canada" they had always believed in had never really existed, save in their own heads. Thus, if it was true that Quebecers felt no deep or abiding loyalty to the larger Canada, and Ontarians were largely using Confederation to cement their economic mastery over others, it was possible, just possible, that westerners had been made the patsies of Confederation.

The reaction of people who have been made fools of is not to reexamine objectively what the world is like; it is to lash out in anger at those who have made fools of them. And so the first reaction of westerners to change in Quebec in the early 1960s was anger and fear and doubt, and that old, latent frontier desire to start over again with a clean political and social slate.

This reaction was exacerbated by the discovery that Pierre Trudeau was not particularly interested in the kind of country westerners wanted: there was no room in his bilingual, bicultural design for regional control over our own destiny.

What is starting to happen in the West now—to be sure, only in a small, but growing, part of the populace—is that people are beginning to find it possible not to be bitter about Quebec, hence about Canada.

Our resentment at Quebecers was largely unjustified: if we had paid more attention to what they had always said they wanted and less to what we hoped they wanted, we would never have assigned them a role they didn't want to play in the first place.

Why should westerners be bitter to discover that Quebecers basically want to run their own affairs and control their own destiny? Isn't that what westerners have wanted and fought for?

Now that we can at least agree on some basics about this country—something Canadians haven't been able to do for generations—perhaps we can start having an honest discussion. Perhaps we can even start liking each other and respecting each other as equals.

Now that we know there are not two solitudes in Canada, but many, we can all stop pretending that this is a united nation, or indeed a nation at all, in the modern tight-knit nation-state sense of the word. It is really a collection of fairly parochial regions held together by a tenuous sense of shared consciousness and a fear of American or other outside domination—but each area pursuing its own identity and its own sense of destiny.

What I am saying is that within a few years it will be possible for a large number of westerners to cease being bitter about Quebec's "betrayal" of the national dream in this country. It will be possible to reexamine what this country is really like and how it might be reconstituted. The time to sketch out the parameters of this discussion is now.

Equality or Independence?

I am arguing that the West today is in a condition of latent political rebellion. To understand how this is possible one must first of all contrast unrest in the West with the course of unrest in Quebec. If the shared experiences of a people are what form their collective consciousness and identity, then it is possible to understand why Quebecers and westerners both feel they have a destiny of their own, even if the two destinies differ.

Quebec has gone through distinct phases in its relationship with the rest of Canada in this century. The first phase, more or less coinciding with the reign of the Union Nationale, was a time of political stagnation but vast social and economic change—the old agrarian, church-dominated society in Quebec was breaking down under the impact of industrialization and urbanization. It was a time of resistance to change at the political level because the Union Nationale wanted to maintain its political power and this power depended upon the preservation of a Quebec society that was an imperfect realization of the dream of those who wanted an uncorrupted Christian culture with deep roots in the family and the soil.

By the late 1940s and 1950s the Union Nationale could no longer cope with the forces of economic and social change. The inward-looking isolationism of Quebec, aimed at insulating the province from the corruption of The World, slowly gave way to a newer kind of isolationism shared by those better-educated, more ambitious urban Quebecers who did not want the serenity of the village and the security of the parish, but rather a piece of the action. (This, I realize, is far from an original interpretation of modern Quebec history.) If Quebec was "Separatist" prior to the 1950s, then her separatism was a very cautious and defensive kind of feeling: a desire to be let alone. The kind of separatism that developed in the 1960s, culminating with the Parti Québécois, was a more fiery kind of modern nationalism in which the motivation was to gain control of Quebec's destiny. By the late 1960s it was becoming obvious that Quebecers could go only so far within Confederation towards being *maitre chez nous*.

The exploding higher-education system in Quebec was turning out a turbulent and ambitious new intelligentsia and this class, long the social base of the serious separatist movements, saw its own interests tied in deeply with the jobs and opportunities—especially in the government—that would become available in a nationalist independent State.

There are a number of parallels between this evolution and the evolution of western unrest.

The first important experience that shaped the consciousness of the West was the Frontier: the people who came to the West were the dissatisfied, the restless, the nonconformists, the ambitious young who felt cramped in the traditional societies, whether in Galicia or Upper Canada.

The most important single feature of the Frontier was its loneliness and isolation. It was not only possible for people to join together for mutual protection, and innovate, it was absolutely necessary; the rigours of the climate dictated it. This, remember, was the last Frontier in North America, colder, windier, drier, vaster than the American West; until almost the turn of the century by-passed by the great waves of agricultural settlement because it was considered too inhospitable to man.[8]

In the open fields and in the minds of men there was, and is, more room in the West. Hence the proliferation of cults, political protest movements, religious sects. Most of the interesting and significant political innovation in Canada has begun in the West. Why? In contrast to Quebec, Ontario, and the Maritimes, the West is not borne down by the weight of too many traditions. Men brought with them to the West their own precedents and examples, their own culture; but in the cold fresh air of the Frontier it was experiment and experience that shaped our institutions. Thus, while religion played a vital part in shaping the consciousness of both Quebec and the West, in Quebec it was The Church; in the West, it was the churches.

Westerners and Quebecers have had some common experiences with Canada. The most obvious was their common experience of Ontario. Both groups know what it is like to be sneered at and viewed as bumpkins. The prevailing stereotype of the Québécois and the westerner has some common traits (or at least it had): both are humble, loyal, charming in a folksy sort of way, superstitious, and somewhat ignorant. But while the stereotype of Quebec has, it seems, faded somewhat in Ontario, certain stereotypes of the West are still held. One of them is the image of a sea of blowing short grass between the Lakehead and Vancouver, punctuated by some interesting characters and grain elevators.

The most alarming thing about the West's historical experience for the Canadian centralist has been the tendency of westerners to think of history in radical terms, i.e., as something to be seized and shaped by free men. Because he typified this attitude, Louis Riel was the first westerner. Confronted with a distant, arrogant, and unheeding government and the crisis of his people, he took history into his own hands. Like those westerners—Aberhart, Woodsworth—who later acted in a similar way, Riel was not out-argued, he was simply out-gunned.

The rise of the Progressives after the First World War, and of the CCF and Social Credit during the Depression proved that the West was a fertile seed bed for a deeply humanist view of life and change. All three had their roots in distinctly western conditions and raised deeply challenging questions about the organization of power and privilege in Canada. All three were met with conniving. The Progressives were very coolly, and very efficiently, seduced. The Socreds were beaten back with constitutional coercion. The most important questions that were raised by Social Credit and the CCF were never answered—they were either co-opted by establishment parties ("we just had this brilliant idea . . . family allowances!!") or shelved by the Second World War.

Today, a sense of down-troddenness is a central part of the western folklore. This sense of injustice has been communicated from the older generation of the 1930s to its children. It has been revivified and sharpened by the frustrations and irritations all westerners have encountered in recent times. Westerners share a long heritage of revolt against injustice. The protest movements in the 1920s and 1930s showed that economic crisis could eat quickly into westerners' sense of loyalty to the nation by outraging their sense of fairness and equity. Even a perceptive eastern journalist like Peter Desbarats therefore errs when he draws this kind of distinction between Quebec separatism and the regionalism of other parts of Canada:

> If Manitoba today were confronted with a choice, if it could be proved beyond doubt that the national good demands some sacrifice of important Manitoba interests, Manitoba would accept the sacrifice. So would Newfoundland or the Maritime Provinces, partly for financial reasons but mainly because there is a common belief that independence is impractical and that federation with some continental power is essential. Even British Columbia . . . subscribes to primacy of national interest . . . but separatism in Quebec . . . is far removed from regionalism. It is an authentic nationalism warring continually in the heart of almost every French-Canadian with his sense of loyalty to the Canadian nation.[9]

This same tension between national loyalties and regional loyalties exists in the West today and, while it is less agonizing than Quebec's, the difference is less than Desbarats might think.

This is what we mean by "the unfinished revolt." Twice before—in the North-West and during the Depression—the West rebelled against the status quo and seriously challenged its role in Canada. Both times, this rebellion produced short-term gains but failed to realize its ultimate objective—a radically reordered Confederation. Today, the basic resentments that in earlier times burst into flame are growing again.

This is political raw material of the most combustible kind. It could erupt into a new regional political party like the Ralliement Creditiste; it could become the basis for a stunning comeback by the federal Tories, provided they were able to find a leader capable of getting the western pulse; it could simply smoulder, awaiting a spark. Given a prolonged regional recession or a lengthy political crisis at the national level, it could burst into a nationalist flame of its own.

At any given point in time during "normal" conditions, the notion of an independent West is somewhat unreal. In normal times, every westerner must wrestle with a deep suspicion that western independence is really too trivial a problem, measured first against the problems of Canada and second against the very marginal role that Canada plays in the modern world. Does it really *matter* what happens to five and one-half million people west of the Lakehead?

It clearly matters less than whether an American civil war spills across our border or nuclear war breaks out or we have another Depression. And if Canada is destined for eventual absorption by the United States, what difference does it make whether we negotiate the final surrender as one nation or several?

But we must insist upon our right, indeed our responsibility as free men and women, to try to shape our own destiny. And the good things the West does represent deserve to be preserved in some kind of political order. Westerners are therefore confronted with a "lesser of evils" dilemma.

The lack of "positive" attributes of Canadian culture, other than those qualities we do not share with Americans, seems less of a problem for Canadian writers and intellectuals than it did ten years ago: our culture may be less spectacular than America's, but it is obviously freer and more humane. Confronted with a choice between attempting to preserve those differences through a united Canada or allowing the present injustice under which the West labours to lead us into seeking western independence, the onus lies upon the western critic to show that remaining within Canada is the greater evil. I personally doubt that it is.

Conscientious westerners must therefore try to make Canada work, but in a more just fashion. If, however, it becomes obvious that Canada is not a viable proposition politically, or if the present injustice deepens, I see no very persuasive moral argument for the West trying to integrate itself into a burning building.

Therefore:

1. We must strive for a more justly constituted Canada;

2. If Canada loses her political viability, the West must strike out against the odds to try and build an independent State in this corner of North America.

How would a more just Canada be constituted? It would begin by recognizing John Calhoun's great insight into the weakness of all federative states that delegate powers to a central authority—namely, that the regions must then have institutional safeguards against the unfair exercise of the central power by evanescent majorities.

Calhoun confronted the drive of northern manufacturers to impose a punitive tariff on southern agriculture in the United States in 1832. Striking out at this proposed tariff, which was designed to benefit northern manufacturers and which clearly worked to the detriment of southern agriculture, he wrote:

> There are two different modes in which the sense of the community may be taken; one, simply by the right of suffrage, unaided; the other, by the right to a proper organism. Each collects the sense of the majority. But one regards numbers only, and considers the whole community as a unit, having but one common interest throughout; and collects the sense of the great number of the whole, as that of the community. The other, on the contrary, regards interests as well as numbers—considering the community as made up of different and conflicting interests, as far as the action of the Government is concerned; and takes the sense of each, through its majority or appropriate organism, and the united sense of all, as the sense of the entire community. The former of these I shall call the numerical or absolute majority; and the latter, the concurrent or constitutional majority.[10]

This is what Riel revolted against in the very beginning: a decision-making system in which the naked power of majorities determined all. In a democracy built on the concept of concurrent majorities decisions on national policy would not be based simply on a count of heads, which ultimately comes down to a calculation of who is stronger. Instead there would be a balancing and compromising of interests, especially regional interests. Such a balancing would lead to a conviction in all parts of Canada that the rights of people in *each* region had been respected.

The surest way of insuring this kind of democracy in Canada is to reduce the power of the central government to dictate to the regions or provinces.

If westerners had the necessary constitutional authority and power to protect their vital interests, they would be far less susceptible to those who whisper that we should strike out on our own.

What would such a Canada look like?

I am not a constitutional theorist and this is not the place to sketch out a detailed constitutional blueprint. I would suggest, however, that the New Confederation would have several salient features:

First, there would be some form of institutional safeguard for regional prerogatives—perhaps a reformed senior chamber for the House of Commons, electing an equal number of representatives from each region of the country, to counterbalance representation by population.

Second, there would be a nationwide guaranteed income plan, financed by the federal government, to replace the present ineffective patchwork-quilt of regional incentives and regional development programs. The plan would create a modest level of guaranteed income, sufficient to enable one to live at a spartan but healthy level. Beyond that the problem of "regional inequality" would be left to the working of the free market and stepped-up programs of manpower retraining and mobility grants by the federal government.

Third, there would be a reformed judiciary with provision for regional nominations. Such a judiciary would be more capable of interpreting the jurisdiction of the federal and provincial authorities fairly and credibly.

Last, there would be a modification in the distribution of constitutional powers to prevent an excessive accumulation of power by the federal government. The central clause in a revised constitution would limit the spending by the federal government to a certain percentage of the gross national product. This would restrain any temptation to move into too many areas and, more importantly, compel the federal authorities to periodically reexamine their spending priorities in light of available funds. It would also ease the growing pressure on the provincial authorities, who are saddled with some of the most expensive government responsibilities—particularly education and health—but who have too little access to direct taxation. The present "Peace, Order and Good Government" clause of the BNA Act, which assigns all residual powers to the federal government, would, finally, be replaced with a clause designating all residual powers to the regions or provinces.

There are two arguments against this proposal: the first, which Pierre Trudeau mounted in 1968 against "special status" for Quebec, that too much devolution of power will destroy Canada by weakening vital central powers; the second, mounted by Peter Boothroyd in *the unfinished revolt: Some Views on Western Independence*, that regionalization will victimize the poor and speed up American conquest of Canada.

To those who raise the charge that decentralization will destroy Canada by weakening vital central powers, I reply that *not* to decentralize these powers will destroy Canada more surely—because it is anger at the injustices the present system has perpetrated upon people in the regions that is tearing this country apart.

To those who charge that regionalization will not solve the problem of powerlessness—that while powerlessness is a serious moral problem in Canada, it is a class and not a regional phenomenon—I reply that I do not underestimate this point. I would only point out that *all* kinds of powerlessness are morally important. The problem of regional powerlessness is more neglected today than other kinds.

We could, surely, solve the class powerlessness problem by some kind of socialist restructuring of society and still fail to solve the problem of regional powerlessness. I am no more anxious to be ruled by the Ontario Federation of Labour than by the Ontario Association of Manufacturers.

I would go further and argue that political centralization in Canada actually *reinforces* the tendency of the powerful in our society to concentrate their power and ignore those who are powerless in the locales. For a variety of reasons, provincial governments in the West have often been more sympathetic and responsive to the needs of Native people, for example, than the federal government. Alberta–a "free enterprise" province–had a superb community development program and special housing programs for the aged long before they were even thought of at the federal level. Alberta and Saskatchewan were the first two provinces in Canada with medicare programs, even before the federal government got into the act. One reason for this is likely the fact that the populist protest movements which came out of the Canadian West were somewhat to the left of their American counterparts.[11]

Let us assume that our drive for a more justly constituted Canada is thwarted, or that Canada begins to disintegrate politically, beginning with Quebec–or both. What then?

The question of an independent West would then have to be squarely confronted.

Would a thinly spread-out, thousand-mile-wide entity with fewer than six million people be politically viable on the same continent as the United States? (The answer, I expect, is less obvious than it may first seem. Such a nation would lack credibility–but then so does Canada; and so does Israel. Severance from Canada might, by the very act of reducing western numbers, heighten the region's "siege consciousness" and thus our unity and determination to survive. It is this very kind of siege consciousness–this sense of being surrounded by more than two hundred million aliens–that has made it possible for Quebec to retain so much of her identity. Whether, in the long run, *any* effective resistance to continentalism is possible–by either Quebec or the West–is a moot point.)

Would the four western provinces unite, placing their hopes on their shared history, or would British Columbia elect to go it alone?

Should we talk about a common market relationship with Ontario, or would we be better to go it entirely by ourselves?

Political questions aside, could the economic base in the four western provinces sustain independence?

These questions cannot yet be answered. Put so baldly, they even sound bizarre. And of course they are–for the moment. They are not "serious" questions as this is being written.

But we live in very fluid times. Two days before the act, who anticipated the upsurge of FLQ terrorism, with its incalculable consequences for Canada? I am haunted by the fear that Canada may rupture more suddenly than anyone now thinks possible, forcing us to ask these questions, and answer them with unseemly haste. Surely it makes sense to begin turning them over in our minds now, while we still have time to make sense of them.

If there is a message, it is that the Canadian Dream is in far more trouble than many Canadians–especially in Ontario, the centre of Canadian opinion making–realize.

This book probably underplays the real bitterness that westerners have often felt in past, and still frequently feel today, towards their role in Canada. For more than two generations it has not been possible to get a fair hearing in this country for the western

259

case; the general reaction of the national media has been the kind of sneering viciousness displayed by Douglas Fisher and Harry Crowe in their column in the Toronto *Telegram* during the last Tory leadership convention, when they characterized westerners as the most depraved and mean-spirited reactionaries in the nation. In a nation, as in a marriage, there are some things said which can never be forgotten or forgiven.

The deepness of this bitterness is attested to by the fact that it remains today, when the worst and most blatant excesses that provoked it are gone. I wasn't even born when the dark days of the 1930s led to those terrible times when thousands of men and women were driven from their farms by the mortgage companies, a generation of our youth spent their best years riding the rails and waiting in soup lines, and the cries of human needs were met with constitutional buck-passing and pious reminders that the rich, too, were forbidden to sleep under bridges. I wasn't there, but I know the ineradicable scars they left on the souls of the people of my father's generation.

But the time for bitterness is past. Canada is in deep trouble today and may well founder from the consequences of past acts. This is not something I celebrate: Canada has not been a bad country for me and I would not greet her death with celebration. It is, alas, a country torn by strong regional loyalties—so torn by them, in fact, that those in each region are forced by the rules of the national power-game to fight as hard as they can for the interests of their own area. Those who do not fight go to the wall.

This essay is written in defence of the interests of a neglected region in this country. If, by pressure of circumstances, this region were forced to seek its own political identity, there would be no room for bitterness—only sadness.

Notes

1. For the record, I have found westerners less hostile to Canadian National. Whether this is because of its superior passenger services or something else, I don't know. It is a matter of record, however, that in its dealings with Alberta cities attempting to redevelop downtown railway lands, CN has been much fairer and more flexible than Canadian Pacific.

2. From my standpoint, the match was at best a draw; at worst, a TKO for the Research Department.

3. The importance of VHF versus UHF broadcasting on educational television is that a vast majority of TV receivers now in use can receive VHF; only a much smaller and slowly growing proportion are capable of receiving UHF.

4. Since the initial CRTC decision the commission has announced a slight modification of this principle, which will allow residents of Edmonton, Saskatoon, and other centres to receive a nominal amount of cross-border U.S. broadcasting via cablevision.

5. My own personal feeling is that I admire the French deeply and I am frequently ashamed of my own inability to speak French. Our French courses in public schools have created little proficiency in the language and a great deal of disdain for it. This is tragic. If we could do our national history over again I would opt for a multilingual education beginning in grade one for everyone in the country. A true multilingual nation would be a joy, full of human variety and colour. We could have used the French culture out West to break down the dour Scottish domination of our ethos. But today it is too late. A minority will learn French voluntarily, as a labour of love; a few will learn for business or career reasons. But this number will always be small as a percentage of our total population, and little that the government can do by way of financing special schools or other programs will enlarge it significantly.

6. But the reader may ask: why cannot the West emulate Quebec and send "three wise men" to Ottawa to take over the leadership of an existing national party and equip it with a new set of priorities? There are two obvious reasons why "working through existing channels" in this way

is unrealistic at the present time: one, we don't have a Pierre Trudeau, or even a Jean Marchand, to send; two, unlike Quebecers, westerners do not have a tradition of acting in concert politically, three provinces together to achieve common ends. Perhaps, it is the individualism of the frontier, or what is left of it. In any case, even *if* the three prairie provinces could act in concert at the federal level, they lack the sheer *numbers* to have enough impact.

7. This may have something to do with the fact that our major communications networks are run from the East and, economically, for the East. In the magazine field, Peter Gzowski made a noble attempt to get *Maclean's* out of its Toronto ghetto and for a while succeeded, before he left. The phenomenon with which he wrestled was the West as a quaint land of political eccentrics—with the *Maclean's-Chatelaine* ploy of the late 1960s, the put-on (Edmonton as the home of a sensational culture boomlet). The first was insulting, the second was patronizing; neither was just.

8. The first thing my grandfather did on his first return to Ontario from the West in 1912 was to dig up and bring back to Edmonton some sugar maples. Every spring for several years, he planted them out and each winter the blizzards killed them back to the ground. Finally, he surrendered to the realization that the West is different. The sugar maple—our national tree—won't grow here. Symbolic?

9. Peter Desbarats, *The State of Quebec: A Journalist's View of the Quiet Revolution* (Toronto: McClelland & Stewart, 1965), 178–79.

10. From a debating standpoint I regret having to call upon John Calhoun for support because, although his argument has great power, his solution—interposition of local authority—was untenable and he eventually became a defender of slavery. I hope the critical reader will resist the temptation to conclude that western radicals believe in slavery. Actually, they believe in abolition.

11. This is one reason American right-wing radicalism has never managed to take root in the Canadian West. There have always been more public social services programs north of the border and less of an ideological obsession with "free-enterprise."

Western Alienation and Political Culture

DAVID ELTON AND ROGER GIBBINS

Reprinted with deletions from Richard Shultz, Orest M. Kruhlak, John C. Terry, eds., *The Canadian Political Process*, 3rd ed. (Toronto: Holt, Rinehart and Winston, 1979), 82–97, by permission of the authors.

The existence of strong regional identities was given special recognition and enshrined in Canada's constitution by the Fathers of Confederation through the establishment of a federal system of government. This political action was taken in response to the geographical, economic, and social realities of Canada as they existed at the time of Confederation. Today, the impact of these same factors on Canadian politics is no less significant, particularly in western Canada. Physical isolation from the Canadian heartland, the wheat economy, the unique ethnic composition and immigrant history of the population, and the frontier experience of prairie settlement have set western Canada apart and created a regional unit with interests and needs in direct opposition to those of central Canada. Regional distinctiveness, regional integration, and a sense of threatened regional self-interest have in turn forged a unique regional political consciousness. This "moulding influence of plains geography and plains economy"[1] has generated a political culture in western Canada that stands apart from the broader political culture of English Canada.

The political distinctiveness of western Canada is attested to by its history of political radicalism and revolt. Beginning in 1921, large numbers of prairie voters turned their backs on the traditional political parties rooted in central Canada and created in their place the Progressive Party of Canada, the United Farmers of Alberta, the Social Credit Party, the Co-operative Commonwealth Federation, the Manitoba Progressive movement, and other political organizations. Events and movements outside electoral politics, such as the Winnipeg General Strike, the Social Gospel, and the On-to-Ottawa Trek, offer further evidence of a regionally distinctive political style and outlook.

The impact of these regionally based political movements and their control of provincial governments have led many scholars to examine the regional orientation of Canadians in detail, not only from a legal, geographical, or economic point of view but also from a cultural perspective.[2] For example, a group of political scientists undertook a national public-opinion study shortly after the 1974 general election—a study that, among other things, identified the degree of provincial and regional orientation among Canadians.[3] In an article entitled "Public Orientation to Regions and Provinces," Jon Pammett examined the data generated in this study and concluded that "many Canadians are used to thinking of Canada in terms of its component parts, its regions."[4]

More specifically, Pammett concluded that western Canadians are much more likely to think of Canada in regional terms than are other Canadians and that they feel their provincial governments are more important in affecting their lives than is their national government.[5] The findings of this study support the hypothesis that a regionally distinctive political culture still exists in western Canada.

It is our contention that the core of this western political culture is alienation. Although western alienation has its roots in an agrarian society that has by and large disappeared, the economic, political, and partisan unrest of the past is sustained by contemporary grievances, some of which reach back into the past and some of which are more recent in origin. Moreover, the coals of western alienation are regularly fanned by provincial politicians in the West, who find that to do so is very much to their electoral advantage.

Our task in this article is fourfold. First, we will discuss the contemporary nature of western alienation and will provide some empirical evidence garnered from survey research carried out in Alberta. Second, we will explore the historical roots of western alienation, its contemporary sources of sustenance, and the continuity between the two. Third, we will examine the role played by electoral politics in the maintenance and promotion of western alienation. Finally, we will examine the place of western alienation within the broader Canadian political culture. The nub of our argument will be that western alienation represents a demand for greater inclusion in, rather than withdrawal from, the broader Canadian society and thus that this alienation is radically different in nature from contemporary nationalist movements in Quebec.

Contemporary Western Alienation

Western alienation has little in common with more general forms of political alienation.[6] It does not reflect apathy, withdrawal, or estrangement from the polity *per se;* provincial governments have been enthusiastically supported by their electorates. Neither is contemporary western alienation associated with the usual clientele of alienation—the dispossessed, the poor, the economically and socially marginal. If anything, the public articulators of western alienation have tended to be wealthy and successful individuals. In a *Saturday Night* article on "the new Albertans," Christina Newman has neatly captured the creed of such individuals: "What Albertans want is to control their own destiny and to be recognized for what they are—not seen as imitators of Texans or enviers of easterners, not as loudmouths, rednecks, soreheads, or cowboys but as hard working, urban-dwelling, richly deserving, sweetly reasonable S.O.B.'s."[7] The sense of meaninglessness often associated with political alienation is also missing from western alienation; on the prairies the political decisions of the national government are seen as all too predictable, almost conspiratorial. Finally, the very pervasiveness of western alienation within the prairie population mitigates against the linking of western alienation with psychological traits or personality needs. The acquisition by individuals of orientations as widely shared as western alienation is more readily accounted for by models of social learning and socialization than by psychological explanations.

For these and other reasons, then, it is inappropriate to conceptualize western alienation as a particular form of a more universal phenomenon, political alienation. Rather, western alienation is a regional political ideology of discontent. By this we mean that western alienation embodies a socially shared set of political beliefs—a set with some degree of cultural expression and intellectual articulation, with a recognized history and constituency, and with recognized proponents and representatives. Western alienation is thus a central part of the political culture of the Canadian West.

The beliefs and grievances woven into the fabric of western alienation have not remained constant over time. There has been, for example, a shift away from earlier agricultural issues, these having been resolved, ameliorated, or reduced to a position of marginal importance by the numerically dominant urban population of western Canada. Within the last decade there has also been a growing feeling that Quebec and its concerns have come to play too large a role in national politics and that this role is being played directly at the expense of western Canada. Certain of the grievances harboured by the West have not changed with time, however—specifically, that western Canada is consistently outgunned in national politics and that as a consequence the region has been economically exploited by central Canada.

A number of studies done in Alberta have measured the components of western alienation and the degree to which it characterizes the Alberta electorate.[8] In 1976 Gibbins conducted a province-wide survey of the Alberta electorate. Researchers visited the homes of 502 randomly selected adults and presented a battery of statements commonly heard in western Canada.[9] The intention was to determine the extent to which these statements tapped the disposition of respondents, so the respondents were asked to state the degree to which they agreed or disagreed with each of the statements presented in table 1. As the table makes abundantly clear, western alienation was not a marginal disposition in the Alberta population of 1976...

Table 1

Western Alienation in Alberta, 1976

	Percent of Sample	
	Agreeing	Disagreeing
	Strongly or	Strongly or
Statement	Moderately	Moderately
The economic policies of the federal government seem to help Quebec and Ontario at the expense of Alberta.	73.7	9.6
Because the political parties depend upon Quebec and Ontario for most of their votes, Alberta usually gets ignored in national politics.	77.1	13.9
During the past few years the federal government has made a genuine effort to overcome problems of economic discrimination against Alberta.	32.1	45.0
In many ways Alberta has more in common with the western United States than it does with eastern Canada.	62.5	18.9
Most eastern Canadians seem to feel that Canada ends at the Great Lakes.	64.5	16.3
Alberta benefits as much from the industries of the East as eastern Canada benefits from Alberta's natural resources such as oil.	23.9	62.7
It often seems that Alberta politicians are not taken seriously in the East.	71.3	13.5

If one part of Canada suffers we all suffer, and if one region prospers, we all share in the prosperity.	32.1	56.8
Albertans have to unite behind one party to get anything out of Ottawa.	63.9	18.3

Number of respondents=502.

To show that western alienation exists, and that indeed it is a pervasive element of the western Canadian political culture, is not to explain why it exists. To find this explanation we must examine the historical roots of western alienation, learn what nourishes it now, and explore the connection between the two.

The Economic Background of Western Alienation

Throughout the history of the West there has been a widespread belief that the resource-rich prairies were being exploited by central Canada, and the imagery evoked by former Alberta Premier Harry Strom still strikes a deep resonance within the prairie region:

> We have always had a sense of economic exploitation. This notion has marked all political parties in the West. The cartoon that has captured these sentiments is one of a large cow standing on a map of Canada munching grass in Alberta and Saskatchewan with milk pouring from a bulging udder into the large buckets in Ontario.[10]

Western Canadian historians have documented time and again the manner in which central Canadian business interests have, with the help of the national government, exploited the West at the expense of the resident regional population.[11] The problems that each province has had to deal with can be traced to the development in the 1870s of what has become known as John A. Macdonald's National Policy.[12] The three main elements of this policy were:

> 1. the encouragement of immigration through the development of national land-settlement policies;
> 2. the development of a national transportation system to facilitate the development of the West and aid eastern industrial development; and
> 3. the establishment of high tariffs to encourage the development of industry that would provide jobs for Canadians and generate profits for Canadian entrepreneurs.

The second two elements of this policy are by and large still in effect today and make up the primary economic issues that currently generate western discontent with Confederation.

From the day the first Canadian Pacific Railway freight rate schedule was published in 1883 there has been evidence of deliberate discrimination against the West.[13] Western interest groups, members of Parliament, and provincial governments have denounced this discrimination, even taken drastic and unilateral action in defiance of national policy, but have never been able to rectify the situation. Federal-government spokespersons, on the other hand, have used the principle of "fair discrimination" to justify the freight rate structure. In areas where there are competing transportation facilities, such as water transportation, rail freight rates are set at a competitive level, even if the rates are so low as to result in an operating loss. Operational losses in competitive areas, or on uneconomical sections of the railroad such as those bridging

265

the Canadian shield, are recouped through the charging of higher rates where there is no competition. Because of the monopoly that railroads have on the shipment of commodities both to and from the prairie region, prairie residents have continually found themselves at the very apex of Canada's freight rate structure. Victoria and Vancouver residents have suffered less from this policy because the alternative of water transportation through the Panama Canal forces the railroads to fix lower rates on shipments from central Canada to West-Coast ports.

There was some modification of the freight rate structure around the turn of the century, the most important development being a federal-government subsidy for the building of a line through the Crow's Nest Pass. In response to this subsidy, the CPR agreed in 1897 to reduce its western freight rates on a wide range of products, creating what has become known as the Crow's Nest Pass Agreement. The significance of the Crow's Nest Pass Agreement did not become apparent until after World War I, when by Order in Council agreement was set aside to permit railroads to increase their rates. This action was one of the main catalysts of the election of Progressive Party candidates across the West and the creation of a minority government in Ottawa. In his efforts to maintain the support of the Progressives after the 1921 election, Prime Minister Mackenzie King struck a compromise with the prairie MPs by restoring the original Crow's Nest rates for unprocessed cereal grains. This action was welcomed by western Canadians and provided considerable relief to farmers in the 1920s. Unfortunately, however, the Crow's Nest Pass rates have caused problems in other areas of the western Canadian economy.

Western Canada's present-day grain farmers jealously guard the lowest single transportation rate on any commodity in North America—the statutory rates on unprocessed grain fixed by the Crow's Nest Pass Agreement. In partial compensation for the loss incurred as a result of this anomaly, the railways have over the years sought and received across-the-board rate increases on all other types of commodities. One of the most frustrating aspects of these increases to western Canadians is that, although on the surface horizontal rate increases seem equitable, in practice they further exacerbate the "fair discrimination" policy on all processed grain and nongrain commodities. For example, if a 25 percent increase is granted on a commodity that costs 20 cents per hundredweight in central Canada and 40 cents per hundredweight in the West, then the increase in the transportation cost of that commodity in the central region will be 5 cents, compared with a 10-cent increase in the western region. For manufacturing companies in the West, a difference of this magnitude often means an inability to compete in the marketplace with eastern manufacturers. The long, drawn out hearings held by the Canadian Transportation Commission in the mid-1970s pertaining to the rapeseed-crushing industry concerned this very issue.

As long as western Canada's economy was based primarily on the production of unprocessed grain, the national transportation policy was tolerable. The higher costs of shipping processed goods to and from the region were compensated for by the maintenance of the Crow's Nest Pass rates. However, as urbanization increased and new primary and secondary industries sought to locate in the West, the discriminatory rate structure became one of the major obstacles to the success of attempts by local and provincial governments to encourage economic growth through diversification. The rate-structure issue has become particularly troublesome in the 1970s. At the Western Economic Opportunities Conference in 1973, proposals were made by the four western provinces to amend the national transportation act and establish an equitable pricing technique, but to date there have been no major changes in the "fair discrimination" policy. Peter Lougheed's statement to WEOC in 1973 is still valid today: "In [the four western premiers'] judgment the greatest single impediment standing in the way of the development of western Canada's full potential is transportation freight rates which discriminate against the West."[14]

Western Canada's concern over tariff policy is just as deep-rooted and ongoing as the freight-rate issue. Tariffs on imported goods have aided the industrialization of central Canada and in so doing have promoted both jobs and profits. The same tariffs, however, have forced western Canadians, and indeed all Canadians, to pay a higher price for imported goods. Such higher prices are particularly irksome in western Canada, however, because the compensatory jobs and profits created by the tariffs have not flowed to the West in any proportionate manner and because western Canadian prices have already been inflated by higher transportation costs. If the National Policy had been equitable in the regional allocation of costs and benefits, there would have been little complaint from western Canada. But, because the benefits flowed to central Canada and the costs to the West, the picture is quite different.

Western grievances regarding bilateral trade are easily understood. At present Canada allows processed beef into the country duty-free, yet western packing plants cannot ship customer-ready cuts of beef into the Pacific Northwest because of the competitive disadvantage caused by a 10-cent U.S. import duty. A similar situation exists regarding rapeseed oil. Access to the Pacific Northwest markets for Alberta's petrochemicals is also effectively blocked due to protective U.S. tariffs. Western elites, led at present by Alberta's Premier Lougheed, continue to argue that, unless action is taken to reduce these trade barriers, the development of viable secondary industry in the West will not take place.

In 1973 the federal government denied the western premiers' request that they be allowed to send observers to the international meeting in Geneva on the negotiation of a new General Agreement on Trade and Tariffs (GATT). Alberta's premier nonetheless went to Geneva in 1977, with the blessings of his fellow western premiers, to discuss trade and tariff policy with Canada's negotiators. In addition, western spokespersons have for a number of years attempted to encourage the development of bilateral agreements with the United States and spent considerable time and effort meeting with both Canadian and U.S officials in the hope of generating support for freer trade relations between the two countries. At the May 1977 annual meeting of the four western premiers in Brandon, Manitoba, the provinces released a 235-page report prepared by their Departments of Industry that identified the precarious position of industry in the West.[15] A multitude of products were discussed, including metals, chemical products, wood and paper, processed agricultural commodities, and agricultural equipment. The underlying argument presented in the document was that western Canada would benefit considerably from the initiation by Canada of a freer trade policy, particularly in the area of manufactured goods.

As the western Canadian economy has expanded and diversified beyond an agricultural base, many historical grievances—such as those over freight rates—have persisted. In addition, as the resource base of the prairie economy has spread from the soil itself to the oil, natural gas, potash, and mineral wealth lying beneath it, new grievances have emerged. Conflicts between Alberta and Ottawa over the price and marketing of energy resources have become legendary, and Saskatchewan has run up against national institutions, most notably the Supreme Court, in its development of the potash and petroleum industry. More generally, 1974 federal-government changes in the tax position of resource companies, and the payment of provincial royalties thereby, played a major role in fanning the coals of western alienation.

Economically, western Canada has suffered from both discriminatory and nondiscriminatory national policies. Speaking to the Toronto Canadian Club in 1977, Saskatchewan Premier Allan Blakeney pointed out that the natural resources regulated by the federal government are those located in western Canada. In a speech worth quoting at length, he enunciated a commonly held western perspective:

> We in the West find it passing strange that the national interest emerges only when we are talking about Western *resources* or Eastern *benefits*. If oil, why not iron ore and steel products? If natural gas, why not copper? If uranium—and we in Saskatchewan may well be Canada's biggest uranium producer in a few years—if uranium, why not nickel?
>
> And, to add insult to injury, we in the West are now being told by the Federal Minister of Transport that the national interest demands a rail transportation policy in which the user pays the full cost. What user will pay the most under that kind of system? Land-locked Saskatchewan. Air transport is subsidized. The Seaway runs monumental deficits. Our ports are all subsidized. Truck transportation is subsidized by many provincial highway systems in Canada. But in rail transportation—the one on which we depend—we are told that the user must pay.[16]

Unfortunately, there are no simple reparations available for the economic grievances of western Canada. Admittedly, the western Canadian economy has been booming in recent years, and there have been some major accommodations between Ottawa and the western provinces. Examples are the federal government's participation in the Syncrude tar sands development in northern Alberta, the federal tax breaks received by Syncrude, and the relatively amicable agreements between Ottawa and Edmonton on increases in the price of energy resources during the period 1975 to mid-1978. Economic prosperity has only strengthened political discontent, however, as western Canadians search fruitlessly for both a degree of political power commensurate with their new economic strength and a solution to seemingly intractable economic problems.

There is little likelihood that economic friction between the West and the national government will ever be eliminated. Pessimism on this account springs from the fact that western Canada remains a thinly populated economic hinterland within both the Canadian and North American market economies. As economist Kenneth Norrie has pointed out, "many of the Prairie grievances must be interpreted as dissatisfaction with a market economy rather than with discriminatory policies of the federal government."[17] Thus, the West's position on the economic periphery continues to generate regional grievances—grievances that are directed at the national government if only for want of a better target.

To extend Norrie's argument, the abolition of discriminatory national policies alone will not fundamentally alter the economic position of western Canada. What is required is positive national government intervention in the market economy—promotion, through public policy, of western economic goals that cannot be met by a free-market company. Given the relative weakness of western Canada in national politics, however, the prospects of this intervention's happening are remote. Here it must be remembered that Ontario alone contains almost twice the population of the three prairie provinces combined. Thus, even the removal of discriminatory national policies seems a distant prospect at best.

The economic fate of western Canada has always depended on forces external to the region or beyond the control of western Canadians. Some of these, such as drought, frost, and the state of foreign markets, can only be borne with stoicism and a faith that next year things will be better.[18] However, a national government of which western Canadians have been a part but never the master has been more difficult to tolerate. The control by outsiders of public policies vital to the West has given rise to anticolonialism as a major thread in the fabric of western alienation. The fact that the major levers of public policy in such matters as international trade, tariffs, and transportation rest outside the prairies, and largely in the hands of Ontario and Quebec, has been particularly aggravating for provincial leaders in the West. David Smith's discussion of Premier Ross Thatcher's problems leading up to the 1971 Saskatchewan provincial election illustrates the point:

> Frustration was all the greater because the problems demonstrated what had always been true of Saskatchewan's economy but had frequently been ignored by advocates of private enterprise and individual initiative: that the economy responded to, indeed was determined by, external forces largely immune to the control of provincial leaders.[19]

In the negotiations on constitutional change presently under way, western Canadian political leaders face a dilemma that has been with the West since its political creation. Should the West bargain for greater regional power *within* the national government, knowing full well that the region's relatively small population (approximately 18 percent of the national total) cannot ensure favourable policy treatment given the essentially majoritarian framework of the national government? Or, alternatively, should the West seek a transfer of power to the provincial governments? Although constitutionally protected provincial powers are relatively safe from the intervention of the national government and the central Canadian electorate, the awkward fact remains that many of the policy areas of continuing concern to the West—international trade, transportation, and so on—fall naturally within the jurisdiction of the national government and thus cannot be successfully addressed by the individual provinces. A satisfactory constitutional solution seems to be extremely evasive, even given the best of faith and intentions among all participants in the process of constitutional change.

Western Alienation and Antipathy Towards Quebec

Antipathy towards Quebec has long been a pillar of western alienation. The nature of the antipathy has changed over time, however, as the focus of western hostility has shifted across a number of distinct, though interrelated, targets. Initially, French Canadians were perceived as a troublesome ethnic and religious minority in western Canada—one that constituted a serious impediment to the assimilation of a large and polyglot immigrant population. Quebec itself was seen as both a willing partner with Ontario in the economic exploitation of western Canada and a near-seditious obstacle to the pursuit of national goals (as, for example, in the conscription crises of World Wars I and II). More recently, the focus of antipathy has shifted to the federal government's bilingualism and biculturalism programs, to the federal government's apparent fixation on national-unity questions to the exclusion of concern for western Canada, and to the prominence of Quebec MPs within a national government almost devoid of prairie representation. Western Canadians feel ignored, although the attention of the federal government has not always been beneficial, as David Smith notes: "After a decade of singular devotion to Quebec's problems, the federal government is viewed from the prairies, in the conflict over oil and natural gas, as once again turning its guns and not its ear to the West."[20]

The focal point of contemporary western Canadian hostility is bilingualism. The prairie electorate, firmly in the Conservative camp and generally distrustful of the Liberal government, needed a lot of convincing that bilingualism was either necessary or desirable. Unfortunately, national-government leaders made little attempt to explain the rationale or political necessity for programs such as the Official Languages Act. In the attempts that were made, little sensitivity was displayed towards the multicultural character of the prairie population or towards the region's history of conflict with language legislation. As a result, when bilingual signs began to appear in national parks, when bilingual labelling appeared on consumer products, and when air controllers struck over the introduction of French, misunderstanding and anger grew like wheat under a warm prairie sun. Even metrication was seen as another aspect of bilingualism. Graham Smith, editor of Calgary's *North Hill News*, complained about the heavy cost of implementing "the French metric system."[21] As James Gray explains, "It was the heavy-handed way in which Ottawa pursued its goals in the West, its universal proliferation of an alien language, that made it easy for Westerners to assume Ottawa's intention was to 'jam French down our throats.'"[22]

In a 1974 survey conducted in Calgary by Gibbins, a strong correlation was found between western alienation and antipathy towards Quebec.[23] In that study, western alienation was measured in a manner very similar to that reported earlier, whereas antipathy towards Quebec was measured by the following types of agree/disagree statements:

Because the federal government is afraid of Quebec's separating, Quebec gets more than its fair share from Ottawa.

French Canadians have made Canada a more interesting country by contributing a second language and culture.

In Ottawa lately, it seems that French Canadians are getting most of the important jobs.

Overall, the most highly alienated individuals in the sample were also the most antagonistic towards Quebec. Interestingly, however, an index of orientation towards French Canadians constructed through the use of semantic-differential scales had only the most modest relationship with the Western Alienation Index. The implication is that, although hostility towards the political role and power of Quebec constitutes an important complement to western alienation, hostility towards French Canadians *per se* does not. Western Canadians are not bigots; rather, they are, in the main, reacting to a political situation that they find unjust and frustrating.

Antipathy towards Quebec is heightened by the seeming inability of western Canadians to affect the policies or partisan composition of the national government. In the 1974 national election, for example, the Liberal Party had secured 128 seats—just five short of a majority—before ballots were even counted west of the Great Lakes. If the prairie provinces had failed to elect a single Liberal MP (they elected five), the Liberal Party would still have enjoyed a comfortable majority. Thus, western Canadians find that their support—steadfast since 1958—for the Conservative Party is insufficient to propel that party into national office. The Liberal dominance in Quebec, on the other hand, appears to have given the Liberal Party a stranglehold on national office. The end result is that antipathy towards Quebec, and western alienation itself, have been overlaid by the partisan hostility of the Conservative prairie electorate towards the national Liberal government. Fortunately, through the 1976 Alberta survey discussed earlier, we can examine this relationship between western alienation and political partisanship more closely.

Western Alienation and Political Partisanship

If western alienation embodies a distrust and dislike of the national government, then it stands to reason that Conservatives on the prairies will be more alienated than Liberals. For Liberals, the national government is, in an important partisan sense, *their* government, despite the paucity of western Canadian Liberal MPs. For Conservatives, on the other hand, and for New Democrats, the national government may be disliked not only from a regional perspective but also on partisan grounds—that is, because it is a Liberal rather than a Conservative or New Democratic government. Thus we would expect political partisanship to be an important factor in the accentuation or moderation of western alienation among members of the prairie electorate. This factor is of particular importance when one bears in mind the generally Conservative hue of the prairie electorate; if Conservative partisanship exacerbates western alienation, the effect will be a general one indeed.

In Gibbins's 1976 survey of the Alberta electorate, respondents were asked the following question: "As far as national politics are concerned, do you usually think of yourself as Conservative, Liberal, NDP, Social Credit, or what?" Respondents identifying with one of the four major parties were then asked: "How strongly Conservative (or whatever) do you generally feel—very strongly, fairly strongly, or not very strongly?" Together, these two questions constitute a standard measure of political-party identification. They allow us to divide up the Alberta sample into Conservatives, Liberals, New Democrats, and so forth, and, in the case of self-identified Liberals and Conservatives, there were enough respondents to permit distinctions between the varying strengths of party identification...

The lowest levels of alienation were to be found among Liberals and independents, with the strength of Liberal Party identification being negatively correlated with the strength of western alienation. Conversely, among respondents identifying with the Conservative Party, the strength of party identification was positively correlated with the level of alienation. Thus, weak Liberal and weak Conservative identifiers had very similar levels of alienation, whereas strong Liberals and strong Conservatives were poles apart.

The relatively low levels of alienation found among political independents may be accounted for by the fact that they, like western Liberals, do not carry a *partisan* grudge against the national government. It should also be noted, however, that the close similarity in levels of alienation between Liberals and independents raises the suspicion that many of the independents in the sample may have been closet Liberals—individuals who, although predisposed towards the Liberal Party, find the Liberal label too heavy a cross to bear in the overwhelmingly Conservative climate of Alberta.

In summary, western alienation appears to be intensified by partisan considerations; supporters of opposition parties—particularly strong supporters of the Conservative Party—are alienated from the incumbent *Liberal* administration in Ottawa as well as from the national government *per se*. There is, however, a chicken-and-egg difficulty

271

with this finding. Take, for example, those individuals who identify with the Conservative Party. It may be that Conservatives are relatively alienated from the national government because their party has been excluded from that government for the past fifteen years. They do not see the national government as their government, they dislike the direction of its policies, they dislike its leader, and they generalize their partisan dislikes to a broader sense of regional disaffection—a generalization that is aided by the Conservative hegemony across the prairies. If this explains the character of the relationship, then the election of a Conservative government to power in Ottawa would sharply reduce existing levels of alienation in western Canada. However, it may also be the case that highly alienated individuals have gravitated towards the Conservative Party, seeing it as a means through which they can express their dissatisfaction with the national government. If this is the case, the election of a national Conservative government would in itself do little to reduce levels of western alienation unless that government were able to overcome the long-standing western Canadian grievances.

Although the linkage between political partisanship and western alienation has been demonstrated only for Alberta, it is likely that similar patterns exist within the electorates of Saskatchewan and Manitoba. It would be surprising if Conservatives in these two provinces turned out to be less alienated than their Liberal counterparts . . .

Western Alienation and Electoral Politics

Western alienation was initially the product of events and circumstances lying outside the arena of electoral politics; nevertheless, the sentiment has been repeatedly exploited within that arena. Although it may be overly cynical to state that party organizations on the prairies deliberately foster western alienation, fanning the coals of western alienation has been a common and very effective electoral strategy, frequently used in conjunction with attacks on the national affiliations of provincial opponents. In recent years, for example, the provincial Liberal Party in Alberta found its affiliation with the national Liberal Party to be a crippling handicap. Thus in 1977 all organizational links between the provincial and national party were severed—a step that had been taken for many of the same reasons by the Quebec Liberal Party a decade earlier. However, similar surgery within the minds of provincial voters will be more difficult to perform.

David Smith's history of the Liberal Party in Saskatchewan has thoroughly documented the perils and pitfalls of provincial affiliations with national party organizations. In the 1971 provincial campaign, for example, the New Democrats used an agricultural-policy report by the national Liberal government as an effective club against the provincial Liberal government. "To the retort that the task force had nothing to do with Saskatchewan Liberals, the NDP replied that 'a Liberal was a Liberal' and that if the provincial voter wanted to protest about the task force and its recommendations, about the LIFT programme, and about the state of western agriculture generally, he should vote for the NDP."[24]

The earlier CCF government in Saskatchewan was so successful in attacking the provincial Liberals through the national Liberal Party that the former contemplated breaking with the national party.

> A break would deprive the CCF of one of its favourite pastimes—imputing blame to provincial Liberals for federal government actions. As long as the present situation continued, the CCF could continue to debate federal issues on the premise that the provincial Liberals were somehow responsible for them.[25]

As Smith's discussion of the Saskatchewan CCF makes clear, western alienation can be used by provincial governments to reduce opposition parties to a state of virtual irrelevance in provincial campaigns. Perhaps the best contemporary example of this was the 1975 provincial election campaign in Alberta. Premier Peter Lougheed built the Conservative campaign around the call for a mandate to strengthen the provincial government's hand in energy-pricing negotiations with the federal government; in effect the Conservative slogan for the campaign was "Vote for Alberta."[26] The Conservative strategy placed provincial opposition parties in an extremely uncomfortable position. When they tried to discuss purely provincial issues, the opposition parties were dismissed by Lougheed as "carping critics" who were ignoring the main issue of the day. When forced into a discussion of federal-provincial energy policies, the opposition parties had little ground on which to stand; to endorse the position of the Alberta government was to declare themselves redundant, and to appear to support the federal government was suicidal. Thus the alienated disposition of the Alberta electorate enabled the Lougheed Conservatives to derail the opposition campaigns and to turn the election into a two-way fight, with the provincial Conservatives leading the Alberta electorate into battle against the federal Liberal Party. The provincial opposition parties had the unenviable choice of being either standard-bearers for the Conservatives or passive spectators.

Since the 1975 election, Lougheed has continued to seek national opponents and has by and large ignored the provincial opposition parties—something that is easily done given that the Conservatives hold sixty-nine of the seventy-five provincial seats. In July 1977, returning from an extended overseas tour, Lougheed launched a vigorous attack on the Canadian Wheat Board, charging that it was being out-hustled in foreign markets. Also in 1977, the CBC aired *The Tar Sands*, a fictionalized documentary that cast some doubt on the motives and success of the Lougheed government in its negotiations with the Syncrude consortium. The next day Lougheed announced his intention to sue the CBC. What is interesting to note in light of the present discussion is the way in which Lougheed placed the lawsuit within the rubric of western alienation: "I want to see them come out here to our courthouse from Toronto and answer to questions on how that program was produced."[27]

Provincial politicians have not merely exploited the resource of western alienation but rather have actively cultivated it for the electoral opportunities it could yield. In this respect Richard Simeon notes that "to maintain support, a provincial government is motivated to accentuate the degree of internal unity, and to exaggerate the extent of difference with Ottawa, and to divert political conflict onto an external enemy"[28]—the 1975 Alberta election campaign to a tee. Provincial governments, then, do more than simply respond to western alienation; western alienation is to a significant degree sustained and manipulated by provincial party organizations.

Western Alienation and Canadian Federalism

Interestingly, there are some significant similarities between western alienation and contemporary Québécois nationalism—similarities captured in a remark by Canada West Foundation President Stanley Roberts: "Just like Quebec, we want to be *maitres chez nous*—masters in our own house."[29] The concern in the West with federal-government intrusions into provincial areas of jurisdiction, and the push for greater provincial autonomy, are concerns not unlike those expressed by Quebec premiers from Maurice Duplessis to René Lévesque. Premier Peter Lougheed, in a March 1977 speech to the

Alberta Progressive Conservative Party, drew a number of parallels between the positions of Alberta and Quebec on Canadian confederation.

> Just as Albertans want more control over their destiny—primarily for economic reasons—Quebecers, I sense, want also more control over their destiny, essentially for cultural and linguistic reasons. Hence, just as Albertans want more government decisions made in Edmonton than in Ottawa, I think Quebecers, for different reasons, but somewhat similar motives, want more government decisions made in Quebec City, and fewer in Ottawa.[30]

The parallels become superficial, however, when the fundamental underlying differences come to light. Despite the call for greater provincial autonomy, western Canadians have persistently sought greater inclusion in the national political, social, and economic fabric. As J.A. Archer has pointed out, western Canadians, despite serious economic grievances, "feel deep economic concern with, and strong emotional ties toward, the modern Canada they did so much to create."[31] Although western Canadians maintain a political subculture that is oriented primarily towards strengthening of regional political processes, they also maintain a commitment to their national government. The evidence available suggests that western Canadians do not want to see any substantial reduction in the powers of their national government. Take for example the data from a 1969 public-opinion study undertaken by Elton of preferences regarding the jurisdictional responsibilities of the two levels of government. The data in table 2 make it very clear that there is almost no support for a drastic reduction of federal-government powers.[32] Less than 5 percent of the population would favour provincial-government jurisdiction over basic national responsibilities such as foreign affairs and banking. Furthermore, there is evidence that many Albertans would like to see greater federal activity than presently exists in such areas as education and natural resources.

Table 2

Jurisdictional Preferences of the Alberta Electorate*

Government Responsibilities	Federal Gov't. Percent	Provincial Gov't. Percent	Both Gov'ts. Percent	Doesn't Matter Percent
Foreign affairs	88	3	6	2
Banking and paper money	89	4	5	1
Inflation	69	9	18	2
Old-age pensions	68	18	9	5
Family allowance	58	22	6	12
Indians	49	24	24	2
Broadcasting (radio/TV)	46	23	15	15
Unemployment insurance	40	44	11	4
City Government	6	81	7	3
Hospitals and asylums	22	59	16	2
Building Roads	8	59	31	1
Primary & secondary ed.	25	56	17	2
Medical care	25	55	16	3
People on welfare	20	54	24	2

Property and civil rights	33	38	26	3
Natural resources	33	37	28	1
Income taxation	60	17	19	4
Housing	27	40	30	1
Air & water pollution	41	20	36	2

*Responses of 567 individuals to the question "Which level of government do you think should look after the following matters?"

Given the preferences of western Canadians, it is understandable that representatives of western Canada refrain from pushing their discontent too far—from discussing or advocating separatism. Rather than argue the merits of separation, westerners argue only for the development of equitable national policies and the maintenance of a classical federal system of government. The rhetoric of Alberta's Premier Lougheed is a good example of this type of argument. The premier punctuates his rather frequent attacks on the federal government with reminders that he is first and foremost a Canadian and only secondly an Albertan. This statement is quickly followed by the assertion that a stronger West will make a stronger Canada.[33] The latter assertion not only justifies opposition to a national policy that is insensitive to western development but also legitimizes the maintenance and development of a regional identity. Note also a 1977 speech by Saskatchewan Premier Allan Blakeney:

> Let me begin by saying I do not subscribe to the proposition that Easterners, whether born in or out of wedlock, should freeze in the dark. Most of us in western Canada would agree—and have agreed—that the national interest demands . . . that Canada should have first claim to our depleting energy resources.[34]

Premier Blakeney may well be a more enthusiastic supporter of the national interest and the existing federal arrangements than are some of his western colleagues, but the point is that western Canadian politicians still speak of, and believe in, the national interest. Although the promotion of the national interest in the past frequently imposed heavy financial costs on the West, western Canadians have not lost faith in national aspirations and goals that transcend provincial and regional concerns. They simply demand that western Canada have a greater say in the establishment of such aspirations and goals. Here the gulf between western alienation and Québécois nationalism is immense.

Nor are other differences hard to find. Whereas Québécois nationalism embodies the demand for some form of political independence, separatism has been at best a fringe element of western alienation. Take, for example, the following findings from Alberta, supposedly the hotbed of separatist sentiment in western Canada:

> The 1969 provincial survey conducted by Elton found that only 5% of the respondents expressed interest in even discussing the merits of separation.[35]

> In a 1974 Calgary survey conducted by Gibbins only 8 of 221 respondents expressed even the most cautious support for separatism.[36]

> In early 1977 the *Calgary Herald* commissioned a survey of 300 randomly selected Calgarians in which 2.7% said yes and 93.7% said no to the question "Would you like Alberta to separate?"[37]

The weakness of separatist sentiment within the general public is reflected also by the absence of organizational champions of the separatist cause. Certainly nothing with even a glimmer of similarity to the Parti Québécois has existed; nor has there been a prairie equivalent to the St. Jean Baptiste Society in Quebec. From time to time separatist parties have been formed, but they have attracted no more than a handful of active supporters. Never has a separatist organization made any dent whatsoever in prairie electoral politics.

In summary, the political culture that has evolved in western Canada is both attributable to and compatible with Canada's federal character. Although regional attachments and identities are strong in western Canada, they are not preemptive of a strong national identity. Nor has significant support for separatism emerged from widespread antipathies towards the national government, the Liberal Party, central Canada, and Quebec. At heart, the western Canadian political culture is federalist; the desirability and utility of both national and provincial governments are accepted, even though intrusions of the former on the latter constitute a constant irritant, especially to provincial political elites. Western Canadians today seek, as they have continually done in the past, a better deal within rather than without Canada. But the quest seems to be without end. The relatively small regional population means an inevitable weakness within the national government and a continued position on the economic periphery. Partisans will continue to win advantage by throwing fuel on the coals of western alienation. It seems as though western alienation will sustain a distinctive political culture on the prairies for as long as the wheat shall grow.

Notes

1. George F.G. Stanley, "The Western Canadian Mystique," in *Prairie Perspective*, ed., P. Gagan (Toronto: Holt, Rinehart and Winston, 1970), 14.

2. See Mildred Schwartz, *Politics and Territory: The Sociology of Regional Persistence in Canada* (Montreal: McGill-Queen's University Press, 1974); and David Bercuson, ed., *Canada and the Burden of Unity* (Toronto: Macmillan, 1977).

3. For a description of the sampling design, see Lawrence LeDuc, Harold Clarke, Jane Jenson, and Jon Pammett, "A National Sample Design," *Canadian Journal of Political Science*, Vol. 7, No. 4 (December 1974).

4. Jon Pammett, "Public Orientation to Regions and Provinces," in *The Provincial Political Systems*, eds., David J. Bellamy, Jon H. Pammett, and Donald C. Rowat (Toronto: Methuen, 1976), 98.

5. Ibid., 87.

6. For an expanded discussion of the following points, see Roger Gibbins, "Western Alienation and the Alberta Political Culture," in *Society and Politics in Alberta*, ed., Carlo Caldarola (Toronto: Methuen, 1979).

7. Christina Newman, "The New Power in the New West," *Saturday Night*, September 1976, 18.

8. For example, see Roger Gibbins, "Models of Nationalism: A Case Study of Political Ideologies in the Canadian West," *Canadian Journal of Political Science* (June 1977), 341–73; R.R. Gilsdorf, "Western Alienation, Political Alienation, and the Federal System," in *Society and Politics in Alberta*, ed., Carlo Caldarola; and Thelma Oliver, "Aspects of Alienation in Alberta" (Paper presented at the Canadian Political Science Association Annual Meeting in Edmonton, Alberta, 1975).

9. For methodological details, see Gibbins, "Western Alienation and the Alberta Political Culture."

10. Harry E. Strom, "The Feasibility of One Prairie Province," in *One Prairie Province?* ed., David K. Elton (Lethbridge, Alberta: *Lethbridge Herald*, 1970), 32.

11. For an extended bibliography on this subject, see Alan F.J. Artibise, *Western Canada since 1870: A Select Bibliography* (Vancouver: University of British Columbia Press, 1978), 21-27.

12. Much of the material in this article dealing with the national policy was prepared by David Elton for *Legion* magazine, September 1978, 20, and is included herein with permission.

13. For a more extended and insightful article pertaining to transportation, see T.D. Regehr, "Western Canada and the Burden of National Transportation Policies," in David Bercuson, op. cit., 115-41.

14. Statement by Premier Lougheed, 25 July 1973 (mimeographed, Office of the Premier, Government of Alberta).

15. "Industrial Sector in the Multi-Lateral Trade Associations," Brief submitted jointly by the Western Provinces of Saskatchewan, British Columbia, Manitoba, and Alberta to the Government of Canada (Dept. of Business, Development & Tourism, Government of Alberta, 1977).

16. Allan Blakeney, "Resources, the Constitution and Canadian Federalism," in *Canadian Federalism: Myth or Reality*, 3rd ed., ed., J. Peter Meekison (Toronto: Methuen, 1977), 181.

17. Kenneth H. Norrie, "Some Comments on Prairie Economic Alienation," in *Canadian Federalism*, ed., Meekison, 325.

18. Jean Burnet, *Next Year Country* (Toronto: University of Toronto Press, 1951).

19. David E. Smith, *Prairie Liberalism: The Liberal Party in Saskatchewan, 1905-1971* (Toronto: University of Toronto Press, 1975), 314.

20. David E. Smith, "Western Politics and National Unity," in *Canada and the Burden of Unity*, ed., Bercuson, 143. [Also see p. 43 in this volume.]

21. *North Hill News*, 3 September 1975, 1.

22. *Calgary Herald*, 31 July 1976, 7.

23. Gibbins, "Models of Nationalism," 360.

24. Smith, *Prairie Liberalism*, 318.

25. Ibid., 208-209.

26. David Elton, "Alberta," in *Canadian Annual Review, 1975*, ed., John Saywell (Toronto: University of Toronto Press, 1976), 215-19.

27. *Calgary Herald*, 14 September 1977, 1.

28. Richard Simeon, "Regionalism and Canadian Political Institutions," in *Canadian Federalism*, ed., Meekison, 302.

29. *Calgary Herald*, 5 December 1977, A1.

30. *Calgary Herald*, 12 April 1977, 7.

31. J.A. Archer, "The Prairie Perspective," in *One Country or Two?* ed., R.M. Burns (Montreal: McGill-Queen's University Press, 1971), 231.

32. David Elton, "Public Opinion and Federal-Provincial Relations: A Case Study in Alberta," in *Canadian Federalism*, ed., Meekison, 49-63.

33. For example, see *Calgary Herald*, 12 April 1977, 7.

34. Blakeney, "Resources, the Constitution and Canadian Federalism," 179.

35. Cited in David V.J. Bell, "Regionalism in the Canadian Economy," in *Politics: Canada*, 4th ed., ed., Paul W. Fox (Toronto: McGraw-Hill Ryerson, 1977), 82.

36. Gibbins, "Models of Nationalism," 358.

37. *Calgary Herald*, 26 February 1977, A1.

The West as a Political Region

NELSON WISEMAN

Reprinted from Ronald G. Landes, ed., *Canadian Politics: A Comparative Reader* (Montreal: Prentice-Hall, 1989), 308–324, by permission of the publisher.

Regionalism is both an abstract academic concept and a continuing policy concern. Social scientists tell us that regionalism is a function of size and diversity and that it exists in all territorially based societies. Geographers, economists, historians, sociologists, and political scientists have demonstrated that the study of regionalism transcends the boundaries of any single discipline. Regionalism is a ubiquitous component of political life in all but micro-states like Andorra, Liechtenstein, and San Marino. Canada has less history and more geography than Italy, but both states exhibit regional variations within themselves. These variations often lead to political tensions and conflict. In no state are people, their beliefs, and their economic activities spread evenly, like jam, across its terrain. Unlike people and governments, however, regions do not have identities, interests, or aspirations. Perhaps "regionalism" signifies little by itself beyond a spatial dimension to politics (Elkins and Simeon, 1980: xi).

A region might be recognized and defined by its shared characteristics. Quebec may be considered a distinct region because the overwhelming majority there are francophones of French ethnic origin. The majority of those in the regions of west Montreal and the Eastern Townships, however, have been anglophones of non-French descent. From a more distant yet concentric perspective, Quebec is but one region in a country that, in turn, is but part of an international regional military alliance (NATO). Thus, there are different levels of regional analysis. There are also different levels of comparative analysis. Has regionalism, as a source of political conflict, increased in Canada while decreasing in other western industrial states? Or do the cases of the United Kingdom, Spain, and Belgium suggest nothing exceptional about the Canadian case, however unique it might be? Is Quebec regionalism more or less of a threat to Canadian unity than western Canadian regionalism?

If we accept regional analysis as a helpful, indeed essential, key to understanding Canada's politics, the next questions might be: What are the regions? What defines and differentiates them? What are political expressions of regional differences in demography, economy, and culture? How do political parties and institutions reflect regional differences? The five-region concept—Atlantic Canada, Quebec, Ontario, the Prairies, and British Columbia—is the one most commonly applied by social scientists (e.g., Schwartz, 1974; Bellamy et al. 1976, part I). Sometimes, as in survey research, provinces might be grouped together because that increases a sample's size and facilitates comparative analysis. Other times, the concept of "provincialism" competes

278

with or replaces "regionalism." There are some good reasons for this: provinces have governments, capitals, and flags. Regions have none of these.

Nevertheless, regions are acknowledged in Canada's supreme law. The title of Part III of the Constitution Act, 1982, for example, refers to regional disparities. Regions are recognized in Canada's written and unwritten constitution in the composition of the Senate, the Supreme Court, and the federal cabinet. Regions were recognized in such historical federal legislation as the Maritime Freight Rates Act of 1927 and the Prairie Farm Rehabilitation Act of 1935, and since the 1970s have featured prominently in such statutes as the Unemployment Insurance Act and the Regional Development Incentives Act.

Some political scientists (e.g., Wilson, 1974; Jenson, 1976) have suggested that as regional societies and economies mature and become more integrated into a national society and economy, regionalism will diminish as a political factor. The expectation is that class will become more salient in politics than region. This "modernization" thesis is based broadly on the European, especially British, experience over the past two centuries. Canada's 1988 federal election, however, confirmed premodern patterns. Voting behaviour was not deregionalized. Quebec behaved as a region and the NDP appeared, as the CCF had from the 1930s through the 1950s, as a western regional party.

Regionalism in voting has also been expressed within provinces. The 1988 Manitoba provincial election, for example, was decidedly postmodern. Beginning in the 1960s, the NDP on the left and the Conservatives on the right operated in a polarized two-party system that imitated the British and British Columbia experiences. The Manitoba Liberals, who in 1981 actually disappeared from the legislature for the first and only time in this century, could be written off as the victims of "modernization" (Wilson, 1975). In 1988, however, the Liberals rose like the phoenix and the NDP sank from government to third party. Retrospectively, class voting has been more evident in Manitoba's past than its present (Wiseman and Taylor, 1982). Regionalism, in contrast, persists: all the Liberal seats but one are in Winnipeg, while most of the Conservative seats are concentrated in the rural areas, and the NDP now appears more as the party of the far-flung and Native North.

Is the West a political region? Yes, no, and perhaps. Constitutional framers perceived the West as a region both in the distribution of Senate seats (twenty-four for each of four main regions) and in the aborted Victoria Charter amending formula of 1971. Perhaps these perceptions of the West as a region were a figment of a central Canadian imagination. The experience with the federal-provincial equalization formula, which determines fiscal capacity, suggests the lack of a single region: BC and Alberta over the long term have been "have" provinces, Saskatchewan has been a swing province—a recipient some years and not others—and Manitoba has been a chronic "have-not" province (Black, 1977: 88). We might designate the West as a single political region or as four provincialized regions, with an intermediate possibility having BC and the prairies as two regions. Politicians, bureaucrats, and citizens often refer to the "West," and western premiers sometimes behave as if it were a region: in 1965 the three prairie premiers began to meet annually as the Prairie Economic Council. Since 1973 they have been joined by BC's premier to form a Western Premiers' Conference. Their common concerns generally revolve around their heavy reliance on natural resources and their frustration with the federal government's transportation, trade, taxation, and monetary policies.

These issues and the question of the West's influence in federal institutions contributed in the 1980s to the rise of regionally conscious western protest parties: the Reform Party, the Confederation of Regions Party, West-Fed, and the Western Canada Concept. Although these parties have floundered, regionalism has nevertheless been reflected in voting behaviour. Since the 1950s, the West alone among the regions has consistently and vehemently rebuffed the federal and most provincial Liberals. In federal voting behaviour, region has counted far more than other variables such as gender, age, and income. Women in Saskatchewan and British Columbia, for example, have been more willing to vote NDP than women in Quebec or Atlantic Canada. Thus, the West is a region that matters politically because, in at least some political respects, it has behaved in a distinctive manner.

The existence of a western political community, however, is problematic. In terms of popular culture, the West is little more than a geographic demarcation, merely the territory on the Pacific side of an arbitrary cartographic feature—the Manitoba/Ontario border. Western Canadians, like Canadians generally, have become more rather than less similar in their tastes, from television programs to fast foods (Gibbins, 1985: 82). Survey researchers have attempted to determine the content of regional political consciousness. They have found that in many respects western attitudes are similar to national attitudes, while in other respects they are different. Westerners, like most other Canadians (but not most Newfoundlanders) think of themselves as Canadians first rather than as primarily westerners, Manitobans, and so on (Kornberg et al. 1982: 38). Westerners are more likely than Atlantic Canadians or Quebecers, however, to say their "first loyalty" lies with Canada rather than their own province. Western public opinion does not favour a drastic reduction in federal power, although westerners—again like other Canadians, except in this case, Ontarians—"feel closer to" and may have more trust in their provincial governments than in their federal government (Clarke et al. 1980: 57).

Westerners have in common, at varying levels of intensity, a sense of separateness from and frustration with central Canada. Nevertheless, there has never been more than minuscule support for either separatism or American annexation. More Albertans and British Columbians, in comparison with other Canadians, believe that their province either bears undue burdens or receives less than its fair share of benefits from the federal system. The attitudes of Manitobans and Saskatchewanians on this question, however, are about the same as those of Ontarians (Kornberg et al. 1982: 41). Thus there are differences, as well as similarities, in the attitudes of residents of the different western provinces.

Whatever attitudinal similarities there might be among westerners, the four western provinces are studies in contrast in their histories, ethnic composition, and political cultures and behaviour (Galbraith, 1976; Wiseman, 1981). Treating them as a single region is akin to trying to tie four watermelons together with a single piece of string. British Columbians would protest being lumped together with the prairie provinces. They have been more aloof and isolated, detached from and relatively disinterested in the hostility emanating from the prairies against central Canada (comprising Ontario, Quebec, and the federal government). BC had a corporate frontier requiring wage labourers in a resource hinterland of one-company towns (Robin, 1978); the prairies, an agrarian frontier requiring homesteading farmers.

These differences have been reflected politically. BC has a long history of strong support for socialist and labour parties, but the United Farmers of British Columbia were a sorry joke compared to the United Farmers of Alberta, the United Farmers of Manitoba, and the Saskatchewan Grain Growers' Association of the 1920s. In the apparently similar prairie provinces, there has been little popular support for the notion of a single prairie political unit. In one survey on the subject, westerners were less approving of the idea than Canadians as a whole (26 percent versus 28 percent) and more disapproving (63 percent versus 52 percent) (Canadian Institute of Public Opinion, 1970). If there were more public sympathy for a western political union, it would have to contend with institutional barriers and elite opposition. How many premiers, MLAs, ministers, and deputy ministers would be keen to surrender their positions even if they believed that a single, larger province (with one premier, fewer MLAs, and one minister and one deputy per department) would strengthen the West's clout with the federal government and other regions? Furthermore, the history of prairie political protest reveals a broad spectrum of ideological responses to the same perceived injustices: between the 1930s and the 1960s, a right-wing Social Credit Party scored repeated successes in Alberta, a left-wing CCF ruled Saskatchewan, and an amorphous coalition of Liberals, Progressives, Conservatives, and Social Crediters held sway in Manitoba. In BC, Social Credit and the NDP have long been engaged in so-called modern politics: a polarized symbiotic dance of right and left.

We enhance our appreciation of the West as a distinct political region if we keep it constantly in comparative perspective. Regional identity is not and cannot be as strong in the West as it is in Quebec, because the West, unlike Quebec, is not a "distinct society." The West shares its language and other aspects of its cultural heritage with Anglo-America generally and English Canada specifically. Where the Québécois have resisted assimilation, westerners have sought integration, on better terms, in the national political and economic systems. Ontarians, in further contrast, have had neither set of concerns. Like Atlantic Canada, the West has been a peripheral economic hinterland for central Canada; but it is quite unlike Atlantic Canada in its legacy of social heterogeneity and frontier openness. This fed a contentious ideological component in western Canadian politics, whereas Atlantic Canadian party politics has never risen far above contests between "ins" and "outs" with little differentiation in terms of platforms, programs, and philosophies. Unlike Atlantic Canada and Ontario, the West has produced third parties throughout this century. Unlike Quebec, where nationalist parties like the Union Nationale and the Parti Québécois have represented a distinct nationalist consciousness, the idea of a western "nationalist" or separatist party begs the question of "what nation?"

Society and Economy

The French as well as the British saw the West as their frontier, and set out to exploit its resources and to settle it. Part of Confederation's rationale was the development of the West, to keep it out of America's reach. The areas known as Rupert's Land and the North-West Territories were transferred to Canada from the Hudson's Bay Company and British control in the late 1860s. Then Ontario farmers, the CPR, and an influx of Britons between the turn of the century and World War I ensured that the 49th parallel would not collapse under American pressure. But the interests of westerners and easterners diverged over the legacy of the National Policy and on such issues as Ottawa's control over prairie resources and public lands, which were only transferred to provincial control in 1930. Because Laurier's government thought the West's numbers might come to rival Ontario's or Quebec's, two provinces were carved out of the Territories in 1905—Alberta and Saskatchewan—rather than one (Smith, 1976: 47). Western wheat fuelled the national economy in the first quarter of this century, and western oil, gas, minerals, hydro power, and forests helped to fuel it in the third quarter. In between, national communication links came to depend less on the railway and the economy came to depend less on wheat.

Demographically, the West was once a cultural polyglot lacking a common political heritage. This promoted an orientation to the future rather than the past as in Quebec and Atlantic Canada. The West—especially BC and Alberta—has been a parvenu culture, an upstart society that offers the prospect for a dramatic rise from low to high status, from indebtedness or little money to riches and new money. Diverse national origins also made the West a natural hotbed for new and radical political parties. The West's formative labour unions were composed mainly of unskilled immigrants led by veterans of British, especially miners', unions. Ontario's early unions, in contrast, were composed mainly of highly skilled craftsmen and were relatively conservative. In further contrast, much of Quebec's union movement began and operated under the tutelage of the church and in self-imposed isolation (Lipsig-Mummé, 1984: 294).

The growth of the West was spectacular. At one time, just over a century ago, pamphleteering boosters predicted that Winnipeg might become not just Canada's capital, but the British Empire's (Owram, 1981: 48). Alberta and Saskatchewan each grew by over 500 percent in the first decade of this century. Their ethnic diversity was graphically reflected in the bloc farm colonies that looked like patches on a map. In 1913 Canada received one immigrant for every eighteen in the population, and most of them by-passed central Canada and headed directly west. For a long time, the majority of westerners were born elsewhere. As recently as the 1970s, fewer than half of British Columbians were born in the province (Statistics Canada, 1974, table 34). The lingering flavour of that province's British Edwardian legacy is reflected in the very title of Victoria's newspaper, the *Times-Colonist*.

Of all Canada's regions, the West is the least British (especially the prairies) and the least French (especially BC). In descending numbers, the noncharter groups are German, Ukrainian, Scandinavian, Dutch, and Polish. In BC, the Chinese are the third-largest group. Alberta and BC are the least Catholic of provinces. The West is also home to about 70 percent of Canada's Native people. The West's multicultural diversity, and its distance from Quebec, help to explain its historical antipathy to a dualistic conceptualization of Canada and to the maintenance and expansion of French language rights. The attitude of many European-origin pioneers was that if they could assimilate into the anglophone majority, so should the French, who, at least in terms of numbers, did not warrant a "special status."

Over time, populations and their relative political weight have shifted. Where BC grew by nearly 400 percent between 1931 and 1981, Saskatchewan grew by only 5 percent. BC was Canada's second least-populated province in 1901, but its third most populated in 1951. Saskatchewan, in contrast, went from third to sixth in population between the 1930s and 1970s. As in the late 1920s, westerners in the late 1980s make up about 30 percent of the national population, but whereas the majority of them lived in Manitoba and Saskatchewan in the 1920s, about three-quarters now live in Alberta and BC. The Depression and the mechanization of agriculture contributed to an outflow of a half-million people from Saskatchewan between the 1920s and 1970s. Today most westerners, like most Canadians, are city dwellers. Westerners are now so assimilated that the "ethnic" label carries neither stigma nor benefit. Political power is no longer the preserve of Anglo-Saxons, as it was in the first half of the century. Unlike their grandparents, contemporary westerners are more similar and native than diverse and foreign. This is reflected in the West's attitude to multicultural programs: once supportive, it is now tempered by the feeling that these programs largely benefit Ontario's newer, post-World War II immigrants (Smith, 1981: 174).

Political economists have described the West as a resource hinterland in a quasi-colonial relationship to a central Canadian metropolis or heartland (Macpherson, 1953; Phillips, 1978). The common characteristic of the various western staples—from wheat and lumber to oil and hydroelectricity—has been that their prices and demands are largely determined abroad. The expansionary-recessionary veerings of a market-driven resource economy have produced cycles of boom and bust, optimism and despair. When Canada's centre of economic gravity temporarily moved westward in the 1970s, many Albertans felt that their resources were being looted by artificially low, federally imposed prices and the National Energy Program of 1980. The centre-periphery relationship of central Canada to the West was historically reflected—in western eyes—in federal and corporate policies. Those policies encouraged the export of unrefined raw resources, forced westerners to buy finished manufactured goods from central Canada, determined the pace and pattern of capital investment, sacrificed western interests for those of the heartland in international economic relations, physically linked the West and East by a transportation system centrally controlled and operated, and protected corporations (the banks, the CPR) from both foreign and hinterland competition (Smiley, 1980: 263).

Nevertheless, however earnestly western provincial governments have attributed economic difficulties to federal policies, there have always been substantial nonpolitical impediments to economic development. In the North American economic scheme, the Canadian West is distant from large markets and is sparsely populated. The necessary objective conditions for a large manufacturing base are absent. Despite a major effort to aid industrialization through Alberta's and Saskatchewan's Heritage Funds, the percentage of westerners engaged in manufacturing is lower than that of Atlantic Canadians. Interventionist efforts by provincial governments have, arguably, neither diversified nor strengthened the West's economy. Nevertheless, per capita personal incomes in the West are near the national average (somewhat lower in Manitoba and Saskatchewan), and Alberta's ranked second nationally in 1986 (Statistics Canada, 1988: 93). Whereas the national and British Columbia per capita income that year was about $17,000, it was nearly $18,000 in Alberta, and slightly below $16,000 in Manitoba and Saskatchewan. In contrast, it was only $11,600 in Newfoundland and well under $14,000 in the Maritime provinces. All this suggests that large-scale manufacturing is perhaps neither necessary nor possible in sustaining high incomes and a buoyant regional economy.

Philosophies and Parties

The West more than any other region has proposed new political institutions, new philosophies, new political parties, and innovative public policies. The prairies in particular have strong democratic, populist, and cooperative traditions. Canadian women first gained the franchise in Manitoba in 1916. In the early part of the century, populists agitated for "direct legislation" and, in Alberta, for something called "group government." The former idea was imported from the United States, where it also went by the label of "the initiative, referendum, and recall," the idea being that the popular will should dictate and reverse the will of elected parliamentarians. All three prairie provinces passed laws accommodating "direct legislation," but the Manitoba version was struck down by the Judicial Committee of the Privy Council as *ultra vires* in 1920. In the 1930s Alberta's Social Credit government repealed its recall bill when a movement arose to recall its premier. Social Credit's early proclamations in support of popular sovereignty, and its critique of parliamentary sovereignty as dictatorial and undemocratic, came to naught; it operated in a conventional, orthodox parliamentary manner both in the legislature in Edmonton and on Parliament Hill. An echo of Alberta's plebiscitarian instincts came in the early 1980s when its government called for referenda to settle constitutional issues, and again in the late 1980s when it proposed the popular election of senators.

"Group government" and "nonpartisan" politics were championed during and after World War I. The former was formulated and articulated by the American-born leader of the United Farmers of Alberta (UFA). The idea was representation in government based on occupational groups. In power, however, the UFA cabinet operated conventionally; the idea faded. A Non-Partisan League was formed to parallel the successful North Dakota model, and a self-proclaimed "Non-Partisan" government—actually, a coalition of parties—ruled Manitoba in the early 1940s. One nonpartisan objective was to weaken, if not eliminate, the hold of federal parties over their MPs. In the provinces, the nonpartisan enthusiasts quickly encountered the reality that cabinet-parliamentary government could not work without parties. Nonpartisanship was not part of British Columbia's political life except in urban municipal politics, where it served as an antisocialist vehicle for Liberals, Conservatives, and Social Crediters.

The cooperative thrust on the prairies was reflected in the very name of the Co-operative Commonwealth Federation (CCF), although most cooperators in Alberta and Manitoba were and are not socialists. In 1930 two platform planks of the United Farmers of Canada (Saskatchewan Section) summed up both its socialist orientation and its Britishness: "Abolition of the competitive system and substitution of a cooperative system of manufacturing, transportation, and distribution," and "Free trade with [Britain] the mother country" (Lipset, 1968: 106). In recent years, the three prairie wheat pools—all cooperatives—have handled most of the prairies' grain and generated annual revenues in excess of $3 billion (29 Dec. 1988, *The Globe and Mail*). The prairie provinces have been leaders in the public ownership of utilities such as telephones (since 1908 in Saskatchewan and 1906 in Manitoba); in creating provincial government enterprises, from air services and automobile insurance to potash and oil development (between the 1940s and 1970s in Saskatchewan); in the innovation of social programs like Medicare (in the 1960s); and in renovations in policy-making structures such as a cabinet level Planning Board (in 1945). In BC, cyclical unemployment helped feed labour militancy, labour-socialist parties, and such syndicalist organizations as the One Big Union, which was founded in Calgary (where both the CCF and Social Credit were also born) and was prominent in the Winnipeg General Strike in 1919.

The West was particularly receptive to new and sometimes radical ideas because many of its settlers arrived directly, without spending time in the East. They had no background in Canadian politics nor in the established political parties. For some, the West represented opportunities for economic advancement and individual achievement. For others, it represented opportunities for creating social egalitarianism through a more equitable distribution of wealth. The West's political culture, therefore, has been more polarized than that of Ontario or Atlantic Canada, where ideological conflict has been relatively muted or absent. This is evidenced by BC Social Credit's being driven by an "ultra-conservative ideology" (Dyck, 1986: 337). As well, the West is the only region in English-speaking North America where self-proclaimed "democratic socialists" have come to power.

Some western Conservative governments have, like NDP governments, been policy activists. Their rationales for activism, however, have diverged. In the 1970s Alberta's Conservative government and Saskatchewan's NDP government responded in quite different ways to similar frustrations over federal resource policies and Supreme Court decisions. This was partially owing to different circumstances, but also to different ideologies. In Alberta, a newly ascendant class of indigenous business entrepreneurs, young urban professionals, and a growing number of government bureaucrats and administrators supported the provincial government's "province-building" strategy (Pratt and Richards, 1979). That strategy sought to strengthen provincial control over resources, reduce dependence on both political and economic forces in central Canada, and diversify the provincial economy before oil and gas reserves were depleted. Saskatchewan moved in the same directions, but did so by expanding the public sector through the creation of Crown corporations. Neither Alberta's free-enterprise nor Saskatchewan's social-democratic ideology was incongruent with the creation of joint public-private ventures. In some cases, as with Pacific Western Airlines, the Alberta government purchased an enterprise (and then was happy to privatize it) in support of the further private development of the provincial economy.

Western experimentation with new political parties has been, in part, an expression of regional discontent. In 1921 the Progressives forever shattered the established party system by winning thirty-eight of the prairies' forty-three seats and another twenty-four seats in Ontario. They wanted to remake federal political institutions and to render the federal government more sensitive to western agrarian concerns. In pursuit of the latter objective, however, the national Progressive leadership was co-opted and defused by Mackenzie King. The CCF and Social Credit then arose in the West in the 1930s. Although they represented more than regional protest—the CCF actually wanted to strengthen federal powers and Social Credit wanted to manipulate them in monetary policy—both appeared as parties of regional discontent. This was the odd output of the single-member constituency, simple plurality, or first-past-the-post electoral system. It generously rewarded Social Credit's concentration of votes in Alberta and simultaneously deprived the CCF and then the New Democratic Party of more seats in other parts of the country, especially Ontario, where they consistently captured a healthy share of the national vote (Whitehorn, 1985: 195).

In western provincial politics, the CCF-NDP and Social Credit have been rooted in fundamentally different constituencies. Social Credit was always more popular in the countryside than in the cities, while the reverse has been the case for the CCF-NDP. As in other provinces, rural areas were systematically overrepresented on electoral maps, sometimes by statute, sometimes by gerrymander, sometimes by neglecting to redistribute for decades. The distribution of seats is now nearer to the principle of one person, one vote, but anomalous results are still possible: in 1986, for example, Saskatchewan's Conservatives won a majority government even as the NDP captured a plurality of the popular vote. It lost because it was virtually shut out of the rural areas. So too was the Alberta NDP, despite its sixteen seats, in both the 1986 and 1989 provincial elections. In Manitoba, the CCF-NDP has never won a constituency in the southwestern wheat belt, whereas all the Social Crediters elected between the 1930s and 1960s represented farm districts. In office, Social Credit, in both its Albertan and British Columbian manifestations, became a self-proclaimed bulwark against creeping socialism. BC never needed an agrarian protest party because the provincial government gladly catered to agricultural interests long before Social Credit appeared.

Between the 1950s and the 1980s, elected federal Liberals were scarce in the West. The Liberals rejected the West, as much as it rejected them, by devising an electoral strategy that built on a Quebec base and played to the swing seats of metropolitan southern Ontario. The tactic made political sense because that area gained more and more new seats; today, Manitoba and Saskatchewan combined have fewer MPs than the greater Toronto area. During the Pearson and Trudeau years, therefore, the West's frustrations were doubly exacerbated: although it repeatedly rejected the Liberals, they kept winning office and consequently had too few western MPs for the cabinet. Western premiers and governments, like Alberta's Conservatives, could appeal to popular alienation from Liberal Ottawa by running provincial campaigns against the federal government ("Vote for Alberta," declared the PCs in 1975) rather than the provincial opposition parties. The reappearance and resurgence of provincial Liberals in Manitoba and Alberta in the late 1980s suggested both their resilience and a tempering of ideological polarization.

Institutions and Constitutions

Western provincial party systems, unlike those in Atlantic Canada and Ontario, did not parallel the federal party system between the 1920s and 1980s. Parties, therefore, failed to knit together in an intimate way the issues on which federal and provincial politics turned. In the Mulroney era, some federal-provincial parallelism emerged in western party systems. In the late 1980s, Conservatives were in power in Ottawa, and all three prairie provinces, and their Social Credit kin governed BC. The organizational and policy differences between federal and provincial parties of the same name, however, ensure continued divergence and conflict. In 1989 this was reflected in the refusal of Manitoba's provincial Conservatives to endorse the federal Conservative Meech Lake Accord.

The brokerage theory of Canadian parties holds out the prospect that regional differences may be accommodated and resolved within the major federal party caucuses. In theory, every party caucus would contain westerners as well as easterners, farm as well as labour spokesmen, anglophones as well as francophones, and so forth. In theory, the parties would act as vehicles or mechanisms for integration, for resolving tensions produced by Canada's social and economic diversity. In practice, however, the major parties in the Pearson-Trudeau era became regionally identified: the Liberals with Quebec, the Conservatives with the West. The parties have had to operate, moreover, within the inescapable parameters of tight party discipline in a cabinet-parliamentary form of government. This makes western MPs appear to be more responsive to their party whips and leaders than to their constituents or their conscience. The older parties easily weathered the West's assault—however virtuous—on their power because Parliament's operation assumes, indeed encourages, the functioning of competing, well-disciplined parties. Political institutions such as the party system, the electoral system, and British-style cabinet government have thus reinforced rather than mitigated regionalism as a source of conflict (Simeon, 1975).

The federal system was specifically devised to reconcile regional and national interests. Federalism in practice, however, has exacerbated rather than alleviated western alienation. The federal government is not organized to represent regional interests in the way that the United States government is with its powerful Senate. The Canadian Senate, in contrast, lacks legitimacy and status. It was designed to be undemocratic. The unsatisfactory incorporation of western interests into national policy making in Ottawa has promoted their articulation at federal-provincial conferences, especially the summitry of First Ministers' Conferences. Such forums, unlike other institutions, are 40 percent Western, 40 percent Atlantic, and only 20 percent central Canadian. The very substantial jurisdictional powers of provincial governments—from social policy to economic development to constitutional politics—have helped western provincial governments, and the parties and elites that drive them, to shape, mould, and reinforce regional protest. Unlike western MPs, western premiers, independently powerful and unfettered by their parties, speak loudly on the public record in defence of provincial interests. This contributes to citizens' seeing premiers and their governments, rather than MPs, as the foremost spokesmen for regional interests.

The West's influence in national politics declined steadily after the 1920s and until the 1970s, when its economy boomed, its population expanded, and its consent was required for constitutional change. Part of the price Saskatchewan exacted in exchange for giving Trudeau his Charter of Rights was Section 92A, reversing two Supreme Court decisions that undermined provincial control over resources. Alberta bargained for, and won, the authorship of the amending formula. Commodity market forces in the 1980s, however, dampened the significance of constitutional refinements. The influence of western provincial governments today is arguably less than it was in the 1970s. Simultaneously, the influence of western MPs—most of whom are in the Conservative government caucus—has increased. Western provincial governments sometimes banded together in assaulting federal government policies, and they appeared collectively as the strongest opponents of Ottawa's powers in the 1970s. It is noteworthy, however, that in some areas—such as energy pricing and fiscal equalization—they were unable to agree among themselves. Manitoba, for example, was, like Ontario, unsupportive of Alberta's push for world oil prices for domestic production.

An area that appears relatively devoid of ideological differentiation has been constitutional politics. Even in this case, however, Conservatives—in contrast to New Democrats—argued in 1981 for entrenching property rights in the Charter. Both socialist and conservative western premiers were leery of an entrenched Charter and insisted, along with Atlantic premiers, on the "notwithstanding" clause, which permits the legislative override of some key Charter provisions. Generally, Manitoba's government, of whatever stripe, has been more supportive of a strong central government than its more westerly neighbours. Howard Pawley, for example, threatened to scrap the Meech Lake Accord if it threatened to lessen federal spending powers in areas of provincial jurisdiction (Elton, 1988: 361).

The West's discontent with federal government institutions, like its discontent with the federal party system, has not and cannot be abated permanently. Institutional reform does not come easily or quickly and a western sense of inequality and relative powerlessness will persist. In liberal democracies, power is closely linked to building majorities and to relative populations. There are and always will be many more people in central Canada. No amount of institutional reform will alter greatly either the regional balances of population or the location of primary and secondary industries. The West has always pursued respect and status within, rather than outside, the national political and economic systems. Western frustrations, however, have been translated into provincial government demands for more power. Some federal powers, such as trade, monetary, and interprovincial transportation policies, cannot and should not be transferred to regional or provincial authorities. Some western Canadians, especially in Alberta and BC, have pinned their hopes and directed their efforts to a reconstructed Senate. Implicitly, they point to the American model, but neglect to note that state governments are relatively weak and passive. It is doubtful that westerners desire the same fate for their provincial governments.

The West's Future as a Political Region

The West's future will be much like its past. Neither a western political union within Canada nor a separatist West is on the agenda. Provincial governments are happily and popularly well entrenched. A spate of analyses in the 1970s and 1980s asserted "crises" in Canadian politics induced by regionalism—specifically, Quebec's election of a separatist party and the West's vociferous discontent with made-in-Ottawa policies. They suggested the imminent or potential breakup of Canada. Retrospectively, these pronouncements were somewhat alarmist. In the late 1980s, regionalism appeared relatively quiescent and on the wane. Nevertheless, the West and Quebec will in the future continue to foment political tension, if not crisis. The West will also continue to be the region least sympathetic to francophone interests.

Western regional discontent is a chronic, not a temporary, condition. Its symptoms have no quick remedies, for they are the cumulative product of distance, perception, imbalance, and experience. Once upon a time, the "bad guys" were the banks and the CPR. More recently, they have been federal agencies like the National Energy Board, the CBC, the federal departments from Transport and Agriculture to Finance and Fisheries. Westerners recognize that some federal government initiatives in the past have aided them—from agricultural price supports and low freight rates for grain to research programs and aid in the development of export resources. But these efforts, in the future as in the past, will not detrimentally affect central Canadian interests, whereas federal policies often detrimentally affect western interests (Bercuson, 1977: 9).

Westerners are accustomed to and expect to be given short shrift when their interests clash with those of central Canada. They might become upset, but they are not surprised. When the Mulroney government in its first term awarded the massive CF-18 fighter maintenance contract to a Montreal rather than a Winnipeg firm, the cries of protest and a sense of betrayal spread westward beyond Manitoba's border. Although the western bid was cheaper, technically superior, and preferred by the federal bureaucracy, the federal Conservatives reneged on their earlier election promises to make such decisions on the cold, calculating basis of businesslike criteria (Campbell and Pal, 1989: 20). As a consequence, they plummeted in the polls, but only temporarily.

As long as there is a West and people live there, they will think of themselves as separate and apart from the East. This is not so much a threat to Canadian unity as it is the simple reflection of Canada's rich diversity. Westerners might feel wronged, but they will not turn to separatism. Despite perceived injustices, westerners will continue to feel positive about Canada and their Canadian identity. Simultaneously, they and their provincial governments will complain bitterly, take the federal government to task, and seek better terms and conditions for themselves. In the first half of this century, the West produced third parties as instruments to sensitize the federal government to western concerns. In the second half, modernized provincial governments have become the vehicles to assert provincial preferences in competition with the federal government.

References

Bellamy, D.J., Pammett, J.H., and Rowat, D.C. (Eds.) (1976). *The Provincial Political Systems.* Toronto: Methuen.

Bercuson, D.J. (Ed.) (1977). *Canada and the Burden of Unity.* Toronto: Macmillan.

Black, E.R. (1977). *Divided Loyalties.* Montreal: McGill-Queen's University Press.

Campbell, R.M., and Pal, L.A. (1989). *The Real Worlds of Canadian Politics.* Peterborough: Broadview Press.

Canadian Institute of Public Opinion. (1970, 9, 11 September). *The Gallup Report.*

Clarke, H.D., et al. (1980). *Political Choice in Canada.* Toronto: McGraw-Hill Ryerson.

Dyck, R. (1986). *Provincial Politics in Canada.* Scarborough: Prentice-Hall.

Elkins, D.J., and Simeon, R. (1980). *Small Worlds: Provinces and Parties in Canadian Political Life.* Toronto: Methuen.

Elton, D. (1988). Federalism and the Canadian West. In R.D. Olling and M.W. Westmacott (Eds.), *Perspectives on Canadian Federalism* (346–63). Scarborough: Prentice-Hall.

Galbraith, G.S. (1976). British Columbia. In D.J. Bellamy, J.H. Pammett, and D.C. Rowat (Eds.), *The Provincial Political Systems* (62–75). Toronto: Methuen.

Gibbins, R. (1985). *Conflict and Unity.* Toronto: Methuen.

Jenson, J. (1976). Party Systems. In D.J. Bellamy, J.H. Pammett, and D.C. Rowat (Eds.), *The Provincial Political Systems* (118–31). Toronto: Methuen.

Kornberg, A., Mishler, W., and Clarke, H.D. (1982). *Representative Democracy in the Canadian Provinces.* Scarborough: Prentice-Hall.

Lipset, S.M. (1968). *Agrarian Socialism: The Cooperative Commonwealth Federation in Saskatchewan* (rev. ed.). Garden City, NY: Anchor.

Lipsig-Mummé, C. (1984). The Web of Dependence: Quebec Unions in Politics before 1976. In A.G. Gagnon (Ed.), *Quebec: State and Society* (286–313). Toronto: Methuen.

Macpherson, C.B. (1953). *Democracy in Alberta: Social Credit and the Party System.* Toronto: University of Toronto Press.

Owram, D. (1981). Reluctant Hinterland. In L. Pratt and G. Stevenson (Eds.), *Western Separatism* (45–64). Edmonton: Hurtig.

Phillips, P. (1978). *Regional Disparities.* Toronto: James Lorimer.

Pratt, L., and Richards, J. (1979). *Prairie Capitalism: Power and Influence in the New West.* Toronto: McClelland and Stewart.

Robin, M. (1978). British Columbia: The Company Province. In R. Martin (Ed.), *Canadian Provincial Politics* (28–60). Scarborough: Prentice-Hall.

Schwartz, M.A. (1974). *Politics and Territory: The Sociology of Regional Persistence in Canada.* Montreal: McGill-Queen's University Press.

Simeon, R. (1975). Regionalism and Canadian Political Institutions. *Queen's Quarterly,* 82(4), 499–511.

Smiley, D. (1980). *Canada in Question: Federalism in the Eighties.* Toronto: McGraw-Hill Ryerson.

Smith, D.F. (1976). The Prairie Provinces. In D.J. Bellamy, J.H. Pammett, and D.C. Rowat (Eds.), *The Provincial Political Systems* (46–61). Toronto: Methuen.

Smith, D.F. (1981). Political Culture in the West. In D. Bercuson and P.A. Buckner (Eds.), *Eastern and Western Perspectives* (169–82). Toronto: University of Toronto Press.

Statistics Canada. (1974). *Population, 1971 Census.* (Catalogue 92-727, Vol. 1, Part 3). Ottawa: Statistics Canada.

Statistics Canada. (1988, June). *National Income and Expenditure Accounts.* Ottawa: Statistics Canada.

Whitehorn, A. (1985). The CCF-NDP: Fifty Years After. In H.G. Thorburn (Ed.), *Party Politics in Canada* (5th ed.) (192–204). Scarborough: Prentice-Hall.

Wilson, J. (1974). The Canadian Political Cultures: Towards a Redefinition of the Nature of the Canadian Political System. *Canadian Journal of Political Science,* 7(3), 438–83.

Wilson, J. (1975). The Decline of the Liberal Party in Manitoba. *Journal of Canadian Studies,* 10(1), 24–41.

Wiseman, N. (1981). The Pattern of Prairie Politics. *Queen's Quarterly,* 88(2), 298–315.

Wiseman, N., and Taylor, K.W. (1982). Voting in Winnipeg during the Depression. *Canadian Review of Sociology and Anthropology,* 19(2), 213–36.

7

WESTERN PROTEST IN THE NINETIES

Introduction

The power of western protest was confirmed in the 1990s by the ascent of the Reform Party of Canada led by Preston Manning. Founded in Winnipeg in late 1987, headquartered first in Edmonton and then in Calgary, the party has come to exemplify the western protest tradition in this decade.

George Melnyk examines the roots of the party and traces them back to the unsuccessful separatist movements of the late 1970s and the conservative tradition of Alberta. Although the party did not elect any representatives in the 1988 federal election, it is expected to win a significant number of seats in the 1993 federal election.

The party has expanded beyond its western base and is now active in Ontario and the Maritimes. If past experience of other western protest parties is any indicator, the attempt of the Reform Party to widen its base will result in the same mainstreaming and deradicalization experienced by Social Credit in Alberta. Western reform of Canada would mean the renewal of Canadian conservatism.

Journalists Don Braid and Sydney Sharpe examine the western discontent that gave rise to the Reform Party in the late 1980s and consider what made the region amenable to the Reform Party's slogan of "The West Wants In." They point out how the need for equality in Confederation has resulted in the West's prominent role in Senate reform, espousing the Triple-E Senate concept.

As Canada's constitutional crisis ebbs and flows after the failure of the Meech Lake Accord (destroyed by two hinterland provinces, Manitoba and Newfoundland) and Quebec's demand for distinct status clashes with western demands for provincial equality, the issue of the breakup of Canada hovers over everyone, waiting for yet another solution.

Western protest is a key ingredient in the multifaceted equation of Canadian federalism and if the interpreters of western protest are to be believed, it will ultimately play a key role in shaping the nature of Canadian unity.

Region and Reaction: The Western Right

GEORGE MELNYK

Western Canada has always had its conservative forces. Since the 1970s these forces have been spread over a wide ideological spectrum from a moderate right-of-centre approach to reactionary and racist attitudes. In the 1980s the main vehicles of conservatism in the region were right-wing provincial governments under Conservative and Social Credit Party control, bolstered after 1984 by a Conservative government in Ottawa. But these governments, both provincial and federal, were mainstream phenomena and created a social and economic agenda brokered through a wide range of viewpoints and social forces. This meant that reactionary elements became alienated from the established party of conservatism (the PCs) because it did not fulfil their desires or espouse their radical viewpoints.

In the late 1970s alienation from the mainstream conservative parties in the West was expressed primarily by the western separatists, who called for some form of independent state in the region. By the end of the 1980s these alienated conservatives abandoned western separatism and resurfaced in the Alberta-based Reform Party of Canada led by Preston Manning, son of the former Social Credit premier of the province. The party, officially formed in October 1987, espoused a rather contradictory platform: federalist but pro-Western, right-wing but anti-Conservative Party. This transformation of the western right from separatists to federal reformers is the curious path that right-wing western regionalism has taken as it moved from the provincial-rights phase of postagrarian regionalism in the 1970s—when western interests were led by provincial premiers and separatism was an extreme manifestation of this regionalism—to a new phase of third-party protest politics in the 1980s. The achievement or lack of success of this third-party protest movement in Ottawa will be an important barometer of right-wing power in the 1990s.

Western Separatism 1971–1981

Three major forces provided the context for western separatism during the 1970s. First, the rise of Quebec separatism in the 1960s, resulting in the creation and eventual military defeat of the FLQ in 1970 and the election of René Lévesque's sovereignty-association Parti Québécois in 1976, served as an incentive to western separatist demands. In this period the Quebec push for independence was associated with left-wing, socially progressive forces composed of students, labour, and intellectuals. The western right found inspiration in Quebec's constitutional demands for self-determination but rejected its left-liberal social policy. It adopted the form of independence but replaced the social substance.

Second, the West, due to high energy prices, was a rich and powerful region during the 1970s, and its provincial governments of both left (Blakeney) and right (Lougheed) clashed repeatedly with the federal government over fiscal and jurisdictional matters. This created a climate of East-West hostility that fed the separatist movement. The "fight against Ottawa" and its Trudeau Liberals was a basic tenet of provincial-rights regionalism in the 1970s and a generator of western separatism.

Third, the centralist federal government under the Trudeau Liberals provided a focus for conservative opposition in such areas as bilingualism, federally mandated social programs such as Medicare, and economic programs such as Canadian ownership of the energy industry. Except for a brief period in 1979/80, the Trudeau Liberals remained firmly in power from 1968 to 1984, enabling western separatism to gain a certain legitimacy by encouraging anti-Ottawa, anti-Liberal, and anti-French sentiments to coalesce under the umbrella of separatism. These same attitudes would reappear in the Reform Party a few years later.

These three underlying factors—Quebec separatism, western provincial rights, and Trudeau Liberalism—were gone by the mid-1980s and western separatists with them, but extremism remained, unable to find a home in the mainstream "Conservative Revolution" that came to Canada in the 1980s. Enter the Reform Party, a late-1980s creation that cannot be properly understood until the main features of western separatism of the 1970s are identified.

The first western separatist group, the Western Canada Party, was founded in 1970 in British Columbia, but became defunct in 1972. The founder resurrected himself in 1976 with newspaper ads calling for "a new nation" in the West but then he disappeared again. Also in 1970, Lethbridge, Alberta, was host to a conference examining the idea of "one prairie province." Soon-to-be-premiers Peter Lougheed and Allan Blakeney attended and voiced their opposition to this type of regional unification, while the sitting Social Credit premiers of Alberta and British Columbia were much more positive about the idea. Of course, when elected, Lougheed and Blakeney set the 1970s agenda for a provincially based western regionalism and the one prairie province idea fell by the wayside.

Up to 1973 the prairie West was viewed as a disadvantaged region because of its "backward" agricultural base. Events including that year's failed "Western Economic Opportunity Conference" were typical of the federal government's welfare approach to the region. But it was the OPEC oil embargo of 1973, which placed oil prices on a steep climb, that changed the region's position in Confederation. Wealth flowed into Alberta in particular, setting the stage for the energy wars between Ottawa and the western provinces that lasted into the Conservative victory of 1984. This battle over revenue-sharing and pricing and resource-ownership and provincial power resonated throughout the next ten years as the West fought against a "national" policy in energy that subsidized central Canadian industry and consumers.

After the failure of the W.E.O. Conference, a right-wing think-tank called the Canada West Foundation appeared. Based in Alberta, but with a regionwide mandate, it received both public and private funding and called for a constitutional rearrangement that would increase the power of the West in Confederation. The foundation played an intellectual role until the mid-1980s as a monitor of western alienation and economic grievance and as an advocate of a reformed, elected Senate of equal provincial representation.

Another group that surfaced in this period was the Independent Alberta Association based in Calgary. Its leader was a former president of the Independent Petroleum

Association of Canada, representing the small producers and drillers in the energy industry. In 1977 the group renamed itself the Western Nationalist Association, but it never progressed to the stage of running candidates.

British Columbia's involvement in the separatist movement materialized through its 1975 Committee for Western Independence founded by Doug Christie, a lawyer who made his career defending anti-Semitic Holocaust deniers across Canada. Christie's poor showing in the 1979 BC provincial election (he polled a meagre 280 votes) evidenced the low appeal of the group.[1] In 1976 a parts distributor in Vancouver restarted the Western Canada Party, which had existed briefly from 1970–72. These groups eventually coalesced into the Western Canada Concept Party led by Christie.

Three events occurring in the late 1970s resulted in a short-lived outburst of separatist sentiment in 1980. These events included the election of the PQ government in Quebec, the Trudeau government's Task Force on Canadian Unity, and the heightened sense of economic grievance created by the energy wars, culminating in Ottawa's declaration of the National Energy Program. In 1979 a Canada West Foundation poll showed 3 percent of western Canadians were proseparatist, but by the end of 1980 that figure had risen to 9 percent, and a CBC poll that year listed proseparatist feeling at 14 percent.[2] This response can also be attributed to the shifting of power in Ottawa. In 1979 the Trudeau government was defeated and the Conservatives, under Albertan Joe Clark, formed a brief minority government, but its defeat in 1980 and the reelection of the Trudeau Liberals exasperated the western right once again.

Evidence of this exasperation was obvious. For example, the Independent Alberta Association, renamed the Western Nationalist Association, claimed a membership of five hundred in 1978, but in 1980 it came under the leadership of one Elmer Knutson, a former Tory, who turned it into the Western Canada Federation or West-Fed. Although the "fed" referred to a Canada of autonomous regions, in the popular mind it bespoke more of being "fed up." West-Fed received substantial media coverage, becoming familiar to a national audience, as did Doug Christie's Committee for Western Independence, renamed the Western Canada Concept, when one of its rallies in Edmonton drew 2,700 people. A third major group in the 1980 resurgence of western separatism was the Unionist Party, led by the former head of the Saskatchewan Progressive Conservative Party, Dick Collver. He called for the West to join the U.S., where he subsequently went to live. But within the year both West-Fed and the W.C.C. were turning into mere shadows of their 1980 selves. On 15 December 1980, *The Globe and Mail* accurately described western separatism as "primitive and confused, groping for a platform and searching for a leader."

With its gradual disappearance in the 1980s, the failed separatism of the 1970s and early 1980s came to rest in the right-wing regional protest movement known as the Reform Party of Canada. There are a number of reasons why this occurred, as I shall outline below.

The year 1980 witnessed the defeat of the sovereignty-association referendum in Quebec and meant that the days of the PQ government were numbered. Quebec would soon be under the control of the profederalist Robert Bourassa and his Liberal Party. Separatism's role as a catalyst to western grievances virtually disappeared. The West also faced its first recession in a decade in 1981/2, marking the beginning of the end of a provincial rights era founded on the wealth of rising prices for both natural resources and agricultural production. In the 1980s the former unity of OPEC lay in shambles and energy prices dropped dramatically. In addition, Blakeney suffered defeat in 1982 and Lougheed left in 1984. Clearly the provinces were not in the driver's seat, and the economic decline the region experienced in the 1980s contributed to the demise of western separatism. It is obvious that buoyant conditions encourage right-wing western separatism because of the sense of power and self-importance that wealth gives, but once the wealth vanishes, separatism no longer seems a viable option. This pattern is also evident in Quebec separatism, which flourished in the days after the Meech Lake Accord died. In the 1980s separatism was fed by a strong Quebec economy, but began to dissipate with the onset of the 1991 Canadian recession.

During the 1971–81 period, then, western separatism had developed several salient characteristics. First, it was a separatism of wealth and power, i.e., it was based on the new wealth and dynamic of a regional economy experiencing a boom. It was a time when the regional bourgeoisie was flying high, and the West's new political muscle and regional wealth gave it a sense of self-assuredness and of being a powerful national player that the disadvantaged West of the agrarian period never had.

Second, it was a separatism of disenchanted conservatism—a right-wing protest against bilingualism, national social policy standards, and the "socialism" of the Liberal Party in Ottawa and the provincial premiers. It also had a white racist component. Its extreme conservative agenda was not surprising when one considers that the movement was led by small businessmen whose self-made entrepreneurial ethic was antiunion, anti-nonwhite immigration, anti-French, and antigovernment intervention. Their conservative socioeconomic agenda was not in command in the 1970s, but the Conservative Revolution for privatization and dismantling of the social welfare state led by Margaret Thatcher and Ronald Reagan and followed by Brian Mulroney in the 1980s offered a haven for right-wing conservatism. However, the extreme conservatism of the separatists was not welcome in the official political institutions of the Conservative Revolution (the Progressive Conservative Party) and so sought a new home.

The third characteristic of western separatism was its context of crisis. Its appeal was strongest when the region was in transition from the powerful 1970s to the weak 1980s and the Trudeau Liberals were being blamed for the demise. The forced imposition of the National Energy Program made provincial power appear ineffective, and the cause of western separatism attracted the protest sentiment.

Once the West was deep into the recession of the 1980s, when the darling of the regional bourgeoisie, Dome Petroleum, went bankrupt and was bought by the U.S. energy giant, AMOCO; when Pioneer Trust, the Principal Group, and the Northland Bank, all pillars of new regional financial power, collapsed with the fall of real estate values, separatist appeal likewise collapsed. When the West's inflated hopes for power and influence disappeared, the dreams of western separatists went with them.

Fourth, separatism was a discredited fringe phenomenon that did not have any real influence on electoral politics whatsoever in the 1970s. Its only elected representatives were two former Tories turned Unionist (promoting union with the U.S.) who disappeared in the 1982 Saskatchewan provincial election that brought in Grant Devine's Conservative government. One W.C.C. MLA had been elected in rural Alberta in 1982 but was defeated in 1986. Unlike the channelling of separatist feeling in Quebec into support for one major party—the Parti Québécois—and its legitimizing election victory in Quebec in 1976, western separatism lacked electoral legitimacy or a single-party focus. In the 1982 Saskatchewan provincial election the Western Canada Concept drew a mere 3.3 percent of the vote.

Fifth, separatism was primarily an Alberta phenomenon because its membership was largest there, followed in second place by British Columbia, where a large number of retired Albertans live. It had limited appeal in both Saskatchewan and Manitoba, and so it was logical that Alberta should prove to be the base for the return of the far right in the late 1980s.

Sixth, separatism was an anglophone white movement in the West that sought to maintain a conservative white society when Canada was beginning to undergo a period of major Third World immigration that was changing the urban landscape of the country. It also represented a negative feeling towards the francophone Canadian minority and its linguistic and cultural demands as a founding people.

These same six features resurfaced in the Reform Party of the late 1980s.

From Separatism to Reform 1981–1991

In an essay entitled "Understanding Separatism" that appeared in the January 1981 issue of *NeWest Review* when western separatism was at its peak, I wrote:

> I believe that the crisis of the regional bourgeoisie will be resolved so that its power and relationship vis à vis Central Canada will be brought back in line with its historical position of subservience.[3]

This did in fact happen in the 1980s, when western economic development took a nose dive and the once powerful were made weak. The collapse of energy prices, whose dramatic rise in the 1970s had created the powerful regional bourgeoisie in the first place, broke western power. The regional bourgeoisie, dependent on these high prices (created not by the West but by OPEC) fell with them. The old economic base of agriculture, superseded by the postagrarian energy economy, suffered from a lowering of state subsidies, long-term low prices for grain, and massive farm debt based on inflated 1970s land values. Energy and agriculture—the two pillars of the western economy—were cut down and with them political power, embodied in weak western premiers who were subservient to the conservative agenda of the federal government and its handouts.

Linking the demise of separatism with the decline of the regional bourgeoisie and the western economy in the 1980s and the rise of the Conservative Revolution in Canada points to two conclusions. A separatism based on wealth and power could not survive in an era of regional impoverishment and decline because the essence of separatist rhetoric rested in the region's ability to sustain an independent economy. Also, the Conservative Revolution, as embodied in the two 1980s provincial Conservative governments in the West and in the election of a federal Conservative government, was seen at first as fulfilling the hopes of the extreme right; separatism was no longer needed. But in a few years, the compromises made by the established mainstream governments produced an alienated minority in the West that viewed other areas of the country, especially Quebec, as receiving favoured status.

This alienated minority did not turn to the now discredited and unfulfilled western separatism of the 1970s, but instead created a new movement that retained its conservative character but opposed a Conservative Party rooted in Quebec via its leader, Brian Mulroney. This new movement evolved through disillusionment with the Mulroney agenda and presented itself as prowestern. It called for a realignment of political power to give the West "equality" within Confederation, which no Quebec-based party could.

The movement gained instant recognition and more authority and membership in one year than a decade of separatist groupings had. It did so by maintaining that it was a grassroots and mainstream protest that was pro-Canadian. It absorbed and focused the former divisions, gaining a momentum similar to the Parti Québécois in the 1970s.

The conditions that gave rise to the Reform Party were: the continued Quebec orientation of the new federal Conservative government; the inability of a declining provincial-rights regionalism under weak western premiers to express western aspirations; an Alberta economy that began to move upward again in the latter 1980s with increased gas exports to the U.S.; and the anti-Quebec feeling aroused in English Canada during the Meech Lake constitutional negotiations and agreement. The right in the West viewed the Accord as a sop to Quebec and welcomed its defeat. The overwhelmingly negative reaction in Quebec to the defeat of Meech Lake gave Quebec separatism centre stage once again and, of course, this challenged the West as Ottawa sought to create a new accommodation.

In the mid-1980s the Confederation of Regions Party laid the groundwork for a more moderate western separatist position. This fringe party expressed the ideas W.A.C. Bennett had presented in his paper to the One Prairie Province Conference of 1970, calling for an amalgamation of provinces into regional governments, which would then make up a new Canada. Best known for its anti-French ideas, the party made inroads in the 1991 New Brunswick election, where the francophone Acadian minority had won major concessions in the 1980s. The Confed Party showed that a western-based party that was national in orientation rather than western nationalist had a greater appeal within the region as well as potential outside of it.

The nonviability of western nationalism as a vehicle for the right meant that disenchanted western conservatives needed a new home, and they found it in 1987 when the Reform Party came into being at a founding convention in Winnipeg. Right-wing disenchantment centred on the Quebec issue, which included numerous scandals among Quebec Conservative MPs, Quebec's Bill 101 that restricted English language use, and pro-Quebec favouritism in Ottawa patronage.

A 1990 book on western alienation suggested a "strong connection" between the membership of the Reform Party and the remnants of Western Canada Concept and other western independence groups of the early 1980s.[4] The authors of the book also pointed out that in a 1990 survey of Reform Party members, 48 percent were over the age of sixty and 38 percent were retired—a demographic profile precisely the same as that of the earlier western separatists.[5] Journalist Denise Harrington in her 1981 article "Who Are the Separatists?" stated that "the separatists of 1980 are mostly middle-aged or elderly. The hardcore supporters are rural residents."[6]

A telling photograph appeared in *The Globe and Mail* in 1989 showing Reform Party leader Preston Manning flanked by two aged farmers during a tour of Manitoba.[7] This was the same "constituency of the old" that had been attracted to right-wing separatism. Intolerant and fundamentally disenchanted with modernity, it called for the preservation of the old ways. Mr. Manning, then forty-eight, had the youthful vigour to make their old ideas feel potent once more. One newspaper article mentioned that of about ten thousand British Columbia members of the party, 50 percent lived on Vancouver Island, a favourite retirement haven for prairie farmers.

The roots of the Reform Party go back to Social Credit and to Preston Manning's father, the long-time Social Credit premier of Alberta, Ernest Manning, an evangelical radio preacher and associate of Aberhart, the first Social Credit premier of Alberta.

Social Credit's conservatism has always found a ready audience among elderly white anglophones from the West.

Reform Party ties to populist right-wing ideology are summarized in a 1967 book entitled *Political Realignment: A Challenge to Thoughtful Canadians*, which the Mannings wrote, calling for a new conservatism that would unite Social Credit's right-wing western populism with the establishment conservatism of the Tory party. They also go back to the *One Prairie Province* book edited in 1970 by University of Lethbridge political scientist David K. Elton. Elton became president of the Canada West Foundation in 1980, and the foundation was one of the organizations that Preston Manning was associated with as he struggled to create a vehicle for his views. The foundation's proposal for a Triple-E Senate became one of the cornerstones of the Reform Party program and a specific western initiative for constitutional reform. *One Prairie Province*, which summarized the conference of the same name, clearly pointed out that western disenchantment was primarily a right-wing phenomenon and that its main focus was federal restructuring and not separatism.

Preston Manning was fundamentally an outsider in the period of provincial-rights regionalism led by Peter Lougheed, but once Lougheed was gone from the political stage, a new populist party for national reform was free to come out of the West. The Reform Party of Canada has been described as "a federal party with the greatest popular momentum in the West since the Progressives in the 1920s."[8] The party appealed to the same constituency as the separatists, but was based on the slogan "the West wants in" as opposed to the West wanting out, which is what the separatists had preached. Its mythology, articulated over and over by its leader, was that the Reform Party was a grassroots populist movement that was sweeping out of the West to change the nation for the better just as previous "reform" movements had.

When Manning formed the party, the western provinces were in conservative political hands, and he insisted that it run only in federal elections so as not to split the conservative vote provincially. He preached power in Ottawa as an answer to the failed provincial-rights regionalism of the 1970s. Only through Ottawa could the West achieve justice. Manning had not been part of any of the separatist parties, and while they were having their brief strut on the stage of history in the late 1970s he had created something called the Movement for National Political Change, which never went anywhere at the time but did reflect his basic vision. In 1986, when disillusionment with the federal Conservatives was on the rise in the West, Manning joined with former head of the Canada West Foundation, Stan Roberts, to organize a convention in Vancouver that would be a prelude to the founding of a new political party. Manning had lived in Edmonton and vicinity most of his life and it was here that he found his start-up funds. With $100,000 from Francis Winspear, a retired Edmonton accountant, and financial support from retired Edmonton construction magnate John Poole, among others, the Reform Association of Canada was launched.

The reactionary news journal *Alberta Report*, spread the message of the new party and the credibility of its evangelical Christian leader. Membership skyrocketed. In 1989, newspaper reports claimed that the party's annual budget stood at $750,000, membership at twenty-five thousand, and that the leader was being paid a salary commensurate with this status. By the spring of 1991 membership was at sixty-two thousand and the party budget had grown accordingly. Projections for 1991 surpassed $3 million.[9] This kind of performance was the complete opposite of the separatist phenomenon.

Although the founding convention had been in Winnipeg, the headquarters of the party were in Edmonton, where the party leader lived. After his defeat in the 1988 federal election when he ran in the riding of Yellowhead against former prime minister Joe Clark, his archrival, the party leader and the party headquarters moved to Calgary, a city with a more amenable right-wing constituency and business class than Edmonton, which had had a strong NDP base since 1986. The Reformers elected their first MP in 1989 in an Alberta by-election and also elected Alberta's first senator, a retired lieutenant-general and former associate deputy minister of defence, Stan Waters, who died in 1991. Lieutenant-General Waters spent about $200,000 on his election campaign, far surpassing the other candidates. With right-wing credentials from Social Credit to *Alberta Report* to retired generals, basing the party in Alberta was both a natural development and a strategic necessity if the party was to survive and the movement to grow.

The *Calgary Herald* reported that just two years after its founding a Reform Party survey of its members indicated that 76 percent were former members of the Progressive Conservative Party and that 20 percent had formerly supported Social Credit.[10] The article went on to say that 76 percent of the party members who responded to the survey were forty-five or older and 73 percent were male. It was obvious that this "grassroots" movement was a movement of middle-aged and elderly white males and that it was receiving funding from elements of the regional Alberta bourgeoisie who wished to support a native son.

The western separatist movement had been strongest in Alberta and British Columbia, and the Reform Party followed this pattern with a majority of members in Alberta followed by British Columbia. Of the party's twenty-eight thousand members in 1989, fifteen thousand were in Alberta and eight thousand in British Columbia, with Saskatchewan and Manitoba making up the other five thousand. In 1992 Alberta and British Columbia continued to lead.[11] The party preached the usual right-wing demand for fiscal restraint, less government, cuts in spending, balanced budgets, a war on the federal deficit, etc. It also opposed bilingualism and special status for Quebec at the expense of the other provinces and, of course, it called for Senate reform and equality for the West within Confederation. Manning kept the party purely federal in orientation and away from providing any challenge to the ruling right-wing regimes in Alberta, Saskatchewan, British Columbia, and Manitoba that would split their conservative support. This proved a real challenge in Alberta because the polls showed the party was capable of replacing the Conservatives provincially. Manning's goal was to entrench the party in Ottawa first and then use this credibility as a mainstream right-wing force to unseat either left-of-centre provincial parties that may by then be in power in the West or to replace corrupt or dispirited right-wing regimes that were dying out, such as the Conservative Party of Alberta under Don Getty.

Western disenchantment with Ottawa was the main driving force of the party. Its leader was intent on creating at minimum a right-wing "bloc" in Ottawa from the West that would hold a balance of power, and at maximum replacing the Conservatives as the government. In either case the fortunes of his party continue to seesaw with those of the Conservatives—as one goes up the other goes down. Because the West as a region could not provide sufficient seats to form a federal government the Reform Party began a move towards Ontario in preparation for the 1993 federal election.[12] Again building on right-wing disenchantment with Ottawa over Quebec, which has been the main political issue after Meech Lake, the Reform Party sought to broaden its regional base to a national one and thereby confirm its pro-Canadian identity. In early 1992 national polls gave the Reform Party greater popularity than the Conservatives, but as the federal Conservatives began to move up in the polls, Reform Party support did not.

This undeviating drive for federal power by a regionally based party was the western version of the Bloc Québécois, which was made up of disenchanted Quebec Conservative MPs who created this political vehicle after the Meech Lake fiasco.[13] In both cases, a regional constituency was seeking a presence in Ottawa that did not require it to make any compromises the way an established national government had to as it balanced various regional interests. This purity was compromised when Ontario became part of the Reform election strategy in 1991.

By including Ontario in its political mandate in 1991, the Reform Party sought to become "national" in the sense of representing the contradictory interests of Ontario and the West. The ambition and vision of its leader caused a fundamental shift away from being a true regional party to a classic Canadian protest movement with national aspirations and responsibilities. His obsession with federal politics and Ottawa made him use the Reform Party's regional base for broader goals. By forsaking its purely regional focus, the Reform Party adopted a national umbrella whose inherent conflicting interests could only be reconciled through a unifying right-wing ideology and a constitutional restructuring that was anti-Quebec. It was no longer a true western voice, yet its base remained in the region.

In the period after the 1988 federal election the national media took the Reform Party seriously and focused on its leader as a man who was neither extreme nor eccentric.[14] It viewed the party as a "federal" party and so acknowledged it as legitimate. In 1990, front-page stories appeared in *Maclean's, Saturday Night,* and *The Globe and Mail.* Manning was no longer simply the darling of the regional *Alberta Report.* After being invited to speak to the Toronto establishment in the fall of 1990, Manning was welcomed into the bosom of Bay Street.

Armed with this new national identity, Manning developed the theme that an old Canada was dying and a new Canada was being born.[15] He claimed that while the Reform Party represented the new, the Conservatives stood for the old. In the post-Meech Lake constitutional crisis this theme made superficial sense. Everyone was talking about a new Canada. But what was this Reform Party "newness" except fiscal tightfistedness, total support for the Free Trade Agreement that was deindustrializing central Canada, provincial control over social programs, unacceptability of special status for Quebec, and the end of official bilingualism? In essence it was little more than an accelerated Conservative Party agenda.

Curiously, and in a broader sense, one can also compare the Reform Party to the Quebec Creditistes led by Caouette in the 1960s. The Creditistes were a right-wing populist group that did not fit into a Conservative Party but were a keen ally of theirs on certain social programs. They disappeared with their leader, around whom the party was built. With its rural and elderly supporters, the Credististe movement represented threatened conservative values in Quebec. The roots of Reform are strikingly similar and its political scenario may end up being similar as well.

The Reform Party has been described as a "populist crusade," which gives it a certain purity and righteousness and a housecleaning mandate.[16] But this crusade is on track to pragmatic politics. Crusades conveniently die out once they capture the citadels of power and the crusaders themselves are comfortably seated in the positions held by their foes. And what is one to make of a crusade of the elderly if that is what the party remains? What kind of new Canada will the old create? (In the 1990s the

Reform Party tackled its geriatric and white profile by making an effort to appeal to younger and nonwhite voters, especially in Ontario, with limited success.)

The Reform Party is not a mainstreaming of former western separatism; it represents the resurgence of right-wing ideology in a new western protest mode that has given itself a national mandate. Western separatism had failed conservative ideology because it had a divided, fanatical, and incompetent political leadership and structure. In building a single nonseparatist party around a credible leader, right-wing ideology had found a suitable western vehicle for its political aspirations at a time when the federal Conservatives could not provide one. However, by 1992 the Reform Party had not been able to move beyond its minority base and seemed to have, perhaps only temporarily, reached a plateau. It had failed to reach its goals in a major fundraising drive in late 1991, and Bay Street did not seem as interested in Reform conservatism in early 1992 when Mulroney might yet win on the Quebec front and also carry through on the expanded Free Trade Agreement that would include Mexico.

Because the Reform Party has a large, growing membership base, a substantial budget, and a respected leader with a responsible image, it has surpassed the fringe appeal of the old separatist groups. Its constituency is much larger now and so its policies are more opaque and constructed to encourage a range of interpretation. Everything is couched in the language of mainstream moderation in order to capture votes and expand its political base. It arrived on the scene when there were no competitors, and in a few short years it has nicely monopolized the disenchanted right in the West and is making inroads into Ontario where recession has caused a great deal of disenchantment after the boom of the 1980s. The ties with western separatism have not been overcome, but rather transformed through a dialectical process in which two opposing characteristics have been synthesized into a single feature.

To begin with, the old separatism had been a separatism of wealth and new western power, but the Reform Party came out of a period when wealth and power and the West's former political and economic leadership had dissipated. It filled the vacuum in the West created by the failure of the provincial-rights phase of postagrarian regionalism to give the West the power it had sought in Confederation by promising that its call for a regional party to reform Ottawa was a better answer than both the old separatism and provincial-rights regionalism. The party leader claimed that it was the western protest tradition that was resurrecting itself to send a new political message of change to Ottawa. This hit a responsive chord in the West because it removed itself from both separatism and provincialism, neither of which had much credibility any longer. There may have been disappointment over the party's 1991 move into Ontario, but the western constituency of the Reform Party had no place else to go. The leader said he could work his reforming miracle in Ottawa only with the help of Ontario's electors. Under the current system the West couldn't reform Ottawa alone.

Western separatism was a separatism of the alienated right. The Reform Party was certainly a right-wing phenomenon combining reactionary and racist elements with general regional discontent over Ottawa and anglophone opposition to Quebec demands. But the old separatism was a statement of extremes that devoured itself through its own rhetoric, while the new party worked to eliminate extremism in its language. It put the same right-wing tendencies in mainstream language and viewpoints, and the leader stressed the party's opposition to extremism.

The old separatism was a separatism of crisis arising out of the failure of the provincial-rights regionalism of the 1970s to produce control over the regional economy. The Reform Party arose at a time when there was nothing like the crisis of 1980, but it was positioned to take advantage of the crisis created by the federal Conservatives and their dependence on Quebec voters. While the old separatism tried to emulate Quebec's sovereignty demands for the West, the new party articulated a pro-English Canadianism claiming the old could be made new again.

The party thrives on an atmosphere of crisis. In fact, it depends upon it. Should that atmosphere disappear it will need to transform itself out of its crisis mould into another political manifestation, either by becoming a casualty of history or reentering the Conservative Party mainstream. Because the sense of political crisis lessened in early 1992 and economic concerns replaced constitutional ones, the Reform Party seemed to falter. Should an atmosphere of crisis return at any point, the fortunes of the party will rise dramatically.

Western separatism was a fringe phenomenon. Although the Reform Party claims mainstream status, it is at present a fringe phenomenon in Ottawa, unable to attract any sitting Conservative MPs the way the Bloc Québécois has. So it combines the characteristics of a mainstream protest movement with those of a fringe party. It displays opposing characteristics, as any true synthesis must. The 1993 federal election will indicate if this right-wing, populist, antiestablishment movement will enter the canon of Canadian third-party protest politics and become a permanent feature of Canadian politics like the CCF/NDP did, or whether its existence will be brief like that of the Creditistes.

The old separatism was based in Alberta and British Columbia. This is also true of the Reform Party, but by rejecting separatism the party also has rejected the western regionalism that underlies it and is trying to turn itself into a national party by appealing to the alienated white anglophones of Ontario and the Maritimes. So it has synthesized the regionalist base of the former movement with the need for a national focus in order to hold power in Ottawa, where, in its view, all things are possible. By using the West as a base, a tool rather than an end in itself, it has surpassed the limitations of the separatist vision.

The old separatism was a movement of aging white anglophones in the West. This was also the constituency of the Reform Party in its early years, but no party can come to significant power or acceptance with such a narrow base and so the new party, in moderating its policies and obfuscating its ideological roots, is expanding beyond this group while ensuring that it does not alienate its founding core. When the party went to Ontario in 1991, it used the same strategy it used in the West of appealing to middle-aged and elderly white anglophone conservatives as a base for its constituency organizations and then expanding from that limited group.

The Reform Party has succeeded in both retaining and surrendering certain features of the old movement. Essentially, it retained popular right-wing ideology and jettisoned unpopular western separatism. And should the political climate move against right-wing attitudes Reform will mostly likely move in that direction as well since it will have power rather than ideology as its main concern. Becoming a popular party of the right means its continued existence as a federal party will depend on its making compromises similar to those made by the Conservative Party. In its modus operandi, it has developed a methodology of going beyond its founding base, of reinterpreting its mandate to suit a new goal and yet it has been able to retain followers attracted by its initial message.

Conclusion

Why did the West of the 1970s produce western separatists who went nowhere politically, and the 1980s produce a Reform Party that has entered Canadian politics in the 1990s with great hope and real potential for political office? Don Braid, an experienced Alberta political commentator, wrote that "Western separatist sentiment is almost always a by-product of good times, when people are feeling feisty and secure enough to indulge their passion," but they quickly move from "open defiance to quiet surliness" when the good times disappear.[17] This is certainly an important factor, but more important is the history of western regionalism in which separatism has been an occasional, short-lived, and generally unpalatable component. It is the historic unacceptability of separatism in the canon of western regionalism that ensured that the western right would have to find a new venue for its sentiments if it wanted to capture political power.

The passage from the 1970s theme of a "New West" to the 1990s theme of a "New Canada" occurred because separatism was a nonstarter in the West, while the protest tradition was, in the words of political scientist John Richards, one of "a half-century of political reform" calling for devolution of power to the regions but nothing more.[18] What was revolutionary about the separatists was their refusal to consider either the provincial structure or the federal structure as an adequate vehicle for western aspirations. What is mainstream about the Reform Party is that it accepts and focuses on federal power and may go provincial if it does well in the federal election of 1993.

Both the western separatists and their successor, the Reform Party, are fundamentally antiregionalist. The separatists substituted western nationalism for western regionalism, calling for an independent national state (western regionalism is fundamentally an autonomist movement for regional equality within established national boundaries) and the Reformers began with a regional stance and profile but quickly changed to a national one under the argument that western interests can only by achieved through Ontario's support. Although both movements based themselves in the West and claimed to articulate western grievances, they did so in a way that was essentially against the interests of the region: the separatists by calling for a new political entity that no doubt would have united with the United States, and the Reformers by sacrificing the region's needs for national power. The Conservative Revolution of the 1980s has given power to the right in the West; the Reform Party is positioned within that revolution and will rise and fall with its success in the 1990s.

What did not appear in the West in the 1970s or 1980s was a left-wing regional party that represented a socially progressive but strictly western orientation. The NDP retained its monopoly on left-wing political expression. The mid-1980s attempt by western NDP MPs to challenge the federal Broadbent leadership failed. The chance of a new left-wing populist movement with a radical socioeconomic agenda based on regional self-determination increases as New Democrat provincial governments fail to make fundamental advances in regional economic and political power.

The western right has tried everything from provincial-rights to separatist ideology to federal third-party protest politics, and none have fulfilled western aspirations. At some point a new regional left will have its chance to seek a solution to western grievances.

Notes

1. Denise Harrington, "Who Are the Separatists?" in Larry Pratt and Garth Stevenson, eds., *Western Separatism* (Edmonton: Hurtig, 1981), 27.

2. George Melnyk, "Understanding Separatism," *NeWest Review*, Vol. 6, No. 5, Jan. 1981, and Pratt and Stevenson, *Western Separatism*, 39 and 40.

3. Melnyk, "Understanding Separatism," 15.

4. Don Braid and Sydney Sharpe, *Breakup* (Toronto: Key Porter, 1990), 37.

5. Ibid., 38.

6. Pratt and Stevenson, *Western Separatism*, 33.

7. *The Globe and Mail,* 2 Dec. 1989, D2.

8. Ian Pearson, "Thou Shalt Not Ignore the West," *Saturday Night,* Dec. 1990, 38.

9. *The Globe and Mail,* 2 Dec 1989, D2, and 8 April 1991, A1; *Calgary Herald,* 8 April 1991, A3.

10. *Calgary Herald,* 29 Oct 1989, E3.

11. *Maclean's,* 29 June 1992, 12.

12. John Dafoe, "Reform Party Ponders Move to far reaches of the East," *The Globe and Mail,* 16 Feb. 1991, D2.

13. Stevie Cameron, "Reform Party: Looking for the next target," *The Globe and Mail,* 25 Oct. 1989, A7.

14. *The Globe and Mail,* 10 March 1990, A1.

15. *The Globe and Mail,* 24 May 1990, A7.

16. *Maclean's,* 29 Oct. 1990, 31.

17. Braid and Sharpe, *Breakup,* 43.

18. *NeWest Review,* Feb./Mar. 1991, 29.

Outsiders Looking In

DON BRAID AND SYDNEY SHARPE

Reprinted from Don Braid and Sydney Sharpe, *Breakup: Why the West Feels Left Out of Canada* (Toronto: Key Porter, 1990), 203–215, by permission of the publisher.

Westerners want only one small thing from Canada—equality. They long to be equal partners in a truly united land that includes Quebec, pleases the Maritimes, and deals fairly with all provinces. Despite the intermittent rage of separatism, the hostility over language, the resentment towards Ontario and Quebec, and the rise of the Reform Party, regional equality is the one basic demand of most westerners. Granting it would go a long way towards easing all the other problems, which are merely symptoms of the larger one. Equality is a small demand to make, surely, of a country that calls itself democratic and fair-minded.

And yet, our lopsided system is so entrenched that the most powerful forces in the country won't even admit that inequality exists. Ontario premier David Peterson has suggested that Prince Edward Island should not have as many Senate seats as Ontario. PEI has so few people, after all—only 130,600, compared to 9,667,600 in Ontario, at the beginning of 1990. Like many Ontarians before him, Peterson misses the whole point. PEI needs Senate equality *because* its population is so small. Its small band of four MPs is hardly likely to overwhelm Ontario's army of ninety-nine in the federal Parliament. Virtually powerless in the House of Commons, its citizens have little protection against unfriendly federal policies. They are forced to rely on Ottawa's generosity, an uncertain thing at best. Why then is Ontario worried by the thought of PEI, with its full provincial status, having an equal voice at one level of government? Does Canada's mightiest province really fear that the tiniest will plunder Ontario's resources, steal its industry, end its economic dominance? Surely not. To people in smaller provinces, Ontario's resistance reveals a fierce, unbending desire to dominate the country for all time. The only other explanation is an insensitivity so deep it numbs the mind. The true answer, one suspects, is a combination of both, mixed with Ontario's complacent belief that it really does speak for all English Canada.

The most vivid expression of this Ontario attitude, perhaps, came in an article printed in *The Globe and Mail* in early 1990 by Joseph Eliot Magnet, a specialist in constitutional law and minority rights at the University of Ottawa law faculty. Writing about the opposition of Manitoba and Newfoundland to the Meech Lake Accord, Professor Magnet stated: "Two pip-squeak provinces representing less than five per cent of Canadians, going back on their signatures, will ruin Meech Lake and imperil the noble Canadian experiment." This is an odd view, in light of the very first sentence of Meech Lake, which said the agreement "would recognize the principle of equality of all the provinces" (even the pip-squeaks). The central Canadian authorities, as usual, presume they hold the keys to the "noble Canadian experiment," when all they speak for is their own opinion. And their love of minority rights obviously doesn't extend to small provinces with a minority of the population.

California, with nearly thirty million people, does not pretend to wield such power over Alaska, which has fewer than one million. Both send two senators to Washington. New York, with twenty million, doesn't try to strip senators from Rhode Island, with its one million souls. The United States, with its deep sense of national pride implanted in all the states, is a powerful argument for regional equality. America works well as a federal nation, whatever one might think of its foreign policies and social problems. But the example is lost on most central Canadian leaders. Mention it and they have a series of easy rebuttals. "Oh, our provinces are too big... There aren't enough of them... That's the American way, not ours... You can't transplant an elected Senate to a British parliamentary democracy."

These are excuses, not answers, and every one is bogus. Australia grafted such a Senate to the British system nearly ninety years ago. There are only six states; the largest, New South Wales, has nearly six million people; the smallest, Tasmania, has fewer than half a million. Somehow, Australia doesn't collapse under this terrible burden of regional equality. Its states and parties still squabble, but Australia is a far more united country than Canada, with a deeper sense of national identity. Australians have succeeded in nationalizing a diverse country that covers a whole continent; Canadians have only managed to regionalize theirs.

Until quite recently, though, the idea of Senate reform was regarded in Ottawa as a crackpot issue—a "rural eccentricity," in Gordon Robertson's striking phrase. To some politicians and mandarins it still is. They believe they can make the country work with the proper combination of good will, good works, and legislative tinkering. When the federal Tories took power in 1984, bubbling with lust for "national reconciliation," these ideas propelled them with missionary zeal. A government with 211 seats from all parts of the country could surely please everyone, they thought. The delusion lasted for about two years before regional brawls began to pummel them bloody. After six years, even the sunniest Conservative had to admit that the nation had almost come unglued. Good will isn't enough to govern this country. Neither is generosity. Pierre Trudeau could have told the Conservatives that much (although he didn't always demonstrate much of either). The tensions are too powerful to be reconciled by any government, however generous. Ultimately, when regions divide, our leaders always pull back to defend their bases in the provinces with the most seats. This discredits government MPs from the provinces that lose out, creates yet another image of central Canada against the rest of the country, and helps divide us further. Only a saint could resist this temptation to pull back to the power centres, and Canada has never been run by saints.

The smaller provinces do not need any more of the temporary good will that can vanish as quickly as the sun slips behind a cloud. This is a kind of political welfare that creates only dependency and resentment. What the provinces need are the tools to fight for themselves, at the centre of power, on an equal regional footing—the tools of self-respect. The obvious first step is an equal, elected, and effective Senate. Properly built, it would help replace strict party discipline with a measure of old-fashioned horse-trading, a useful western art. If the prime minister wants Ottawa to help pay for a new car plant in Ontario, he should have to submit the enabling bill to a Senate with real authority. A majority of senators might say, "Sure, you can have that, but next up is the Polar 8 icebreaker in British Columbia, or the fixed link from Prince Edward Island to the mainland. Forget us and you won't get another vote for years." A National Energy Program would have to be modified before it could pass. A better policy would result, and regional anger would diminish. The prime minister and the cabinet would no longer take the full rap for every decision, and even a leader like Mulroney might begin to hear a cheer or two in the smaller provinces. This is how the United States divides regional development, placates regional emotion, and holds the president above the messiest parts of the domestic fray. Government projects and private developments are spread over many states because of horse-trading in the Senate. Even when a state loses a battle, its residents always know two things: the system wasn't hopelessly stacked against them, and somebody will need their Senate votes another day. This method isn't perfect, but it certainly works better than the inequity that prevails in Canada.

Long-standing objections from Ontario appear not only selfish but shortsighted, because in the long run the biggest province would probably benefit most from regional equality. The western premiers whose bleating annoys Ontarians would have their guns spiked by senators doing the regional job properly in Ottawa. The capital, an Ontario city after all, would enjoy even more prestige and authority as the real site of central government. With more action in Ottawa and less in the provincial capitals, Toronto would cement its role as the media centre of English-speaking Canada. Ontario would still be the logical site for the auto industry and many corporate headquarters. And as the smaller provinces began to develop more evenly, the market for Ontario products would grow too. Most of all, Ontario would still have the most seats in the House of Commons, and thus enjoy the most overall influence (which it deserves, having the most people). Westerners should have no illusions about this; an American in Idaho might feel roughly equal to a Californian, but she still knows who carries the hammer in the House of Representatives. Similarly, an elected Senate will never give a farmer in Prince Edward Island the same regional influence as a stockbroker on Bay Street. But the Islander would at last make his voice heard.

The Canadian nationalists who believe Senate reform is a plot for diluting central authority are exactly wrong. A Triple-E Senate is really a centralizing device, a way of refederating the country with more authority in the national government. The benefit to the small provinces, of course, is that they would have equal clout in one level of that authority. This is the essence of real federalism in large countries like Canada, the United States, and Australia. The big centres might lose a struggle once in a while, but that's the nature of the game. As political scientist Roger Gibbins notes, true federalism forces a few defeats on the population centres. They can fight, and mostly they will win because of their larger representation in one chamber. But they can no longer control every outcome through majority rule, or arrogantly assume the role of paternal gift-giver. A nationalist who can't see the justice in this is really an apologist for dictatorship by numbers.

Quebec's fears about Senate reform are easier to understand and much more valid. Quebecers fear that a Triple-E Senate would make them merely one of ten, not distinct at all, subject to one defeat after another on vital issues of cultural survival. The whole notion of provincial equality, in fact, raises the deepest Quebec fears of being swamped by the rest of Canada. This is why the equality provision in Meech Lake always seemed so odd and contradictory beside the distinct society clause. The best proposals on Senate reform all recognize these Quebec concerns and address them. The Alberta report on the Senate, for instance, suggests that all changes affecting French and English should be subject to a double majority veto. This means that a majority of all senators, combined with a majority of francophone senators, could stop any such bill. An even better proposal might be to allow a simple majority of the French speakers to approve or reject any language law affecting Quebec. If movement towards Triple E began in earnest, Quebec might be surprised at how accommodating westerners would be.

After all, Quebec and the West have been silent partners throughout much of Confederation. René Lévesque and Peter Lougheed forged an alliance based on mutual respect and provincial understanding. Lévesque well understood what the loss of resource control meant for Quebec's autonomy. Today Robert Bourassa and the four western premiers share a hidden trust that surfaces whenever Ottawa challenges provincial controls. In the spring of 1990, for instance, Quebec Communications Minister Liza Frulla-Hébert brought the twenty-year Quebec-Ottawa battle for control over communications to the West. She wasn't there to tap the lines of the West's provincially owned telephone networks. Frulla-Hébert wanted western support for a series of provincial telecommunications guidelines that federal minister Marcel Masse couldn't ignore.

Quebec-West support over telecommunications is only the latest in a series of bonds these two solitudes have created. Bureaucrats from both areas consult each other on mutual matters involving Ottawa wresting power from the provinces. These alliances are based on a collective quest for equality. Most westerners have never wanted to thwart Quebec's desires; they are simply angry at having their own ignored for so long, while Quebec's get most of the attention.

Westerners have come to these views slowly, painfully, after many years of agonizing over their role in the country. Often they were accused of being disloyal, even un-Canadian, for disputing the official view of the country. Some feel as guilty as a cleric with lewd thoughts for harbouring feelings that seem to threaten national unity. Official history is powerful and daunting; it holds that only one difference in Canada counts, the one between French and English. Quebecers clutch this opinion almost blindly, admitting to no meaningful variation within "English Canada." This popular Quebec belief is also a useful official position, because it always carries Quebec's grievances above any in the rest of Canada. The Quebec view influences policy makers in Ontario, who know better, but happily agree because it nicely fits their self-image as keepers of the national flame, English version. Federal leaders agree because they don't have the courage to reach for a vision of the whole country; Joe Clark and John Diefenbaker were crushed when they tried. The only bow to other differences is a patronage-ridden multiculturalism that now divides rather than unites. We are locked in an archaic notion of Canada that rings false to almost every western ear. Yet when westerners say what seems true to them, they are branded with all the old labels: crackpot, bigot, nation-wrecker.

John Foster, a brilliant University of Alberta historian, notes that whole generations of westerners know nothing of central Canada. They came directly to the West from other lands, never visit Ontario or Quebec, and see Canada only through western eyes. Quebec is a mythical land off to the East, and Ontario is merely a name stamped on the back of half the things they buy. "These people include British ranchers, American cowboys, Highland Scots, Ulster Irish, Ukrainians, Germans and many others," Foster says. "They have no family ties whatever in Central Canada." When tensions rise, Foster adds, such people are the most likely to become separatists. The official vision of Canada sends them one powerful message—they aren't included.

Yet there are western pioneers alive today who did as much to build Canada as any *habitant* in eighteenth-century Quebec, or any Englishman in nineteenth-century Ontario. They created the parts of modern Canada that were forged in the early twentieth century—the frontiers of the West. Indians and Métis often helped them clear the land and start their farms. (The contribution of the Native people is almost forgotten today, even by westerners, but many regions could not have been opened to farming without their help.) Many of their original houses still stand today from the farms around Winnipeg to the valleys of the British Columbia interior. All these groups—Natives, Ukrainians, Scandinavians, Germans, even the British who came West—ask the same questions: "Aren't we founders, too? What about *our* Canada? Who speaks for it? Why do we always hear of anglophone and francophone? What kind of country is this that tells me a language I never hear is more important than the one my parents speak?"

To the keepers of official history, these voices flirt with bigotry. They threaten the national myth of duality, so they must be silenced. Prime Minister Mulroney, with typical Quebec testiness, is forever flaring up at such signs of "intolerance." But these voices rise from anger, hurt, and confusion, not usually from hatred (although some do). They are the voices of outsiders flailing at a system that consigns them to a secondary place in Canada. If westerners had full political rights in Canada, the French in the West might find themselves getting fairer treatment. Mature citizens can afford to be generous. It's the deprived who resort to meanness.

This would certainly be welcome to western francophones, often the chief victims of regional anger and bitterness. The West isn't free of pettiness or instinct for revenge, and western French speakers often find themselves paying, politically and socially, for ancient grudges against Quebec. Yet Quebec has abandoned them shamefully, as Robert Bourassa's language pact with the western leaders showed very clearly. Neither anglo nor ethnic, with few allies in western provincial governments, little protection from Ottawa, and no help at all from Quebec, western francophones are adrift without anchors, forced to assimilate or fall back on their withering communities. This trend is certain to accelerate as the country retreats deeper into its language ghettos. It's hard to imagine a sadder fate for the proud, brave people who first opened the West to homesteading as missionaries and explorers. If the country hadn't gone so badly awry, if westerners felt more equal and less threatened, the francophones might enjoy the dignity and respect they deserve. Instead, they are just as often told to "go back to Quebec," even though their families might have been in the West for five or six generations.

Westerners always know what they think, but often they know surprisingly little about the real history of their region. John Foster once got a powerful shock when he tried to change the way Alberta high schools teach history. Sitting on a committee to revise the curriculum, he suggested that textbooks be written from a western viewpoint, with less emphasis on two founding races, the deification of John A. Macdonald, and all the old standards of Canadian history. He was turned down flat by the other members, all westerners. They didn't have the nerve to challenge the powerful tenets of "national history," the meat-and-potatoes fare of English-Canadian schools for more than half a century, even though most of them must have felt the tension between this history and their own view of the world.

In the schools, the result of this tension is curious and destructive. Young westerners learn one view of Canada in the classroom, but hear another at home, in the street, at the corner store. In school, they learn that Canada is a compact of the two founding races. At home, the Ukrainian kid listens to his mom and dad say his people are first Canadians, too, because they opened whole regions of Canada. In school, they hear that English and French are the official languages. But in many western schools, the lesson might be taught in Ukrainian or German. In the classroom, they hear that Canada is a great nation of equal citizens from sea to shining sea. Yet their parents, their friends, and even the premier of their province might complain every day that Ontario and Quebec run everything.

Because of this dissonance, Foster notes, "many westerners don't believe in formal history. They subscribe rather to folk history, beer-parlour history, the kind of history that is concerned with image. There's a clear division between western folk history and formal history, and when that happens, folk history always wins." It can be accurate and is often useful, he maintains, because it helps people explain and identify themselves within the country.

The main lessons of folk history are similar across the West. Ottawa can't be trusted. Your best friend, if you send him to Ottawa as an MP, can't be trusted. The prime minister might seem friendly for a while, but Ontario or Quebec will always yank his leash before he gets carried away. Official bilingualism is an expensive policy that matters only to Quebec and Ontario. Quebec and its eternal worries are more important to Ottawa than all four western provinces together. Western complaints, especially about language and the constitution, are dismissed as intolerant. Ontario wants cheap western resources and all the industrial growth for itself. Ottawa makes sure this happens, and placates the West with handouts that don't begin to compensate for the wealth sucked out of the region for a hundred years. Grant Notley, the late leader of the Alberta NDP, caught the profound sense of distance and alienation when he said: "Ottawa is three thousand miles from Alberta, Alberta is three million miles from Ottawa."

There's an element of truth in every one of these beliefs, but they're often stated with no sense of nuance because westerners lack knowledge of their past. Students on the prairies still learn, from texts printed in Ontario, that Louis Riel was a rebel whose chief benefit to Canada was to bring the Mounties to the West and consolidate the frontier. There's no mention of the vital fact that some of the things Riel demanded are still valid western grievances today. The crucial matter of resource control is largely ignored, and so is most history of the Progressives, Social Credit, the CCF, the United Farmers, and other movements that arose to do battle with Ottawa. If the history doesn't concern the national Tories and Grits, it probably won't be in the text. Western children might learn of these things, but only if their teacher is energetic and knowledgeable enough to go beyond the textbook.

The culprit here is the economics of school-text production and sales. The big companies, all in Toronto, want to sell their books right across the country. This almost forces them to stick to "national history," because a chapter on, say, the CCF in Saskatchewan might lose them sales in Ontario or the Maritimes. This leaves the old myths: English and French build Canada together, the railroad binds a happy nation, Macdonald rescues the West from grasping Americans. Ontario students get their regional history because so much of it is officially endorsed as national history. But children in the so-called regions can be left in woeful ignorance of their heritage, and that, of course, has its own charm for the keepers of the myth.

Today the genie is out of the bottle. Westerners have a new sense of purpose, a passionate desire to win their way into Canada at last. Senate reform has quickly become one weapon. Others are the region's growing sophistication and expanding economic base. If the rest of Canada can recognize these facts and somehow accept the West on equal terms at last, Wilfrid Laurier will be right, although a century late—the twenty-first century will belong to Canada. But if the West is ignored yet again, left to fester and stew, this country will forever be a mere shadow of its potential, and ultimately no country at all. The test for Canada is this: do Ontario, Quebec, and Ottawa have the courage to give up some small part of their control for a far greater good, a truly united Canada?

The choice is theirs. Westerners can only knock at the door and wait, outsiders looking in, hoping that others stop the drift towards breakup.

Printed in Canada